METHUEN'S
MANUALS OF PSYCHOLOGY

(Founder Editor C. A. Mace 1946-1968)
General Editor H. J. Butcher

The Experimental Study of Freudian Theories

The Experimental Study of Freudian Theories

HANS J. EYSENCK
and
GLENN D. WILSON

Institute of Psychiatry
University of London

METHUEN & CO LTD
11 New Fetter Lane London EC4

First published in 1973
by Methuen & Co Ltd, 11 New Fetter Lane, London EC4P 4EE
First published as a University Paperback in 1976

Printed in Great Britain
by Willmer Brothers Limited Birkenhead

ISBN 0 416 78010 5 (hardback edition)
ISBN 0 416 70470 0 (paperback edition)

Distributed in the USA by
HARPER & ROW PUBLISHERS, INC.
BARNES & NOBLE IMPORT DIVISION

Contents

'They reason theoretically, without demonstration empirically, and errors are the result.'

MICHAEL FARADAY

Acknowledgements

The authors and publisher thank the following for their permission to reprint material from the sources listed below.

The Williams & Wilkins Company and the authors for Chapter 16 by Howard M. Wolowitz and Samuel Wagonfeld, from *Journal of Nervous and Mental Disease*, 146 (1968), 18–23 (©Williams & Wilkins Company 1968), and for Chapter 19 by J. Wolpe and S. Rachman, from *Journal of Nervous and Mental Disease*, 130 (1960), 135–48 (© Williams & Wilkins Company 1960). Duke University Press and the authors for Chapter 3 by Gerald S. Blum and Daniel R. Miller, from *Journal of Personality*, 20 (1952), 287–304, Chapter 6 by Calvin Hall, from *Journal of Personality*, 31 (1963), 336–45, Chapter 7 by Bernard J. Schwartz, from *Journal of Personality*, 24 (1956), 318–27, Chapter 8 by Irving Sarnoff and Seth M. Corwin, from *Journal of Personality*, 27 (1959), 374–85, Chapter 9 by Calvin Hall and L. Van de Castle, from *Journal of Personality*, 33 (1965), 20–9, Chapter 18 by Harold S. Zamansky, from *Journal of Personality*, 26 (1958), 410–25. Cambridge University Press and the authors for Chapter 4 by Paul Kline, from *British Journal of Medical Psychology*, 41 (1968), 299–305, Chapter 17 by Yizhar Eylon, from *British Journal of Medical Psychology*, 40 (1967), 317–32. The American Psychological Association and authors for Chapter 5 by Alvin Scodel, from *Journal of Consulting Psychology*, 21, No. 5 (1957), 371–4, Chapter 10 by David S. Holmes, from *Journal of Personality and Social Psychology*, 22, No. 2 (1972), 163–70, Chapter 11 by George Levinger and James Clark, from *Journal of Abnormal and Social Psychology*, 62, No. 1 (1961), 99–105, Chapter 12 by Joseph Adelson and Joan Redmond, from *Journal of Abnormal and Social Psychology*, 57 (1958), 244–8, Chapter 13 by Harry F. Gollob and Jacob Levine, from *Journal of Personality and Social Psychology*, 5, No. 3 (1967), 386–72. The American Psychosomatic Society and authors for Chapter 15 by Marvin Stein and Perry Ottenberg, from *Psychosomatic Medicine*, 20 (1958), 60–5, The Journal Press and author for Chapter 1 by Leon J. Yarrow, from

The Journal of Genetic Psychology, 84 (1954), 149–62. Headley Brothers Ltd. and the authors for Chapter 2 by Frieda Goldman-Eisler, from *Journal of Mental Science*, 97 (1951), 765–82, and Chapter 20 by S. B. G. Eysenck, from *Journal of Mental Science* 102 No. 428 (1956), 517–29. *Perceptual and Motor Skills* and M. Soueif for Chapter 14, from *Perceptual and Motor Skills*, 35 (1972), 945–6.

Foreword

In view of the great interest aroused by psychoanalytic notions in the years from 1930 to 1960, it seems odd that very little was done experimentally to put these views to the test. A few summaries of such attempts exist, such as those by Sears (1943), Rapaport (1942), MacKinnon and Dukes (1962) and Orlansky (1949) but on the whole belief in Freud's conceptualizations was based on faith rather than proof. This is very much in line with Freud's own attitude, as revealed in his famous postcard to Rosenzweig, dated 1934 and reproduced in Postman's book (1962, p. 702). This is a reply to Rosenzweig's account of his attempts to study repression experimentally, an account he had sent to Freud. Freud states: 'I cannot put much value on these confirmations because the wealth of reliable observations on which these assertions rest makes them independent of experimental verification.' He added graciously: 'Still, it can do no harm.' Nothing could demonstrate more clearly the non-scientific character of Freud's thinking (of which he was of course well aware, as Ernest Jones points out in his biography); in his view experiments were not needed to confirm his hypotheses, nor could they infirm them. No other discipline claiming our attention has ever so clearly and decisively cut itself off from experimental testing of its theories – even astrology and phrenology make claims which are empirically testable.

In spite of Freud's disclaimer, many psychologists have followed Rosenzweig's example rather than Freud's precept, and have attempted to test Freudian theories along experimental lines. In this book we are concerned with the most important of these studies; the studies in question are reprinted in full, and we have in each case added a critical discussion which raises questions of statistical treatment, of sufficiency of controls, of alternative interpretations, and all the other types of comments which would normally be found in a discussion of experimental studies. We have treated these studies in exactly the same way as we would have treated studies in any other area in psychology, adopting the same standards of adequacy of design and statistical treatment, of representativeness of population tested and reasonableness of conclusion drawn. We have looked at the rigour with which the experimental consequences were deduced from the theory, and we have tried to point out the extent to which the results can be said to support or disprove the theory. This has not always been easy, because Freudian theories have changed over the years, and also because different interpretations of these theories are possible. In each case the reader will have to decide whether our interpretations, comments and criticisms are or are not reasonable and fitting; the format adopted lends itself particularly well to this type of judgment, giving the reader a chance to look at each study as it is presented by the author, before turning to the comments and criticisms.

Everything of course depends on the care adopted in choosing the particular articles to be reprinted; it would be easy to choose poor, silly and worthless papers, and score an easy victory by pointing out their many defaults. There is probably no other field of psychology where critical scrutiny of editors and referees has been so much missing as in this; the quality of work looked at by us has been truly appalling. Nevertheless, there are a handful of papers where by general consent of people whose judgment we value, and whose knowledge and expertise is unquestioned, Freudian theory has been adequately tested, and been found to emerge successfully from the ordeal; we have relied in our choice very much on favourable comments made by such people as Kline (1972), Lindzey and Hall (1965) and Vetter and Smith (1971). We believe that we have chosen for inclusion in our book only articles which are widely believed to be the most convincing, the best designed, and the most conclusive among those which confirm Freudian theories.

We have concentrated on articles favourable to Freud for one very obvious reason, which is explicated by Kline (1972) as follows: 'Failure to confirm the theory can always be blamed on the test. Test validity on the other hand automatically implies the validity of the theory.' Thus there is imbalance involved in the testing of Freudian theories to which we should be very much alive. If we fail to confirm the theory, we blame the test – we do not dismiss the theory. If we do confirm the theory, we accept the test – although it may be the very same one we dismissed on another occasion, when it failed to confirm the theory. Along these lines, it would seem, Freud cannot lose. Nevertheless, we have accepted the challenge in the hope that by doing so we would be able to better evaluate Kline's (1972) final statement, after reviewing much of the experimental evidence available: 'It seems clear that far too much that is distinctly Freudian has been verified for the rejection of the whole psychoanalytic theory to be possible.' It would not be of much help if we reprinted and criticized mainly studies with negative outcomes; these would not enable us to pass judgment on Kline's assertion. Only by looking at the studies with the most positive outcomes, exhibiting the best available technical treatment, and acknowledged to constitute the most persuasive evidence for Freudian theories, can we hope to come to any worthwhile conclusion. The existence of many studies with negative outcomes must of course not be forgotten, but failure may be due to many causes, and consequently such studies are inherently less interesting than successful ones – however unjust this may be!

A few articles have been included where the outcome was in fact negative; we have done this in the belief that these articles touch upon the very heart of Freudian theorizing; and that the studies are directly relevant to a proper evaluation of psychoanalytic theory. In these cases there is no real question of possibly blaming the 'test' used, because no particular psychological test was in fact employed; the studies looked directly at certain deductions made by Freud himself from his theories, as applied, e.g. to the effects of different types of therapy. It is of course still possible to argue about the applicability of prediction and criterion used, and we have tried to put the relevant arguments in perspective in our discussion following these papers. Similarly, we have looked in detail at the type of evidence which Freud himself regarded as the strongest support of his theories – detailed case histories. We have tried to show in our discussion that it is permissible to regard such studies as truly experimental attempts (in the tradition of Pavlov and Skinner) to control conditions and vary single parameters in such a way as to produce a predicted outcome; the tradition is different from the more common statistical approach, but no less scientific.

Some readers may object to our use of the term 'experimental' in the title of this book; several of the studies here quoted are correlational or observational in character, rather than experimental in the narrowest sense. It is possible to hold that an experiment is performed only when all conditions are rigidly controlled, with the exception of the independent variable, which is systematically varied to permit measurement of concomitant changes in the dependent variable. It would be safe to say that such a conception of experimental psychology is intimately tied to the outmoded S-R paradigm, and it is equally safe to say that such experiments simply do not exist in psychology. We are dealing with the much more complex paradigm S - O - R - C, where S and R as usual stand for stimulus and response, while O stands for organism and C for contingencies (positive or negative reinforcement contingent upon R). Given the infinite variability of O, any notion that all conditions can be rigidly controlled is simply futile; as Eysenck (1967) has shown, the S-R sequence depends to a large and not always realized degree on O (personality in humans, strains in rats and other animals). Under these conditions, the term *experimental* either cannot be used at all (in its most strict sense), or else it must be used in a much broader sense which would include the type of work here reported. We are aware that many experimental psychologists would not agree with our usage, but we feel that the argument set out above puts a not entirely unreasonable case for the slight break in tradition which may be involved.

We believe that this book fills a very real gap in the psychological literature. There are several books and articles which summarize the experimental literature in this field, but all of these essentially interpret and evaluate the evidence – indeed, that may be regarded as their main function. Yet this is an unsatisfactory situation for the reader who either has to accept the authors' interpretation and evaluation, or else hunt up for himself several hundred articles and books, spread over many journals often difficult to get hold of, and then make a thorough study of these. By reprinting the articles commonly regarded as the most persuasive, we enable the reader to come to an independent conclusion about the value of this work; our comments are meant to help him consider certain possible criticisms, alternative hypotheses, and different conclusions, but leave him free to go back to the original to evaluate in turn our comments. This is a salutary process which should enable the reader to look with a more critical mind at other papers purporting to support or disprove Freudian hypotheses; we feel that one important place for this book would be in courses dealing with abnormal psychology, personality and social psychology, areas where Freudian theories have always played an important part, but where a critical outlook has not always been paramount. We are not concerned so much that readers should agree with our evaluations (which may of course very well be mistaken), but rather that readers should develop critical habits of evaluation. If these newly developed critical habits are turned against us, and our discussions, so much the better – all science is based on informed criticism, leading to theoretical dialogue, leading to further experimentation. It is our hope that in the future such experimentation may aspire to a better quality than that which has been so characteristic of the past.

Institute of Psychiatry,
University of London
1 January 1973

REFERENCES

EYSENCK, H. J. (1967) *The Biological Basis of Personality.* Springfield, Ill.: Charles C. Thomas.

KLINE, P. (1972) *Fact and Fantasy in Freudian Theory.* London: Methuen.

LINDZEY, G. and HALL, C. S. (1965) *Theories of Personality: Primary Sources and Research.* New York: Wiley.

MacKINNON, D. W. and DUKES, V. F. Repression. In L. POSTMAN (ed.), *Psychology in the Making.* New York: Knopf, 1962.

ORLANSKY, H. (1949) Infant care and personality. *Psychol. Bull.,* 40, 1-48.

POSTMAN, L. (ed.) (1962) *Psychology in the Making.* New York: Knopf.

RAPAPORT, D. (1942) *Emotion and Memory.* Baltimore: Williams & Wilkins.

SEARS, R. R. (1943) *Survey of Objective Studies of Psychoanalytic Concepts.* New York: Social Science Research Council.

VETTER, H. J. and SMITH, B. D. (1971) *Personality Theory: A Source Book.* New York: Appleton-Century-Crofts.

Introduction

A title concerning the experimental study of Freudian concepts immediately raises certain questions in the minds of most readers, which require an answer. Is the nature of Freudian theories such that they can with advantage be considered *scientific*? Are they sufficiently *clear-cut* to permit testable deductions? Even if deductions can be made from Freudian theories, is it in fact possible to *falsify* these deductions? Granting the possibility of such falsification, can this be done by means of experimental studies properly so called, or are we reduced to observational studies and single case histories? What in fact is the scientific status of Freudian theories, and of psychoanalysis in general? These are some of the questions which have in the past been raised by many people, psychologists, philosophers, medical men, psychiatrists, and not least psychoanalysts themselves. We cannot pretend to know the answers to all of these questions, but we can at least suggest certain approaches which may turn out to be useful, and we can quote and discuss what others, possibly better equipped than ourselves, have had to say in this connection.

We may with advantage begin with Karl Popper (1963), probably the greatest living philosopher of science, and a self-confessed friend of psychoanalysis. He describes his own co-operation with Adler during the latter's social work in Viennese child guidance clinics, and his gradual disillusionment with psychoanalytic theory regarded as a scientific hypothesis. He found that, comparing Adler's and Freud's theories, 'I could not think of any human behaviour which could not be interpreted in terms of either theory. It was precisely this fact – that they always fitted, that they were always confirmed – which in the eyes of their admirers constituted the strongest argument in favour of these theories. It began to dawn on me that this apparent strength was in fact their weakness.' (p. 35). Popper gradually began to work out his philosophical theory of science as implying in essence the falsifiability of a theory; theories which cannot be falsified by any experimental or observational procedure are not scientific theories at all (Popper, 1959), they can explain everything and predict nothing. He came to the conclusion that Marx's theories (about which he also had had considerable doubt) were scientific and had in fact been disproved in part; with psychoanalytic theories the position was entirely different.

> The two psychoanalytic theories were in a different class. They were simply non-testable, irrefutable. There was no conceivable human behaviour which could contradict them. This does not mean that Freud and Adler were not seeing certain things correctly; I personally do not doubt that much of what they say is of considerable importance, and may well play its part one day in a psychological science which is testable. But it does mean that those 'clinical observations' which analysts naively believe confirm their theory, cannot do this any more than the daily confirmation which astrologers find in their practice. And as for Freud's epic of the Ego, the Super-ego, and the Id, no substantially stronger claim can be made for it than for Homer's collected stories from Olympus. They contain most interesting psychological suggestions, but not in a testable form. (p. 37).

Popper goes into some detail with respect to his refusal to allow clinical observations to be considered as evidence, but his general attitude will be clear from what has been said, without going into further detail.

Kuhn (1970), perhaps the only philosopher of science whose stature at the moment is comparable to that of Popper, agrees with him on the question of the scientific status of psychoanalytic theory. 'Examining the vexing cases, for example, psychoanalysis or Marxist historiography, for which Sir Karl tells us his criterion was initially designed, I concur that they cannot now be properly labelled 'science'.' And to quote just one more leading authority, B. A. Farrell (1964), who has specialized in this field and has copiously written on the scientific status of the Freudian opus (Farrell, 1951, 1961), says explicitly: 'Can we say that psychoanalytic theory is a scientific theory – that it embodies scientific knowledge of the mind? No, it is either just false or utterly misleading to say this.' Farrell gives two reasons to support this refusal to regard psychoanalytic theory as scientific; the first is that most of the supporting evidence for the theory comes from the use of the psychoanalytic method, the validity of which has not been established, and which he regards as very doubtful indeed, and the second is that the theory is 'not sufficiently determinate, logically or empirically'. Readers who wish to pursue these points will no doubt wish to consult the original papers; many other eminent philosophers, not on the whole unfriendly to the psychoanalytic endeavour, could be quoted to the same purpose. There is remarkable unanimity among those best qualified to judge that psychoanalysis is not in fact a scientific theory.

It would ill become us to contradict these experts in a field in which we are but tyros; nevertheless there are certain arguments which may be made in reply. Popper's notion of falsifiability as the essential demarcation criterion which can decide between scientific and non-scientific theories is open to many difficulties in its application; readers should consult the excellent symposium on *Criticism and the Growth of Knowledge* (Lakatos and Musgrave, 1970) which contains a spirited debate on precisely this point. Astrology and phrenology are both clearly falsifiable; does this mean that astrologers must be accorded scientific status? Are theories in fact rejected because deductions from them are falsified? As the symposiasts point out time after time, all theories contain numerous anomalies which would appear to falsify that theory; yet theories continue to flourish in spite of their anomalies. Copernicus predicted stellar parallax to follow from his heliocentric theory, but none was observed by his contemporaries, or even his successors; it was first observed in 1838 (Kuhn, 1957). Yet by this time the heliocentric theory had been universally accepted, in spite of this outstanding anomaly. Harvey put forward his theory of the circulation of the blood, but no intermediaries were found between the arteries and the veins; capillaries were not discovered until some fifty years after his death (Keele, 1965). In spite of this apparent falsification, his doctrine had been widely accepted by that time. Even the great Newton could not fit the motions of the moon into his system, and failure still dogs the footsteps of those who try to account for Mercury's aberrations.[1]

[1]The precession of the perihelion of Mercury fails to fit in with Newtonian theory, and although LeVerrier tried to account for it in terms of an inferior planet, none such has ever been found. Einstein's general theory of relativity predicted the observed precession within an error of 1 per cent, and this provided the most precise experimental support of Einstein's general theory. His prediction, however, assumed the sun to be round, which has since been found not to be so, the sun being oblate by 1 part in 2,000; this raises the observational error to an unacceptable 8 per cent. The best-fitting theory at present is that of Dicke and Brans, but astronomers are not ready at the moment to consider the problem solved. Thus Mercury's precession still defies theoretical explanation.

Yet Newton's system was universally revered as the greatest example of the application of scientific method. The list could be extended indefinitely; falsifiability in its simple form is not an acceptable demarcation criterion, and requires to be made considerably more sophisticated than the casual reader often imagines.

What the argument boils down to, essentially, is the simple question of whether the Freudian system is sufficiently determinate to permit testable deductions to be made. If the answer is no, then the system is unscientific, and such books as this are *a priori* useless. If the answer is yes, then such books as this are clearly of great use and value. Unfortunately no clear answer can in fact be given; such an answer would presuppose some solution to the problem posed by the additional question of just how rigorous a deduction requires to be before it is admitted in the high court of the philosophers of science. Consider an historical precedent, presented by Newton (1704) himself, in Query 17 to his *Opticks,* Book III, part 1. This query has a bearing on the controversy of the nature of light; is it corpuscular, as Newton thought, or does it partake of the nature of waves, as Thomas Young (*inter alia*) proposed, many years after Newton's death? Wood (1954), in his biography of Thomas Young, puts the problem thus:

> Reflection and refraction occur simultaneously. When a beam of light falls on a water surface, some is transmitted and some reflected. How is this to be explained? On the wave theory it is quite simple – the phenomenon is common to all kinds of wave. Some of the energy of the wave is transmitted and some reflected. What of the corpuscles? Why do some pass on and some come back if they are at all identical? Here we have a good example of the ad hoc hypothesis. And it is supplied by no less a person than Newton himself. He suggested that when the corpuscles reached the boundary, some were in a 'fit of easy transmission' and some in a 'fit of easy reflection'. What happened at the surface depended on the fit of the moment. It is difficult for us to take this theory seriously, but certainly Newton did, and he even suggested waves as the predisposing cause of the fits:
>
> 'And in a like manner, when a ray of light falls upon the surface of any pellucid Body, and is there refracted and reflected, may not waves or vibrations or Tremors be there excited in the refracting or reflecting medium at the point of incidence? And do they not overtake the Rays of Light, and by overtaking them

successively, do they not put them into the Fits of easy Reflexion and easy Transmission described above?'

Now, with all due deference to our greatest scientist, this statement clearly fudges the issue so completely that no prediction is in fact possible which would decide between the corpuscular and the wave theory. By making the quite arbitrary assumption of the existence of 'fits of easy reflection' (which are nowhere derived from other parts of the theory, and for which it would be impossible to find any method of testing), Newton gets out of his particular difficulties very much in the manner of Freud postulating reaction formation in order to account for the fact that observation showed exactly the opposite sort of effect to that derived from his theory. But would this lead us to dismiss Newton as unscientific, and his theory as useless? Newton was of course accused by French physicists of being non-rigorous and inventing meaningless and impossible concepts (such as action at a distance); it was not until 150 years after his death that Cauchy, in his *Cours d'analyse,* made Newton's calculus into a rigorous body of knowledge. There are usually no blacks and whites in this type of work, only greys shading over more or less to the one side or the other; would it be reasonable to make *ex cathedra* judgments about Freudian theory when the same sword might cut off so many other, worthy heads? We merely raise this question, not being competent to answer it. Perhaps the ultimate answer must come, not from philosophers at all, but from experimental psychologists. If they feel that they are in a position to make testable deductions from psychoanalytic theories, and if these tests turn out successful, then it would be hard for the philosophers to rule these deductions and verifications out of court. Much would depend on the reaction of psychoanalysts themselves; if the deductions were in fact falsified, would they accept the verdict of empirical science, and change their theories, or abandon them, or would they rather re-interpret the theories so as to make them fit in with the findings?

There seems to be no doubt that many psychologists have in fact assumed that Freudian theories are sufficiently clear-cut to make prediction possible, and many deductions from such theories have been made and tested. We would regard it as slightly absurd to reject these studies on *a priori* grounds, and to refuse for philosophical reasons to look at them, and prefer to examine them as carefully as we would deductions and experiments resulting from Hullian theory, or Pavlovian theory – deductions and experiments which in many cases could also be regarded as perhaps less rigorous than might be considered desirable! We would not like our refusal to accept *in toto* the philosophical condemnation of Freudian theorizing as 'unscientific' to imply an arrogation of philosophical competence beyond our modest abilities; what we feel, rather, is that philosophical considerations make up only one of many aspects of the problem, and that others are perhaps more important from the point of view of the experimental psychologist.

There has of course been a good deal of discussion among psychologists, philosophers and psychoanalysts on these points; the work of Cheshire (1964), Ellis (1950), Farrell (1961), Feigl and Scriven (1956), Hook (1959), MacIntyre (1958), Pumpian-Mindlin (1952), and Wisdom (1953) being perhaps among the best known. It would be out of place here to discuss these issues at great length; our position is not dissimilar to that of Miles (1966), whose little book *Eliminating the Unconscious* attempts to recognize the legitimate claims of psychoanalysis while refusing to grant it an *imprimatur* to cover all its sins by reference to the special training given by psychoanalysts. The tenor of his conclusions can be gathered from the following brief quotation:

> The main thesis ... is that psychoanalysis is capable in principle of being a rational, systematic study. Whether we also say that it is 'scientific' depends on how widely or otherwise we use the term 'scientific'. For my part I see no good reason for restricting this word to those enquiries which have the experimental rigour of the chemistry and physics laboratory; I would prefer to extend it to any study where general conclusions are supported by a systematic study of the evidence. (p. 23).

Miles goes on to draw a distinction between the essentials and the 'mere trappings' of scientific respectability, and concludes that

> There is no justification for assuming that the only valid scientific work is that done in the laboratory, or that scientific respectability is possible only when there is the deliberate setting up of experimental conditions; the ideal of repeatability is in theory a sound one, but in psychoanalysis as in many other enquiries it is an ideal which cannot be realized; on the other hand, accurate recording, generalization, quantification, and the exclusion of alternative explanations are all desirable objectives and as far as

> psychoanalysis is concerned are capable in principle of being achieved. (p. 24).

We would agree with these sentiments, adding that what we have attempted in this book has been to bring together those studies which by common consent have gone farthest to achieve these aims of accurate recording, generalization, quantification, and the exclusion of alternative explanations; in addition, we have given preference to those studies which have involved the deliberate setting up of experimental conditions. We cannot claim to have anything novel to say with respect to the philosophical points raised by Popper and Kuhn; all we can say is that in our view the contents of this book are of interest to psychologists and psychoanalysts alike, and possibly even to philosophers, and that one's judgment of psychoanalysis as a science must ultimately rest more on the kind of critical consideration we have here given to some two dozen empirical studies, than on *a priori* judgments as to the possibility of studying Freudian concepts empirically.

There are one or two points which require discussion. The first of these relates to the statement often made by psychoanalysts, when confronted by psychologists and others who wish to carry on experimental work on Freudian concepts or to discuss the validity of Freudian theories, that only those who have undergone the process of a training analysis are fit to do any of these things. We would hold the opposite view; a training analysis has the effect of biassing the mind of the trainee to such an extent that he cannot under any circumstances be relied upon to observe and report accurately anything relating to the doctrines which he has received during his analysis. This belief is apparently shared by Glover (1952), who for some sixteen years was Director of Research of the London Institute of Psychoanalysis; this is what he writes:

> Whatever may be the ideal of training analysis, it is indisputable that the margin of scientific error introduced by factors of transference and counter-transference is extremely wide. It is scarcely to be expected that a student who has spent some years under the artificial and sometimes hothouse conditions of a training analysis and whose professional career depends on overcoming 'resistance' to the satisfaction of his training analyst, can be in a favourable position to defend his scientific integrity against his analyst's theory and practice. And the longer he remains in training

> analysis, the less likely he is to do so. For according to his analyst the candidate's objections to interpretations rate as 'resistances'. In short there is a tendency inherent in the training situation to perpetuate error.

Precisely. And this error-producing process is then recommended to searchers after truth in this field!

It is for this reason of course that we have laid stress on experimental studies; these alone can have the objectivity, the detailed description of conditions and results, and the requisite statistical elaboration to make proper judgment possible. The majority of psychoanalytic writings are lacking in these essential safeguards, and hence are not of much value for those searching after truth. Here again Glover bears witness from the psychoanalytic side:

> We may start with four working assumptions: first, that psychoanalytical research is almost totally unorganized; second, that the conditions of clinical analysis and of analytic training militate against objectivity in research; third, that in consequence a large proportion of current theorizing and clinical finding is little more than unchecked speculation; and fourth, that so far no system exists whereby the scientific authority of the research workers can be distinguished from the prestige of senior analytical practitioners and teachers.

And Glover ends his report by saying: 'It would save a good deal of fruitless effort and much disappointment if we recognize that one of our first tasks, without which research is threatened with stagnation and sterility, is to settle down to the long and arduous task of defining terms, verifying criteria and developing reliable statistics.' In this task, we would add, the question of whether the research worker has or has not received a training analysis does not seem very relevant; far more important would seem a good training in experimental method, research design, and statistical enquiry.

Another point which must be considered is a suggestion made by Cioffi (1970), and extensively documented by him. He argues that psychoanalysis is a pseudo-science; this he defines as being constituted 'not merely by formally defective theses but by methodologically defective procedures . . . The notion of a pseudo-science is a pragmatic and not a syntactic one.' Cioffi argues that underlying all the defects of psychoanalytic theory is 'the same impulse: the need to avoid refutation'. As he goes on to say,

> it is characteristic of a pseudo-science that the hypotheses which comprise it stand in an asymmetrical relation to the expectations they generate, being permitted to guide them and be vindicated by their fulfilment but not to be discredited by their disappointment. One way in which it achieves this is by contriving to have these hypotheses understood in a narrow and determinate sense before the event but in a broader and hazier one after it on those occasions on which they are not borne out. Such hypotheses thus lead a double life – a subdued and restrained one in the vicinity of counter-observations and another less inhibited and more exuberent one when remote from them. (p. 474).

Cioffi gives several examples; we will look at just one of these.

Cioffi starts off by saying that our confidence in Freud's reconstructions of his neurotic patients' infantile sex life might be justified by the accuracy of those portions of the reconstructions which are held to characterize childhood in general, thus being capable of confirmation by the contemporary observation of children. Freud himself seems to concur when he writes, in his 'Three Essays in Sexuality': 'I can point with satisfaction to the fact that direct observation has fully confirmed the conclusions drawn from psychoanalysis and thus furnished good evidence for the reliability of the latter method of investigation.' (Freud, 1958, p. 594.) And on many other occasions Freud says explicitly that his clinically derived theses regarding the infant's sexual life could be tested by systematically observing the behaviour of children. In his case history of 'Little Hans' he refers to the observation of children as a 'more direct and less roundabout proof of these fundamental theories', and speaks of 'observing upon the child at first hand, in all the freshness of life, the sexual impulses and conative tendencies which we dig out so laboriously in the adult from among their own debris'. (We have included in this book a detailed examination of the case of Little Hans, partly to enable the reader to check on statements of this kind.) Cioffi goes on to say of Freud that

> he even implies that the facts to which he has called attention are so blatant that one must take pains to avoid noticing them. For example in his paper 'The sexual theories of children' he says 'one can easily observe' that little girls regard their clitoris as an inferior penis. In his paper 'The resistances to psychoanalysis' he writes of the Oedipal phase: 'At that period of life these impulses still continue uninhibited as straightforward sexual desires. This

> can be confirmed so easily that only the greatest efforts could make it possible to overlook it. (p. 478).

Cioffi quotes other statements by Freud, but the point is clear: the hypotheses advanced on the basis of adult analysis, relating to the vagaries of childhood libidinal tendencies, can be directly observed in young children, and indeed are difficult to overlook. 'The further one carried these observations on children, the more self-evident the facts became and the more astonishing was it too that so much trouble was taken to overlook them.' (Freud, 1925).

What happens when an impartial, well-trained psychologist of some eminence studies a number of children in the greatest detail, with Freudian hypotheses specially in mind? The answer is found, e.g. in Valentine's (1942) book on the *Psychology of Early Childhood.* He concluded (to cut a very long story short) that 'from every point of view – the preferences for M or F at different ages, by boys or girls, the reasons for changes in preferences, the influence of discipline, the occasions for jealousy – all these give ample reasonable explanations of the facts and supply no evidence of the supposed Oedipus complex.' (p. 330). As regards the strength and general influence of sexual factors in early childhood, Valentine's conclusions are equally negative. He concludes by saying that

> whether the ideas of infantile sexuality reported by patients are indeed (a) suggested by psychoanalysts – as Freud at one time himself suspected – or (b) are entirely or partly the patients' own interpretations of and exaggerations of relatively slight sensations and impulses, or (c) whether they are largely true but only in a few abnormal cases, this is not the place to discuss. But the fact that the reports of patients, which Freud himself took at first to be facts, proved to be mere fantasies, is very significant. (p. 351).

In other words, the most careful observation of children, carried out over a long period of time, utterly failed to reveal any of the phenomena so confidently claimed as 'self-evident' and said to be 'confirmed so easily'. Many other observers could be quoted here as having come to the same conclusion, but our point here is not to disprove Freud's theories, but rather to see how he deals with disconfirmation.

As Cioffi goes on to point out, 'on occasions when Freud is under the necessity of forestalling disconfirmatory reports he forgets the so-easily-confirmable character of his reconstructions of infantile life and insists on their esoteric only-observable-by-initiates status!' This is what Freud has to say in the preface to the fourth edition of the 'Three Essays on Sexuality': 'None . . . but physicians who practise psychoanalysis can have any access whatever to this sphere of knowledge or any possibility of forming a judgment that is uninfluenced by their own dislikes and prejudices. If mankind had been able to learn from direct observation of children these three essays could have remained unwritten.' Cioffi comments that 'this retreat to the esoterically observable in the face of disconfirmatory evidence is a general feature of psychoanalytic apologetic'. Such a retreat would of course render the observation of children futile for the purpose of validating psychoanalytic method.

> Freud's peripheral awareness of this would account for a lack of candour in his expositions. The expression 'direct observation' alternates with 'direct analytic observation' as if they were synonymous, so that it only becomes clear after several rereadings that when Freud speaks of 'the direct observation of children' he is referring to the psychoanalytic interpretation of infantile behaviour. That is, Freud, in attempting to dispel our doubts as to the validity of psychoanalytic method by appeals to 'direct observation', proffers us a copy of the same newspaper, this time with his thumb over the banner. (p. 480)

We would not dismiss Cioffi's case out of hand; his presentation should be read in detail before any conclusion is arrived at by the reader. The evidence clearly is inconclusive; it is possible that Freud deliberately wrote in such a manner as to make disproof impossible, but it is also possible that these contradictions arose in the course of a very busy career, stretching over many years, in which Freud wrote millions of words, constantly correcting himself and presenting new and changed theories. Certainly Freud's choice of words is often curiously indecisive, as if he were afraid to say something that could be tested in any rigorous way. Cioffi urges us to 'consider the idioms in which Freud's interpretations are typically phrased. Symptoms, errors, etc. are not simply *caused by* but they "announce", "proclaim", "express", "realize", "fulfil", "gratify", "represent", "imitate" or "allude to" this or that repressed impulse, thought, memory, etc.' True, these phrases might have been used to avoid refutation, as Cioffi suggests; they might also have been used because Freud was a great writer, unwilling to follow the practice of experimental psychologists and use identical phrases each time a similar thought required expression. Clearly there is but one way out of this difficulty; let us give Freud the benefit of the doubt, and interpret what he says as being precisely what he intended to say. Thus when he proclaims that simple observation of child behaviour can verify psychoanalytic hypotheses, we are quite justified to do what Valentine did – observe children under relevant circumstances, as closely and as accurately as possible. If the results disconfirm Freud, then we must accept this as a genuine disconfirmation; if we now argue that only observations made by trained psychoanalysts are relevant, then we would indeed seem to justify Cioffi's accusation, and deservedly be regarded as outside the pale of science. We would extend this argument to the contents of this book as a whole; we have done Freud the honour of treating him as a man searching for truth, expressing his thoughts freely and as best he could, without any notion of 'avoiding refutation'. This does not prejudge the outcome in any way, and seems to be the only way in which to examine any person's contribution. If the reader, or the critic, now tries to argue away negative findings by reference to 'hidden' meanings in Freud's writings, this trust is broken, and Freud's theories become impossible to verify or disprove; in other words, they cease to have any scientific interest.

A last point on which much has been written, and which is crucial to our organization of this book, relates to the hierarchical structure of psychoanalytic theory (Rapaport & Gill, 1959). Criticisms of psychoanalytic theory are often directed towards the higher, metapsychological portions of the theory, rather than against the lower, more empirical ones; it may be possible to come to agreement on the latter, on the basis of experimental study, while any agreement on the former is perhaps out of the question. Rapaport and Gill suggest four layers or stages: 1. Empirical propositions, such as that around the fourth year of life boys regard their fathers as rivals. 2. Specific psychoanalytic propositions, such as that the solution of the Oedipal situation is a decisive determinant of character formation and pathology. 3. General psychoanalytical propositions, such as that structure formation by means of identification and anti-cathexes explains theoretically the consequences of the 'decline of the Oedipus complex'. 4. Metapsychological propositions, such as those of the general psychoanalytical theory which explains the Oedipal situation and the decline of the Oedipus complex as involving dynamic, economic, structural, genetic and adaptive assumptions. Kline (1972) points out that the testing of any Freudian concepts must address itself to the empirical basis, i.e. the empirical and specific psychoanalytic propositions. 'It seems pointless to criticize the metapsychology of psychoanalytic theory on the grounds of internal inconsistency, or untestability of the hypotheses, before establishing whether or not the empirical data, which the metapsychology seeks to subsume, are well founded or not.' (p. 3). This is a reasonable point of view, and one which we have adopted in this book. If the basic propositions of the theory can be validated, then is the time to worry about the highest-order propositions, and the difficulties to which they give rise; if validation fails, then the highest-order propositions fail *ipso facto*, and need not worry us any further.

So much, then, for our introductory remarks; it will be seen that we have left open quite a number of questions which have been discussed at great length by many knowledgeable and gifted people, without any great agreement. We believe that to search for answers which would be acceptable to all the philosophers, psychologists and psychoanalysts working in this field would be a task of supererogation; such answers are not to be found by the customary experimental researches of the scientist, and hence may not be sufficiently factual to be worth pursuing. We believe that an actual examination of the manner in which experimental psychologists have tried to formulate testable deductions from Freudian concepts and theories, and the way in which they have carried out their experiments, is more informative than any amount of philosophizing. If these empirical studies come up with important new knowledge, then few people will worry about the 'scientific' nature of Freudian thinking; if they instead fail to provide any such knowledge, then no amount of philosophical justification will rescue the theories involved from oblivion. By their fruits shall ye know them – these are the fruits of Freudian thinking, tested and tried by the best available experts; what conclusion do they permit? We shall try to answer this question in the Epilogue, after we have considered some two dozen studies in detail; the reader will no doubt formulate his own conclusions, and it will be interesting to see whether these different views agree or disagree in the end.

REFERENCES

CHESHIRE, N. M. (1964) On the rationale of psychoanalytic argumentation. *Brit. J. Med. Psychol.*, **37**, 217-30.

CIOFFI, F. (1970) Freud and the idea of a pseudo-science. In M. R. BORGER and F. CIOFFI (ed.) *Explanations in the Behavioural Sciences*. Cambridge: Univ. Press.

ELLIS, A. (1950) An introduction to the principles of scientific psychoanalysis. *Genet. Psychol. Monogr.*, **41**.

FARRELL, B. A. (1951) The scientific testing of psychoanalytic findings and theory. III. *Brit. J. Med. Psychol.*, **24**, 35-51.

—— (1961) On the character of psycho-dynamic discourse. *Brit. J. Med. Psychol.*, **54**, 7-21.

—— (1964) The status of psychoanalytic theory. *Inquiry*, **7**, 104-23.

FEIGL, H. and SCRIVEN, M. (1956) The foundations of science and the concepts of psychology and psychoanalysis. *Minnesota Studies in the Philosophy of Science*, Vol. 1. Minneapolis, Minn.: Univ. of Minnesota Press.

FREUD, S. (1925) *Collected Papers*, Vol. 4. London: Hogarth Press.

—— (1958) *The Basic Writings of Sigmund Freud*. New York: Knapp.

GLOVER, E. (1952) Research methods in psychoanalysis. *Int. J. Psychoanal.*, **33**, 403-9.

HOOK, G. (ed.) (1959) *Psychoanalysis, Scientific Method and Philosophy*. New York: Univ. Press.

KEELE, K. D. (1965) *William Harvey*. London: Nelson.

KLINE, P. (1972) *Fact and Fantasy in Freudian Theory*. London: Methuen.

KUHN, T. S. (1957) *The Copernican Revolution*. Cambridge, Mass.: Harvard Univ. Press.

—— (1970) Logic of discovery or psychology of research? In LAKATOS and MUSGRAVE (1970), see below.

LAKATOS, I. and MUSGRAVE, A. (1970) *Criticism and the Growth of Knowledge*. Cambridge: Univ. Press.

MacINTYRE, A. C. (1958) *The Unconscious*. London: Routledge & Kegan Paul.

MILES, T. R. (1966) *Eliminating the Unconscious*. Oxford: Pergamon Press.

NEWTON, I. (1704) *Opticks*, Book III, part 1, query 17. London.

POPPER, K. R. (1959) *The Logic of Scientific Discovery*. London: Hutchinson.

—— (1963) *Conjectures and Refutations.* London: Routledge & Kegan Paul.

PUMPIAN-MINDLIN, E. (ed.) 1952 *Psychoanalysis as Science.* New York: Basic Books.

RAPAPORT, D. and GILL, M. M. (1959) The points of view and assumptions of metapsychology. *Int. J. Psychoanal.* **40,** 153-62.

SEARS, R. R. (1943) *Survey of Objective Studies in Psychoanalytic Concepts.* New York: Social Science Research Council.

VALENTINE, C. W. (1942) *The Psychology of Early Childhood.* London: Methuen.

WISDOM, J. (1953) *Philosophy and Psychoanalysis.* Oxford: Univ. Press.

WOOD, A. (1954) *Thomas Young.* Cambridge: Univ. Press.

PART ONE

Psychosexual development

I

Leon J. Yarrow (1954)[1]

The relationship between nutritive sucking experiences in infancy and non-nutritive sucking in childhood

The Journal of Genetic Psychology, 84, 149-62

THE PROBLEM

Thumbsucking is of interest both from clinical and theoretical points of view; from the clinical standpoint because of the problems it creates in parent-child relationships, and from a theoretical point of view because of its implications for the psychoanalytic theory of orality.

It is generally accepted that most infants engage in some sucking of the thumbs or fingers during the first few months of life, either in the process of exploring the world through the mouth or as a reaction to hunger or other deprivation. The point, in terms of age or frequency, at which this exploratory or substitutive sucking becomes an anxiety-evoking stimulus to the parent varies greatly, dependent upon the cultural milieu of the parents, as well as upon their conscious and unconscious attitudes toward orality. It is well known to pediatricians, psychiatrists and psychologists that thumb- or fingersucking after one or two years of age arouses strong anxieties in many parents, and leads to counter-anxieties and guilt feelings in the children engaging in this activity.

There have been a few investigations (Davis *et al.*, 1948; Kunst, 1948; Levy, 1928, 1934; Roberts, 1944; Sears & Wise, 1950) which have attempted to study some of the factors in the etiology of prolonged thumbsucking, but much of the vast literature on the subject has been speculative. Moreover, statements in the literature

[1]Child Research Council, University of Colorado School of Medicine. The author wishes to express his appreciation to Dr Alfred Washburn for providing an environment facilitating research, and to Dr John Benjamin for many constructive criticisms and suggestions.

by 'experts' (pediatricians, psychologists, psychiatrists and orthodontists) on the causes and methods of treatment have often been contradictory. One common maxim has been that weaning should not be started too early lest the child turn to thumbsucking as a substitute. This implication – that there is a relationship between duration of feeding on the breast or bottle and the occurrence of thumbsucking – is one of the hypotheses tested in this investigation.

Orality and its manifestations and vicissitudes form a significant part of the content of psychoanalytic theory. The child's experiences during the oral stage of development, the balance of gratifications and frustrations during this period, and the ease or difficulty with which he progresses from this to the subsequent developmental stages are considered crucial for his personality development.

The present study deals with only one aspect of orality – the physical act of sucking. 'Orality' in its broad sense in psychoanalytic theory has more varied and subtle manifestations than those involved in the act of sucking. The psychological aspects of oral deprivation and gratification based on affectional relationships (Abraham, 1927a; Ribble, 1939; Spitz, 1946) are not considered in this report.

This study would also seem to have implications for the specific hypotheses concerning the mechanisms of fixation and regression, basic concepts in psychoanalytic theory. Fixation on, or regression to, a mode or zone characteristic of a given developmental stage is presumed to be dependent upon one or a combination of the following stimulus conditions – extreme frustration or excessive gratification during the appropriate stage. Recent literature (Hartman, 1950) has emphasized 'phase specificity', that is, that the organism is most vulnerable to a given type of frustration or over-gratification at the appropriate developmental stage. Thus, during the period of greatest oral sensitivity, oral deprivation or oral over-gratification would be most likely to create the conditions for fixation or later regression. Thumbsucking beyond early infancy might be considered an expression of at least a partial fixation at the oral stage of development.

The present study is concerned with the relationship between deprivation and gratification in the early feeding situation and non-nutritive sucking habits in childhood. This study deals with single variable relationships, and does not attempt to test the broad psychoanalytic theory of orality. However, the isolation of some simple relationships can perhaps suggest a clearer formulation of more complex, multi-variable relationships.

SUBJECTS

The subjects were 66 children, 28 boys and 38 girls, chosen from the population of children participating in a longitudinal research project conducted by the Child Research Council.[1] The children were born between 1935 and 1948. Study of these children began at birth, and is still in progress. Only those children whose records contained adequate information on the relevant variables were included in the study. These variables were age of weaning, reaction to weaning, presence or absence of thumbsucking, and duration and severity of thumbsucking.

PROCEDURE

The data included in this study were obtained by interviews with the mother by a psychologist or pediatrician. To reduce retrospective errors, only information on behaviour and events which occurred within six months of the time of the interview was included in the study.

The interviews with the mothers covered a variety of aspects of development – physical, motor, language, social, personality, etc. In studying any aspect of behaviour or development, all of these variables are to some extent relevant. For the purposes of this study only those data were included which were directly relevant to the limited hypotheses formulated for the study. The following information was selected from the records available on the children:

1. The child's attitude during feeding.
2. The vigour of sucking on breast or bottle. (Based on mothers' reports. No direct observations were available).
3. General appetite.
4. Feeding disturbances.
5. Age of weaning from breast or bottle or complementary feeding.

[1]The Child Research Council population at present consists of 170 children. There are two chief criteria governing the admission of the children to the Child Research Council programme. First, that the parents be sufficiently interested in the programme to maintain a high level of co-operation. Second, that there be a high probability that the family will be permanent residents of the community.

The group is not a representative sample of the total population of the community: it is quite homogeneous in class status and socio-economic level. The families are from a middle to upper middle social class group, most of the fathers being engaged in professional or managerial occupations. The educational level of the parents is above that of the general population.

6. Reaction to weaning from breast or bottle.
7. Usual feeding time on breast or bottle during first six months.
8. Age when thumbsucking was first reported.
9. Age of cessation of thumb or fingersucking.
10. Vigour of thumb or fingersucking.
11. Conditions under which thumb or fingersucking usually occurred.
12. Parents' attitudes toward thumb or fingersucking.
13. Parents' methods of handling thumb or fingersucking.

For purposes of statistical analysis of the data, the qualitative information on feeding and oral behaviour obtained from interviews with the mothers was rated. The following ratings were made:

1. *Reaction to weaning.* Reactions to weaning were rated on a three-point scale: 1 = no observed reaction; 2 = moderate reaction; 3 = strong reaction.

Examples of moderate reaction: 'No reaction (to weaning) but was fussy about taking milk for a few days.' 'No effect, although at first the baby did not get enough milk.' 'No reactions except not drinking as much milk as usual.'

Examples of strong reaction: 'Cried for about half an hour for a week on going to bed.' 'Had an aversion to liquids for almost five months, he reacted so strongly.' 'Took about a week before he accepted the idea. When he saw the cup coming, he would cry.'

2. *Severity of thumbsucking.* Severity of thumbsucking was rated on a three-point scale: 1 = none or mild thumbsucking; 2 = moderate thumbsucking; 3 = severe thumbsucking.

Examples of mild thumbsucking: 'No thumbsucking now (five months). There was a little for a few months.' 'Sucks fingers occasionally when he wakes up before feeding.'

Examples of moderate thumbsucking: 'Starts sucking thumb as soon as mention is made of going to bed.' 'Sucks when unhappy and frustrated.' 'Sucks when hungry, tired and occasionally when unoccupied.'

Examples of severe thumbsucking: 'Sucks much of the time when unoccupied.' 'Sucks all of the time . . . a strong habit.'

RESULTS

Basic Data on Feeding and Thumbsucking

a. Breastfeeding. Of the children studied, 46 (70 per cent) had some breastfeeding experience. For the group as a whole breastfeeding was of short duration. The median age of weaning from the breast was 2.3 months, with a range from one week to ten months. In this group, the boys were weaned almost a month earlier than the girls, the median age of weaning for the girls being 2.6 months; for the boys, 1.8 months. Only one child was weaned directly to the cup. Two were weaned from a complement of breast and bottle to the cup.

b. Bottlefeeding. The median age at which the children in this group were weaned from the bottle was 12.9 months, with a range from six months to thirty-eight months. As was the case with weaning from the breast, the boys were weaned from the bottle earlier than the girls; the median age for the girls being 14.5 months, and for the boys, 11.6 months.

c. Thumbsucking. Sixty-four per cent of the children in the group were reported as having sucked their thumbs at some time. There were slight sex differences in incidence of thumbsucking, its occurrence being reported in 66 per cent of the girls and 54 per cent of the boys.

Of the total group of thumbsuckers, 63 per cent had begun this practice before three months of age; 90 per cent had begun by six months of age. The age at which thumbsucking was discontinued ranged from one month to more than eight years. Fourteen per cent of the children who sucked their thumbs had discontinued by six months of age. Twenty-eight per cent of the thumbsuckers had stopped by one year. By four years half of the group of thumbsuckers was still engaging in this activity. By six years 75 per cent of the children who had sucked their thumbs had discontinued the practice. Six children (14 per cent of the group), one boy and five girls, were still doing some thumbsucking after seven years.

Relationship between Thumbsucking and Feeding Variables

Tables 1-1 to 1-5 show the distribution of cases for each of the variables of the feeding situation in relation to the duration and severity of thumbsucking. For the statistical analyses, chi-square tests of significance (McNemar, 1949) were computed comparing the children at the extremes in thumbsucking and at the extremes on each of the feeding variable. Since theoretical frequencies in each cell were small, the Yates' correction for continuity was applied.

a. Relationship between duration of breastfeeding and thumb-

sucking. It has been assumed (by some pediatricians and psychologists) that infants who are breastfed for a reasonably long period of time are less likely to become problem thumbsuckers than babies who have had no or little breastfeeding experience. This is based on the hypothesis that the child who receives his nourishment from the breast is able to obtain more adequate gratification of his sucking needs than the bottle-fed child. Recent literature (Goldman, 1948) also suggests that the breastfed child as a result of the close physical contact with the mother obtains more 'mothering', and consequently has his affectional needs more adequately gratified. If one considers oral gratification in both its restricted and its broader sense, i.e. including affectional gratification, then one might predict a lesser likelihood of thumbsucking among the children with long breastfeeding experience.

To test the above hypotheses, comparisons were made between the children who had no breastfeeding experience and those who were breastfed for a period of months beyond the median of the group (three months). Chi-square test applied to the cases at the extremes in severity and in duration of thumbsucking indicated no statistically significant differences, $P = .20$ for severity of thumbsucking; $P = <.20$ for duration of thumbsucking. On the other hand, comparison of children who were not breastfed with those who were breastfed for six months or longer showed that of the 6 children in the latter group, none continued thumbsucking beyond infancy, whereas of the 20 children who had no breastfeeding experience, 7 sucked their thumbs for more than five years. Chi-square analysis, utilizing Yates' correction for continuity, showed no statistically significant difference in severity or duration of thumbsucking; Chi-square = 2.399, $P = >.10$ for severity; Chi-square = 2.362, $P = <.10$ for duration[1] (Tables 1-1 and 1-2).

These statistical findings do not support the hypothesis that lack of breastfeeding is likely to be a significant factor in the causation of thumbsucking. The direction of the findings, however, suggests that a long period of breastfeeding may be a prophylactic against thumbsucking, although the number of cases is too few to permit any definite conclusions.

On the hypothesis that early cessation of breastfeeding may be experienced as a stronger frustration to the child than no breastfeeding at all, comparisons were made between the children who had a short

[1] '*t*' test applied to these data indicated no statistically significant differences.

period of breastfeeding and those who had a long breastfeeding experience. Of 21 children who were breastfed for less than two months, 13 stopped thumbsucking during infancy, and 5 continued this practice after five years. Of the 6 children who were breastfed for more than six months, none was engaging in thumbsucking at five years. Chi-square analysis gives an insignificant level of confidence, Chi-square = 0.6524.

TABLE 1.1. *Relationship between duration of thumbsucking and duration of breastfeeding.*

Duration of breastfeeding	Duration of thumbsucking No T.S.	To 1 year	Between 1-5 years	More than 5 years
None	5	3	5	7
0 – 2 months	8	5	3	5
2 – 3 months	2	2	2	2
3 – 6 months	6	0	0	5
6 months plus	5	1	0	0

TABLE 1.2. *Relationship between severity of thumbsucking and duration of breastfeeding.*

Duration of breastfeeding	Severity of thumbsucking None to mild	Moderate to severe
None	11	9
0 – 2 months	16	5
2 – 3 months	4	3
3 – 6 months	7	5
6 months plus	6	0

b. Relationship between age of weaning to the cup and thumbsucking. For statistical comparisons, the children were divided into two groups, the early-weaned and the late-weaned. Weaning to the cup before one year was considered early, whereas weaning after sixteen months was considered late.

Chi-square tests showed no significant differences between the early- and late-weaned children in duration of thumbsucking (Chi-square = 1.854, $P = .20$). A larger proportion of the late thumbsuckers, however, were among the late-weaned children. Of 29 children weaned before one year, only 3 continued thumbsucking after five years; whereas of 22 children weaned after sixteen months 6 were still engaging in non-nutritive sucking after five years.

There is a similar, but stronger trend on the ratings of severity of thumbsucking. Of 29 children weaned before one year, 6 were rated as moderate or severe thumbsuckers; whereas of the 23 children weaned after sixteen months, 9 were in the moderate or severe category. These differences are significant at the 10 per cent level of confidence (Chi-square = 2.155). Although this probability is not sufficiently large to reject the null hypothesis, these findings would certainly lead one to question the assumption that early weaning to the cup is conducive to prolonged or severe thumbsucking (Table 1-3).

TABLE 1.3. *Relationship between age of weaning to the cup and thumbsucking.*

A. DURATION OF THUMBSUCKING

Age of weaning	Age of cessation of thumbsucking: No T.S.	Before 1 year	1 – 5 years	After 5 years
Before 12 months	13	5	8	3
12 – 16 months	4	3	1	7
After 16 months	8	4	4	6

B. SEVERITY OF THUMBSUCKING

Age of weaning	Severity of thumbsucking: None to mild	Moderate to severe
Before 12 months	23	6
12 – 16 months	7	7
After 16 months	14	9

c. Relationship between age of weaning to cup and reaction to weaning. There are significant differences between the early-weaned and the late-weaned children in reaction to weaning. The late-weaned children show a more severe reaction to weaning than the early-weaned children. Chi-square test applied to the cases at the extremes of the group in weaning time showed differences significant beyond the 1 per cent level of confidence (Table 1-4).

Sears has theorized on the basis of similar findings (Sears & Wise, 1950) that the sucking drive is strengthened by prolonged gratification. The stronger frustration reactions at weaning by the late-weaned groups are considered to be a function of the greater strength of the drive which has been frustrated. Although the data on weaning reactions are in agreement with Sears' findings, their adequacy in supporting Sears' interpretation can be questioned. Ratings of strength of protest at weaning, based on parents' reports of the child's behaviour at the time, can be considered only rough indices of the degree of frustration experienced by the child. Inferences from parents' reports regarding the degree of frustration experienced by the child are complicated by individual differences in children's modes of reaction to frustration. The vigour of protest at weaning may also be a function of developmental level, with the older child being able to express more forcefully than the younger his dislike of a change in the feeding routine.

TABLE 1.4. *Relationship between age of weaning and reaction to weaning.*

	Reaction to weaning	
Age of weaning	None	Moderate to severe
Before 12 months	21	6
12 – 16 months	6	6
After 16 months	5	9

d. The relationship between thumbsucking and feeding time in infancy. To test the relationship between amount of direct sucking gratification obtained during early infancy and severity and duration of thumbsucking, comparisons were made of children with different amounts of time on the breast or bottle per feeding.

TABLE 1.5. *Relationship between thumbsucking and feeding time.*

A. AGE OF CESSATION OF THUMBSUCKING

Feeding time (in minutes)	No T.S.	Before 1 year	1 – 5 years	After 5 years
5 – 15	2	0	1	6
15 – 20	0	6	2	3
More than 20	3	6	2	0

B. SEVERITY OF THUMBSUCKING

Feeding time (in minutes)	None	Moderate to severe
5 – 15	2	7
15 – 20	6	5
More than 20	10	1

Data on feeding time – the number of minutes on the breast or bottle – during the first six months were available on only 31 subjects. These data indicate that a significantly larger number of children who had short feeding times in early infancy developed severe thumbsucking habits. Of 11 children who had more than 20 minutes of sucking time on the breast or bottle during infancy, 9 had stopped thumbsucking before one year. There were 9 children with less than 15 minutes of feeding time; of these 6 persisted in thumbsucking after five years. Chi-square test showed these differences to be significant at the 2 per cent level of confidence. Similarly significant differences ($P = .02$) were found with regard to ratings on severity of thumbsucking (Table 1-5).

DISCUSSION

The data of the present study on feeding time support the hypothesis that severe thumbsucking represents a substitute form or oral activity, arising from inadequate satisfaction of the sucking drive during early infancy. These findings on feeding time are in agreement with those of Levy (1928, 1934) and Roberts (1944).

Levy studied the relationship between the thumbsucking habits and the feeding histories of 122 children. The data were obtained through retrospective interviews with the mothers of these children. He concluded that 'the severity of the thumbsucking habit is in proportion to the insufficiency of sucking time' (during feeding). He found, too, that there were no thumbsuckers among the children who had used artificial pacifiers.

In a follow-up of the latter investigation under more controlled conditions, Levy studied the sucking habits of three pairs of puppies who were given different feeding experiences. One pair of puppies was breastfed by the mother, the other two groups were bottlefed. Of the bottlefed puppies, one group was allowed a long sucking period during feeding, and extra sucking on an artificial nipple after feeding. The other group had a short sucking time and no extra-nutritive sucking. The puppies with the shortest amount of sucking time did the most extra-nutritive sucking, the breastfed puppies, the least amount of sucking.

Roberts studied the relationship between feeding time and thumbsucking of a group of 30 infants between 7 and 8 months of age, half of whom were thumbsuckers, and the other half, non-thumbsuckers.

She concluded that 'the amount of time spent in sucking is the primary determinant of the habit of sucking the thumb or fingers'.

It would seem a logical deduction from these findings on feeding time that early weaning would be associated with greater extra-nutritive sucking. The data of this study do not support this commonly held assumption; rather the direction of the findings tends to support Sears' hypothesis that a long duration of breast or bottle feeding strengthens the oral drive, and thereby leads to increased extra-nutritive sucking. This hypothesis was based on the findings of two studies. Davis, Sears, Miller, and Brodbeck (1948) found that breastfed infants developed a stronger sucking response at the end of 10 days than did the infants fed by cup or bottle. In a later study by Sears and Wise (1950) on the effects of infant feeding experiences on sucking, an attempt was made to test the Freudian hypothesis that the lips and mouth become erotogenic as a result of the association of the act of sucking with the act of food-taking. The findings of greater frustration reactions among the late-weaned children were interpreted in terms of a reinforcement hypothesis, i.e., that the sucking drive is strengthened by practice at the breast or bottle.

The present findings on feeding time and age of weaning to the cup – that is, a short period of feeding time in infancy and a late age of weaning are both associated with prolonged thumbsucking – would seem to be incompatible in terms of a simple reinforcement theory of sucking. These findings can perhaps be reconciled by the introduction of an additional hypothesis, that is, that the strength of oral drive varies at different levels of development. It can be hypothesized that during early infancy, i.e., during the oral phase of development, the need for sucking is at its greatest intensity. Inadequate gratification of this need, as a result of short feeding periods, during this stage of development may lead, in accordance with psychoanalytic theory, to a fixation on this mode of gratification. On the other hand, continued satisfaction of this drive at a stage of development when its strength is waning, i.e. by late weaning from breast or bottle, may create conditions of overgratification, and, again in agreement with psychoanalytic theory, may result in a fixation on this mode of gratification. The role of overgratification in the fixation of a response tendency has not been so extensively studied as has frustration. Moreover, the point at which satisfaction of a need becomes overgratification has not been clearly defined in psychoanalytic theory. Further research on this point is needed. Animal experimental studies can be expected to further clarify this issue.

Insofar as the above interpretation is tenable, the findings of this study offer support of the hypothesis of 'phase specificity', that is, the special sensitivity of the organism to a particular type of frustration at a given developmental stage. There are many interesting theoretical and practical derivatives of this hypothesis with regard to personality development. It suggests the likelihood that experiences which might be 'traumatic' or decisive for character formation at one time in the early life history of the child may be attenuated in importance at another period of development.

An earlier study which provides a specific test of this hypothesis is that by Hunt (1941) on the effects of infant feeding-frustration upon hoarding in the adult rat. He found that adult rats which had been deprived of food at the age of 24 days showed significantly more hoarding behaviour than a group of litter mates which had been frustrated at a later age. These findings suggest that the timing of the frustration is of decisive importance for the determination of later modes of response.

Sucking deprivation and gratification, for the purposes of this study, are defined chiefly in terms of the stimulus conditions, that is, in terms of the amount of opportunity for sucking. However, it is likely that constitutional differences in the strength of 'oral drive' may be the basis for quite different reactions to the same stimulus conditions of deprivation or gratification. For example, Sears' hypothesis (Sears & Wise, 1950) that a long period of breast or bottle feeding strengthens the oral drive might have to be modified if it were shown that infants already showing a strong drive in the early weeks of life were the ones who succeeded in obtaining long periods of breast or bottle feedings. Current studies concerned with methods for discriminating in infants initial differences in strength of oral drive, present at birth, offer an approach to a more adequate consideration of this variable (Escalona & Leitch, 1948-9). Further longitudinal study of basic constitutional differences in 'oral drive' can be expected to contribute to a more thorough understanding of the relationship between early sucking deprivation and non-nutritive sucking.

The fact that the etiological importance for thumbsucking of insufficient feeding time in early infancy has been emphasized in this report does not suggest that this is the only factor operating in the determination of thumbsucking. There is considerable clinical evidence to indicate that thumbsucking is complexly determined by a number of variables. It is so frequent in infancy that it can be considered a normal expression of a 'sucking instinct'. In later childhood it may be symptomatic of a variety of states – boredom, frustration, generalized anxiety or insecurity. However, these states may be only precipitating conditions for the expression of behaviour rooted in earlier conditions of deprivation or overgratification. The fact that some children choose this type of response – thumbsucking – under these conditions suggests a predisposition based on earlier experiences.

It is recognized that in isolating single variables for the study of a specific hypothesis, one does not negate the axiom of a complex interdependence of variables in the determination of behaviour. Such simplified analysis is justified insofar as it stimulates the building of larger hypotheses, and gives impetus to further research based on consideration of the interaction of a larger number of variables.

SUMMARY

Study of the relationship between early feeding experiences in infancy and thumbsucking in childhood was made by the analysis of longitudinal data on a group of 66 children. The major findings were:

1. There were no differences in duration or severity of thumbsucking between children who had no breastfeeding and those who were breastfed for a period beyond the median of the group (three months). There was a tendency, however, for the children who were breastfed over the longest period of infancy (more than six months) to show less severe thumbsucking and to discontinue this activity at an earlier age than children with little or no breastfeeding experience.

2. There was no significant relationship between age of weaning to the cup and duration or severity of thumbsucking. There was a definite tendency, however, for more severe and more prolonged thumbsucking among the late-weaned children.

3. Significant differences were found between early- and late-weaned children in reaction to weaning, with more of the late-weaned children showing a severe reaction than the early-weaned.

4. There was a significant relationship between severity and duration of thumbsucking and the amount of time per feeding during the first six months. The children with the shortest feeding times were the most severe and most persistent thumbsuckers.

COMMENT

This would seem to be a carefully conducted empirical study of the relationships among a number of childrearing and child behaviour variables. Yarrow himself makes no excessive claim for the study; he notes that it 'does not attempt to test the broad psychoanalytic theory of orality' but 'deals only with one aspect of orality – the physical act of sucking'. He expects, however, that it might have 'implications for the specific hypotheses concerning the mechanisms of fixation and regression'. We have included the paper here because both Caldwell (1964) and Kline (1972) consider it to be the most sophisticated and central study among a number supposedly demonstrating that failure to get enough nutritive sucking experience at the oral phase in early infancy leads to other forms of oral activity such as thumbsucking in later childhood. According to Kline (p. 77) 'this is powerful support for the concept of oral erotism as it is described in Freud (1905)'.

Although the results of Yarrow's study are unquestionably very interesting we have certain misgivings concerning the interpretations that have been placed upon them by the author and others. The first thing to note about the results is that two of the most central hypotheses failed to obtain confirmation. The amount of breastfeeding that a child had been given did not predict either the duration or severity of thumbsucking in later childhood, nor was there any significant relationship between age of weaning to the cup and the duration or intensity of thumbsucking. Much of Yarrow's discussion is devoted to 'definite tendencies' that unfortunately were not statistically reliable; we shall restrict our comments to the two relatively minor and tangential findings that did achieve significance. These were: (1) late-weaned children showed a more 'severe reaction to weaning' than early-weaned children, and (2) children who had short average feeding times, whether on bottle or breast, showed greater severity and persistence of thumbsucking.

Before going on to consider some non-Freudian explanations of these findings (particularly the second finding, which seems more relevant to the oral fixation hypothesis) it is necessary to point out that although empirical, Yarrow's study cannot be regarded as an adequately controlled experiment in the strict sense of the term. For one thing, the methods of childrearing were freely chosen by the parents in the sample rather than randomly assigned to them by an experimenter. Therefore, Yarrow is not able to rule out the possibility of genetic links between the behaviour of the parents and behaviour of their children. Insufficient or overindulgent feeding on the part of the mother might reflect a personality characteristic in her (e.g. general neuroticism) which is also manifested in the child as severe or prolonged thumbsucking. (Here is one alternative explanation of the feeding-time/thumbsucking connection; others more plausible are outlined below.)

Secondly, the behaviour of the infants must surely have influenced the way in which they were treated by their parents. This raises a very important question which Yarrow has completely ignored – that of the direction of cause and effect in the relationship he has observed. For example, the finding that late-weaned children showed a more severe reaction to weaning might have arisen because certain children were allowed to remain on the bottle or breast longer than they would otherwise have been *because they reacted strongly against weaning*. Similarly, we might well question whether a short feeding time necessarily implies 'inadequate gratification' as the author supposes. Are we to believe that the short-feed mother actually snatched the bottle away from the child before it was finished? More likely, she withdrew it following cues from the child indicating that it had had enough (e.g. vomiting). Most mothers and pediatricians are aware that infants vary enormously both in the rate at which they extract milk from the bottle or breast and in the amount they require to take in before reaching satisfaction. It seems probable, then, that feeding time was determined at least as much by the child as by the mother.

A fully controlled experiment, then, would require that feeding practices be chosen randomly for the children (not by their parents) and strictly adhered to regardless of the reaction of the child. Such an experiment is of course impractical and inhumane, so we must sympathize with Yarrow to some extent. He might, however, have attempted to investigate also the factors determining differences in feeding practices adopted by different parents.

Concerning the relationship between shortness of feeding time and amount of thumbsucking in later childhood (really the only positive finding which bears at all on the Freudian theory of oral eroticism) we have already suggested one alternative explanation – that of a genetic connection between the mother's behaviour and that of the child. Another possible explanation of this finding that was not considered by Yarrow is implicit in the suggestion that the short feeding times might have been determined by the child rather than the mother. If we were to postulate a generalized 'sucking drive' which varies from one child to another independently of the amount of food required for appetite satisfaction, then the infant who sucks very hard on the breast or bottle (thus showing a short feeding time because gratification point is reached more quickly) would also tend to be the child who shows more persistent and severe thumbsucking. Here we have a second genetic hypothesis which would quite comfortably explain Yarrow's finding.

Both Yarrow and Kline argue that this study is a particularly critical one because it favours the Freudian theory of oral erotism against reinforcement theory, which they see as the main alternative in this area. In particular they claim that the discovery that thumbsucking is related both to brief feeding during infancy *and* late weaning (even though the latter relationship was non-significant) cannot be explained in terms of reinforcement theory. In fact, it can, and quite readily. One of the best established laws of conditioning is that intermittent reinforcement makes for greater resistance to extinction of a response than continuous reinforcement (cf. the success of poker machines in sustaining lever-pulling behaviour). If, as we have suggested, early withdrawal of the bottle from the infant sometimes leaves the child gratified and sometimes not, then types of sucking behaviour that are *never* reinforced by appetite reduction (e.g. thumbsucking) would be expected to persist longer than would have been the case if bottle or breast sucking had *always* led to satisfaction rather than frustration.

Finally, we should mention the most parsimonious of all the non-Freudian explanations of Yarrow's finding that have not previously been considered. All of Yarrow's data was obtained from retrospective reports by the mothers, and even though a limit of six months was placed on the time that was permitted to elapse between the events concerned and the interview in which they were recorded, we must nevertheless allow for some distortion due to the effects of motivation on memory. Now if we are to assume a 'social desirability' factor which leads some mothers to want to impress the doctor more than others, then the mother that reports that her child does little thumbsucking is also likely to be the mother who reports that she spent a great deal of time patiently feeding her infant, and that the infant was weaned to the cup very early.

There are certain other reasons for feeling dubious about the method by which the results of this study were obtained, e.g. there is no mention of any of the children having used pacifiers (dummies) at any stage, nor any statement that they did not – so it is difficult to assess the possible influence of this factor, but in any case, enough has been said to throw doubt on the Freudian interpretation of the results themselves. The alternative explanations that we have suggested are all *ad hoc* and possibly no more plausible than the Freudian theory of oral fixation; nevertheless, until they have been discounted Yarrow's study can hardly be regarded as powerful support for psychoanalytic theory.

REFERENCES

ABRAHAM, K. (1927a) The influence of oral eroticism on character formation. In *Selected Papers on Psychoanalysis.* (Translated by D. BRYAN and A. STRACHEY.) London: Hogarth Press.

—— (1927b) A short study of the development of the libido viewed in the light of mental disorders. In *Selected Papers on Psychoanalysis.* London: Hogarth Press.

—— (1927c) The first pregenital stage of libido. In *Selected Papers on Psychoanalysis.* London: Hogarth Press.

BAKWIN, H. (1948) Thumb and fingersucking in children. *J. Pediat.*, **32**, 99-101.

BALDWIN, A. L. (1945) An analysis of some aspects of feeding behaviour. *J. Genet. Psychol.*, **66**, 221-32.

CALDWELL, B. M. (1964) The effects of infant care. In M. L. and L. W. HOFFMAN (eds.), *Review of Child Development Research*, Vol. 1. New York: Russell Sage Foundation.

DAVIS, H. V., SEARS, R. R., MILLER, H. C. and BRODBECK, A. J. (1948) Effects of cup, bottle, and breast feeding on oral activities of newborn infants. *Pediatrics*, **2**, 549-58.

ESCALONA, S. K. and LEITCH, M. (1 Dec. 1948—30 June 1949) Early phases of personality development: a non-normative study of infant behaviour (abstract). *Research Relating to Children: An Inventory of Studies in Progress.* Children's Bureau, Federal Security Agency.

FREUD, S. (1930) Three contributions to the theory of sex. *Nerv. and Ment. Dis. Monogr. Series*, No. 7.

GLOVER, E. (1925) Notes on oral character-formation. *Int. J. Psychoanal.*, **6**, 131-54.

GOLDMAN, F. (1948) Breastfeeding and character formation. *J. Pers.*, **17**, 83-103.

—— (1950) Breastfeeding and character formation: II. The etiology of the oral character in psychoanalytic theory. *J. Pers.*, **19**, 189-96.

HARTMAN, H. (1950) Psychoanalysis and developmental psychology. *Psychoanal. Study Child*, **5**, 7-17.

HUNT, J. MCV. (1941) The effects of infant feeding-frustration upon adult hoarding in the albino rat. *J. Abnorm. Soc. Psychol.*, **36**, 338-60.

KLINE, P. (1972) *Fact and Fantasy in Freudian Theory*. London: Methuen.

KUNST, M. S. (1948) A study of thumb and fingersucking in infants. *Psychol. Monogr.*, No. 3.

LEITCH, M. (1948) A commentary on the oral phase of psycho-sexual development. *Bull. Menninger Clinic*, **12**, 117-25.

LEVY, D. M. (1928) Fingersucking and accessory movements in early infancy. *Am. J. Psychiat.*, **7**, 881-918.

—— (1934) Experiments on the sucking reflex and social behaviour of dogs. *Am. J. Orthopsychiat.*, **4**, 203.

—— (1937) Thumb or fingersucking from the psychiatric angle. *Child Devel.*, **8**, 99-101.

MCNEMAR, Q. (1949) *Psychological Statistics*. New York: Wiley.

MASSLER, M. and WOODS, A. W. (1949) Thumbsucking. *J. Dent. Child.*, **16**, 1-9.

NEWTON, N. R. and NEWTON, M. (1950) Relationship of ability to breast feed and maternal attitudes toward breast feeding. *Pediatrics*, **5**, 869-75.

NORVALL, M. A. (1946) Sucking response of newborn babies at breast: 50 cases. *Am. J. Dis. Child.*, **71**, 41-4.

ORLANSKY, H. (1949) Infant care and personality. *Psychol. Bull.*, **46**, 1-48.

PEARSON, G. H. (1948) The psychology of fingersucking, tongue-sucking and other oral 'habits'. *Am. J. Orthod.*, **34**, 589-98.

RIBBLE, M. (1939) The significance of infantile sucking for the psychic development of the individual. *Nerv. and Ment. Dis.*, **90**, 455-63.

ROBERTS, E. (1944) Thumb and fingersucking in relation to feeding in early infancy. *Amer. J. Dis. Child.*, **68**, 7-8.

ROSS, S. (1951) Sucking behaviour in neonate dogs. *J. Abnorm. Soc. Psychol.*, **46**, 142-9.

SEARS, R. R. (1943) *Survey of Objective Studies of Psychoanalytic Concepts.* New York: Soc. Sci. Res. Council.

SEARS, R. R. and WISE, G. (1950) Relation of cup feeding in infancy to thumbsucking and the oral drive. *Am. J. Orthopsychiat.*, **20**, 123-38.

SPITZ, R. A. (1946) Anaclitic depression. *Psychoanal. Study Child*, **2**, 313-42.

SWINEHART, E. W. (1938) Relation of thumbsucking to malocclusion. *Am. J. Orthod.*, **24**, 509-21.

2

Frieda Goldman-Eisler (1951)[1]

The problem of 'orality' and of its origin in early childhood

Journal of Mental Science, 97, 765-82

INTRODUCTION

The concept of 'orality' as used in this paper indicates a certain constellation of traits or habitual reactions which are, or are assumed to be, derivatives, whether direct or modified, of behaviour patterns characteristic of early childhood. The importance of the mouth as the first erotogenic zone and as the organ generating fundamental attitudes of giving or receiving, waiting or being impatient, and hoping or despairing, has been stressed by psychoanalysis. According to psychoanalytic theory, the oral phase, that is, the first period of libidinal development, plays a most important part for later character development in as far as gratification, or frustration, of the oral impulses is assumed to have a determining influence on character-formation in later life.

SUMMARY OF PREVIOUS WORK

This hypothesis was put to the test by the writer, and some of the results of this work have been reported with the full details of the investigation in two previous articles (Goldman, 1948, 1950) which are summarized below.

The investigation proceeded in two steps:

(*a*) Working out the diagnostic tool by which syndromes or oral character traits corresponding to those described by psychoanalysts

[1]Department of Psychology, Institute of Psychiatry, Maudsley Hospital.

might be detected, and (*b*) relating these to the subjects' date of weaning.[1]

The Syndromes of Oral Pessimism and Oral Optimism

To carry out the first of these steps, verbal rating scales for 19 traits mentioned by psychoanalytic writers as having an oral connotation were administered to 115 adult subjects. These traits were: optimism, pessimism, exocathexis, endocathexis, nurturance, passivity, sociability, aloofness, oral agression, autonomy, aggression, guilt, dependence, ambition, impulsion, deliberation, change, conservatism, unattainability. They are given in full in the Appendix, together with definitions of the trait names, and the coefficients of their respective reliabilities and of the internal consistency of each item. A type pattern or ideal character profile was then set up in the following manner.

After computing from standardized test measurements the correlation of each of the traits with all others, an intercorrelation table was arranged with optimism at the one end of the list of traits and pessimism, which had meaningfully the highest negative correlation at the other end (see Table 2-1).

A type pattern was set up, conforming to the two antithetical clusters which emerged from the intercorrelation table: optimism, exocathexis, nurturance, sociability, and ambition correlating positively at one end of the distribution, and pessimism, passivity, aloofness, endocathexis, autonomy, and oral agression constituting the opposite pole. The persons whose measurements corresponded most closely to the above clusters were selected, whether their scores on optimism and the related traits were positive and those on pessimism and its correlates negative, or the other way round. Those who showed positive scores for the first group of traits were called 'oral optimists', and those who showed positive scores for the second group of traits 'oral pessimists'. In this way twenty 'oral optimists' and twenty 'oral pessimists' were selected, the qualification for these categories being that their scores should show at least 8 out of the 11 characteristic traits clustering in the expected antithetical direction. The scores for the 20 'oral pessimists' and the 20 'oral optimists' were then totalled – after the signs of the optimists had been reversed – and averaged.

[1]This was obtained by asking the subjects' mothers at what age (in terms of months) the subjects had been finally taken off the breast.

TABLE 2.1

	Opt.	Exc.	Nurt.	Soc.	Amb.	Change	Unatt.	Delib.	Imp.	Cons.	Dep.	Guilt.	Aggr.	Auto.	Endo.	Oral.	Aloof.	Pass.	Pessim.
Opt.	..	..	..	..	..	..	..	..	..	..	..	..	..	..	..	..	..	..	..
Exc.	·51	..	..	..	..	..	..	..	..	..	..	..	..	..	..	..	..	..	..
Nur.	·46	·35	..	..	..	..	..	..	..	..	..	..	..	..	..	..	..	..	..
Soc.	·20	·31	·17	..	..	..	..	..	..	..	..	..	..	..	..	..	..	..	..
Amb.	·27	·14	—·17	—·11	..	..	..	..	..	..	..	..	..	..	..	..	..	..	..
Change	·16	—·05	·30	·21	·01	..	..	..	..	..	..	..	..	..	..	..	..	..	..
Unatt.	—·34	—·22	·06	—·01	·22	·32	..	..	..	..	..	..	..	..	..	..	..	..	..
Delib.	—·11	·05	·00	—·15	—·26	—·35	—·02	..	..	..	..	..	..	..	..	..	..	..	..
Imp.	—·38	—·16	—·05	·08	·04	·44	·13	—·75	..	..	..	..	..	..	..	..	..	..	..
Cons.	·21	—·19	—·11	—·50	—·15	—·50	—·14	·42	—·39	..	..	..	..	..	..	..	..	..	..
Dep.	—·10	—·15	—·22	·39	—·32	·04	·11	·19	—·36	·06	..	..	..	..	..	..	..	..	..
Guilt	—·15	·00	—·02	—·20	—·09	·12	·24	·23	—·17	·21	·47	..	..	..	..	..	..	..	..
Aggr.	—·31	—·16	—·27	—·17	·00	·00	·28	—·38	·35	—·05	—·05	—·16	..	..	..	..	..	..	..
Auto.	—·23	—·47	—·29	—·20	·07	·17	·07	—·12	·19	—·20	—·11	—·47	·10	..	..	..	..	..	..
Endo.	—·29	—·60	—·16	—·40	·16	—·04	·32	·08	·04	·20	·21	·05	·08	·31	..	..	..	..	..
Oral.	—·36	—·07	—·19	—·19	—·23	—·02	—·07	—·42	·12	—·14	—·08	—·13	·33	·10	—·09	..	..	..	..
Aloof.	—·37	—·55	—·65	—·50	—·09	—·29	—·02	·05	·00	·20	—·07	·05	·24	·41	·33	·12	..	..	..
Pass.	—·48	—·34	—·43	—·01	—·40	—·01	—·25	—·16	·21	·02	·17	—·01	·32	·06	·03	·37	·44	..	..
Pessim.	—·63	—·55	—·22	—·34	·05	—·14	—·02	·27	—·10	·16	—·02	·38	·11	·13	·20	·11	·37	—·03	..

The measurements (in standard units) which appear in column I and II of Table 2.2 are presented graphically in Figure 2.1. The standard measures at the scale on the left express the saturations of the type with the traits. The relative symmetry of the two graphs or profiles supporting the assumption that the traits form a bipolar syndrome seemed to justify the pooling of the two groups.

TABLE 2.2

Traits	I Upper group (Pessimists)	II Lower group (Optimists)	III In standard measure Total	IV Average
Pessimism	+1·417	−0·894	+46·23	+1·155
Passivity	+0·966	−1·134	+42·01	+1·050
Aloofness	+0·826	−0·685	+30·23	+0·755
Oral aggression	+0·862	−0·335	+23·94	+0·598
Endocathexis	+0·687	−0·485	+23·44	+0·586
Autonomy	+0·919	−0·234	+23·08	+0·577
Aggression	+0·445	−0·339	+15·69	+0·392
Guilt	−0·025	−0·587	+11·23	+0·280
Dependence	+0·364	−0·151	+10·31	+0·257
Conservatism	+0·135	−0·167	+6·06	+0·151
Unattainability	−0·052	+0·204	+5·13	+0·128
Impulsion	+0·194	+0·337	+2·86	+0·071
Deliberation	−0·092	−0·072	−0·40	−0·010
Change	−0·091	+0·395	−9·74	−0·243
Ambition	−0·309	+0·223	−10·66	−0·266
Sociability	−0·695	+0·536	−24·63	−0·615
Nurturance	−0·958	+0·611	−31·38	−0·784
Exocathexis	−0·952	+0·701	−33·07	−0·826
Optimism	−1·192	+1·086	−45·57	−1·139

This procedure may be criticized on the ground of what might be called its impurity of method. If the aim of the investigation was to test a psychoanalytic hypothesis, namely the relation of oral character types to weaning, it would have been more strictly logical to set up the ideal or hypothetical profile which was to serve as the criterion of orality, without reference to the actual intercorrelation table, but directly from psychoanalytic description. However, there were difficulties in the way of following this course. For although psychoanalytic writers agree with respect to the basic oral traits, different writers put different emphasis on different traits or combinations of traits. Syndromes are sometimes suggested, but on other occasions traits are enumerated singly without a clear idea being given of how they combine, or whether in fact they invariably do combine. Moreover, the psychoanalytic theory is phrased in a descriptive and qualitative form, so that it was still incumbent upon the investigator to find its quantitative expression. Thus, while psychoanalytic

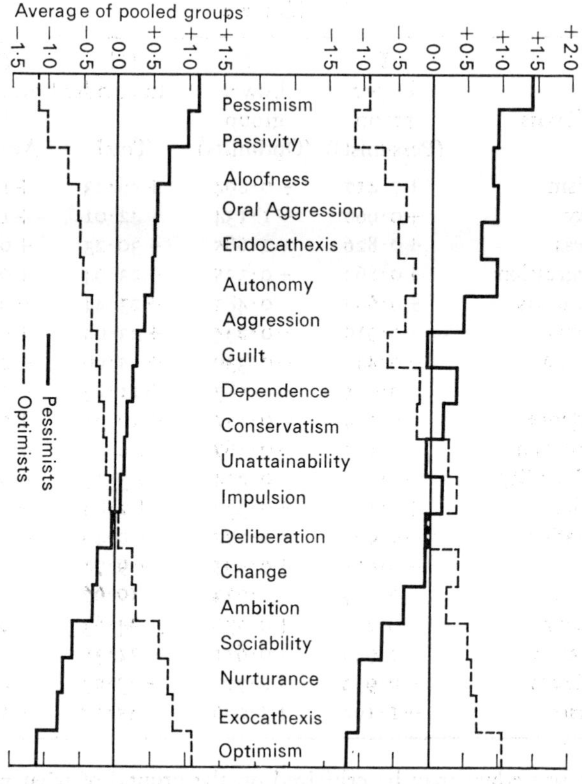

Figure 2.1. Upper part: trait profiles derived from the measurements of 20 Pessimists and 20 Optimists. Lower part: ideal type profiles of oral Pessimism-Optimism based on the measurements of the pooled groups. Scale in standard measures.

literature was responsible for the selection of the particular traits tested, their quantitative expressions have emerged from the intercorrelations of tests. As it happened these were very much, though not entirely, what one would have expected on the basis of the theory. Indeed, when the type pattern extracted in this way, both for oral pessimism or, conversely, oral optimism, was compared with the orally gratified and the orally ungratified types as described by psychoanalytic writers, a close correspondence was found. A detailed juxtaposition of the test results with the psychoanalytic theory is to be found in a previous article (Goldman, 1948). All test measurements, except those for impulsion, deliberation and unattainability, were in the expected direction. In particular those traits which had impressed themselves on psychoanalysis as of oral origin most clearly, namely excessive optimism or alternatively pessimism, the passive-receptive attitude (tests: passivity, neg. nurturance); narcissism (tests: aloofness, autonomy); and generosity (test: nurturance) were represented by the highest quantitative assessments (see Table 2.2).

Breastfeeding and Oral Pessimism-Optimism (Goldman, 1950)

The assumption of an oral history underlying the oral character was tested in the following way: Each subject's test scores on the 19 traits were correlated with the 'ideal' type profile, and this correlation coefficient, indicating the degree of correspondence of this individual's own profile to the type profile, was taken as his score in oral pessimism (or optimism). An analysis of variance was then carried out comparing the scores in oral pessimism of those who had been weaned early (i.e., not later than four months of age) with those who had enjoyed breast-feeding for a longer period. (The choice of the critical period of four months was suggested by the observations of Margaret Ribble, 1950, who had found that infants adjusted considerably better to deprivation after than before this date.) The mean score in oral pessimism for the early-weaned group was +0·139, and for those weaned later −0·181. The difference was significant beyond the 1 per cent level of probability. The correlation between early weaning and pessimism was ·271, and when the early weaners were compared only with those who had enjoyed a full measure of breastfeeding, i.e., nine months and more, it was ·305; when they were compared with those who had enjoyed an excessive period of breastfeeding, i.e., more than nine months, it was ·368, the scores in oral pessimism of the early weaners being +·138, and of the excessive feeders −·346.

While the above results confirm the psychoanalytic theory of oral character types in most of its essential aspects, one important characteristic, the significance of which as an oral trait ranks extremely high in psychoanalytic literature (Abraham, 1942; Glover,

1925), forms an exception. This is the trait of impatience, measured in this investigation by the scales of impulsion, and, negatively, deliberation. These two scales make practically no contribution to the oral pessimist type profile, and the intercorrelation table of traits shows that it is outside the optimist or pessimist clusters. Its independence suggested a second bipolar factor, and the table was therefore submitted to a factor analysis (simple summation method). Two factors were extracted and their saturations with each of the 19 traits are given in Table 2.3. The two columns of saturations are plotted in Figure 2.2.

TABLE 2.3

	F_1	F_2		F_2
Aloofness	·709	·164	Impulsion	·782
Endocathexis	·513	·160	Autonomy	·600
Pessimism	·501	−·059	Aggression	·476
Passivity	·387	·204	Oral aggression	·318
Conservatism	·353	−·438	Change	·275
Dependence	·347	−·244	Passivity	·204
Early weaning	·337	·129	Unattainability	·201
Aggression	·235	·476	Rejection	·164
Oral aggression	·193	·318	Endocathexis	·160
Deliberation	·178	−·776	Ambition	·139
Extreme weaning			Early weaning	·129
(early and very late)	·167	·059	Extreme weaning	·059
Guilt	·163	−·376	Sociability	−·012
Autonomy	·150	·600	Pessimism	−·059
Unattainability	·054	·201	Nurturance	−·184
Impulsion	−·052	·782	Dependence	−·244
Ambition	−·219	·139	Optimism	−·280
Change	−·253	·275	Exocathexis	−·297
Sociability	−·489	−·012	Guilt	−·376
Nurturance	−·585	−·184	Conservatism	−·438
Optimism	−·694	−·280	Deliberation	−·776
Exocathexis	−·701	−·297		

The first factor corresponds to the type profile of oral pessimism and correlates with it ·694. It differs from it in as far as factor I is most highly saturated with aloofness, which is only third in importance in the type; and passivity takes fourth place as against second place in the type. Moreover oral aggression and autonomy, which were fourth and sixth place respectively in the trait heirarchy of the type, move to tenth and eleventh place, thus contributing little to the factor. (We shall see below that these latter traits appear prominently in factor II.)

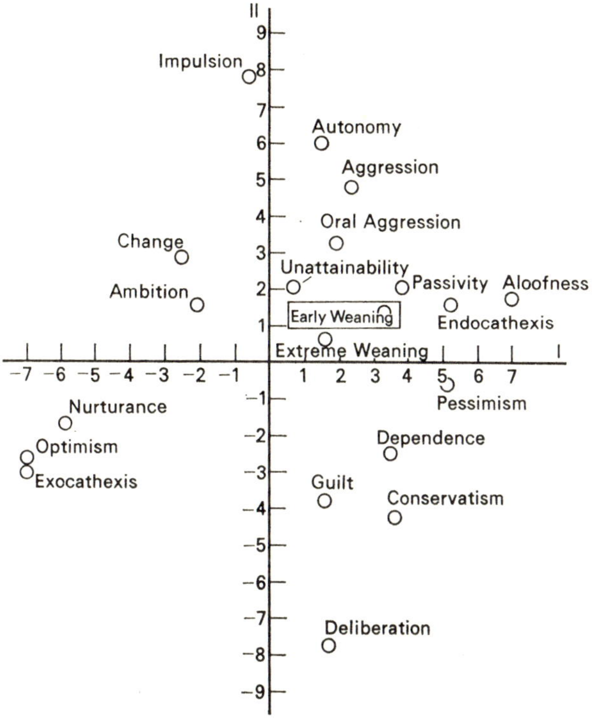

Figure 2.2. *Plot of the factor loadings of* 19 *tests with reference to factor axes I and II.*

An analysis of variance discriminating between the two groups of early- and late-weaned subjects on the basis of factor scores of this first factor showed the difference to be significant beyond the 1 per cent level of probability. The correlation between weaning and factor 1 being ·287 as against ·27 for the type pattern showed that the factor gave only an insignificantly better prediction than the type.

FACTOR II OF IMPATIENCE-AGGRESSION-AUTONOMY AND ITS RELATION TO BREASTFEEDING

Our main interest in this paper however, belongs to factor II. A person who would be highly saturated with this factor would be characterized by extreme impulsiveness and a disinclination to wait or refrain from action (impulsion, ·761; deliberation, – ·766), by independence or a disinclination to conform (autonomy, ·560), by agression, general and oral (aggression, ·479; oral aggression ·303), and by a tendency to change, to seek the new, rather than to stick to the well-known and familiar (change, ·267; conservation, – ·436). Aloofness (·234), passivity (·214), the desire for unattainable (unattainability, ·209), and withdrawal (endocathexis, ·160; exo-cathexis, – ·316) also contribute to the syndrome but to a much smaller extent. Pessimism plays an insignificant role in this factor. Recalling psychoanalytic writers on the subject, particularly Abraham and Glover, there is no doubt that a person like the one described above contains in his personality what these writers considered to be essential aspects of the oral character. None of the psychoanalytic writers have, however, discriminated between two different and independent oral syndromes as are suggested by our two independent factors, although there are implicit suggestions of an active reaction as compared with a passive submission to oral frustration (Abraham, 1942).

The question remains to be answered what the relation of factor II to oral frustration is. The idea that 'oral frustration, oral impatience, oral sadism, are inseparable' (Sharpe, 1950) is a firmly entrenched tenet of the psychoanalytic theory of orality. As factor II is highly loaded with impatience (impulsion) and aggression (sadism), its relation to weaning (if early weaning be taken as a measure of oral frustration) should demonstrate with what degree of confidence such a statement as the above may be made. Again factor scores were computed, showing the degree with which each individual was saturated with factor II, and the two weaning groups compared for differences. Although the differences were in the expected direction, those subjects who had been weaned early having a mean factor score of ·0344, and those weaned late (after four months of breast-feeding), a mean factor score of – ·0234, the analysis of variance showed that these differences were not significant; nor were the differences between the early-weaned subjects and those who had been given breastfeeding for nine months and longer. In other words, our data do not confirm the psychoanalytic contention that oral frustration, impatience and oral aggression are inseparable or even related. Clearly early weaning seems to have not nearly as much bearing on the impatience-aggression syndrome as it had on the syndrome of pessimism, passivity, aloofness and endocathexis.

However, a hypothesis treated as a fact by so many careful and highly trained (although of course also highly indoctrinated) observers and stated again and again with the utmost confidence, must still command attention. A further analysis of the data was therefore undertaken. This analysis was based on factor scores of oral pessimism (factor I). The sample was divided into four groups: impulsive and early-weaned, non-impulsive and early-weaned, impulsive and late-weaned, and non-impulsive and late-weaned subjects. Those who had scores on factor II higher than ·200 were apportioned to the impulsive group; those whose factor scores were below ·200 to the non-impulsive. The mean scores of oral pessimism for each of these groups are given below:

	Mean	Numbers in group
Early impulsive	516·7	8
Early non-impulsive	427·7	22
Late impulsive	413·6	11
Late non-impulsive	341·2	49

An analysis of variance was carried out comparing the differences between these groups. The F-ratio was 4·38, significant at the 1 per cent level of probability. T-tests were then calculated in order to compare the individual groups. Table 2.4 shows the results.

The greatest difference, significant at the 1 per cent level, can be observed between the early-impulsive and the late non-impulsive group, and the difference between the early impulsive and late impulsive groups is significant at the 5 per cent level. These, one might argue, are the differences between early and late weaning, quite independent of any effect of the factor of impulsiveness. This, however, does not explain the following features in the above array: (*a*) that no significant difference exists between the early non-impulsive and the late impulsive group, and (*b*) the consistency of the decrease in oral pessimism as the scale moves from those who are impulsive as well as early-weaned towards those who are neither.

For the purpose of further clarification, frequency distributions for the early and late weaning groups were plotted along the oral pessimism scale of factor I, saturations showing the location on this

TABLE 2.4. *Analysis of variance testing the difference between early-weaned impulsive, early-weaned non-impulsive, late-weaned impulsive, and late-weaned non-impulsive subjects with respect to oral pessimism (factor I).*

Source	Degrees of freedom	Sum of squares	Mean square
Between groups	3	281,657·5	93,885·8
Within groups	86	1,843,670·9	21,438·0
	89	2,125,328·4	

F = 4·38 (F for 3 and 80 df. at 1 per cent level = 4·04)

T-TESTS

	Early impulsive	Early Non-impulsive	Late impulsive	Late Non-impulsive
Early-impulsives				
Early non-impulsives	1·47			
Late impulsives	1·52	0·26		
Late non-impulsives	3·14*	2·30†	1·48	

* Significant at the 1 per cent level
† Significant at the 5 per cent level

scale of the members of the impulsive groups of early as well as of late weaners (Figure 2.3). From these we can see that of the eight impulsive subjects in the early-weaning group, seven are above the mid-point of oral pessimism. (It may be noted that the one who is not is an extreme optimist). The distribution of late weaners, on the other hand, shows the impulsive subjects to be distributed all along the scale from optimism to pessimism.

The proportions of impulsive and non-impulsive subjects in the two weaning groups and in the total sample are presented in Table 2.5. From this it may be seen that among those who had been weaned early, the proportion of pessimists, with an impulsive and aggressive personality, to optimists of the same disposition, was 7 : 1; while the ratio of pessimists to optimists among those with a placid disposition (non-impulsive, non-aggressive) was 11 : 11 or 1 : 1. No such contrast exists among the group of subjects who had enjoyed long breastfeeding, testifying to the fact that over the whole sample the two factors of oral pessimism and impulsion-aggression are independent.

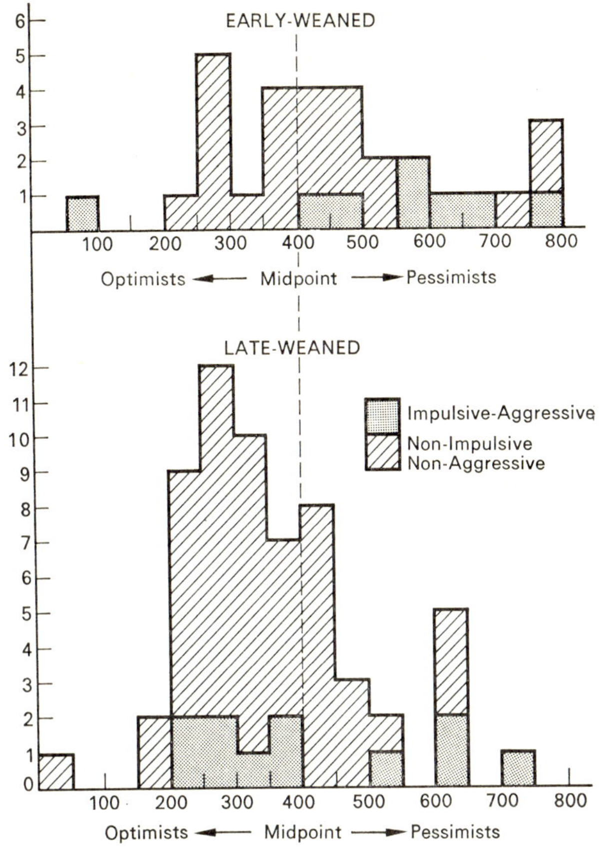

Figure 2.3. Frequency distribution for early and late weaning groups plotted along the Oral Pessimism scale of factor I.

TABLE 2.5.

	Early-weaned		Early-weaned total	Late-weaned	
	Pessimists	Optimists		Pessimists	Optimists
Impulsive	7	1	8	4	7
Non-impulsive	11	11	22	15	34
Sums	18	12	30	19	41

	Late-weaned total	Bottlefed		Bottle-fed total	Total sample
		Pessimists	Optimists		
Impulsive	11	3	1	4	23
Non-impulsive	49	2	4	6	77
Sums	60	5	5	10	100

Whether this relatively greater predominance of early-weaned oral pessimists over optimists among the impulsive-aggressive individuals (7 : 1), as compared with the equal balance of the same types among placid individuals (11 : 11), is a matter of chance, or has any significance, is a question which must be left to a further investigation; the above numbers are too small to justify any conclusion. A suggestion emerges from our samples that there may be two types of early-weaned pessimists: one who is aggressive at the oral level, impulsive, and also generally aggressive, and the other who is neither particularly aggressive nor impulsive. The former corresponds much more closely to the classical conception of the aggressive, impatient, dissatisfied oral character as described by Abraham (1942) and Glover (1925) than does our original oral pessimist type profile.

The emphasis in psychoanalytic literature on the impulsive-aggressive oral pessimist may possibly be due to the fact that this type of person being the more active will more frequently be found in the psychoanalytic consulting room than the orally unaggressive individual.

SUMMARY

1. Previous work was summarized showing that a type pattern derived from 19 trait scales and corresponding to the syndrome of oral pessimism as described by psychoanalytic writers was significantly related to early weaning, oral optimism being significantly related to late weaning.

2. The 19 traits measured were: optimism, pessimism, exocathexis, endocathexis, nurturance, passivity, sociability, aloofness, oral aggression, autonomy, aggression, guilt, dependence, ambition, impulsion, deliberation, change, conservatism, unattainability.

3. An intercorrelation table based on the trait scores of a hundred subjects was computed and submitted to a factor analysis. Two factors were extracted.

4. Factor I corresponded in most aspects to the syndrome of oral pessimism as described by psychoanalysts, and correlated ·694 with the previously derived type pattern. It was, however, poorly saturated with impulsion, aggression and autonomy, which psychoanalysts consider to be important traits of oral character. It was significantly related to early weaning.

5. Factor II was highly saturated with impulsion, aggression and autonomy. It was not significantly related to early weaning.

6. Individuals who had high scores on factor II and who had been weaned early had significantly higher scores on factor I (oral pessimism) than the rest of the sample.

7. A suggestion to be investigated emerges that the concurrence in an individual of early weaning and of the characteristics of impulsiveness-aggression-autonomy, as defined in factor II, may possibly promote the development of oral pessimism.

APPENDIX

The Traits

(Reliability coefficients are presented in parentheses following the description of each trait.)[1]

Optimism: Optimism and pessimism are antithetical expressions in character-formation of an omnipotent and magical relation to reality. Optimism deriving from this unconscious source would be upheld by the individual against reasonable expectation (r=·90).

Pessimism: Inability to accept frustrating experiences as part of reality. Defence against disappointments through summary and advance resignation, anticipation of disappointment (r=·74).

Passivity: Passive-receptive attitude, hedonism, indolence, self-indulgence (r=·81).

Desire for the unattainable: Intense desire to climb combined with a feeling of unattainability, of difficulty in achievement, of the insuperable, grudging incapacity to get on (r=·78).

Displaced oral aggression (verbal): Aggressive use of speech, 'omnipotent valuation of speech', 'incisive speech'. Question 7, although not referring to speech but to the oral expression of rage or the motor accompaniments of oral activity, was included in this scale.

Its correlation of +·52 with the total score of the scale seems to confirm that there is a common factor operating in primary oral aggression and aggressiveness in speech (r=·76).

Aggression: The desire to injure or inflict pain, to overcome opposition forcefully, to fight, to revenge an injury, to attack, to oppose forcefully (r=.78).

[1]The reliability of each scale was measured by the split-half method of correlating odd and even numbered items and corrected by the Spearman-Brown prophecy formula.

Aloofness: Negative tropism for people, attitude to rejection (r=·73).

Ambition: Tendency to overcome obstacles, to exercise power, to strive to do something difficult as well and as quickly as possible, to attain a high standard, to excel one's self (r=·68).

Autonomy: Those who wish neither to lead nor to be led, those who want to go their own way, uninfluenced and uncoerced. Independence of attitude (r=·88).

Dependence: Tendency to cry, plead or ask for nourishment, love, protection or aid. Helplessness, insecurity (r=·56).

Guilt: 'Conscience', inhibiting and punishing images, self-torture, self-abasement (r=·90).

Change: A tendency to move and wander, to have no fixed habitation, to seek new friends, to adopt new fashions, to change one's interests and vocation. Inconsistency and instability (r=·71).

Conservatism: Adherence to certain places, people, and modes of conduct. Fixation and limitation. Enduring sentiments and loyalties, persistence of purpose; consistency of conduct; rigidity of habits (r=·56).

Impulsion: The tendency to act quickly without reflection. Short reaction time, intuitive or emotional decisions. The inability to inhibit an impulse (r=·82).

Deliberation: Inhibition, hesitation and reflection before action. Slow reaction time, compulsive thinking (r=·87).

Exocathexis: The positive cathexis in practical action and co-operative undertakings. Occupation with outer events: economic, political and social occurrences. A strong inclination to participate in the contemporary world of affairs (r=·72).

Endocathexis: The cathexis of thought or emotion for its own sake. A preoccupation with inner activities, feelings, fantasies, generalizations, theoretical reflections, artistic conceptions, religious ideas; withdrawal from practical life (r=·73).

Nurturance: Tendency to nourish, aid, and protect a helpless object. To express sympathy, to mother a child, to assist in danger (r=·79).

Sociability: Tendency to form friendships and associations; to join, and live with, others. To co-operate and converse socially with others. To join groups (r=·70).

The rating scales for 19 character traits

	Optimism	
Rating scale:	Rel. coeff. r = ·90	rt.[1]
1. Nothing is impossible to a willing heart		·74
2. In the end justice will prevail		·60
3. Every cloud has a silver lining!		·63
4. There is sure to be enough to go round		·92
5. Ill luck is good for something		·52
6. Atomic energy will bring progress and happiness to humanity		·54
7. Most people can be trusted		·47
8. The world is a wheel and it will all come round right		·73
	Pessimism	
Rating scale:	Rel. coeff. r = ·74	rt.
1. It is misery to be born, pain to live, grief to die		·76
2. Greed and lust are the most powerful motive forces of mankind		·44
3. Hardly anyone cares much what happens to you		·48
4. "Oh life! thou art a galling load Along a rough, a weary road"		·64
5. There is sure to be a snag somewhere		·41
6. Real friends are hard to find		·52
7. Accept the present evil, lest a greater one befall you		·58
8. Hope only brings disappointment		·58
	Passivity	
Rating scale:	Rel. coeff. r = ·81	rt.
1. It is better to sit still than rise and fall		·44
2. Oh, for a life of ease and luxury!		·00 (ø = ·41)*
*The ø-coefficient is based on the correlation of the upper and lower quarters of the sample		
3. "An idle life is life for me, Idleness spiced with philosophy"		·60
4. Good luck is more help than hard work		·65
5. Work has no place in paradise		·58
6. It is better to do nothing than make a mistake		·58

[1]Index of internal consistency measured by the tetrachoric correlation coefficient.

7. Comfort is indispensable for a contented life ·50
8. Competition is not for me; it irritates rather than stimulates me ·45

Desire for the Unattainable

Rating scale: Rel. coeff. r= ·78 rt.

1. I like best that which flies beyond my reach ·55
2. I never get what I really want ·80
3. Other people seem to get away with things—I can't ·64
4. How seldom the goal is ever reached in human affairs ·42
5. I often think that other people are more lucky than I am ·38
6. The more you want something the less you get it ·76
7. To attain what we desire means also to realize the vanity of our wishes ·65
8. Life is a wild-goose chase ·84
9. Dreams are the better part of life ·67

Displaced Oral Aggression (*Verbal*)

Rating scale: Rel. coeff. r= ·76 rt.

1. When your anger is aroused do you tend to express yourself in 'strong' language? ·62
2. Do you like colourful invective? ·71
3. Do you tend to make biting or sarcastic remarks when criticising other people? ·66
4. Do you find yourself frequently disagreeing with, and contradicting people? ·73
5. Are you fond of arguing? ·47
6. Do you like a debate to be hard-hitting? ·67
7. When in a rage do you tend to give motor expression to your feelings, such as stamping your feet, grinding your teeth, pushing your fist in your mouth, or biting your fingernails or handkerchief or other objects, or breaking or tearing something? ·52

Aggression

Rating scale: Rel. coeff. r= ·78 rt.

1. If somebody annoys you are you apt to tell him what you think of him? ·76

2. Do you try to get your own way regardless of opposition? ·57
3. If you come across a domineering person are you inclined to put him in his place? ·69
4. Do you often blame other people when things go wrong? ·66
5. Are you considered aggressive by some of your acquaintances? ·80
6. Are you apt to express your irritation rather than restrain it? ·78
7. Do you often let yourself go when you are angry? ·64
8. Are you apt to rebuke your friends when you disapprove of their behaviour? ·59

Aloofness

Rating scale: Rel. coeff. r = ·73 rt.

1. Are you intolerant of people who bore you? ·55
2. Do you maintain reserve when you meet strangers? ·49
3. Do you get annoyed when your time is taken up by people in whom you are not interested? ·78
4. Do you avoid close intimacies with other people? ·58
5. Do you usually keep yourself somewhat aloof and inaccessible? ·60
6. Have you frequently been reproached for your scornful manner in argument, particularly with people whose ideas you considered inferior to your own? ·70
7. Do you often tend to express your resentment against a person by having nothing more to do with him? ·55
8. Do you generally prefer the company of older, talented or generally superior people? ·53
9. Do you find the company of uninteresting people insufferable in the highest degree? ·71

Ambition

Rating scale: Rel. coeff. r = ·68 rt.

1. Do you feel that life can offer hardly any substitute for great achievement? ·66
2. Are you rather set upon accomplishing some valuable piece of work some time in your life? ·77

3. Does your admiration for certain great men inspire you to emulate them in one way or another? ·78
4. Are you employing most of your energies in the pursuit of your career? ·55
5. Do you feel that a far goal is deserving your efforts more than a daily duty? ·72
6. Do you often dream about your future successes? ·52
7. Would you say that ambition is a strong motive force in your life? ·46

Autonomy

Rating scale: Rel. coeff. r=·88 rt.

1. Do you feel that you cannot do your best work when you are in a subservient position? ·52
2. Does it make you stubborn and resistant when others attempt to coerce you? ·60
3. Do you often act contrary to custom or to the wishes of your parents? ·70
4. Do you argue against people who attempt to assert their authority over you? ·58
5. Do you try to avoid situations where you are expected to conform to conventional standards? ·76
6. Do you go your own way regardless of the opinion of others? ·62
7. Are you generally disinclined to adopt a course of action dictated by others? ·55
8. Do you tend to disregard the rules and regulations that hamper your freedom? ·74
9. Do you set independence and liberty above everything? ·44
10. Are you apt to criticize whoever happens to be in authority? ·54

Dependence

Rating scale: Rel. coeff. r=·56 rt.

1. Do you usually tell your friends about your difficulties and misfortunes? ·76
2. Do you think of yourself sometimes as neglected and unloved? ·72
3. Are you rather easily discouraged when things go wrong? ·80

4. Do you sound the opinions of others before making a decision? ·66
5. Do you feel lost and helpless when you are left by someone you love? ·46
6. Are you apt to complain about your sufferings and hardships? ·72

Guilt

Rating scale: Rel. coeff. r = ·90 rt.

1. Do you tend to be rather submissive and apologetic when you have done wrong? ·24 (ø = ·43)
2. Do you feel nervous and anxious in the presence of superiors? ·53
3. Are you sometimes depressed by a feeling of your own unworthiness? ·50
4. Do you often ask yourself: 'Have I done right?' ·73
5. Do you feel sometimes that people disapprove of you? ·52
6. Are you frequently troubled by pangs of conscience? ·60
7. Do you sometimes experience a vague feeling of anxiety as if you had done wrong and would be found out? ·68

Change

Rating scale: Rel. coeff. r = ·71 rt.

1. Do you like variety and contrast; always willing to welcome change? ·50
2. Do you frequently start new projects without waiting to finish what you have been doing? ·50
3. Do you find that novel prospects – new places, new people, new ideas – appeal strongly to you? ·65
4. Could you cut your moorings – leave your home, family and friends – without suffering great regret? ·46
5. Do you find that your likes and dislikes change quite frequently? ·47
6. Are you quick to discard the old and accept the new; new fashions, new methods, new ideas? ·82
7. Are you fickle in your affections? ·52
8. Have you often experienced rather marked swings of mood from elation to depression? ·65

Conservatism

Rating scale: Rel. coeff. r = ·56	rt.
1. Are you somewhat disturbed when your daily habits are disrupted by unforseen events?	·62
2. Do you find that you react with a certain resistance to untested innovations?	·54
3. Do you find that a well-ordered mode of life with regular hours and an established routine is congenial to your temperament?	·82
4. Can you endure monotony without much fretting?	·73
5. Do you prefer to associate with your old friends, even though by so doing you miss the opportunity of meeting more interesting people?	·38
6. Are you usually consistent in your behaviour, going about your work in the same way, frequenting the same preferred places, following the same routes, etc.?	·64

Impulsion

Rating scale: Rel. coeff. r = ·82	rt.
1. Do you often act on the spur of the moment?	·67
2. Are you inclined to express your wishes without much hesitation?	·49
3. Do you often act impulsively just to blow off steam?	·91
4. Are you quick in commenting on most occasions?	·48
5. Do you often do a thing in a hurry just to get it over?	·46
6. When you have to act, are you usually quick to make up your mind?	·42
7. Do you sometimes start talking without knowing exactly what you are going to say?	·68
8. Are you easily carried away by an emotional impulse?	·83
9. Are you apt to say anything – though you may regret is later – rather than keep still?	·78
10. Would you call yourself spontaneous in speech and action?	·74

Deliberation

Rating scale:	Rel. coeff. r = ·87	rt.
1.	Do you repress your emotions more often than you express them?	·47
2.	Do you think much and speak little?	·74
3.	Are you slow in deciding upon a course of action?	·90
4.	Do you usually consider a matter from every standpoint before you form an opinion?	·64
5.	Are you slow to fall in love?	·52
6.	Do you usually make a plan before you start to do something?	·45
7.	When you are confronted by a crisis are you apt to become inhibited and do nothing?	·43
8.	Do you usually do things slowly and deliberately?	·74
9.	Do you dislike making hurried decisions?	·59
10.	Are you good at repartee, quick retorts, snap Judgments? (neg.)	·46

Exocathexis

Rating scale:	Rel. coeff. r = ·72	rt.
1.	Do you find that you can deal with an actual situation better than cope with general ideas and theories?	·62
2.	Do you like being in the thick of action?	·49
3.	Do you like to do things with your hands?	·62
4.	Would you call yourself a practical person?	·60
5.	Would you rather take an active part in contemporary events than read and think about them?	·71
6.	Do you like to have people about most of the time?	·66

Endocathexis

Rating scale:	Rel. coeff. r = ·73	rt.
1.	Are you inclined to withdraw from any kind of action?	·34 (ø = ·50)
2.	Do you prefer to know rather than do?	·57
3.	Do you spend a lot of time philosophizing with yourself?	·75
4.	Do you think more about your private feelings or theories than you do about the practical demands of every-day existence?	·78

5. Would you rather write a fine book than be an important public figure? ·64
6. Do you like above all to discuss general questions – scientific and philosophical – with your friends? ·45
7. Are you more interested in aesthetic and moral values than in contemporary events? ·63
8. Do you find at social gatherings that you don't seem to enjoy yourself as other people? ·53
9. Are you apt to brood for a long time over a single idea? ·56
10. Do you dislike everything to do with money – paying, selling, bargaining? ·34 (ø= ·39)

Nurturance

Rating scale: Rel. coeff. r= ·79 rt.

1. Are you drawn to people who are sick, unfortunate, or unhappy? ·78
2. Do you feel great sympathy for any 'underdog' and are you apt to do what you can for him? ·69
3. Do you often go out of your way to feed, pet, or otherwise care for an animal? ·43
4. Do you enjoy putting your own affairs aside to do someone a favour? ·68
5. Are you considered, by some of your friends, as too good-natured, too easily taken in? ·53
6. Do you enjoy playing with children? ·80
7. Do you find it difficult to lend things (books, money, etc.) to other people? (neg.) ·55

Sociability

Rating scale: Rel. coeff. r= ·70 rt.

1. Do you make as many friends as possible and are you always on the lookout for more? ·83
2. Do you accept social invitations rather than stay at home alone? ·78
3. Do you make a point of keeping in close touch with the doings and interests of your friends? ·50
4. Do you go out of your way to be with your friends? ·52
5. Do you feel that friendship is more important than anything else? ·75

6. Do you enjoy yourself very much at parties and social gatherings? ·74

COMMENT

This study has been selected for inclusion because it appears to be the best-known and most comprehensive attempt to verify the existence of the 'oral' personality syndrome described by psychoanalysts and its hypothesized connection with weaning events in early childhood. By considering the extent to which oral experiences in infancy are reflected in adult personality traits, Goldman-Eisler is supposedly testing a further (and more essentially Freudian) aspect of the psychoanalytic theory of oral fixation than the previous study by Yarrow which was concerned only with thumbsucking in later childhood. The paper reprinted here actually summarizes the results of two previously published studies (Goldman, 1948 and Goldman, 1950); the major addition in this paper is that of a more sophisticated use of the technique of factor analysis in classifying the traits hypothesized to comprise the oral character.

The theory of the oral personality and its childhood origins investigated in this study was derived from Freud (1938) and various other psychoanalytic writers, especially Abraham and Glover. In her 1948 paper, Goldman-Eisler outlines it as follows:

> Oral character traits are assumed to originate from repressed or deflected oral impulses which are dominant during the nursing period and which have undergone transformation into certain permanent behaviour patterns by the processes of reaction-formation, displacement, or sublimation. Two main syndromes of bipolar significance seem to emerge . . . The basic conditions for the development and fixation in character of the one or the other syndrome are assumed to be the experiences of gratification or frustration attached to the oral stage of libido development (p. 86).

According to analytic writers, the *orally gratified type* is characterized by 'imperturbable optimism, generosity, bright and sociable conduct, accessibility to new ideas, and ambition accompanied by sanguine expectation.' By contrast, the *orally ungratified type* is distinguished by 'a profoundly pessimistic outlook in life, sometimes accompanied by moods of depression and attitudes of withdrawal, a passive-receptive attitude, a feeling of insecurity, a need for the assurance of getting one's livelihood guaranteed, and ambition which combines an intense desire to climb with a feeling of unattainability, a grudging feeling of injustice, sensitiveness to competition, a dislike of sharing and an impatient importunity'. These two character types are more usually referred to as *oral optimists* and *oral pessimists* respectively. Oral pessimism is hypothesized to result either from frustration during the nursing period or overindulgence, i.e. both early weaning and unusually late weaning are assumed to be traumatic.

The results from the Goldman-Eisler study that bear most directly on this theory of orality are summarized in her Diagram 2.2, which shows the position of the various personality traits as well as two weaning measures in relation to the two orthogonal factors that were necessary to account for their interrelationships. The fact that two factors are necessary to describe the organization of a set of traits that were chosen on the assumption that they would fall along a single dimension of oral optimism-pessimism is clear disconfirmation of the first Freudian hypothesis. As Goldman-Eisler notes (p. 46), the data 'do not confirm the psychoanalytic contention that oral frustration, impatience and oral aggression are inseparable *or even related*' (italics ours). It is interesting to compare this statement by the author with the comments of Kline (1972): On p. 14 he cites these results as 'tentative support' for the psychoanalytic theory of the oral syndrome; later on it is just plain 'support' (p. 30), and on p. 48 he concludes that 'Goldman-Eisler has better supported the existence of the oral syndrome than its hypothesized aetiology'. At least this last comment may have some truth in it; let us consider the evidence in this connection.

The only significant relationship between adult personality and weaning practice was that between early weaning from the breast and factor I (the second part of the Freudian hypothesis – the effect of extremely *late* weaning on personality development failed to obtain confirmation). Although Goldman-Eisler identifies factor I with 'oral pessimism' it actually loads on all the trait descriptions that might be called 'negative', 'neurotic' or 'undesirable', but especially withdrawal and pessimism. Thus we have a correlation between people who are unsociable and unhappy with mothers who took them off the breast relatively early, and might therefore be called 'rejecting' mothers. Could this not result from a genetically transferred personality tendency, e.g. neurotic introversion? Once again, we have a case in which an environmental explanation of a correlation between parent and child is preferred when there is absolutely no evidence that would enable us to discount the genetic alternative. Yet, generally speaking, there is stronger evidence for genetic determinants of personality than there is for the influence of environmental factors (Eysenck, 1967).

Kline has other objections to the methodology of the study, like the fact that the feeding data were retrospective and at least fifteen years old (he is incorrect in saying that they were obtained from the subjects themselves – actually they were obtained from their mothers), and that no evidence was presented to support the validity of the questionnaires employed to assess the personality traits. These are sound criticisms but insignificant compared to the one that we have made; after all, Goldman-Eisler did get a positive result no matter how much error variance was involved, and this does require explanation. There is, however, no reason that we can see for preferring a psychoanalytic explanation over the more parsimonious genetic one.

This might not matter particularly if there was other good evidence to support the psychoanalytic position. But even Kline, whom we regard as fairly uncritical, is forced to make the following summary statement (1972, p. 93): 'From the considerable number of studies attempting to relate infant-rearing procedures to personality development *only two studies give even slight support to the Freudian theory*' (italics ours). According to Kline, these are: the Goldman-Eisler study that we have just discussed, and another by himself (Kline, 1968) relating to the anal character. The evidence provided by this latter study is considered later in the book (Chapter 4).

REFERENCES

ABRAHAM, K. (1942) The influence of oral eroticism on character-formation. In *Selected Papers*. London: Hogarth Press.

BERGLER, E. (1934) Zur Problematik des Oralen Pessimisten. *Imago*, **20**, 330-76.

EYSENCK, H. J. (1967) *The Biological Basis of Personality*. New York: C. C. Thomas.

FREUD, S. (1938) Three contributions to a theory of sex. In *The Basic Writings of Sigmund Freud*. New York: Modern Library.

GLOVER, E. (1925) Notes on oral character-formation. *Int. J. Psychoanal.*, **6**, 131-53.

GOLDMAN, F. (1948) Breast-feeding and character-formation. *J. Pers.*, **17**, 83-103.

—— (1950) the aetiology of the oral character in psychoanalytic theory. *J. Pers.*, **19**, 189-96.

KLINE, P. (1972) *Fact and Fantasy in Freudian Theory*. London: Methuen.

RIBBLE, MARGARET M. (1950) Infantile experience in relation to personality development. In J. MCV. HUNT (ed.), *Personality and the Behaviour Disorders*. Vol. 2, pp. 621-51. New York: Ronald Press.

SHARPE, ELLA (1950) Hamlet. In *Collected Papers on Psycho-analysis*. London: Hogarth Press.

3

Gerald S. Blum and Daniel R. Miller (1952)

Exploring the psychoanalytic theory of the 'oral character'[1]

Journal of Personality, 20, 287-304

In these days of sophisticated discussion on how to study psychoanalytic theory we feel somewhat defensive concerning the methods we are about to describe.[2] Not only did we confine ourselves to conventional techniques in psychology's stockpile but we used as many as we could. This approach was designed to test whether the theory *can* be phrased in operational terms amendable to traditional types of experimentation.

The topic we chose to investigate was the theory of 'oral character'. On one hand, there is sufficient agreement in the psychoanalytic literature to provide a starting point from which to formulate hypotheses. On the other, this aspect of the theory is admittedly incomplete. The combination made the area seem especially promising for experimental exploration.

Various clinical manifestations of oral passivity are summarized by Fromm in the following selected excerpts describing what he calls the 'receptive orientation':

> In the receptive orientation a person feels 'the source of all good' to be outside, and he believes that the only way to get what he wants – be it something material, be it affection, love, knowledge, pleasure – is to receive it from that outside source. In this orient-

[1]This project was supported by a grant from the Rackham School of Graduate Studies at the University of Michigan. The following individuals participated in the planning and execution of the study: Edith B. Bennett, Marvin A. Brandwein, James Chabot, Elizabeth Douvan, Stanley C. Duffendack, Glenn D. Garman, Maizie Gurin, J. Edwin Keller, Louise Morrison, Otto Riedl, E. Robert Sinnett, Ezra H. Stotland, William D. Winter, and Marion P. Winterbottom.

[2]Based on a paper presented at the 1950 American Psychological Association symposium on 'Experimental Approaches to Psychoanalytic Theory'.

ation the problem of love is almost exclusively that of 'being loved' and not that of loving . . . They are exceedingly sensitive to any withdrawal or rebuff they experience on the part of the loved person . . . It is characteristic of these people that their first thought is to find somebody else to give them needed information rather than to make even the smallest effort of their own . . . they are always in search of a 'magic helper'. They show a particular kind of loyalty, at the bottom of which is the gratitude for the hand that feeds them and the fear of ever losing it. Since they need many hands to feel secure, they have to be loyal to numerous people. It is difficult for them to say 'no', and they are easily caught between conflicting loyalties and promises. Since they cannot say 'no', they love to say 'yes' to everything and everybody, and the resulting paralysis of their critical abilities makes them increasingly dependent on others.

They are dependent not only on authorities for knowledge and help but on people in general for any kind of support. They feel lost when alone because they feel that they cannot do anything without help . . .

This receptive type has great fondness for food and drink. These persons tend to overcome anxiety and depression by eating or drinking. The mouth is an especially prominent feature, often the most expressive one; the lips tend to be open, as if in a state of continuous expectation of being fed. In their dreams, being fed is a frequent symbol of being loved; being starved, an expression of frustration or disappointment . . . (Fromm, 1947, pp. 62-3).

COLLECTION OF DATA

Having delimited our field of investigation, we were then faced with decisions concerning subjects and specific techniques. In regard to subjects, we chose to work with humans rather than animals. Generalizations from animal behaviour are largely by way of analogy. Furthermore, the complexities of interpersonal relationships cannot be fully duplicated in animal work. A second division concerned normal versus abnormal subjects. We chose the former because of the frequently heard objection that a theory derived largely from abnormal subjects must be shown to be applicable to normals. A third decision involved the desired age level of the subjects. The selection finally centred on eight-year-olds, since children in the latency period have the double advantage of being relatively free of the rampant psychosexual conflicts of earlier childhood on one hand, and of crystallized adult defences on the other. The experimental group consisted of the eighteen boys and girls in the third grade at the University of Michigan during 1948-9.

To test the hypotheses formulated from the literature, we first had to select a criterion measure of orality. This operational definition consisted of nonpurposive mouth movements recorded at various times over the three-week period of the research. Trained observers followed the children individually during eight two-minute intervals as part of a time-sampling procedure. They tallied such oral activities as thumbsucking, licking the lips, tongue-rolling, and bubbling. In addition to these routine classroom observations, the same activities were noted in an experiment on boredom tolerance (see Section X). All children were ranked on both measures and a final average ranking computed.[1]

Data on the dependent variables were collected by the following methods: teacher ratings, time-sampling, sociometrics, and experimental situations. Wherever feasible, we employed several approaches to test each hypothesis. Since the theory postulates that all individuals fall along a continuum of orality, rank-order correlations (corrected for ties) were calculated to measure the association between variable and criterion.

TESTING THE HYPOTHESES

Each of the following sections presents the statement of a hypothesis, the design worked out to test it, and the subsequent results.

I. *Extreme interest in food*

A. Hypothesis

Since the oral character is emotionally involved with eating beyond the dictates of simple hunger, he will consume extreme amounts of oral supplies and evince great interest in related activities. Accordingly, positive correlations are predicted between the orality criterion (mouth movements) and variables measuring interest in food.

B. Methods

1. Ice cream consumption. Our measure of consumption of oral supplies was the amount of ice cream eaten after hunger

[1]These two measures of mouth movements correlated ·61 with each other.

satiation. The children all ate lunch together. The meal, provided by the school, was dietetically planned and ample for all the children. Upon conclusion of a short rest period which followed lunch, they were offered an unlimited supply of vanilla ice cream contained in one-ounce paper cups packaged especially for the study. The carton of ice cream was placed on a table in the centre of the room by a female graduate student who supervised the distribution of cups. Each child was allowed to take one whenever he wished. However, only one cup at a time was permitted and that in return for an empty one. No limit was placed on how much a child ate. The carton was kept in the room for the entire forty minutes devoted to arts and crafts, during which period observers recorded the exact number of cups consumed by each child. This procedure was repeated daily over three weeks. From these data averages were computed. The range in any one day's session was quite startling, varying all the way from no cups to thirty-nine for a single child. The absence of any parental complaints concerning illness or lack of appetite was a pleasant surprise in view of the inability of the observers, even at the end of the most frustrating days of the experiment, to eat more than five or six cups without discomfort.

2. Eagerness at lunch time. The regular teacher and five practice teachers were given a scale describing various kinds of behaviour typical of oral children. They were asked to write the names of the children who occurred to them spontaneously as they read each of fourteen items.[1] At the completion

[1]Following is the complete list of questions: (1) Which children do you think get discouraged or give up most easily when something is difficult for them? (2) Which children do you think are most able to take care of themselves without the help of adults or other children? (3) Which children get the blues most often? (4) Which children would you most like to take with you on a two-week vacation? (5) Which children tend to ask the teacher for help most often, even when they know how to do the task? (6) Which children are most eager to have other children like them? (7) Which children display their affections most openly to the teachers? (8) Which children's feelings seem to be most easily hurt? (9) Which children seem to be always eager to help even when they are inconvenienced? (10) Which children seem to accept the suggestions of others almost without thinking twice? (11) Which children appear most impatient to eat at lunch time, as if eating were particularly important to them? (12) Which children make a special effort to get the teachers to like them? (13) Which children would you least like to take with you on a two-week vacation? (14) Which children seem most concerned with giving and receiving things?

of the form they were asked to reconsider each item and to increase all shorter lists of names to five. Among the questions was: 'Which children appear most impatient to eat at lunch time, as if eating were particularly important to them?'

C. Results

Mouth Movements

1. Ice cream	.52	P<.05
2. Eagerness at lunch time	.51	P<.05

These figures strongly support the predicted association between orality (mouth movements) and interest in food.

II. *Need for liking and approval*

A. Hypothesis

In terms of the theory, a significant relationship should be found between degree of orality and the need for liking and approval.

B. Methods

1. 'Which children are most eager to have other children like them?' (Teacher item 6)
2. 'Which children make a special effort to get the teachers to like them?' (Teacher item 12)
3. Approaches to teachers for approval. (Time-sampling item)
4. Approaches to children for approval. (Time-sampling item)
5. Attention to observers. (Time-sampling item)

C. Results

Mouth Movements

1. Eagerness for others' liking	.68	P<.01
2. Efforts for teachers' liking	.10	N S[1]
3. Approaches to teachers for approval	.44	P<.10
4. Approaches to children for approval	.24	N S
5. Attention to observers	.36	P<.20

Viewing these correlations as a whole, the hypothesis seems to be fairly well supported. Although only two are significant beyond the 10 per cent level, all are in the positive direction.

III. *Dependency*

A. Hypothesis

Closely allied to the preceding hypothesis is the prediction of a positive correlation between orality and dependency.

[1]Not significant.

B. Methods

1. 'Which children do you think are most able to take care of themselves without the help of adults or other children?' (Teacher item 2)
2. 'Which children tend to ask the teacher for help most often, even when they know how to do the task?' (Teacher item 5)

C. Results

	Mouth Movements	
1. Doesn't take care of self	.50	$P<.05$
2. Asks teachers' help	.10	N S

These results tend to be equivocal, with one correlation being significant and the other not.

IV. *Concern over giving and receiving*

A. Hypothesis

Since gifts represent a form of 'supplies' to the oral character, it is predicted that concern over giving and receiving varies with degree of orality.

B. Methods

1. 'Which children seem most concerned with giving and receiving things?' (Teacher item 14)
2. Generosity without promise of supplies in return. A related prediction held that oral children would be reluctant to give unless attractive supplies were forthcoming. After the distribution of ice cream on the second gift day (see Section 3 immediately following) the class was allowed to use the coloured pencils in a drawing period. Shortly before the end of this session, a strange adult wearing a large, yellow badge marked 'Pencil Drive' entered the room and made a very stirring appeal to give as many pencils as possible to the poor children of the neighbourhood. Each child then went behind a screen and secretly deposited his pencils in the slot of a colourful box marked 'Pencil Drive'. All the new pencils had been marked with pin points, so that the contributions of each subject were readily identifiable. Unfortunately, this coding system was of little aid since only three in the entire class gave new pencils. The rest of the collection consisted of a variegated assortment of battered, chewed-up stumps with broken points – all without identification marks. In order to locate the pencil contributors, a new procedure was

developed which provided the basis for the added experiment described in Section 4 following.

3. Gifts as the equivalent of food. The term 'oral supplies' connotes, in addition to food, tokens of personal recognition. It was hypothesized that, if gifts and food are equivalent supplies, receipt of gifts should result in a diminution of ice cream consumption for the group as a whole. On one occasion the children were each given a box of crayons; another time they received seven coloured pencils which they had chosen as their most desired gift in a rating session the preceding day.
4. Guilt over not giving. The theory leads to the prediction that guilt, typically experienced as a deprivation of supplies, should bring about an increase in the consumption of ice cream. The day after the pencil drive, the teacher agreed to deliver a stern lecture saying how ashamed she was of their stinginess. She was so effective that, before she finished, one boy blurted out that he had meant to give more new pencils and ran to the box to deposit a few. Next the teacher asked the group to retrieve their donations and observers tallied the number of pencils each pupil took back, which provided the data missing in Section 2 immediately above. Shortly afterward the ice cream was distributed and the number of cups counted as usual.

   To relieve the guilt, the pencil solicitor returned later to proclaim happily that the school drive had been 100 per cent successful. He then apologized for not having announced previously that old pencils were not wanted.

C. Results

Mouth Movements

1. Concern over giving and receiving	.46	$P<.10$
2. Lack of generosity	.22	N S

3. Gifts as the equivalent of food. On the crayon day, 14 of the 16 subjects decreased in the number of cups consumed ($X^2=9.00$, $P<.01$); and on the pencil day, 12 out of 15 dropped ($X^2=5.40$, $P<.02$).
4. Guilt over not giving. While there were no significant increases in the actual amount of ice cream consumed after the 'guilt' lecture, certain qualitative observations were noted. The five most oral children in the group sat on the table next to the ice cream carton throughout the whole period, in

contrast to their usual wandering around the room. Since they had apparently been eating up to maximum physical capacity, it was virtually impossible for them to eat significantly more cups than before. Another exceptional feature was the fact that none of the ice cream was left over this time.

Considering the above experiments as a whole, there seems to be fair support for the hypothesis that orality is related to concern over giving and receiving.

V. *Need to be ingratiating*

A. Hypothesis

The oral character, by virtue of his never-ending search for love and approval, tends to behave towards others in a very ingratiating manner.

B. Methods

1. 'Which children display their affections most openly to the teachers?' (Teacher item 7)
2. 'Which children seem to be always eager to help even when they are inconvenienced?' (Teacher item 9)
3. Going out of way to do favours. (Time-sampling item)

C. Results

	Mouth Movements	
1. Displays affection openly	−.28	N S
2. Always eager to help	−.24	N S
3. Goes out of way to do favours	.16	N S

These results clearly negate the predicted association between orality and the need to be ingratiating.

VI. *Social isolation*

A. Hypothesis

According to the theory, the oral character should be infrequently chosen by his peers in view of his passivity, his excessive demands for attention, and his hostility when these demands are not gratified.

B. Methods

In a private interview each child was asked to answer a number of sociometric questions to determine his favourites among his classmates: (1) 'Which children in your classroom do you like best?' (2) 'Which of the children in your classroom would you most like to invite to a party?' (3) 'Which teachers do you like the most?'[1] (4) 'Which children in your class are you good friends with?' Class members were then ranked according to the number of times their names had been mentioned.

C. Results

	Mouth Movements	
1. Social isolation	.68	P<.01

This correlation strongly supports the theoretical deduction that orality and social isolation go hand in hand.

VII. *Inability to divide loyalties*

A. Hypothesis

The theory leads to the hypothesis that the more oral child has greater difficulty choosing between two friends, inasmuch as both represent potential sources of supply.

B. Methods

Several days after the sociometric ratings a measure of divided loyalty was obtained. Each child was interviewed individually and asked to make a number of choices between his two best-liked teachers. The interviewer recorded decision time plus comments, actions, and expressive movements. The protocols were then rated blindly by three judges for degree of indecision.

C. Results

	Mouth Movements	
1. Inability to divide loyalties	−.28	N S

The correlation of this variable with the criterion contradicts the hypothesized association between orality and the inability to divide loyalties.

VIII. *Suggestibility*

A. Hypothesis

From the theory it was anticipated that the oral child, in view of his excessive need for love and approval, would be suggestible in the presence of a potentially supply-giving adult.

B. Methods

1. Upon his arrival in the testing room, the child was told:

[1]Included only for use in Section VII.

'We have some things which we want you to help us try out in order to see if they are right for school children of your age.' The experiment consisted of three parts: tasting a hypothetical cherry flavour in candy, smelling perfume from a bottle of water, and feeling nonexistent vibrations in a metal rod attached to some apparatus.

2. 'Which children seem to accept the suggestions of others almost without thinking twice?' (Teacher item 10)

C. Results

	Mouth Movements	
1. Taste	.50	P<.05
Touch	.00	N S
Smell	.03	N S
2. Accepts suggestions	.11	N S

Except for taste, suggestibility does not appear to be related to degree of orality. The discrepancy between results with taste and with the other items is most easily accounted for by the specifically oral quality of the taste measure.

IX. *Depressive tendencies*

A. Hypothesis

Self-esteem in the oral child is presumed to depend upon external sources of love or supplies. Therefore, the unavoidable frustration of oral demands is said to be experienced as a feeling of emptiness or depression.

B. Methods

1. 'Which children do you think get discouraged or give up most easily when something is difficult for them?' (Teacher item 1)
2. 'Which children get the blues most often?' (Teacher item 3)
3. 'Which children's feelings seem to be most easily hurt?' (Teacher item 8)

C. Results

	Mouth Movements	
1. Get discouraged	.32	P<.20
2. Get the blues	.05	N S
3. Feelings easily hurt	.13	N S

The low correlations between mouth movements and personality characteristics relevant to depression do not support the theoretical prediction.

X. *Boredom tolerance*

A. Hypothesis

Boredom is assumed to be especially disturbing to the oral child because it signifies a lack of available supplies. Therefore he would be expected to show very little tolerance for a boring, unrewarded activity.

B. Methods

In this experiment the child was taken into a room where he was shown a large sheaf of papers containing lines of X's and O's. The examiner then said: 'Your class is being compared with another class in another town to see which class can cross out the most circles.' After giving instructions, the examiner added: 'There are several pages [the examiner leafed through all the sheets]. Don't write your name on the paper. We don't care how much you yourself can do but how much the class can do. All right, you may begin.'

The examiner then left the room. As soon as the child began, an observer casually entered the room, sat at a distance, and recorded all the actions of the subject, such as number of mouth movements and work interruptions. The child was stopped after twenty minutes. Ranks were based on number of lines completed. As mentioned previously, this experiment also contributed to the criterion measure of non-biting mouth movements, which were tallied throughout.

C. Results

	Mouth Movements	
1. Boredom Tolerance	.45	P<.10

While not very high, this figure does provide some support for the prediction that orality and boredom tolerance are positively associated.

XI. *Summary of results*

Ten hypotheses concerning oral character structure have been tested. The results can be summarized in tabular form as follows:

Strong Support	*Fair Support*	*Unsupported*	*Equivocal*
1. Extreme interest in food	1. Need for liking and approval	1. Dependency	1. Need to be ingratiating
2. Social isolation	2. Concern over giving and receiving	2. Suggestibility	2. Inability to divide loyalties
	3. Boredom tolerance		3. Depressive tendencies

The goal of this phase of the research is to check the existing status of the theory, and to make revisions wherever dictated by the evidence. The above data represent the initial tests of hypotheses deduced from the psychoanalytic literature on orality. In general, a fair number of predictions have been supported, some remain questionable, and still others are clearly not supported. Before evaluating specific hypotheses, however, we prefer to await the returns from successive attempts to measure the same variables. It is very possible that any one of the significant correlations may still reflect the influence of chance factors. Also, any one of the insignificant findings may be a function of faulty experimentation rather than incorrect theory. Both of these possibilities suggest the necessity for repeated research along similar lines. Apart from the fate of specific hypotheses, the overall results hold promise for the investigation of psychoanalytic theory by conventional psychological methods.

RELATED EMPIRICAL OBSERVATIONS

Intercorrelations of major variables. In addition to providing data concerning specific hypotheses, the study lends itself to an overall analysis of correlations among the major variables. This supplementary approach seems worth while in view of the postulated communality of the variables. If each variable really measures oral passivity, the table of intercorrelations should demonstrate positive relationships beyond chance expectancy. These data, grouped according to pure oral measures, experimental situations, and behavioural measures, are shown in Table 3.1.

From Table 3.2 we see that the total numbers of significant positive correlations at the 10 per cent, 5 per cent, and 1 per cent levels clearly exceed the chance expectancies. These results suggest the possible existence of a general 'factor' of orality.

Comparative evaluation of methodological approaches. Table 3.3 presents a breakdown of the personality variables into two general

TABLE 3.1. *Intercorrelations of major variables.*

	Pure Oral Measures				Personality						
					Experimental Situations				Behavioural Measures		
	1. Ice cream	2. Eagerness at lunch (T.R.)	3. Mouth activity (T.S.)	4. Mouth activity (B.T.)	5. Suggestibility	6. Boredom tolerance	7. Divided loyalty	8. Generosity	9. Sociometrics	10. Combined teacher ratings[1]	11. Combined time samples[2]
1.		19	67‡	32	30	31	−07	−29	40*	−09	43*
2.			41*	50†	11	34	−18	15	44*	20	01
3.				61‡	04	39	−21	19	61‡	15	55‡
4.					25	44*	−18	32	71‡	20	17
5.						12	44*	−33	36	07	−11
6.							04	25	35	10	−04
7.								−33	03	04	−31
8.									18	45*	09
9.										23	12
10.											−01

* = $P < \cdot 10$
† = $P < \cdot 05$
‡ = $P < \cdot 01$
[1] Does not include 2 [Eagerness at lunch (T.R.)]
[2] Does not include 3 [Mouth activity (T.S.)]

TABLE 3.2. *Number of significant positive correlations among major variables.*

Probability level	Number Expected by Chance	Number obtained
·10	2·75	13
·05	1·38	6
·01	0·28	4

types – experimental situations and behavioural measures. The number of significant correlations for each type with the major variables suggests a probable difference in their relative efficacy. It is true that the same operational variables are not measured in both types.

TABLE 3.3. *Personality measures broken down by the type of approach vs. major variables.*

Personality measures	Probability level	Number positive correlations expected by chance	Number obtained
Experimental Situations	·10	1·70	3
	·05	0·85	0
	·01	0·17	0
Behavioural Measures	·10	1·35	7
	·05	0·68	3
	·01	0·14	2

Nevertheless, the large number of significant behavioural correlations warrants speculation concerning possible causes. Three alternative explanations come to mind. One, the experimental designs were adequate and the negative results are a contradiction of the hypotheses. This possibility does not seem very plausible in the light of the positive theoretical findings with other techniques. Two, the hypotheses are valid and the designs inadequate. No evidence exists for rejecting this alternative, but the marked discrepancy between results with the two approaches, both of which were carefully designed and pre-tested, leads us to question the explanation. Three, the difficulty lies, not in experimental design or theory, but in unreliability inherent in the settings in which the experiments were conducted. The number of observations involved in the experiments were necessarily limited to one session, whereas the behavioural measures were usually accumulated over several time periods. Unavoidable and unpredictable obstacles are bound to arise in the course of experimentation in a natural setting, such as a schoolroom, where the success of each design hinges upon the precision and co-operation of a large number of individuals.

Cases in point are the Love Withdrawal and Can't Say No experiments, both of which had to be abandoned. The hypothesis in the former stated that the oral child should be highly sensitive to withdrawal of love. The 'ice-cream lady' first asked the children in the class to make drawings using themes of their own choice. When the drawings were finished she circulated around the room, praising them all freely. Then she instructed the group to draw a house, each child individually to bring his drawing to her upon its completion.

She lauded half of the drawings, and held them up before the class while commenting on their merits and naming the artists. The other half were received with casual indifference but no criticism. This was the love withdrawal procedure. Finally, she asked the class to draw a picture of a child. The aim of the experiment was to determine the effects of the withdrawal of love upon both drawings and behaviour as recorded by observers.

The experiment was to have been repeated several days later, with a reversal of the treatment of the previously praised and ignored halves. In the actual administration if turned out to be impossible to maintain any kind of order in the class. The children were all excited about an Indian play which they had performed that day before the entire school, and their drum-pounding and war-whooping precluded any systematic, experimental procedure.

The Can't Say No hypothesis dealt with the inability of the oral character to refuse requests from adults for fear of losing their approval. Nine observers entered the library while the class was listening to a fascinating record. Each observer approached a child, tapped him on the shoulder, and said in a neutral tone: 'Come with me'. The reactions to this request were later reported in detail. Like the preceding experiment this one was disrupted by an unforeseen complication. At the last minute the librarian was unable to schedule a record session when the other nine children in the group were to be asked to leave.

In contrast to the above illustrative experiments, the cumulative behavioural measures, on the other hand, were not as suceptible to unforeseen disruptions, since accidental influences on any one day tended to average out in the course of time. For example, differences occurred when ice cream was delivered late, yet this did not seriously alter the final ranking of subjects on the number of cups consumed.

From these speculations, it seems preferable that research designs, when dealing with something as complex as character structure, involve a series of measurements over a period of time.

Exploration of projective instruments. The following four projective techniques were included to explore their suitability as measures of orality: the Rorschach Test (Rorschach, 1942), Thematic Apperception Test (Murray, 1943), Blacky Pictures (Blum, 1949; 1950) and a specially constructed Story Completion Test which had been found to be significantly related to sociometric status in a previous study (Miller & Stine, 1951). Since there had been no previous

TABLE 3.4. *Correlations of Projective Methods with Major Variables.*

	Pure oral measures				Personality						
					Experimental situations			Behavioural measures			
	1. Ice cream	2. Eagerness at lunch (T.R.)	3. Mouth activity (T.S.)	4. Mouth activity (B.T.)	5. Suggestibility	6. Boredom tolerance	7. Divided loyalty	8. Generosity	9. Sociometrics	10. Combined teacher ratings	11. Combined time samples
Rorschach (Objective)	28	19	20	−05	11	41	−03	−11	−13	−10	45
TAT (Objective)	−40	−58	−34	−59	01	−37	33	−21	05	−02	−05
Story Completion (Objective)	−11	−45	−29	−36	08	−20	60	−06	−11	−12	−05
Story Completion (Interpretive)	47	06	33	48	40	37	23	−34	19	−12	06
Blacky (Interpretive)	21	−23	16	25	41	−06	16	−20	28	15	21

applications of the techniques to this topic and age range, attempts at explicit prediction were not made.

Table 3.4 presents the correlations of the various projective methods with the major variables. Analysis of the projectives can be grouped under two broad headings, objective and interpretive. The Rorschach, TAT, and Story Completion (Objective) were all scored by counting the number of oral references, e.g. 'food', 'hunger', 'eating', etc. The Blacky and Story Completion (Interpretive) protocols were ranked according to global impressions of oral passivity. While none of the correlations is very high, it should be noted that the 'objective' approach yielded 22 negative and 11 positive correlations, whereas the 'interpretive' produced only 5 negative and 17 positive ($X^2=10.1$, $P<.01$). Whether this difference can legitimately be attributed to type of scoring approach can be answered only by further investigation.

SUMMARY

This project was designed to explore the feasibility of testing psychoanalytic theory by conventional psychological methods. Hypotheses concerning the 'oral character', deduced from statements in the literature, were examined by means of teacher ratings, time-sampling, sociometrics, and experimental situations conducted in a third-grade class. The operational definition of orality consisted of non-purposive mouth movements recorded by observers. The eighteen subjects were ranked on the criterion and on a series of variables related to specific hypotheses.

The resulting correlations lent strong support to hypotheses dealing with (*a*) extreme interest in food, and (*b*) social isolation. Fair support was given (*a*) need for liking and approval, (*b*) concern over giving and receiving, and (*c*) boredom tolerance. Unsupported hypotheses were (*a*) need to be ingratiating, (*b*) inability to divide loyalties, and (*c*) depressive tendencies; while remaining equivocal were (*a*) dependency and (*b*) suggestibility. Apart from the currently tentative nature of these specific findings, the overall results were interpreted as holding promise for the investigation of psychoanalytic theory by traditional techniques.

COMMENT

This paper has been included primarily because it was selected by Vetter and Smith (1971) as a worthy example of experimental psychoanalysis. According to these writers, the study 'has direct relevance to the . . . matter of the generality of psychoanalytic postulates derived from observations made on a clinical population . . . Blum and Miller were able to validate predictions derived from psychoanalytic theory within a population of normal children'.

Eight-year-old children were chosen for study because 'children in the latency period have the double advantage of being relatively free of the rampant psychosexual conflicts of earlier childhood on one hand, and of crystallized adult defences on the other' (p. 66). Kline (1972), however, all but rejects the study 'because its sample consisted of nine-year-old children' (actually they were eight) 'and it by no means follows, from psychosexual theory, that the adult character traits representative of fixation at various levels will, in fact, manifest themselves in childhood'. Here we have another illustration of the vagueness of psychoanalytic theory; two supposedly expert opinions disagreeing on the predictions that should be made on the basis of psychoanalytic 'orality' theory. If Kline is right, then there would be no need to consider this study any further. We will give Blum and Miller the benefit of the doubt, however (after all, we make no claim to being arbiters in disputes among psychoanalytic theorists), and we will see how their experiment stands up to scrutiny otherwise.

The major results of the study are summarized in Table 3.1, which shows the complete matrix of intercorrelations among the various hypothesized measures of 'orality'. As the authors are aware, this table should show positive relationships beyond chance expectancy. In fact, this *is* found to be the case, although hardly to an extent that justifies identification of a 'general factor of orality'. Of the 55 coefficients in the matrix, only 6 reach an acceptable (.05) level of significance (it is not conventional to accept a .10 significance level). Of these 6, four at least are tautological in the sense that they are relationships among different measures of spontaneous mouth activity and apparent eagerness to eat. (Ice cream consumption × Mouth activity measure 1, Eagerness at lunch × Mouth activity measure 2, Mouth activity measure 2 × Combined time samples, Mouth activity measure 1 × Mouth activity measure 2). Blum and Miller include all of these in their comparison of the expected and observed significance levels, even though the last two correlations amount to nothing more than test-retest reliability coefficients on the time-sampling measures of mouth activity. There is surely nothing 'Freudian' in the discovery that children who smack their lips a lot on one occasion tend to do so on other occasions as well, nor in the findings that children who smack their lips are rated by their teachers as 'eager to eat at lunchtime' and indeed do consume more ice cream than others when given the opportunity. These relationships would be predicted by anybody, regardless of whether or not they were versed in Freud.

This leaves us with only two correlations in the entire matrix that are both statistically significant and theoretically interesting, and these two are redundant because they are both relationships between sociometric rejection and measures of mouth activity (.61 for Measure 1 and .71 for Measure 2). Since these cannot be regarded as separate relationships for the purpose of comparing the number of expected and observed significant relationships in the way that Blum and Miller do, we are effectively left with only *one* relationship to be explained (hardly far removed from the number expected by chance).

If we allow this relationship between sociometric rejection and spontaneous mouth activity as a real finding, then we must question the uniqueness of the interpretation placed upon it by Blum and Miller. Naturally, in view of their theoretical orientation they assume that this finding supports the hypothesis supposedly derived from psychoanalytic theory, that 'the oral character should be infrequently chosen by his peers in view of his passivity, his excessive demands for attention, and his hostility when these demands are not gratified'. Unfortunately for this hypothesis, Blum and Miller find themselves that the oral character as they define him is *not* dependent, suggestible, ingratiating or depressive (all the characteristics that seem most relevant to their hypothesis concerning the mediation between 'orality' and sociometric rejection). Not only do they fail to consider other possible explanations for their finding, but they fail to consider evidence provided by their own study that apparently rules out the Freudian explanation.

If the psychoanalytic explanation is not adequate, can we suggest an alternative? One very simple possibility that could have been easily discounted by collecting appropriate data is that the greedy 'oral' children were fat, and rejected by their peers because of their physical unattractiveness and/or lack of sporting ability. Evidence for such a relationship has been previously reported (Staffieri, 1967). Another possibility involves a reversal of the hypothesized direction of cause and effect; children who are social isolates for one reason or another may take solace in eating and their mouth movements reflect their need for 'substitute gratification'. (In behavioural terms they learn to reduce social anxiety with a reciprocally inhibitory eating response.) Both of these explanations are at least as parsimonious and plausible as that apparently accepted by Blum and Miller, yet neither are considered at any point in their discussion. Characteristically, once the authors have found that Freudian theory fits their finding, that is where they stop thinking. They are not interested in alternative explanations and feel no responsibility to attempt to discount them.

REFERENCES

BLUM, G. S. (1949) A study of the psychoanalytic theory of psychosexual development. *Genet. Psychol. Monogr.*, **39**, 3-99.

—— (1950) *The Blacky Pictures: A Technique for the Exploration of Personality Dynamics.* New York: The Psychological Corporation.

FENICHEL, O. (1945) *The Psychoanalytic Theory of Neurosis.* New York: Norton.

FROMM, E. (1947) *Man for Himself.* New York: Rinehart.

KLINE, P. (1972) *Fact and Fantasy in Freudian Theory.* London: Methuen.

MILLER, D. R. & HUTT, M. L. (1949) Value interiorization and personality development. *J. Soc. Issues*, **5**, No. 4, 2-30.

MILLER, D. R. & STINE, M. E. (1951) The prediction of social acceptance by means of psychoanalytic concepts. *J. Pers.*, **20**, 162-74.

MURRAY, H. A. (1943) *Thematic Apperception Test Manual.* Cambridge, Mass.: Harvard Univ. Press.

RORSCHACH, H. (1942) *Psychodiagnostics* (translation). Bern: Hans Huber.

STAFFIERI, J. R. (1967) A study of social stereotype of body image in children. *J. Pers. Soc. Psychol.*, **7**, 101-4.

THOMPSON, C. (1950) *Psychoanalysis: Evaluation and Development.* New York: Hermitage House.

THORNTON, G. R. (1943) The significance of rank-difference coefficients of correlation. *Psychometrika,* 8, No. 4, 211-22.

VETTER, H. J. & SMITH, B. D. (1971) *Personality Theory: A Source Book.* New York: Appleton-Century-Crofts.

4
Paul Kline (1968)[1]

Obsessional traits, obsessional symptoms and anal erotism

British Journal of Medical Psychology, 41, 299-305

The anal character – that triad of traits, obstinacy, parsimony and orderliness – has long been an eccepted feature of psychoanalytic teaching (Freud, 1908; Abraham, 1923; Jones, 1923; Menninger, 1943). It is claimed, of course, that these traits are defence mechanisms again anal erotism repressed in early childhood by over-enthusiastic toilet-training, hence the name of the syndrome. Menninger (1943) indeed, goes so far as to argue that the anal phase of childhood is the most important influence in the development not only of individuals but also, on account of variations in pot-training methods, of cultures and civilizations. There are clearly two points here worthy of examination. First, is there any objective evidence that a syndrome of traits such as the anal character does in fact occur other than in a few isolated clinical instances? If there appears to be such a constellation of traits, is it in any way related to repressed anal erotism, as psychoanalytic theory claims?

The majority of the psychiatric writers (e.g. Schneider, 1923; Lewis & Mapother, 1941; Curran & Partridge, 1953; Arieti, 1959), it is probably fair to argue, recognize an obsessional personality, which, if not precisely the same as the anal character, inasmuch as there is usually no mention of parsimony, is certainly very similar. This is typically described as careful, meticulous, rigid, bound by routine and slow to make decisions. Nevertheless, the major essays into the psychometry of personality do not recognize either an obsessional or an anal character, as examination of the Cattell 16 PF test (Cattell & Stice, 1958) – which, incidentally, claims to cover all the major variables in the description of personality (Cattell, 1957) – the EPI (Eysenck & Eysenck, 1964) or the MMPI, indicates. It is to be

[1]Institute of Education, Exeter University.

noticed, however, that this last test does contain an obsessional neurosis scale – a measure of obsessional symptoms rather than obsessional traits. Foulds (1965) has recently drawn attention to the distinction between traits and symptoms in the spheres of personality and neurosis. Sandler & Hazari (1961) neatly summarize this position, describing traits as stable and ego-syntonic in nature, whereas symptoms are transient and ego-dystonic. This distinction between traits and symptoms has now quite considerable experimental support (Hazari, 1957; Sandler & Hazari, 1961; Foulds, 1961, 1965; Foulds & Caine, 1958, 1959; Delay, Pichot & Perse, 1962; Pichot & Perse, 1968; Kline, 1967), so it cannot be argued that the MMPI contains a measure of the obsessional personality by virtue of its obsessional neurosis scale.

Thus there is the anomalous position concerning the anal character that it is recognized by clinicians yet neglected by statistical investigators. However, there have been a few attempts to produce empirical statistical evidence for the existence of the anal character, although none have been entirely convincing. Barnes (1952) factor analysed items thought to pertain to anal characteristics and discovered no factor common to them. He concluded that the traits did not therefore form a syndrome in the manner expected from psychoanalytic theory. The Krout Personal Preference Scale (Krout & Tabin, 1954) contains a measure of the anal character. Nevertheless, the validity of this scale has been called into question by the work of both Stagner & Moffit (1956) and Littman *et al.* (1961) and it cannot be regarded as widely acceptable evidence. Grygier (1961), however, has further developed this test and there are two studies which suggest that the anal scales of his Dynamic Personality Inventory have some validity (Barron, 1955; Kline, 1968). In this last study the validity of the anal scales was attested by the fact that they all loaded on a common factor, as would be predicted from Freudian theory. Beloff (1957) constructed an anal scale, the validity of which was derived from item consistency (all the items loaded on a general factor) and from the correlation between self-ratings on the scale and ratings by others. It was concluded from this evidence that the anal character was a meaningful dimension of personality. Hazari (1957) and Sandler & Hazari (1961) factored 40 items from the Tavistock Self-Assessment Inventory and produced two scales: one measuring obsessional traits, the other symptoms. Again the validity of both these scales depends upon item homogeneity and face validity. In the light of the studies on response set (Cronbach, 1946), especially social desirability

(Edwards, 1957), this might be considered insufficient, although Kline (1967) found positive correlations between the Hazari trait scale and the Beloff scale, as well as correlations between the Hazari symptom scale and the MMPI obsessional scale, a result which supports the validity of both the Beloff and the Hazari scales. Thus in these studies there is some objective evidence, suggestive rather than definitive, for the existence of an anal or obsessional personality. In addition, Finney (1961) has produced an anal scale from a factor analysis of the MMPI items, together with some of his own devising. The validity of this scale has been well attested by the work of Delay *et al.* (1962) and Pichot & Perse (1968). Finally, the present writer has produced an anal scale (Ai3), whose validity has been demonstrated by correlations with the Beloff, Hazari and DPI anal scales and in factor analytic studies with the 16-PF, MMPI and EPI, as well as by correlations with ratings for the anal character; results to be published in a later study (Kline, 1969). The items used in this scale may be found in the appendix.

However, if it is admitted that there is some objective support for the existence of a syndrome, there is practically none for the psychoanalytic aetiology. Thus Orlans (1949), surveying the evidence concerning the effects of child-rearing practices on adult personality, is forced to conclude that links between the two are not supported. Hamilton (1929) and Sears (1943), on the basis of ratings for anal traits and childhood memories, offer some slight evidence (by no means conclusive) for the Freudian theory. Beloff (1957), however, in her far more rigorous study, related the anal character not to toilet-training procedures in infancy but to conformity and thus argued that the term 'anal' was a misnomer. However, it may be argued that the fact that no such link was found in this study was due to methodological difficulties rather than to the weakness of the theory. Thus, as Newson & Newson (1963) point out, it is exceedingly difficult to remember the details of pot-training and they regard an interval of a year between its completion and questions concerning it as the maximum to be tolerated for valid results. In the Beloff (1957) study, it will be remembered, this interval must have been at least 15 years. This should mean that child studies, conducted longitudinally (e.g. Huschaka, 1942), should yield better results. However, the anal character and the obsessional personality are adult personality patterns and the fact that such investigations with children have failed to yield the results predicted from Freudian theory can be attributed to this.

There is one further point: these investigations of the anal character regard it as resulting from severe pot-training and the consequent repression of anal erotism. However, this is a gross simplification of the psychoanalytic theory, the popularity of which may be due to the fact that it is easily tested. Thus in the original article Freud (1908) argues that the anal erotism is intensified in the sexual constitution of the anal character, a constitution later referred to by other psychoanalytic writers (e.g. Menninger, 1943) as the anal stamp. In short, in addition to the environmental variable (pot-training) there is the *constitutional* variable (the anal stamp). These constitutional genetic differences are fully discussed in 'Three essays on sexuality' (Freud, 1905), where the claim that individuals vary in strength of their component interests is clearly stated. According to this full formulation of the theory, only when severe training is applied to a child of the anal stamp will the anal character develop. This fact alone is sufficient to account for the failure of those investigations which attempt to correlate pot-training procedures with adult personality traits. There is the further complication that what appears to an objective observer to be the same procedure may be of different severity to children differing in their strength of anal erotism, in much the same manner as one piece of food is of different reward value to a hungry and a sated rat. If this is the case, then the attempt to assess pot-training procedures is valueless and the only method of testing the psychoanalytic hypotheses concerning the anal character would be to correlate the anal characteristics with some measure of the anal erotism itself.

The Blacky Pictures (Blum, 1949) are claimed to test Freudian psychosexual developmental levels projectively, by means of 11 cartoons portraying Blacky, a dog, in a number of family situations considered relevant in psychoanalytic theory to such development. Despite all the well-known caveats concerning projective tests as typified by the Eysenckian claim that they are but vehicles for the riotous imaginations of the clinician, these pictures are particularly suitable for the investigation considered in this paper. Thus the anal dimension is tapped by a picture of Blacky defecating. Even if it is argued that this technique does not reach, as the author of the test claims, the deeper recesses of the personality, it is nevertheless of interest to examine the correlation between responses to what is indubitably an anal situation and scores on measures of characteristics hypothesized as defence mechanism against anal erotism. Positive correlations would have to be admitted as support for the psychoanalytic aetiology, as being the most parsimonious explanations for the observations.

Evidence for the validity of these Blacky Pictures is not strong, partly because many of the studies done with them assume validity. However, a number of investigations do bear on the construct validity of the anal dimension, although there has been no attempt to relate it to the anal or obsessional personality. Construct validity may be claimed for the anal dimension on the grounds that correlations in the predicted direction have been found between it and handwriting variables (McNeil & Blum, 1952), the capacity for verbal recall (Adelson & Redmond, 1958) and stuttering (Carp, 1962), although in this study the findings were contrary to those suggested by Fenichel (1945) in that the anal dimension did not distinguish stutterers, and conditionability (Timmons & Noblin, 1963). Again, in this investigation it is difficult to see the grounds for the claim that anals would be harder to condition than non-anals, a view indeed that is opposed to that of Beloff (1957). This brief summary of the evidence for the construct validity of the anal dimension indicates the problems of this kind of validity with vague constructs. It also shows that the anal dimension is not entirely invalid. Nevertheless, as has been pointed out, even if the validity is denied, the test is still of interest because it constitutes an anal situation.

As regards reliability, the weakness of so many projective tests, despite the gloomy findings of Charen (1956*a*, *b*) inter-marker and between-marker reliability has been shown to be reasonably high (Granick & Schefflin, 1958), so that use of the test is not precluded on these grounds.

Since it has been shown that the failure to link pot-training procedures with the adult obsessional personality can be accounted for both by the methodological problems involved in the collection of pot-training data and by the fact that previous investigations have ignored the anal stamp, it was decided to examine the correlation between three existing measures of the anal or obsessional character and the anal dimension of the Blacky Pictures which, if valid, would appear to be a measure of anal erotism (the anal stamp) and is at least an anal situation.

EXPERIMENTAL PROCEDURE

The Blacky Pictures were administered individually to 46 volunteer students. In addition these subjects completed the Beloff scale, the two Hazari obsessional scales and the Ai3, the anal scale written by the author. The anal dimension of the Blacky Pictures was scored as a measure of anal erotism and correlations between all these measures were computed.

Scoring the Blacky Pictures

There are four components to a score on a Blacky dimension: the story in response to the cartoon, the multiple-choice responses, comments on a cartoon other than that being shown, and preference for a cartoon. The last three are virtually objective and only the story is subjectively marked. Any response that mentioned revenge or aggression against the parents was scored as anal-expulsive; two marks if the language was considered strong, one mark if matter of fact and plain. A similar system was adopted for anal-retentive responses, the criterion content being in this case mention of concealment from parents of the need for cleanliness. The objective questions were simple to score since the neutral responses are indicated by the author of the test. Here the only problem is the classification of the responses into retentive or expulsive which is not always possible. For this reason a third score was derived – anality – the sum of all anal responses, regardless of category, in all four components of the dimension. Support for this procedure comes from the factor analytic study of the Blacky Pictures by Blum (1962) where no distinction was found between the putative expulsive and retentive responses but, rather, these loaded on a common factor. If the cartoon was the most or least liked one mark was scored as it was if during the rest of the test any comment was made relating to the anal cartoon.

Reliability of the scoring

The Blacky protocols were scored blind; that is, they were scored in ignorance of the scores on the objective questionnaires. An independent marker was given the marking scheme for the anal story and his score was correlated with the original score. The inter-marker reliability was very high: 0.94. The few discrepancies were mutually resolved. As has been indicated, the Blacky scores were correlated with those from the questionnaires.

Results

Table 4.1 shows the correlations between the variables.

TABLE 4.1. *Correlations between objective measures of obsessionality and three scores derived from the anal dimension of the Blacky Pictures.*

	Blacky Pictures		
	Anality	Anal-expulsive	Anal-retentive
Beloff scale	0·39**	0·23	0·37**
Hazari traits	0·25	0·21	0·22
Hazari symptoms	0·38**	0·30*	0·27
Ai3	0·60**	0·20	0·40**

* Significant at 0·05 level
** Significant at 0·01 level

DISCUSSION

First, it must be noticed that with three of the four objective scales there are significant correlations in the predicted direction with the measures of anal erotism. Since there is no logical reason why responses to an anal stimulus should correlate with measures of obsessional characteristics, these findings broadly support the Freudian theory. However, it will be best to discuss each scale separately.

The fact that the Beloff scale correlates with the anal-retentive rather than the anal-expulsive score and with the general anal erotism score is in full accord with psychoanalytic theory (Jones, 1923), who makes the distinction between giving (typical of fixation at the early expulsive stage) and retaining (typical of fixation at the later stage). The anal character is then the result of fixation at the retentive phase. Strictly, perhaps, there should be a negative correlation with the expulsive score. The Hazari symptom scale correlates significantly with two of the Blacky scores and only just fails to reach significance with the third. Again this is in accord with theory, since obsessional symptoms are regarded as intrusions of repressed material into consciousness, the result of unsuccessful defence against anal erotism. Thus positive correlations with all the Blacky scores would be predicted. It should perhaps be mentioned that there seems to be little experimental evidence for the validity of the expulsive retentive distinction in the anal dimension of the Blacky Pictures, and it may be the case that both types of response to the anal cartoon are symptomatic of fixated anal erotism in general rather than fixation at a particular stage as suggested in the manual – an interpretation heavily supported by the factor analysis of Blum (1962). The interpretation would certainly suit the correlations with the author's anal scale (Ai3), where the highest relationship was with the general scale, and the lowest with the retentive. This anal objective test, like the Beloff scale, was designed from a search of the psychoanalytic descriptions of the anal character, and thus in terms of face validity, at least, is relevant to many more elements in the syndrome than the more general obsessional scale of Hazari. Thus it is not unexpected to find that it correlates more highly with the Blacky scales.

The fact that the Hazari trait scale fails to correlate significantly with any of the Blacky scales may be a reflexion on the Hazari test rather than the theory since its only validity is face validity and a demonstrated (Hazari, 1957; Sandler & Hazari, 1961) homogeneity of items. Although in a previous study of obsessionality it did appear to be valid (Kline, 1967), the homogeneity of the scale might be due to social desirability and acquiescence, which would then account for its failure to correlate with the Blacky Pictures. Of course, it is true that these same strictures on validity apply to the other Hazari scales and the Beloff scale, although Beloff (1957) did show that self-ratings on her scale correlated with assessment of others using it.

Nevertheless, the fact that three of the scales correlated in the expected direction with responses to the Blacky Pictures must be regarded as evidence in favour of the psychoanalytic hypotheses concerning the aetiology of the anal character. Even if this anal cartoon is nothing other than an anal situation, the fact that positive correlations occur between measures of obsessionality and such a situation still supports the Freudian claims, for, as has been pointed out, there is no logical reason to link responses to a picture of a defecating dog with obsessional traits.

CONCLUSION

This study supports the Freudian hypotheses concerning the aetiology of obsessional traits and symptoms. It also indicates that correlational studies of pot-training and subsequent personality are founded on an oversimplified conception of psychoanalytic theory which accounts for the almost universal failure of empirical studies to support the theory. Clearly the relevant variable is the anal erotism, especially since it is possible that pot-training cannot be assessed by objective criteria. There is clearly a need to develop better tests both of anal erotism and obsessionality.

SUMMARY

The relation of obsessional characteristics and pot-training was examined in the light of psychoanalytic theory. Analysis of the theory revealed that pot-training was only one factor in the aetiology, the other being the sexual constitution of the individual. This was suggested as a reason why empirical studies of the subject have almost always failed to support the theory. Four obsessional scales and the Blacky Pictures as a measure of anal erotism were given to a small sample. Correlations between the objective measures of obsessionality and anal erotism were in the expected direction and Freudian theory was regarded as supported.

APPENDIX

Items in Ai3

1. Do you keep careful accounts of the money you spend? (Yes/No)
2. When eating out do you wonder what the kitchens are like? (Yes/No)
3. Do you insist on paying back even small trivial debts? (Yes/No)
4. Do you like to think out your own methods rather than use other people's? (Yes/No)
5. Do you find more pleasure in doing things than in planning them? (Yes/No)
6. Do you think there should be strong laws against speeding? (Yes/No)
7. There's nothing more infuriating than people who don't keep appointments? (Yes/No)
8. Do you often feel you want to stop people and do the job yourself? (Yes/No)
9. Most people don't have high enough standards in what they do? (Yes/No)
10. Do you make up your mind quickly rather than turn things over for a long time? (Yes/No)
11. Do you think envy is at the root of most egalitarian ideals? (Yes/No)

12. Do you like to see something solid and substantial for your money? (Yes/No)
13. Do you easily change your mind once you've made a decision? (Yes/No)
14. Do you disagree with corporal punishment? (Yes/No)
15. Do you regard smoking as a dirty habit? (Yes/No)
16. Do you often feel like correcting people (even though you may refrain from politeness)? (Yes/No)
17. Only a fool with his money does not think of the years ahead? (Yes/No)
18. Can you usually put your hand on anything you want in your desk or room? (Yes/No)
19. Waste not, want not: every child should have this imprinted on his mind? (Yes/No)
20. Are you tolerant of bossy people? (Yes/No)
21. Do you collect anything? (Yes/No)
22. If you're learning something and progress is slow do you plough grimly on? (Yes/No)
23. Correct sexual behaviour is *the* fundamental part of morality? (Yes/No)
24. Do you continue doing something even when you really know you're not employing the best method? (Yes/No)
25. Is it sheepishness to follow the dictates of style and fashion? (Yes/No)
26. Do you regard the keeping of dogs as household pets as unhygienic? (Yes/No)
27. Vindictive savagery is the motivation of most revolutionaries? (Yes/No)
28. Do you have a special place for important documents? (Yes/No)
29. Do you from time to time enjoy a really big clear out of rubbish, etc.? (Yes/No)
30. Do you often go without rather than feel obliged to anyone? (Yes/No)

COMMENT

Kline (1972, p. 93), in his summary of findings relating to psychosexual personality syndromes, is forced to the following conclusion: 'From the considerable number of studies attempting to relate infant rearing procedures to personality development only two studies give even slight support to the Freudian theory.' These are: the Goldman-Eisler study of the oral character (already discussed) and Kline's own (1968) study reprinted above. Although it is not generally our practice in this book to consider a paper worthy of criticism solely on the recommendation of its authors, this would seem to be a case meriting special treatment. After all, Kline has shown some facility to detect serious shortcomings in the work of other researchers in this area, and is for the most part duly modest about the implications of his own studies; all but this one. These considerations, plus the extreme importance that he attaches to the study indicated by the statement above, led us to the decision to reprint and comment upon it.

Kline rightly draws attention to the distinction that must be made between confirming the existence of a syndrome of traits that might be called 'obsessionality', and the theory that its origin can be traced to 'defence mechanisms against anal erotism repressed in early childhood by over-enthusiastic toilet-training'. The first of these hypotheses is in no sense Freudian. Firstly, its existence was recognized long before Freud, and secondly, an obsessive-compulsive trait cluster comprising an important personality dimension among the population at large was never explicitly postulated by Freud. All that is clearly stated in psychoanalytic theory is that *when* a certain triad of traits – obstinacy, parsimony and orderliness – do occur together, the total character can be explained in terms of the concept of 'oral erotism'. True, the syndrome was supposedly observed with some frequency in the clinic, but this does not necessarily mean that these traits are intercorrelated among the general 'non-neurotic' population. Nevertheless, the evidence presented by Kline in a later paper (1969) and by others (e.g. Foulds, 1965) does appear to confirm the existence of such a syndrome. This trait cluster is probably best described as obsessionality, a label that does not assume a particular aetiological theory as Kline's use of the term 'anal character' does. Among the most central components of the syndrome are orderliness, meanness, cleanliness, punctuality, procrastination, perfectionism, irritability, obstinacy and desire for self-control.

Now what of Kline's evidence relating to the more strictly Freudian hypothesis of a link between this obsessional personality syndrome and anal erotism? Kline is at pains to point out that psychoanalytic theory in this area is more complicated than many researchers have supposed: '. . . in addition to the environmental variable (pot-training) there is the *constitutional* variable (the anal stamp) . . . only when severe training is applied to a child of the anal stamp will the anal character develop' (p. 89). He goes on to argue that all the previous attempts to relate pot-training procedures to obsessionality are valueless because they do not take account of genetic variation in anal erotism; this, he says, is 'alone sufficient to account for (their) failure'. But why should this be so? If two conditions must apply for a certain effect to be observed, then either one by itself will correlate with that effect (except in the unlikely event of a perfect inverse correlation between the two conditions). Strangely, Kline does not seem aware that his own 'logic', if correct, would rule out the possibility of positive results being obtained in his own experiment. After all, he also was concerned with only one side of the coin (the variation in anal erotism), and completely ignored the pot-training variable. Fortunately for him, we prefer to question his logic rather than the potential usefulness of his investigation.

In essence, what Kline found was that high scores on his scale of obsessionality and other similar questionnaires correlated significantly with the degree of disturbance shown by students confronted with a cartoon of a small black dog defecating between the kennels of its parents (relative to their response to a variety of other 'Blacky' cartoons). The correlation with obsessionality held positive for responses to the critical Blacky picture whether they were classified as 'anal-expulsive' (revenge or aggression expressed against the parents) or 'anal-retentive' ('mention of concealment from parents of the need for cleanliness'). Kline concludes that 'this study supports the Freudian hypotheses concerning the aetiology of obsessional traits and symptoms'.

It is difficult to see how he arrives at this conclusion. Earlier in his discussion he admits that since psychoanalytic theory specifically hypothesizes that the anal character results from fixation at the *retentive* phase, 'strictly, perhaps, there should be a *negative* correlation with the expulsive score' (p. 92, italics ours). As with many other psychoanalysts Kline is apparently content to accept any correlation as support for the theory; it doesn't matter if it happens to be in the wrong direction!

In another place he claims that his results must support Freud because 'there is no logical reason to link responses to a picture of a defecating dog with obsessional traits'. Once again it is necessary to question the validity of Kline's logic. His questionnaire contains items relating to concern with cleanliness, e.g. 'When eating out do you wonder what the kitchens are like?' and (believe it or not) 'Do you regard the keeping of household dogs as unhygienic?' Is it really unreasonable to expect answers to these questions to relate to responses to a picture of a defecating dog? Concern with hygiene, cleanliness, tidiness, and self-control (attitudes to which are inevitably tapped by this particular Blacky picture) are clearly central to the obsessional personality syndrome as defined by Kline's questionnaire, and because of this content overlap no Freudian explanation is necessary to account for his results.

One other point is likely to occur to any researcher who approaches Kline's results without Freudian blinkers firmly fixed. He assumes throughout that the picture of Blacky defecating is a measure of 'anal erotism' (also called the 'anal stamp'). Indirectly, we suppose it could be referred to as 'anal', but where is the justification for assuming that it is also 'erotic'. In English, this word refers to love (particularly of a sexual kind); exactly what it means to Freud is not made clear in this paper, and Kline does not appear to feel any responsibility for specifying in what way the Blacky pictures should be regarded as an 'objective measure of anal erotism'. To the non-Freudian it remains nothing more than a rough index of attitudes toward shitting dogs.

In summary, then, Kline's study may be criticized on the grounds that (1) in spite of his conclusion, his results are not in accord with the Freudian hypothesis, (2) his actual results are easily explained in terms of content overlap in the questionnaire and projective measures, and (3) his use of the terms 'anal character' in connection with the questionnaire measure and 'anal erotism' in connection with the projective measure involve unjustified theoretical assumptions. The existence of a cluster of traits that might be called obsessionality or the 'obsessive-compulsive syndrome' has long been established and should not be attributed to Freud – he did not even explicitly hypothesize this as an important dimension of behaviour in the non-clinical (e.g. student) population.

REFERENCES

ABRAHAM, K. (1923) Contributions to the theory of the anal character. *Int. J. Psychoanal.*, **4**, 421-53.

ADELSON, J. & REDMOND, J. (1958) Personality differences in the capacity for verbal recall. *J. Abnorm. Soc. Psychol.*, **57**, 244-8.

ARIETI, L. (ed.) (1959) *American Handbook of Psychiatry*. New York: Basic Books.

BARNES, C. A. (1952) A statistical study of the Freudian theory of levels of psychosexual development. *Genet. Psychol. Monogr.*, **45**, 109-74.

BARRON, F. (1955) The disposition towards originality. *J. Abnorm. Soc. Psychol.*, **51**, 478-85.

BELOFF, H. (1957) The structure and origin of the anal character. *Genet. Psychol. Monogr.*, **55**, 141-72.

BLUM, G. S. (1949) A study of the psychoanalytic theory of psychosexual development. *Genet. Psychol. Monogr.*, **39**, 3-99.

—— (1962) A guide for the research use of the Blacky Pictures. *J. Proj. Tech.*, **26**, 3-29.

CARP, F. M. (1962) The psychosexual development of stutterers. *J. Proj. Tech.*, **26**, 3-29.

CATTELL, R. B. (1957) *Personality and Motivation Structure and Measurement*. New York: World Book Co.

CATTELL, R. B. & STICE, G. (1958) *Handbook to the* 16 *PF Test*. Champaign, Ill.: IPAT.

CHAREN, J. (1956*a*) Reliability of the Blacky tests. *J. Consult. Psychol.*, **20**, 16.

—— (1956*b*) A reply to Blum, G. S. *J. Consult. Psychol.*, **20**, 407.

CRONBACH, L. J. (1946) Response sets and test validity. *Educ. Psychol. Measur.*, **6**, 475-94.

CURRAN, D. & PARTRIDGE, M. (1953) *Psychological Medicine*. Edinburgh: Livingstone.

DELAY, J., PICHOT, P. & PERSE, T. (1962) Personnalité obsessionnelle et caractère dit obsessionel: étude clinique et psychométrique. *Rev. Psychol. Appl.*, **12**, No. 4, 223-62.

EDWARDS, A. L. (1957) *The Social Desirability Variable in Personality Research*. New York: Dryden.

EYSENCK, H. J. & EYSENCK, S. B. G. (1964) *The Eysenck Personality Inventory*. London: Univ. Press.

FENICHEL, O. (1945) *The Psychoanalytic Theory of Neurosis*. New York: Norton.

FINNEY, J. C. (1961) The MMPI as a measure of character structure as revealed by factor analysis. *J. Consult. Psychol.*, **25**, 327-36.

FOULDS, G. A. (1961) Personality traits and neurotic symptoms and signs. *Brit. J. Med. Psychol.*, **34**, 263-70.

—— (1965) *Personality and Personal Illness*. London: Tavistock.

FOULDS, G. A. & CAINE, T. M. (1958) Psychoneurotic symptom

clusters, trait clusters and psychological tests. *J. Ment. Sci.*, **104**, 722-31.

—— (1959) Symptom clusters and personality types among psychoneurotic men compared with women. *J. Ment. Sci.*, **105**, 469-75.

FREUD, S. (1905) Three essays on sexuality. In *Collected Papers*. London: Hogarth Press (1949).

—— (1908) Character and anal erotism. In *Collected Papers*, vol. II, pp. 45-50. London: Hogarth Press (1949).

GRANICK, S. & SCHEFFLIN, N. A. (1958) Approaches to the reliability of projective tests with special reference to the Blacky Pictures test. *J. Consult. Psychol.*, **22**, 137-41.

GRYGIER, T. G. (1961) *The Dynamic Personality Inventory*. London: NFER.

HAMILTON, G. V. (1929) *A Research in Marriage*. New York: A. & C. Beni.

HAZARI, A. (1957) An investigation of obsessive compulsive character traits and symptoms in adult neurotics. Unpublished Ph.D. thesis, University of London.

HUSCHAKA, M. (1942) The child's response to coercive bowel training. *Psychosom. Med.*, **4**, 301-28.

JONES, E. (1923) Anal-erotic character traits. In *Papers on Psychoanalysis*. London: Baillière, Tindall & Cox.

KLINE, P. (1967) Obsessional traits and emotional instability in a normal population. *Brit. J. Med. Psychol.*, **40**, 153-7.

—— (1968) The validity of the Dynamic Personality Inventory. *Brit. J. Med. Psychol.*, **41**, 307-13.

—— (1969) The anal character: A cross-cultural study in Ghana. *Brit. J. Soc. Clin. Psychol.*, **8**, 201-10.

—— (1972) *Fact and Fantasy in Freudian Theory*. London: Methuen.

KROUT, M. H. & TABIN, J. K. (1954) Measuring personality in developmental terms. *Genet. Psychol. Monogr.*, **50**, 289-335.

LEWIS, A. J. & MAPOTHER, E. (1941) In *Price's Textbook of the Practice of Medicine*. London: Oxford Univ. Press.

LITTMAN, R. A., NIDORF, L. J. & SUNDBERG, N. D. (1961) Characteristics of a psychosexual scale. *J. Genet. Psychol.*, **98**, 19–27.

MCNEIL, E. B. & BLUM, G. S. (1952) Handwriting and psychosexual dimensions of personality. *J. Proj. Tech.*, **16**, 476-84.

MENNINGER, W. C. (1943) Characterologic and symptomatic ex-

pressions related to the anal phase of psychosexual development. *Psychoanal. Quart.*, **12**, 161-93.
NEWSON, J. & NEWSON, E. (1963) *Infant Care in an Urban Community*. London: Allen & Unwin.
ORLANS, H. (1949) Infant care and personality. *Psychol. Bull.*, **46**, 1-48.
PICHOT, P. & PERSE, J. (1968) *Analyse factorelle et structure de la personnalité*. Lund: Univ. Press.
SANDLER, J. & HAZARI, A. (1961) The obsessional: on the psychological classification of obsessional character traits and symptoms. *Brit. J. Med. Psychol.*, **33**, 113-21.
SCHNEIDER, K. (1923) *Psychopathic Personalities*. London: Cassell. (Transl. 1948).
SEARS, R. R. (1943) Survey of objective studies of psychoanalytic concepts. *Bull.*, 51. New York: Social Science Research Council.
STAGNER, R. & MOFFIT, J. W. (1956) A statistical study of Freud's theory of personality types. *J. Clin. Psychol.*, **12**, 72-4.
TIMMONS, E. O. & NOBLIN, C. D. (1963) The differential performance of orals and anals in a verbal conditioning paradigm. *J. Consult. Psychol.*, **27**, 283-6.

5

Alvin Scodel (1957)[1]

Heterosexual somatic preference and fantasy dependency

Journal of Consulting Psychology, 21, No. 5, 371-4

With the exception of occasional statements in the psychoanalytic journals, almost no attention has been given to the female body-types considered desirable by adult males, and the psychological correlates of such preferences. It is, indeed, rather curious in light of the numerous attempts to view all behaviour and attitudes from Freudian assumptions that a topic which so preempts the conversation and fantasies of adult males should have been so completely ignored for systematic psychological investigation.

When somatic preferences are discussed in the psychological literature, either in case studies or as part of an exposition of a particular theoretical position, inconsistent conclusions are often reached. Tridon (1922) asserts that men nursed at the breast in infancy are attracted in adulthood to women with well-developed breasts, and that men who have been fed by bottle prefer thin, boyish-looking girls. Breast feeding, presumably a more gratifying experience than bottle feeding, leads to a later preference for women with well-developed breasts who can continue to supply the oral gratifications of infancy. On the other hand, Gorer (1948) states that the fetish that exists for breasts in American culture is a derivative of scheduled feeding in infancy. In this view, then, a preference for large-breasted females is a result of oral frustration rather than oral satisfaction.

Despite such differences, there is little disagreement about the importance of the breast to the concept of orality. In Freud's opinion (1920), the child at the breast formed the prototype of all future love relationships. Illustrative clinical illustrations can be found in cases described by Gero (1936), and Levey (1948). Gero's patient had been

[1]Ohio State University.

separated from his mistress, and it is stated that 'his longing for this woman was not a man's longing for a lost love, but a child's longing for his mother . . . Whenever he thought of his beloved, the aim of his yearning, the lost paradise in his imagination was always the breast' (1936, p. 448). Levey discussed an ulcer patient who 'fantasies the earth, the air, and the universe as composed of breasts, himself floating in a sea of breasts, and the Capitol at Washington as having a breast pinned on it' (1948, p. 163). It seems to be clearly implied that the orally fixated person is preoccupied with the ample, well-developed breast rather than the small breast. By way of a casually stated *ipse dixit* common clinical parlance also speaks of large breast preference as a product of oral fixation.

The present investigation is concerned with the relationship of breast size preference to an allegedly important aspect of orality; namely, dependency. The phrases 'oral passivity' and 'oral dependence' are so frequent in both the psychological and psychoanalytic literature that no documentation is necessary. The instrument used to measure dependency in the present study is the TAT. To be more precise, fantasy rather than overt dependency is being measured, although there is evidence to indicate that fantasy dependency as measured by the TAT correlates significantly with overt dependency when overt dependency is measured by conformity to erroneous group judgments (Kagan & Mussen, 1956).

PROCEDURE

Five male graduate students rated 101 full-length pictures of nude females (obtained from photography and art magazines) along a dimension of breast size. The following rating scale was used:

1. Considerably above average breast size.
2. Slightly above average breast size.
3. Average breast size.
4. Slightly below average breast size.
5. Considerably below average breast size.

By summing the judges' ratings, a range of judgments for all pictures was obtained which extended from 5 to 25. Those pictures with a total rating of 11 or less were defined as large-breasted (LB), those with a total rating of 19 or more as small-breasted (SB). Sixty-five of the pictures met these criteria. Of these 65, 32 were classified as LB, and 33 as SB. Sixty-eight per cent agreement was achieved by the judges in their ratings of the 65 pictures. Ninety per cent agreement was obtained by combining Categories 1 and 2 and Categories 4 and 5.

In order to obtain a higher probability that an experimental subject would select between two females on the basis of breast size, it was necessary to equate the pictures as much as possible in general attractiveness. Otherwise, a subject who usually preferred LB females might on occasion select an SB female because of her greater general appeal. Similarly, the pairing of an attractive LB female with an unattractive SB female could lead a subject to select the former although he generally preferred SB females. To minimize the effect of facial attractiveness, masking tape was placed over the face on each of the pictures. Five additional judges then rated each picture on a six-point scale ranging from 1 (exceptionally attractive) to 6 (exceptionally unattractive). The range of judgments was 8 to 23. The purpose of obtaining these ratings at this time was to determine whether a sufficiently large number of pictures classified as LB and SB would fall within a similar range of attractiveness in order to permit pairing. The distribution of ratings on attractiveness is presented in Table 5.1.

TABLE 5.1. *Distribution of Judges' Ratings on Attractiveness.*

Sum of Five Judges' Ratings	Number LB	Number SB
8 – 12	13	0
13 – 20	17	19
21 – 23	2	14
	—	—
	32	33

It is apparent that LB females were rated as more attractive. The next step consisted of having slides made out of the pictures. Forty-nine of the pictures were converted into black and white 2 × 2 slides with the facial area still masked out. Since conversion of the pictures into slides could conceivably have some effect upon general attractiveness, inasmuch as colour, shading, and lighting and darkness were changed to a degree, a third group of judges, four in number, rated the projected slides on the same six-point scale of attractiveness used previously. A range of ratings was obtained from 8 to 19. For the final sample, 20 slides were selected, 10 LB and 10 SB, all falling within the range of 12 to 15 on attractiveness. The average of the 10 LB slides was 13.2, for the SB, 13.3. An effort was made to match the slides as much as possible with respect to the position of the woman, i.e., to have both members of a pair standing or kneeling, both in profile or front view, etc.

In order to help disguise the purpose of this part of the study, 10 additional pairs, or a total of 20 pairs, were presented to the subjects. The 10 pairs discussed in the previous paragraphs were the only ones used to select subjects on the variable of somatic preference. Of the 10 additional pairs, five were of two LB females, and the other five of two SB females. A table of random numbers was used to determine the order of presentation of the 20 pairs. A crucial pair was presented on the 1st, 6th, 8th, 9th, 13th, 14th, 15th, 17th, 18th and 19th trials. For each crucial pair, the order of presentation of the LB and SB slides was alternated throughout the series.

The subjects were 169 male students enrolled in an introductory psychology course at Ohio State University. They were seen in small groups ranging in number from 5 to 15.

At the beginning of the experimental session, seven TAT cards intended to elicit dependency themes were administered. The cards chosen for this purpose were 4, 6BM, 7BM, 12, 13B, 14, and 18BM. The test was presented as one of creative imagination which the examiner was attempting to standardize (the TAT had not been discussed in the course yet), and subjects were given five minutes to write each story. Aside from these departures, the usual TAT instructions were given. At the conclusion of the TAT administration, and following the distribution of answer sheets, these instructions were read:

> As you may know from your psychology course, Professor Sheldon of Harvard has done considerable research on the different kinds of body-types. We are interested in following up some of his research by finding out what female body-types are generally preferred by the typical American male. One reason for this research is that the kinds of body-types preferred by American men may have some effect on their choice of marital partners, and this in turn can affect the body-types of future generations.
>
> You will be presented with 20 pairs of slides. Each slide contains the picture of an attractive nude female. The numbers on your

sheet stand for the pair number. Following each pair number is an A and a B. The A represents the first slide of the pair that is presented to you and the B represents the second slide of the pair. After looking at both slides of the pair, you are to put a circle around the A if you like the first slide better or put a circle around the B if you like the second slide better. For each pair, you encircle the letter representing the slide you prefer.

You are requested not to talk or make any spontaneous exclamations during the presentation of the slides. The slides must be shown in silence.

The entire sequence of slides required about seven or eight minutes for presentation. Each slide was projected for five seconds, three seconds were allowed between the slides of a pair, and five seconds were allowed between adjacent pairs. Co-operation of the subjects was good and, with rare exceptions, little flippancy was noted. Randomly obtained comments at the end of the experimental session revealed a general lack of awareness concerning the crucial variable in this part of the study.

RESULTS

The distribution of somatic preferences approximated a normal distribution. As previously stated, the judges showed a distinct preference for large-breasted females, but the equation of the two groups for general attractiveness insured the variability which was obtained in the preferences of subjects. Subjects who selected from 0 to 3 of the large-breasted females were defined as the SB group ($N=28$). The LB group was comprised of those who selected from 8 to 10 of the large-breasted females ($N=35$). Inasmuch as the mean number of LB preferences was 5.56, a middle or no-preference group was obtained by selecting those subjects with their five or six large-breasted preferences ($N=57$).

The TAT stories of all three groups were independently scored by the writer and a graduate student in clinical psychology. Neither had any awareness of the subjects' somatic preference ratings at the time of the TAT scoring. Following the procedure of Kagan & Mussen (1956), a story was scored as *D* (for dependency) if the hero sought help from another person in solving a personal problem or was disturbed over the loss of a source of love and affection. In most respects, *D* would be similar to Murray's n succorance. Only one *D* theme was scored for each story so that for any given story *D* was simply scored present or absent. Of a total of 840 stories there was agreement on 782. This 93 per cent agreement indicates considerable reliability in scoring. A third judge arbitrated the 58 stories on which there was disagreement.

The number of *D* themes in the three groups of 120 protocols ranged from zero to six with a median of one. In both the middle and LB groups the distribution of *D* themes was markedly skewed in the positive direction. Chi square was therefore used to test for the significance of difference between groups. The results are given in Table 5.2. For each of the three comparisons the median value was one.

TABLE 5.2. *Chi-square differences between SB, Middle and LB groups in TAT* D *themes.*

	TAT *D* Themes			
Groups	Above Median	At or Below Median	Chi Square	*p*
SB	18	10	6·76	·01
LB	11	24		
SB	18	10	5·70	·02
Middle	21	36		
LB	11	24	·28	·60
Middle	21	36		

The SB group gave significantly more *D* themes than either the LB or middle group. There was no significant difference between the middle and the LB groups.

DISCUSSION

The present result is not what might have been expected on the basis of Freudian theory. In general, the theory has tended to view behaviours as the products of either excessive frustrations or excessive satisfactions (reinforcements) in an earlier period. With respect to the variable under consideration here, most analytically oriented writers who have discussed the matter at all have held that large breast preference is a result of earlier oral frustration. In Levey's discussion of the ulcer patient, for example, it is suggested that the frustrated dependency needs of the patient sought satisfaction in a constant preoccupation with large breasts. Ostensibly, such females should be perceived as potentially more nurturant for basically dependent males if the important determinant underlying such a somatic preference is frustrated dependency.

If the expression of dependency needs in TAT stories can be taken to signify conflicts in this area predicated on the frustration of such needs, and if the absence of these same needs in TAT stories implies experiential reinforcement of them, the present results are more in accord with the view that drive strength is increased by reinforcement. Large breast preference would be regarded as the consequence of continued satisfaction of dependency needs rather than their frustration. Such an interpretation is consistent with the findings of Bernstein (1955). In studying the effects of infantile experiences on later activities, he raised the question of whether it was the child with the greatest amount of sucking practice as an infant who continued to use the sucking act as a preferred mode of behaviour or, rather, the child with the least amount of sucking practice who continued to seek satisfaction through sucking. He found that the amount of sucking reinforcement experienced by the group whose mothers reported resistance to weaning exceeded the sucking reinforcement for the group without weaning difficulty. His results, then, support a reinforcement rather than a frustration theory of drive strength. Sears and Wise (1950) are of the same view in asserting that the strength of the oral drive varies with the number of opportunities for its reinforcement so that the longer the child feeds by means of sucking, the stronger his oral drive will be. The present result is consistent with such formulations if the assumptions concerning the nature of TAT dependency can be maintained.

SUMMARY

The purpose of this study was to ascertain possible relationships between somatic preference (preference for either large- or small-breasted females) and dependency as measured by the TAT. After writing stories to seven of the TAT cards, 169 male subjects were presented with 20 pairs of slides; 10 pairs consisted of a small-breasted and a large-breasted female, previously equated on attractiveness. On the basis of the subjects' selections, large breast preference, small breast preference, and no preference groups were elicited.

The small breast preference group gave significantly more TAT dependency themes than either of the other two groups. Speculations for this result, which is contrary to a widely-held Freudian hypothesis, are offered on the basis of a reinforcement theory of learning.

COMMENT

This paper requires little comment. A clear hypothesis is derived from the psychoanalytic theory of orality: men showing dependency as measured by the TAT should prefer large-breasted women. The experiment is meticulously conducted and the results are significant in the wrong direction. Scodel, therefore, correctly concludes that they are 'contrary to a widely-held Freudian hypothesis'.

Kline (1972, p. 91), however, tries again to argue that a correlation in the wrong direction 'could be regarded as support for the Freudian aetiology of the oral character'. This is how his rescue attempt goes: 'Dependency, of course, is a trait claimed to be part of the oral character, who, according to psychoanalytic theory, should be concerned with breasts. The fact that small rather than large breasts were preferred would have to be attributed to reaction-formation. If we ignore the question of the validity of the TAT we must admit that only psychoanalytic theory could have explained this observed relationship'.

These comments clearly illustrate the unscientific nature of some Freudian theorizing. True, Scodel's results can be 'explained' in terms of the theory if the concept of 'reaction-formation' is invoked, but would this defence mechanism have been called upon if the results had not turned out that way? There was no mention of reaction-formation at the time the hypothesis was formulated. As we pointed out earlier, the fact that Freudian theory 'explains' everything is its greatest weakness, because at the same time it *predicts* nothing. Scodel behaves like a real scientist by making a clear prediction from the outset and accepting his results as disconfirmatory; Kline does not by suggesting that the prediction might be modified following an examination of the results.

In any case, it is not true that 'only psychoanalytic theory' is capable of explaining the result. Contrary to Kline, the author of the paper himself maintains that 'the present results are more in accord with the view that drive strength is increased by reinforcement'. In fact, he offers an alternative explanation in terms of a reinforcement theory of learning that is certainly more parsimonious than the contrived Freudian explanation. In this theory the TAT is presumed to measure not dependency need as such, but the extent to which this need has been frustrated. 'Large breast preference would be regarded as a consequence of continued satisfaction of dependency needs rather than their frustration'.

REFERENCES

BERNSTEIN, A. (1955) Some relations between techniques of feeding and training during infancy and certain behaviour in childhood. *Genet. Psychol. Monogr.*, **51**, 3-44.

FREUD, S. (1920) *Three Contributions to the Theory of Sex.* New York and Washington: Nervous and Mental Disease Publishing Co.

GERO, G. (1936) The construction of depression. *Internat. J. Psychoanal.*, **17**, 423-61.

GORER, G. (1948) *The American People.* New York: Norton.

KAGAN, J. & MUSSEN, P. H. (1956) Dependency themes on the TAT and group conformity. *J. Consult. Psychol.*, **20**, 29-32.

KLINE, P. (1972) *Fact and Fantasy in Freudian Theory.* London: Methuen.

LEVEY, H. B. (1948) Oral trends and oral conflicts in a case of duodenal ulcer. In F. ALEXANDER & T. M. FRENCH (eds.), *Studies in Psychosomatic Medicine.* New York: Roland Press.

SEARS, R. R. & WISE, G. W. (1950) Relation of cup feeding in infancy to thumb sucking and the oral drive. *Amer. J. Orthopsychiat.*, **20**, 123-36.

TRIDON, A. (1922) *Psychoanalysis and Love.* New York: Brentano's. Reprinted in A. TRIDON, *Psychoanalysis and Love.* New York: Permabooks Edition, 1949.

PART TWO

Oedipus and Castration Complexes

6

Calvin Hall (1963)[1]

Strangers in dreams: an empirical confirmation of the Oedipus complex[2]

Journal of Personality, 31, 336-45

The empirical foundations upon which Freud based his theory of personality consisted chiefly of the qualitative analysis of verbal behaviour of patients undergoing psychoanalysis. Although confirmation of hypotheses generated by Freudian theory still comes largely from observations of patient behaviour, other empirical approaches are employed. Among these are observations of infant and child behaviour, cross-cultural studies, responses to projective and objective tests, and controlled laboratory experiments.

One of the principal activities of the Institute of Dream Research is the testing of hypotheses derived from Freudian theory using dreams collected from a large number of persons differing in sex, age, ethnic groups, and other respects. The use of dreams for this purpose is particularly appropriate since from the very beginning of psychoanalysis, dreams and free associations to them have been an important source of data. Freud was convinced that dreaming makes manifest unconscious and otherwise inaccessible roots of personality.

Critics of psychoanalytic methodology have objected to the qualitative, subjective, and anecdotal character of the evidence secured from dreams and free associations of patients. Psychoanalysts have been criticized for generalizing findings obtained from a patient population to people in general.

With the Institute's large collection of dreams it is possible to obviate these criticisms. Objective, quantitative, and repeatable tests of Freudian theory can be made without violating the basic assumptions of the theory.

[1]Institute of Dream Research.

[2]This investigation was supported by a USPHS research grant, No. M-6475 (A) from the National Institute of Mental Health, USPHS.

The investigation to be reported here is a test of the validity of the Oedipus complex. Testable hypotheses were formulated in terms of the contents of reported dreams and associations to these contents.

In the classical exposition of the development of the Oedipus complex, very young children of either sex are described as having a positive cathexis for the mother and a negative one for the father. The father is perceived by the child as an intruder, an unwelcome stranger, and a threat. He is resented and feared. In the course of development, the girl's feelings toward her mother and father diverge from those of the boy's. Recognizing that she lacks a penis and blaming her mother for this deficiency, she turns from the mother to the father. In spite of this turning, the earlier fantasies of the 'good' mother and the 'bad' father are not obliterated. In comparison with the boy whose nuclear Oedipus complex remains fairly constant, the girl is more ambivalent toward both parents. She neither fears nor resents the father as much as the boy does, nor does she love and covet the mother as much as he does.

The primary assumption upon which this investigation rests is that the earliest conception of the father as a resented and feared stranger is represented in dreams by male characters who are not known to the dreamer. The male stranger of the dream, it is asserted, symbolizes the father.

An equally important assumption is that the sleeping person dreams about people who are connected, directly or indirectly, with conflicts, frustrations, insecurities, anxieties, and other emotions which have their inception in early childhood.

The following testable hypotheses were formulated:

1. More strangers in dreams are males than females.

2. There is a higher proportion of male strangers in male dreams than in female dreams.

3. There is a higher proportion of aggressive encounters by the dreamer with male strangers than with any of the following classes of dream characters: (*a*) female strangers, (*b*) familiar males, and (*c*) familiar females.

4. The proportion of aggressive encounters with male strangers is greater for male dreamers than for female dreamers.

5. When Ss are asked to free associate to male strangers who appear in their dreams, they will give more father and male authority figure associations than any other class of association.

METHOD

The data for this investigation were obtained from the content analysis of six groups of male dreams and female dreams. A description of the six groups appears in Table 6.1. Groups 1 through 5 consist of single dreams and Group 6 consists of dream series. The number of dreams in the series ranges from 15 to 21.

TABLE 6.1. *A description of the groups used in this study.*

	Males		Females	
Group	No. Dreamers	No. Dreams	No. Dreamers	No. Dreams
1. (Ages 2 – 12)	105	105	119	119
2. (Ages 13 – 18)	138	138	138	138
3. (Ages 18 – 27)	200	200	200	200
4. (Ages 20 – 24)	200	200	200	200
5. (Ages 30 – 80)	281	281	281	281
6. (Ages 18 – 26)	27	492	28	525

With the exception of some of the dreams reported by young children which were taken down by adults, the dreams were reported by the dreamers themselves on standard report forms. These forms include questions about the dream and about the dreamer.

The dreams were analyzed for characters and aggressions using standard manuals prepared by the Institute of Dream Research (1962a, 1962b).

Although the groups vary in age from two to eighty, none of the hypotheses tested in this investigation is concerned with the age variable.

RESULTS

Hypothesis 1 states that more strangers in dreams are male than female. This hypothesis was tested in two ways:

(1) An analysis of the characters appearing in the dreams (not counting the dreamer) was made. Four categories of characters were identified: known males, known females, male strangers, and female strangers. The hypothesis states that the proportion of male strangers will exceed the proportion of female strangers. The results are presented in Table 6.2. The standard formula for testing the signifi-

cance of difference between proportions was used for Groups 1-5. The statistical treatment of Group 6 consisted of determining the proportions for each individual series, computing the mean and standard deviation for each distribution of proportions, and applying the standard formula for testing the significance of difference between means. If there were reason to believe that the two variables being compared were correlated, the formula for correlated means was employed. In Table 6.2 the differences between the proportions are all in the predicted direction except for the male dreamers of Group 2 who show a reversal and the female dreamers of Group 3 where the proportions are equal. Among the other ten comparisons, eight are significant at the .01 or .001 level. The hypothesis appears to be confirmed.

TABLE 6.2 *Comparison of proportions of male strangers and female strangers for the six groups of dreams.*

	Male Dreamers			Female Dreamers		
	Male Strangers	Female Strangers		Male Strangers	Female Strangers	
Groups	Male Characters	Female Characters	p	Male Characters	Female Characters	p
1	·47	·16	·01	·35	·20	n.s.
2	·24	·35		·32	·14	·01
3	·42	·32	n.s.	·29	·29	
4	·54	·34	·01	·37	·24	·01
5	·51	·25	·001	·36	·27	·01
6	·55	·39	·01	·40	·30	·01

(2) The second method of testing the hypothesis consisted of computing the proportion, male strangers/male + female strangers, and testing the significance of the difference of each proportion from the chance proportion of .50. The results are presented in Table 6.3. All of the proportions except the one for male dreamers in Group 2, exceed .50. Nine of the twelve proportions are significant at the .01 or .001 level, and the hypothesis appears to be confirmed.

Hypothesis 2 asserts that there is a higher proportion of male strangers in male dreams than in female dreams. This hypothesis could not be tested by the first method used in testing Hypothesis 1

TABLE 6.3. *Proportion of male strangers in each of the sex groups.*

	Male Dreams		Female Dreams	
	Male Strangers		Female Strangers	
Groups	Male+ Female Strangers	p	Male+ Female Strangers	p
1	·81	·001	·64	n.s
2	·43		·69	·01.
3	·63	·01	·52	n.s.
4	·71	·001	·67	·001
5	·80	·001	·59	·001
6	·69	·001	·59	·001

because there are more strangers of both sexes in male dreams than in female dreams. Consequently, we compared the proportion, male strangers/male + female strangers, between male and female dreamers. The results are presented in Table 6.4.

With the exception of Group 2, all of the differences are in the predicted direction, but only two of the five differences meet a satisfactory level of significance. By combining the two similar age groups, 3 and 4, the difference is significant at the .05 level. Taking into consideration the relatively small numbers of male strangers in the first five groups, and the fact that in Group 6 which has the

TABLE 6.4. *Comparison of the proportion of male strangers between male and female dreamers.*

	Male Dreamers	Female Dreamers	
	Male Strangers	Female Strangers	
Groups	Male+ Female Strangers	Male+ Female Strangers	p
1	·81	·64	n.s.
2	·43	·69	
3	·63	·52	n.s.
4	·71	·67	n.s.
5	·80	·59	·001
6	·69	·59	·05
Combining 3 and 4	·69	·61	·05

largest number of dreams there is a significant difference, it appears to us that the hypothesis is confirmed.

Hypothesis 3 states that there is a higher proportion of aggressive encounters by the dreamer with male strangers than with any of the following classes of dream characters: (*a*) female strangers, (*b*) familiar males, and (*c*) familiar females. The hypothesis states that the proportions in the first column of Table 6.5 will exceed those in each of the other three columns. This is the case in all of the 36 comparisons except for three. Fifteen of the comparisons are significant at the .05, .01, or .001 levels. In view of the small number of aggressions in some of the groups, these results appear to us to confirm the hypothesis.

TABLE 6.5. *Analysis of aggressions with dream character.*

	Aggressions with Male Strangers	Aggressions with Female Strangers		Aggressions with Familiar Males		Aggressions with Familiar Females	
Groups	No. Male Strangers	No. Female Strangers		No. Familiar Males		No. Familiar Females	
Male Dreamers							
1	·27	·67		·20	n.s.	·16	n.s.
2	·33	·10	·05	·15	n.s.	·18	n.s.
3	·29	·13	·05	·23	n.s.	·23	n.s.
4	·33	·18	·05	·25	n.s.	·15	·01
5	·21	·03	·01	·08	·01	·05	·01
6	·29	·05	·001	·15	·05	·12	·01
Female Dreamers							
1	·40	·27	n.s.	·24	n.s.	·16	·05
2	·31	·23	n.s.	·10	·01	·16	·05
3	·21	·19	n.s.	·15	n.s.	·10	·05
4	·28	·16	n.s.	·21	n.s.	·10	·001
5	·04	·01	n.s.	·03	n.s.	·03	n.s.
6	·15	·10	n.s.	·17		·15	

It will be observed that there are more significant differences for male dreamers than for female dreamers. This is to be expected on the basis of the next hypothesis.

Hypothesis 4: the proportion of aggressive encounters with male strangers is greater for male dreamers than for female dreamers. The proportion, aggression with male strangers/aggression with male strangers + aggression with female strangers, was computed for male and female dreamers in each of the six groups. The results appear in Table 6.6. For Groups 1 and 2, the difference is in the reverse direction from that predicted. For the other four groups, the differences are in the predicted direction but only two of them are significant. However, Group 6, which contains the greatest number of dreams and consequently the greatest number of aggressions, yields a highly significant difference between male and female dreamers. We conclude, therefore, that the hypothesis is confirmed.

TABLE 6.6. *Comparison of the proportion of aggressive encounters with male strangers by male and female dreamers.*

Group	Aggression with Male Strangers / Aggression with Male Strangers + Female Strangers		p
	Male Dreamers	Female Dreamers	
1	·64	·73	
2	·71	·75	
3	·79	·55	·05
4	·82	·78	n.s.
5	·96	·82	n.s.
6	·81	·36	·001

Hypothesis 5 asserts that when subjects are asked to free associate to male strangers who appear in their dreams, they will give more father and male authority figure associations than any other class of association. Free associations were obtained for 10 dreams from each of 12 male college students and 12 female college students. These free associations were collected by Dr Walter Reis (1959) under conditions simulating a psychoanalytic session. Associations were given to all parts of each dream, not just to unknown males.

Thirty-one male strangers were identified in the 120 male dreams. These were all individual strangers, and not groups. One dreamer had no male stranger in his ten dreams. Thirty-three individual male strangers were identified in the 120 female dreams. Three dreamers had no male stranger in their dreams. All of the associations were listed. In some cases, more than one association was given. The associations were classified into the categories shown in Table 6.7.

TABLE 6.7. *Associations by categories.*

Male Dreamers	No.	Female Dreamers	No.
Father	9	Father	12
Stepfather	1	Grandfather	3
Another person's father	3	Uncle	1
Male authority figure or male with power or strength	7	Male authority figure or male with power or strength	2
Dreamer or some aspect of dreamer	13	Priest	1
Miscellaneous	4	Brother	2
		Male cousin	1
		Boy friend	7
		Mother	3
		Male sexuality	2
		Dreamer	1
		Miscellaneous	3
Total	37	Total	38

For male dreamers, the hypothesis states that the sum of categories 1-4 will be greater than either category 5 or 6. The sum of the frequencies for the four categories is 20, which is greater than the frequency for 5 or 6. The difference between the summed frequencies for 1-4 and the larger of the two categories, which is 13, fails to reach a p of .05, however. For female dreamers, the hypothesis states that the sum of categories 1-5 will be greater than the largest of the remaining categories. The sum of 1-5 is 19, and the largest frequency for the remaining categories is 7 for boy friend. The difference between these two frequencies is significant at less than the .01 level.

In view of the small number of cases, we are not willing to conclude that the hypothesis is confirmed. We believe, however, that the addition of more cases will establish its validity.

DISCUSSION

When a theory tells us what we will find if we look in a certain place – and we look there and we do find what has been predicted – then the theory has done its work well. In the present instance, Oedipal theory told us correctly what we would find if we analyzed a population of dreams for certain variables. Had we not found what the theory said, or had the finding been ambiguous and equivocal, then we would have discussed why the theory or the empirical operations failed us, and what steps should be taken to revise the theory or improve the methodology. But what is there to discuss when the findings fulfill the investigator's expectations?

The question is often asked, could not the results obtained have been predicted by another theory? Perhaps. The question is, however, an irrelevant one. An investigator usually has a commitment to, or at least a preference for, a particular theoretical system. Ours is to classical Freudian theory. As long as this theory maintains (*a*) its heuristic value, (*b*) its capacity for making sense out of a wide variety of phenomena, and (*c*) its ability to generate correct predictions, there is no necessity to consider empirical findings from the point of view of other theories.

A discussion of results often involves comparing them with results obtained in comparable investigations. Although empirical tests of hypotheses derived from Oedipal theory have been made (see, e.g. Friedman, 1952), none of them is comparable with this investigation of dreams. Nor is this the place to present a systematic, evaluative review of studies which purport to bear upon Oedipal theory.

What remains to be discussed then are the implications of some findings which appeared, so to speak, 'out of the blue'. Looking at Table 6.7, we see that male dreamers give 13 associations which have a self-reference, i.e. 'I am the stranger' or 'Some aspect of me – my conscience, sadism, or sexuality – is a stranger to me'. One is reminded of A. E. Housman's oft-quoted lines, 'I, a stranger and afraid/In a world I never made'.

In only one instance does a female dreamer give a self-reference association. The sex difference very likely has no great significance because it is probably easier for male dreamers than for female dreamers to identify with male strangers.

Why do young men frenquently conceive of themselves as the stranger in their dreams? Our guess is that when the young boy discovers his parents share certain activities from which he is excluded, the feeling appears that he and not the father is the stranger in the house. Chief among these activities from which he is excluded is the sexual one. But we still think, following Freudian theory, that the father-as-stranger fantasy precedes developmentally the self-as-stranger fantasy, and because of its prior entry it remains potent throughout life for both males and females.

In line with this discussion it is appropriate to look, however briefly, at what is considered by many to be the finest example of the novel form in recent literature. We refer, of course, to Camus' *The Stranger*. Meursault, the hero, is Housman's stranger, although unafraid, living in a world he never made, i.e., an indifferent universe. Camus does not tell us how he got that way; he only shows what happens to him. He is guillotined for killing a man. Had Meursault been brought to the couch rather than to the guillotine, it is our prediction that the impact of primal scene experiences would have been uncovered. The impact consists, we believe, on the one hand, in reinforcing the young boy's hatred of the father-stranger and, on the other hand, in originating the bleak view, 'I am the stranger'. For not only has the father excluded him – that is to be expected – but his mother has, too. The fantasy of being the excluded one, the outsider, would explain Meursault's indifference to his mother as well as the killing of a relative stranger. But this is literary exigesis and not scientific analysis.

Taking another look at Table 6.7 we see that the number of categories under female dreamers is larger than those under male dreamers. We suspect that women make more displacements from the father to other classes of males, e.g., brother, cousin, boy friend than men do. Observe also that in spite of the fact that the stranger is a male, in three instances, women dreamers give the association 'mother'. The mother, according to Oedipal theory, is more likely to be seen as a stranger by her daughter than by her son.

SUMMARY

Five hypotheses, all of them derived from Oedipal theory and all having to do with male strangers in the dreams of males and females, were tested. Four of them were confirmed, and the fifth was marginally confirmed. It is concluded that the male stranger in dreams often represents the young child's fantasy of the father as a hostile stranger.

COMMENT

Kline (1972) describes this study as 'a model of how from general psychoanalytic theory (Oedipus and castration complex) testable hypotheses concerning dream content may be drawn'. His summary of the study was as follows:

> There were four hypotheses: (1) that in all dreams there would be more male than female strangers, (2) that there would be more male strangers in male than in female dreams, (3) that there would be more aggressive encounters in dreams with male strangers, and (4) that such encounters would be more common in male than in female dreams. The basic assumption of these hypotheses is, of course, that a male stranger represents the father. Even for a girl this is true since the castration complex for girls does not entirely wipe out the fantasy of the good mother. All these hypotheses were supported, a finding which strongly confirms Freudian Oedipal theory, in that other hypotheses to account for the results, even of the *ad hoc* variety, are not easy to develop (pp. 113-14).

We think any ingenious psychologist would be able to develop such *ad hoc* hypotheses with considerable ease, but no such feat is in fact necessary; let us take an existing theory of dream interpretation developed by Eysenck (1957) and see how it can cope. There can be no question of 'ad hoc' about this because the theory preceded the data. Quite briefly, this theory asserts that the mind in sleep does not cease to be active, and that this activity, shown in dreaming, continues to be concerned with problems of everyday life; the dream being a more primitive form of mental activity than waking thought, this dream activity expresses itself in pictorial and symbolic form. The function of symbolism is not to avoid the censor; it serves an adjectival function, i.e. it makes more precise the meaning of certain concepts. You may dream of your mother as a cow, or a queen; this signifies her nutritive or disciplinary functions. There is no need to develop this theory here; the reader is referred to the original chapter.

The predictions from such a theory lead to much the same deductions as do those made by Hall from Freudian theory. We normally have more aggressive encounters with male strangers, particularly when we are males ourselves, simply because males are more aggressive, and more so towards other males. Both males and females tend to encounter more male strangers in the course of their work, simply because even nowadays for most women their home is their *point d'appui,* where few strangers intrude, while work is the place where men spend most of their time, and where they are likely to meet male strangers particularly. There may be certain weaknesses in these deductions but they are certainly no worse than those made by Hall. At least they do not involve fine gradations of 'castration complexes' wiping out fantasies of the good mother to a given degree – who would like to quantify that sort of notion? But in any case Kline is wrong in thinking that no alternative theories exist; it is interesting to speculate why he did not discuss them.

It should be noted that Kline quotes, with apparent approval, Hall's statement that it is irrelevant to ask whether any other theory could have predicted his results – the fact is that psychoanalytic theory *did* predict them. One might ask just how rigorous the deduction from psychoanalytic theory really was; would negative results have caused Hall to give up his psychoanalytic beliefs? But above all, note how this statement goes counter to all scientific methodology; no physicist would treat alternative theories so cavalierly. It seems sad that Kline, who in other contexts gives voice to unexceptionable statements of scientific probity, should not point out this curious departure from scientific orthodoxy, and should in fact seem to endorse it. Oddly enough, when an alternative theory is mentioned it is not one that has obtained any degree of support; he briefly mentions a theory attributed to Oswald (1969) that 'the mental content while dreaming is the result of random firing or stimulation of the brain during the REM period while protein is being synthesized' (p. 233). It would be more impressive if a more serious counter-theory had been chosen, e.g. the computer analogy theory of Newman and Evans (1965) which suggests that dreams represent a revision and updating of cognitive processes and memories to incorporate novel material collected by the system in the course of the day.

Kline might read with benefit the recent book by Sutherland and Mackintosh (1971) in which they deal with their own version of a non-continuity theory; for each experiment quoted they go into almost obsessional detail as to how different theories could explain the outcome. That is the way of science, not Hall's; only by following their example are we likely to achieve some form of consensus on Freudian theories and their experimental testing.

REFERENCES

EYSENCK, H. J. (1957) *Sense and Nonsense in Psychology*. Harmondsworth: Penguin.

FRIEDMAN, S. M. (1952) An empirical study of the castration and Oedipus complexes. *Genet. Psychol. Monogr.*, **46**, 61-130.

INSTITUTE OF DREAM RESEARCH (1962a) *A Manual for Classifying Characters in Dreams.* Technical Manual No. 1.

—— (1962b) *A Manual for Classifying Aggressions, Misfortunes, Friendly Acts, and Good Fortunes in Dreams.* Technical Manual No. 2.

KLINE, P. (1972) *Fact and Fantasy in Freudian Theory.* London: Methuen.

NEWMAN, E. A. & EVANS, C. P. (1965) Human dream processes as analogues to computer programme clearance. *Nature*, **206**, 534.

OSWALD, I. (1969) Do dreams have a function? *Paper at Ann. Conf. of Brit. Psychol. Soc.*

REIS, W. J. (1959) A comparison of the interpretation of dream series with and without free associations. In MANFRED F. DeMARTINO (ed.), *Dreams and Personality Dynamics*, (pp. 211-25). Springfield, Ill.: C. C. Thomas.

SUTHERLAND, N. S. & MACKINTOSH, N. J. (1971) *Mechanisms of Animal Discrimination Learning.* New York: Academic Press.

7
Bernard J. Schwartz (1956)

An empirical test of two Freudian hypotheses concerning castration anxiety[1]

Journal of Personality, 24, 318-27

This paper summarizes two studies that employ a previously developed experimentally validated (Schwartz, 1955) measure of castration anxiety to test derivations from psychoanalytic theory. The first study compares homosexual males and normal males in a search for differences in castration anxiety. The second study makes the same comparison for normal men and women.

STUDY I

Male Homosexuality and Castration Anxiety

Freud, in one of his earliest papers (Freud, 1938), suggests that castration anxiety, because of its role in the resolution of the Oedipus complex, is of crucial importance to subsequent object choice. Later papers (Freud, 1924a, b; 1932) repeat his statement without essential modification. He states: 'In extreme cases, this [castration anxiety] inhibits his [the boy's] object choice and, if reinforced by organic factors, may result in exclusive homosexuality' (Freud, 1932, pp. 284-5). Analogously, Horney (1924) states: 'We know that in every case in which the castration complex predominates there is without exception a more or less marked tendency to homosexuality'. Fenichel (1945, p. 326). whose writings may be considered to typify psychoanalytic thinking, states: 'Thus castration anxiety (and guilt feelings which are derivatives of castration anxiety) must be the decisive

[1]These studies were performed as part of a dissertation submitted in partial fulfilment of the requirements for the degree of Doctor of Philosophy, in the Department of Social Relations, Harvard University. I should like to express my most sincere gratitude to Dr Gardner Lindzey, who directed this research.

factor' (i.e., in the genesis of perversion). And again (Fenichel, 1945, p. 330), he states: 'Whenever the difference in the genitals of the sexes is of outstanding importance to an individual, and whenever his relationships to his fellow human beings are in every respect determined by the sex of the others, such an individual is under the influence of a strong castration complex. This is true of homosexual men, analysis of whom regularly shows they are afraid of female genitals.' The above quotations suggest that castration anxiety plays an important role in the personality of the adult male overt homosexual.

PROCEDURE

Subjects

TAT protocols of a group of 20 overt-homosexual males, collected from a college population by another experimenter, were used. This experimenter reported that Ss demonstrated no other gross psychopathology, were not receiving psychotherapy, and seemed to accept their homosexuality. The experimenter reported further that these Ss were *not* commonly known as homosexuals, and did not seem to be overtly fearful of external punishment for their homosexuality.

Twenty TAT protocols of randomly selected males from a college population constituted the control group data. These protocols as well had been previously obtained by another investigator. The two groups were comparable in age, education, and socioeconomic status.

Administration and Analysis of the Thematic Apperception Test

The TAT was administered individually to Ss of both groups. Different TAT cards were used for the two groups, but they shared in common cards 4, 6BM, 7BM, and 18BM, and only these stories were used in the data analysis.

The TAT data were analyzed by means of the content analysis measure of castration anxiety described more fully by Van Ophuijsen (1924). The measure consists of items (i.e. descriptions of behaviour, events, thoughts, or ideas believed related to castration anxiety) which were grouped into nine logically coherent, mutually exclusive categories, as well as into a tenth category dealing with formal characteristics of stories and presumably denotative of nonspecific anxiety. While these items and categories were originally selected on *a priori* theoretical and clinical grounds, six of the categories discriminated reliably between the TAT protocols of normal Ss who had just seen a film designed to provoke castration anxiety and Ss exposed to a neutral control film. These categories are listed below, and may be considered to be an operationally defined index of castration anxiety:

Category 3: Damage to or loss of extensions of the body image. Items include loss of prized possessions which may symbolize the self or parts of the self, such as weapons, machinery, cameras, etc.

Category 5: Personal inadequacy. These are 'lack of competence and strength' items, and include descriptions of the hero as being weak, small, helpless, unable to assert his rights, etc.

Category 6: General repetitive attempts at mastery. These items are concerned with repetitive returning to an area of anxiety in an attempt to master it, and include preoccupation with phallic referents and sexuality, ambivalence (where other items of the measure are involved), exhibitionism, rebellion against threatening authority figures, and repetitive risk-taking.

Category 7: Intrapsychic threat. These items are primarily concerned with guilt, remorse, and expectations of punishment or retaliation.

Category 8: Extrapsychic threat. These items consist in the main of retaliation, punishment, threat, or prohibition from external personal or impersonal sources.

Category 9: Loss of cathected objects. These items are concerned with death, absence, or removal of persons loved by the hero of the story.

The remaining four categories of the measure, though not validated experimentally, are used in these studies because three of these categories (1, 2, 4) are logically and behaviourally closest to the primary representation of castration anxiety, and secondly, these four categories discriminated groups in the validation study, albeit not reliably, in the predicted direction, and the total measure including these unvalidated categories differentiated groups better than did a total score using only the validated categories, and considerably better than any single category. These categories were:

Category 1: Genital injury or loss. Most of these items are unsymbolized representations of actual injury to the genitalia. One item concerns total mutilative destruction of the body.

Category 2: Damage to or loss of other parts of the body. These items include damage to any part of the body other than the genitalia, such as wounds to or operations upon limbs, thorax, or abdomen.

Also included are less specific types of damage, such as beating, torture, or illness.

Category 4: Sexual inadequacy. This category includes items such as impotence, sterility, penile inadequacy, renunciation of hetrosexuality and equation of sexuality with aggression.

Category 10: Formal characteristics of stories. These items include discontinuities in the stories, misspellings, erasures, and 'bad' endings to stories. The items of category 10 are considered indices of anxiety, but are not specific to castration anxiety.

A simple frequency-count system was used in scoring. Each occurrence in the TAT protocol of any item of the measure, or its spontaneous denial, was tallied in one and only one of the first nine categories, but could also be scored in category 10. The number of items of the measure occurring in each story is theoretically unlimited. Only those items of the measure *overtly present* in the stories were tallied: inferences were *not* scored. Interrater reliability of the measure of castration anxiety, using the Pearson coefficient of correlation, was $r=.80$, which compares favourably with reliability indices of other studies using the TAT.

The Link-Wallace method of allowances (Mosteller & Bush, 1954), one-way classification of data, was the statistic used to test the significance of differential occurrence of items between groups. The groups were compared on each category of the measure, on total scores, on the total score of the six validated categories, and on the total score for the nine categories specific to castration anxiety.

RESULTS

Table 7.1 shows the significance of the differences between the overt-homosexual male group and the comparison heterosexual male group on the measure of castration anxiety, as estimated by the method of allowances. Categories 4, 7, 8, and 10 discriminate groups in the predicted direction at the 5 per cent level of risk. The overall total score, the total score of valid categories, and the total score of categories specific to castration anxiety discriminate groups at the 1 per cent level of risk. Differences in categories 5 and 6, though not significant, are in the predicted direction. Category 1 shows no occurrences in either group. Differences in categories 2, 3, and 9 are in a direction opposite to that predicted, and the magnitude of these differences is small. Parallel computations with the more sensitive chi-square technique give analogous results: Categories 4, 7, 8, and

10 are significant at the 1 per cent level, and category 5, not significant with the method of allowances, proves significant at the 5 per cent level.

In summary of these results, the psychoanalytic hypothesis that overt-homosexual males show more intense castration anxiety than comparable normal males is supported.

TABLE 7.1. *Differences between Overt-Homosexual Male and Normal Male groups on the measure of Castration Anxiety.*

	Source	Overt-Homosexual Group Total	Heterosexual Group Total	Differences
Category	1	0	0	0
	2	12	14	−2
	3	1	3	−2
	4	25	6	19*
	5	74	51	23
	6	70	63	7
	7	51	20	31*
	8	92	57	35*
	9	2	5	−3
	10	44	6	38*
Total score		368	225	143**
Total score of previously validated categories (3, 5, 6, 7, 8, 9)		290	198	92**
Total score of categories specific to castration anxiety (1 – 9)		324	214	105**

* Significant at the 5 per cent level of risk, using the method of allowances.
** Significant at the 1 per cent level of risk, using the method of allowances.

STUDY II

Sex Differences and Castration Anxiety

The weight of psychoanalytic theory suggests castration anxiety is of differential importance in the personalities of normal men and women. Freud (1924a, pp. 274-5), speaking of castration anxiety in the female, states: 'She accepts castration as an established fact, an operation already performed. The castration dread thus being excluded in her case . . .' Deutsch (1930) considers the abandonment of clitoral satisfaction, a function of castration anxiety, to be compensated for by the ability to bear a child, and the hope for one in the future; this has the consequence of reducing the amount of castration anxiety the girl experiences. Fenichel (1945, p. 99) states: 'In girls, there seems to be no castration anxiety that could be considered a dynamic force. The idea of having lost an organ cannot condition the same restriction of instinct as the idea that one might lose an organ by instinctual activity. True, many women after their disappointment (i.e., discovery of lack of a penis) have unconsciously built up the fantasy of possessing a penis. But an anxiety concerning a merely fantasied organ cannot have the same dynamic effect as a threat against a real organ. Analysis shows that other and older fears, above all the fear over loss of love, are stronger in women, and in many ways take over the role that castration anxiety plays in men.' This quotation suggests, despite a number of qualifications, that castration anxiety should occurr more frequently or with greater intensity in men than in women.

PROCEDURE

Subjects

The data for this investigation consisted of TAT protocols of 20 matched pairs of male and female Ss. Pairs of Ss were exactly matched for religion and self-ratings of socioeconomic status: 14 of the pairs were identical in age, 6 pairs differed by no more than one year. These protocols were selected from data gathered by previous investigators (Lindzey & Goldberg, 1953) in elementary psychology courses at Boston University.

Administration and Analysis of the Thematic Apperception Test

TATs were group administered, with each slide exposed for 20 seconds, and a five-minute time allotment for writing of stories. Cards 1, 2, 4, 5, 10, 13MF, 14, and 15, applicable to both male and female Ss, were used.

The same procedure of analysis was used in this comparison as in the comparison of the TAT protocols of normal and overt-homosexual males.

RESULTS

Table 7.2 shows the significance of the differences between males and females on the measure of castration anxiety, as estimated by the method of allowances. Categories 5 and 6 differentiate groups in the predicted direction at the 5 per cent level of risk, as do the overall total score, the total score of valid categories, and the total score of categories specific to castration anxiety. Differences in categories 4, 7, 8, 9, and 10, although in the predicted direction, are not significant. The magnitudes of these differences are small, as are those of categories 1, 2, and 3, which are in direction opposite to that predicted. Parallel statistical analysis with chi-square technique again gives analogous results. Category 6 and the three total scores are significant at the 1 per cent level. None of the other categories show change.

These results support the psychoanalytic hypothesis that normal males show more intense castration anxiety than normal females.

TABLE 7.2. *Differences between Male and Female groups on the measure of Castration Anxiety.*

	Source	Male Group Total	Female Group Total	Differences
	1	1	2	−1
	2	11	14	−3
	3	1	3	−2
	4	28	21	7
	5	40	22	18*
Category	6	83	42	41*
	7	33	31	2
	8	72	56	16
	9	14	10	4
	10	5	3	2
Total score		288	203	85*
Total score of previously validated categories (3, 5, 6, 7, 8, 9)		242	162	83*
Total score of categories specific to castration anxiety (1 – 9)		283	200	80*

* Significant at the 5 per cent level of risk, using the method of allowances.

Though the differences between the group totals are significant, the distributions of total scores show considerable overlap between the two groups. One speculative possibility to account for this finding is that the obtained results may be an accurate representation of the differential intensities of castration anxiety in the personalities of males and females, which are probably not as clear-cut as the hypothesis would suggest. Abraham (1927), for example, considers that some manifestations of castration anxiety occur in all women, as do Freud (1932), Horney (1924, 1932), and Van Ophuijsen (1924). Fenichel qualifies his earlier unambiguous statements by saying (Fenichel, 1945, p. 99): 'It is not easy to answer the question about castration anxiety in women . . . the fear that the state of being castrated, thought of as an outcome of a forbidden activity, might be found out often limits the girl's sexual expressions considerably; the idea of having destroyed one's own body is often encountered, as is that of having lost all possibility of bearing children, or at least of having healthy children, and other anxieties which anticipate that the disgrace is found out . . . there are anxieties about anticipated retaliatory genital injuries which replace castration fear. Girls often do not know they have a pre-formed hollow organ in their vagina, and this explains the fantastic fear that their genital longings to be penetrated by the father's organ may lead to bodily injury. Despite all this, the analysis of some women still reveals an unconscious fear that an organ will be cut off as punishment for sexual practices.'

In summary, the obtained results seem to parallel psychoanalytic thinking about the differential role of castration anxiety in the personalities of normal males and females: the ambiguities, qualifications, and lack of specification of magnitude characteristic of much of psychoanalytic theory are reflected in the overlap of the distributions of total score.

Content Differences Between the TAT Protocols of Normal Males and Normal Females

The TAT stories told by males seemed to be characterized by frequent descriptions of male heroes as inadequate, weak-willed, stupid, and incapable of fidelity in marriage. Accompanying this were frequent descriptions of women as prostitutes, or as otherwise immoral, or as demanding and dominating. Their stories were also characterized by a prevailing ambivalence and indecisiveness, and by preoccupation with sexuality. Discontinuities in the stories were frequent, as were story endings concerned with illness, debility, death, loss of possessions or status, etc. These 'bad' endings sometimes did not seem justified by the content of the stories. Thus, the greater intensity of castration anxiety in males was inferred largely from a tendency toward belittling or questioning the adequacy of male figures, and at the same time representing female figures as threatening or immoral.

DISCUSSION

The findings we have just presented suggested certain conclusions concerning our measure of castration anxiety. In the first place the success we encountered in testing propositions derived from psychoanalytic theory in two different areas not only has implications for psychoanalytic theory, but also strengthens the confidence we have in our measure. In any study where an instrument is used to assess a specific variable in order to test a theoretically derived proposition, and the proposition is verified, this not only confirms the derivation, but also suggests strongly that the instrument is indeed getting at the variable it promised to measure. These two studies may therefore be considered a cross-validation of the results of the experimental validation of the measure of castration anxiety (Schwartz, 1955).

Also of interest is the consistent failure of categories 1 (actual genital injury), 2 (damage to other parts of the body), 3 (damage to extensions of the body image), and 9 (loss of cathected objects) to differentiate the groups at question. For the first two categories this lack of sensitivity is coupled with the earlier failure of the attempt to validate them experimentally, and thus constitutes a rather convincing picture of their lack of validity. However, it seems quite possible that the direct and undisguised nature of the material included in these categories would make their incidence unlikely in normal groups. Whether this would be true in psychotic groups and other groups different from those studied remains a question for the future. Our research does not provide any evidence for the validity of these responses, although their rational link to castration anxiety is sufficiently strong to make their inclusion in future investigations seem justified. A further reason for their inclusion in future investigations is statistical: (1) the total measure, including the unvalidated categories, is itself valid and differentiates groups well, and (2), computed intercorrelations among the experimentally validated categories suggest that the categories are all imperfectly correlated predictors of a single underlying variable.

Thus far we have talked only of the significance of our findings for the measurement of castration anxiety. What of their import for psychoanalytic theory? Granted that many alternative hypotheses could be offered to account for the differences we observed, and granted also that our confirmations are made in terms of group differences with considerable overlap between the differentiated groups, it still seems that the capacity of psychoanalytic theory to predict *in advance* the rather complicated findings we observed is encouraging and provides evidence for the crude power of psychoanalytic theory. The crudity of the theory is made clear by the evident difficulty of making an unambiguous derivation in connection with sex differences in castration anxiety. This difficulty is also implied by the fact that the two derivations we chose to test were among the more straightforward of the many conceivable hypotheses that we might have attempted to extract from psychoanalytic theory.

While we choose to view our findings as supplying some support for one of the more controversial aspects of psychoanalytic theory it is evident that these findings are a mere beginning when the immense number of other statements implied by psychoanalysis concerning castration anxiety is considered. The important consideration seems to be that here we have an instrument that is at least partially validated as a measure of castration anxiety and which is sufficiently manipulable so as to lend itself to many research settings.

SUMMARY

This paper presents the results of a test of two derivations from psychoanalytic theory. TAT protocols of comparable overt-homosexual male and normal male groups were obtained, as were TAT protocols of comparable male and female groups. These protocols were scored with a previously validated measure of castration anxiety. Results support the hypotheses that overt-homosexual males show more intense castration anxiety than normal males, and males show more intense castration anxiety than females.

COMMENT

This study is seen by its author as providing evidence in support of the Freudian concept of castration anxiety and its hypothesized involvement in the aetiology of homosexuality. This interpretation is generally endorsed by Kline (1972) who regards it as 'good evidence for the castration complex' and 'limited support' for the link between homosexuality and castration anxiety, and by Vetter and Smith (1971) who reproduce the paper in their book of selected readings in personality theory. Two experiments are reported and we shall consider them in turn.

The first study, according to Schwartz, provides support for 'the psychoanalytic hypothesis that overt-homosexual males show more intense castration anxiety than comparable normal males'. It sounds simple enough and his statistics seem quite adequate, but the meaningfulness of the result depends entirely on his operational definition of castration anxiety. TAT protocols of normal and homosexual males were compared on a number of response categories that were supposed to be related to castration anxiety. The homosexuals gave significantly higher scores on four out of ten categories: (4) sexual inadequacy, including impotence, sterility, penile inadequacy, renunciation of heterosexuality and equation of sexuality with aggression, (7) intrapsychic threat, i.e. guilt, remorse, and expectations of punishment or retaliation, (8) extrapsychic threat, i.e. retaliation, punishment, threat, or prohibition from external personal or impersonal sources, and (10) indications of generalized anxiety. Perhaps these areas do have some kind of tenuous connection with castration anxiety as a Freudian might understand the concept, but it seems clear, regardless of theoretical orientation, that they would have direct relevance to homsexuality. What sort of discovery is it that overt homsexuals 'renounce heterosexuality' more than heterosexuals? In the United States in 1956 homosexuality was both socially proscribed and illegal; is it altogether surprising that homosexuals show greater guilt, remorse, anxiety and fear of punishment or retaliation? It hardly seems that the concept of castration anxiety is needed to explain these associations.

Two other categories from the TAT responses showed higher scores for the homosexual group: (5) personal inadequacy, including descriptions of the hero as weak, small, helpless, unable to assert his rights, etc., and (6) general repetitive attempts at mastery, including preoccupation with phallic referents and sexuality, ambivalence, exhibitionism, rebellion against threatening authority figures, and repetitive risk-taking. Once again, it is easy to see a logical connection with homosexuality – not so easy to see what any of these areas have got to do with castration anxiety.

Schwartz actually scored the TAT protocols for four categories that do have a clear connection with castration anxiety: (1) genital injury or loss, (2) damage to or loss of other parts of the body, (3) damage to or loss of extensions of the body image, and (9) loss of cathected objects. How do these categories make out with respect to the hypothesis? Unfortunately, Category 1 received no score for either group of subjects, while the other three categories showed non-significant differences favouring the heterosexual group (i.e. in the direction contrary to the Freudian hypothesis). How is this finding explained away? Both Schwartz and Kline argue that these categories must have failed to operate as valid measures of castration anxiety because they are too obvious and undisguised. Apparently, then, a valid measure of castration anxiety must look like a measure of something else, e.g. homosexuality. When this measure is subsequently found to correlate with actual homosexuality, the castration anxiety hypothesis is then regarded as supported. This type of logic is not readily acceptable in a scientific context.

In an earlier study (Schwartz, 1955), an attempt was made to demonstrate that the response categories outlined above measure specifically castration anxiety rather than generalized anxiety. Three groups of 18 students each were shown different films. The *castration group* were shown a film of sub-incision rites, the *anxiety group* were shown a film about Negro deprivation, and a seemingly irrelevant *control group* saw a Charlie Chaplin film. Since most of the categories (except for 1, 2, and 4) showed higher scores for the 'castration group' the measure of castration anxiety was regarded as validated. We would regard this demonstration as worthless because there is no way of knowing that the film about Negro deprivation was capable of evoking as much generalized anxiety as the film about sub-incision. In other words, the differences between the castration group and the anxiety group could have been due to differences in the *degree of general anxiety* aroused by two films. In any case, this study could not have told us that the TAT measure was not *also* a measure of homosexuality, and is therefore irrelevant to our criticism of the Schwartz (1956) experiment.

It is hardly necessary for us to go on and point out that exactly the same criticism applies to Schwartz's second experiment, the demonstration that 'normal males show more intense castration anxiety than normal females'. Only two categories of the 'castration anxiety measure' out of the ten show a significant difference in favour of males. These are: (5) personal inadequacy, and (6) general repetitive attempts at mastery. Once again, we do not need Freud or the concept of castration anxiety to tell us that males are more concerned than females with competence, strength, assertion, sexuality, exhibitionism, rebellion against threatening authority figures, and repetitive risk-taking. Although there is some argument about the relative contributions of genetic and cultural factors, everybody is in agreement concerning the manifested differences between males and females in these areas. In this experiment also, the TAT response categories that have an explicit connection with castration anxiety show non-significant differences between males and females, three out of four of them in the wrong direction.

Schwartz concludes thus: 'Granted that many alternative hypotheses could be offered to account for the differences we observed . . . it still seems that the capacity of psychoanalytic theory to predict *in advance* the rather complicated findings we observed is encouraging and provides evidence for the crude power of psychoanalytic theory'. Our examination of Schwartz's two studies leads us to the contrary conclusion that they provide no evidence whatsoever to support either the usefulness of the concept of castration anxiety or its connection with homosexuality. The TAT scores that might be regarded as relevant to castration produced non-significant differences between the criterion groups. The scoring categories that did produce significant differences had no logical or empirical connection with castration, but were patently indices of homosexuality or masculinity.

REFERENCES

ABRAHAM, K. (1927) *Selected Papers of Karl Abraham*. International Psychoanalytical Library, No. 13. London: Hogarth Press.

DEUTSCH, HELENE (1930) The significance of masochism in the mental life of women. *Int. J. Psychoanal.*, 11, 48-60.

FENICHEL, O. (1945) *The Psychoanalytic Theory of Neurosis*. New York: Norton.

FREUD, S. (1924a) The passing of the Oedipus complex. In *Collected Papers,* International Psychoanalytical Library, No. 8. London: Hogarth Press, 2, pp. 269-76.

—— (1924b) The infantile genital organization of the libido. In *Collected Papers,* International Psychoanalytical Library, No. 8. London: Hogarth Press, 2, 244-9.

—— (1932) Female sexuality. *Int. J. Psychoanal.,* **13**, 281-97.

—— (1938) Three contributions to a theory of sexuality. In A. A. BRILL (ed.), *The Basic Writings of Sigmund Freud,* pp. 553-632. New York: Modern Library.

HORNEY, KAREN (1924) On the genesis of the castration complex in women. *Int. J. Psychoanal.,* **5**, 50-65.

—— (1932) The dread of women. *Inst. J. Psychoanal.,* **13**, 348-60.

KLINE, P. (1972) *Fact and Fantasy in Freudian Theory*. London: Methuen.

LINDZEY, G. & GOLDBERG, M. (1953) Motivational differences between male and female as measured by the Thematic Apperception Test. *J. Pers.,* **22**, 101-17.

MOSTELLER, F. & BUSH, R. R. (1954) Selected quantitative techniques. In G. LINDZEY (ed.), *Handbook of Social Psychology,* pp. 289-335. Cambridge, Mass.: Addison-Wesley.

SCHWARTZ, B. (1955) The measurement of castration anxiety and anxiety over loss of love. *J. Pers.,* **24**, 204-19.

VAN OPHUIJSEN, J. (1924) Contributions to the masculinity complex in women. *Int. J. Psychoanal.,* **5**, 39-49.

VETTER, H. J. & SMITH, B. D. (1971) *Personality Theory: A Source Book*. New York: Appleton-Century-Crofts.

8

Irving Sarnoff and Seth M. Corwin (1959) [1]

Castration anxiety and the fear of death [2]

Journal of Personality, 27, 374-85

Beginning with its formulation by Freud (1949), the concept of castration anxiety has been widely invoked by psychoanalytically oriented therapists in their attempts to account for a variety of clinical phenomena (cf. Esman, 1954; Fodor, 1947; Kobler, 1948; Rothenberg & Brenner, 1955; Starcke, 1921). In recent years, several correlational studies have provided some empirical support for the concept of castration anxiety (Friedman, 1952; Schwartz, 1955; Schwartz, 1956). The present experiment was undertaken to contribute further data to aid in the scientific evaluation of the usefulness of the concept. Specifically, this experiment concerns the relationship between castration anxiety and the fear of death.

THE CONCEPT OF CASTRATION ANXIETY

Freud first put forward the concept of castration anxiety in connection with his theory of the Oedipal conflict and the psychological processes employed in its resolution. Briefly, Freud postulated that the male child becomes motivated, at one stage in his psychosexual development, to possess his mother sexually. However, such a desire cannot be countenanced by the child's father. Indeed, the latter threatens to castrate his son if he should persist in his illicit cravings. Presumably, this threat of castration may be made directly and literally, or it may be conveyed indirectly and symbolically. In any case, the threat is perceived by the child and it arouses his intense

[1] Yale University.

[2] The authors wish to thank Professor Arthur R. Cohen for his helpful suggestions in regard to the preparation of this paper.

fear. To reduce this fear, the child must learn to behave in a way which will no longer provoke his father's jealous anger.

From the standpoint of the growing child, the effort to resolve the Oedipal conflict is an ongoing one whose outcome is not conclusively determined until after he has reached adolescence. In the course of this protracted effort, the child may draw upon a number of the mechanisms which are available in his repertoire of ego defence. According to psychoanalytic theory, however, the following three ego defences are of principal importance in the child's struggle to attain mastery over the various facets of the Oedipal conflict: *identification*, *repression* and *displacement*. Identification and repression are employed earlier than the mechanism of displacement. Nevertheless, after these ego defences have been brought into play, they become part of the individual's habitual mode of coping with the Oedipal conflict.

When the conflict emerges during the phallic stage, the child, first of all, identifies with his threatening father. That is, the child adopts his father's sexual taboos and accepts the idea that it is wrong for a son to have sexual desires for his mother. Having internalized his father's prohibitions, the child then represses his sexual feelings for his mother. With this repression, the child ceases to be conscious of any sexual yearning for her.

The repression of sexual desire for the mother is followed by the latency period, a period of several years during which the child's sexual drive is relatively weak and quiescent. During this period, too, the child continues to cement his identification with his father. Hence, for a time, the child appears to be at peace with himself and the Oedipal conflict seems to have been mastered. Inevitably, however, the calm of the latency period is shattered by the onset of puberty. For the physiological changes of adolescence stir up imperative sexual tensions for which some outlet must be found, and sexual desires which had been dormant and unconscious throughout the latency period now tend to break through the barrier of repression which the child had built up against them.

In the throes of his reactivated sexuality, the adolescent may again be inclined to covet his mother. But any such inclination evokes the anticipation of castration which originally induced the child to renounce his mother as a sexual object. The adolescent is obliged to repress any newly awakened sexual desire for his mother, but must find some way of gratifying his urgent sexual cravings. Consequently, he is led to employ still another mechanism of ego defence, displacement. He diverts his sexual interest away from his mother and toward females whom he may consciously covet and pursue without arousing his castration anxiety. In effecting this displacement, the sexually mature male finally succeeds in establishing a lasting resolution of the Oedipal conflict.

Ideally, during the Oedipal period, the child is exposed only to that degree of castration threat which is sufficient to induce the repression of his sexual feelings for his mother alone. When the child attains adulthood, he should experience no anxiety when his heterosexual desires are aroused by any woman other than his mother, for he has learned to anticipate castration only when his mother is the object of his sexual desire. In actuality, however, children are exposed to varying degrees of castration threat; and if the amount of threat has been excessive, the individual may be led to repress his sexual feelings not only for his mother in particular, but also for women in general. In such cases the arousal of his repressed sexuality by *any* female may elicit the anxiety which has become associated with the incipient manifestation of a highly punishable motive. For a man who has suffered excessive threat of castration in childhood, therefore, sexual arousal, even by a female who is not his mother, is likely to evoke the anticipation of castration.

THE PSYCHODYNAMIC RELATIONSHIP BETWEEN CASTRATION ANXIETY AND THE FEAR OF DEATH

Because men differ in respect to the degree of castration threat they have experienced in childhood, they may be expected to respond with differing degrees of castration anxiety to the same sexually arousing stimulus. Indeed, even in the absence of a particular external stimulus, men who, as children, were severely threatened with castration may be subject to chronic anxiety. This anxiety stems from the fact that their chronically repressed desires for sexual contact with women strive continually to break through into consciousness. Naturally, such individuals usually do not know that it is their own sexual motives which stimulate this anxiety, nor are they likely to be aware of the specific danger, castration, which they dread. Nevertheless, their underlying anxiety, as in the case of other strong unconscious effects, may be expected to colour the content of their conscious thoughts, and they ought to become preoccupied with ideas which symbolically reflect the castration anxiety of which they are unaware. Hypochondria is an excellent clinical example of the way in which intense – but unconscious – castration anxiety may be indirectly expressed through a host of conscious fears concerning possible sources of infectious disease or bodily deterioration. Indeed, these hypochondriacal fears may, in some cases, actually focus on infections which could damage sexual organs. However, even in such instances, the individual is not likely to perceive the relationship between his conscious fear and the unconscious castration anxiety which it reflects. His concern tends to be outward rather than inward; and he spends his time and energy in attempts to escape infection.

Just as unconscious castration anxiety may be manifested in conscious fears of bodily injury, it may also manifest itself in a fear of the most extreme consequence of injury: death. Thus, it happens that individuals who are in the best of health and have never actually experienced any serious accident or illness may be obsessed by morbid and unremitting fears of dying or of being killed. These fears may become so acute that the individual is reluctant to go to sleep lest he should never again awaken.

Of course, the conscious fear of death may be developed for a variety of reasons, the most obvious of which concern the aftermath of traumatic events, such as military combat, which might have terminated the individual's existence. Still it would appear, in view of the preceding theoretical account, that an individual who has suffered intense castration threats should have a greater habitual fear of death than an individual who has been less severely threatened. Individuals who have severe castration anxiety ought also to show more fear of death after the arousal of that anxiety than individuals whose castration anxiety is less intense. In arriving at these deductions, we have assumed that people with different degrees of castration anxiety have experienced differential degrees of castration threat for the expression of their sexual feelings. However, we shall not address ourselves directly to an investigation of these presumed developmental differences in this experiment. Instead, we shall focus exclusively on the impact of castration anxiety on the conscious fear of death, after that anxiety has been stirred by the perception of sexually arousing stimuli.

In line with this reasoning, the central hypothesis of this experiment may be stated as follows: *Individuals who have a high degree of castration anxiety will show a greater fear of death after being exposed to sexually arousing stimuli than individuals who have a low degree of castration anxiety.*

METHOD

General Design

The experiment followed a 'before-after' design which provided for the arousal of two levels of sexual feeling among *S*s possessing two degrees of castration anxiety. Castration anxiety was measured in pre-experimental sessions. Thus, the experiment studied the interaction of castration anxiety and sexual stimulation in determining the fear of death.

Subjects

*S*s were 56 male undergraduates of Yale College. They were unpaid volunteers, recruited from among the general college population. *S*s were run through the experiment one at a time in a dormitory room.

Rationale

This experiment was presented to the *S*s as an investigation of some of the psychological factors which influence the appreciation of art. *S*s were told that the investigators were interested in seeing how different individuals react to the same work of art, and how various attitudes and opinions are related to aesthetic reactions. *S*s were informed that they would first fill out a questionnaire which covered a number of opinions pertinent to our research objectives. After they had filled out this questionnaire, *S*s were told that they would be shown several pictures about which they would be asked to write their aesthetic reactions.

The Opinion Questionnaire

The first of the pre-experimental measures consisted of a 22-item Likert-type scale. Included among these 22 items was a seven-item Fear of Death scale and a five-item Morality scale, both of which are described below. The 10 remaining items in the questionnaire were interspersed among the items of these two scales. These 10 'filler' items pertained to various aspects of aesthetic preference. They were included for two reasons: (*a*) to inhibit the emergence of a response set to the other items and (*b*) to support the rationale of the experiment.

*S*s indicated the extent of their agreement or disagreement with each item in the questionnaire. These responses were coded in terms of a six-point scale ranging from +3 (Strongly Agree) to −3 (Strongly Disagree). *S*s were not permitted to take a mid-point on the scale; they were obliged to indicate some degree of agreement or disagreement with each statement.

The Fear of Death Scale (FDS). Since all the items in the questionnaire were devised on an *a priori* basis, and since the FDS measure was the basic dependent variable of the study, it was felt advisable to attempt to weed out those FDS items which were grossly nondiscriminating. Accordingly, after the 'before' measures were collected, an item analysis was performed on the seven-item FDS. Two items failed to discriminate between the high and low scores. Thus, the hypothesis was tested by using a summated score of the five items which were retained.

The following are the five items which comprised the final version of the FDS:

1. I tend to worry about the death toll when I travel on highways.
2. I find it difficult to face up to the ultimate fact of death.
3. Many people become disturbed at the sight of a new grave, but it does not bother me. (reverse scores)
4. I find the preoccupation with death at funerals upsetting.
5. I am disturbed when I think of the shortness of life.

The Morality Scale (MS). The MS was included in the study in order to serve as an internal control for the plausible alternative hypothesis that a post-experimental increase in fear of death might be the result of an increase in guilt following contact with stimuli which violate one's moral values. Such a reaction following sexual arousal could induce an unconscious need for punishment in the guilty *S* and this need, in turn, might express itself in an increased fear of death. The MS consisted of five items dealing with attitudes toward sexual behaviour. The MS items, constructed in the same *a priori* fashion as the FDS and contained in the same questionnaire as the FDS, were also subjected to an item analysis. Since the original MS items discriminated adequately between high and low scorers, they were all retained in the final version of the MS.

The following are the examples of items contained in the MS:

1. Although many of my friends feel differently, I feel that one should wait until he is married to have intercourse.

2. I am frequently disturbed by the complete lack of sexual control in the relationships of my friends and their dates.

The Measure of Castration Anxiety (CA)

After the administration of the scales described above, our measure of castration anxiety was obtained in the following way: *S*s were presented with the so-called castration anxiety card of the Blacky Test (Blum, 1949). This card shows a cartoon depicting two dogs; one dog is standing blindfolded, and a large knife appears about to descend on his outstretched tail; the other dog is an onlooker to this event. *S*s were asked to look at this card and then rank three summary statements which purported to summarize the situation which was depicted. Actually, each statement was composed, on an *a priori* basis, to express a different degree of anxiety, ranging from slight to intense. Thus, *S*s attached a score of 3 to the statement they felt best reflected the emotions of the onlooking dog, a score of 2 to the statement they felt fit the situation second best, and a score of 1 for the statement they felt fit the situation least. The distribution of the scores turned out to be quite skewed: most *S*s assigned a score of 3 to the low CA alternative, a score of 2 to the medium CA alternative, and a score of 1 to the high CA alternative. The 36 *S*s who showed this pattern of scores were placed in the Low CA group. The remaining 20 *S*s were categorized in the High CA group. Below are the summaries used for the Blacky card. (L represents the low castration anxiety statement, M, medium castration anxiety, and H, high castration anxiety.)

L. The Black Dog appears to be experiencing some tension as he watches the scene in front of him. However, the sight of the amputation has little emotional significance for him, and he views the situation in a fairly detached manner.

M. The Black Dog is evidently quite afraid by what is going on in front of him. He is afraid that his tail might be next to be amputated. Nevertheless, he is able to bear up to the situation without becoming deeply upset or overwhelmed by anxiety.

H. The sight of the approaching amputation is a deeply upsetting experience for the Black Dog who is looking on. The possibility of losing his own tail and the thought of the pain involved overwhelm him with anxiety.

The Experimental Conditions

Approximately four weeks after they filled out the 'before' measures, the *S*s participated in the experiment. Since the experimental design called for variation in arousal of sexual stimulation, two experimental conditions were created: High and Low sexual arousal (HAS and LAS). The experimental manipulations were administered individually, with 29 *S*s in the HAS condition and 27 *S*s in the LAS condition.[1]

It was decided that the easiest and most manageable arousal of sexual feelings would be by means of photographs of women. To produce the HAS condition, a series of four pictures of nude women were presented one at a time. These pictures were artistically mounted as if they were prints or lithographs. *E* said that these pictures were designed to study individual differences in aesthetic reactions to the same work of art. To heighten the impact of the arousal, *S*s were given four minutes to write down their reaction to each picture. According to the rationale of the study, this writing was done in order to provide a record of the *S*s responses to the aesthetic qualities of the picture.

In the LAS condition, the procedure was identical except for the fact that four pictures of fully clothed fashion models, taken from a magazine, were used instead of nudes.

After the experimental manipulations, *S*s were required to fill out the following measures which are relevant to the data reported here: a rating scale designed to ascertain whether or not the HAS and LAS conditions succeeded in evoking different intensities of stimulation, the FDS scale, and the MS scale.

The post-experimental check on the sexually-arousing quality of the manipulations indicated that the HAS pictures were clearly perceived as more sexually arousing than the LAS pictures. On a scale ranging from 0 (not at all arousing) to 100 (intensely arousing), the HAS *S*s had an average score of 59, whereas the LAS *S*s had an average score of 35. The difference between these means was well beyond the .001 level of significance. Thus, there can be little doubt concerning the difference in sexual stimulation of the two conditions of arousal.

It may also be relevant to note that, in post-experimental interviews, none of the *S*s indicated that they had been suspicious about our stated research objective. Moreover, although some of the *S*s in the HAS condition could not completely conceal their chagrin or

[1]To insure a sufficient number of HCA *S*s within the HAS and LAS conditions, half of the *S*s were randomly selected from the HCA and LCA *S*s and assigned to the HAS condition. The other half were assigned to the LAS condition. Two *S*s who had been assigned to the LAS condition failed to appear for the experimental session.

embarrassment upon seeing the nudes, they did not doubt that we were interested in studying individual differences in reactions to the pictures.

RESULTS AND DISCUSSIONS

The hypothesis tested in this experiment holds that HCA *S*s will become more afraid of death after exposure to the HAS condition than LCA *S*s. To test this hypothesis, the change in the *S*'s level of fear of death was assessed by comparing their pre-experimental FDS scores with their post-experimental FDS scores. This comparison produced a 'shift' score for each *S*, indicating by what amount and in which direction his 'after' FDS score differed from his 'before' FDS scores. A positive (+) shift score thus indicated that a *S* exhibited more fear of death, while a negative (−) shift score was indicative of a decrease in fear of death.

A *t* test showed that there was no difference between the high and low arousal groups in their initial level of fear of death. However, a strong relationship was found between fear and death and castration anxiety. The phi coefficient is .612, a figure which is significant at the .01 level. This result is in accordance with the anticipations previously stated in the theoretical section. As a result of this relationship, however, the HCA *S*s tended to have higher pre-experimental FDS scores than the LCA *S*s. Consequently, it is clear that HCA *S*s entered the experimental conditions with less possibility for upward movement in the FDS than the LSA *S*s. Conversely, the LCA *S*s had less possibility for downward movement. Therefore, it was deemed advisable to test the hypothesis both with and without attention to the *S*'s initial level of fear of death.

Table 8.1 presents the results pertinent to the basic test of our hypothesis. Without controlling for initial position on the FDS, the predicted difference between HCA and LCA *S*s in mean FDS shift scores under the HAS condition is significant at the .03 level, whereas no statistically reliable difference between the HCA and LCA *S*s is obtained under the LAS condition. A test of the difference between the differences in mean FDS scores (the difference between HCA and LCA *S*s under the HAS condition compared with the difference between HCA and LCA *S*s under the LAS condition) yields a *t* of 4.35. This result, which is statistically significant at beyond the .001 level, appears clearly to indicate that the arousal of sexual feeling interacted with level of castration anxiety in accord with our *a priori* predictions.

TABLE 8.1. *Analysis of Mean FDS Shift Scores. (Differences between HCA and LCA Ss within high, low, and combined levels of pre-experimental FDS under HAS and LAS conditions).*

Strength of sexual arousal	Level of pre-experimental FDS	Strength of castration anxiety: HCA *N*	HCA Mean FDS shift	LCA *N*	LCA Mean FDS shift	Difference between means	*p*
HAS	High and low	11	+3·36	18	+ ·45	+2·91	·03
LAS	High and low	9	−1·11	18	− ·05	−1·06	n.s.
HAS	High	8	+1·88	6	+ ·33	+1·55	n.s.
	Low	3	+7·33	12	+ ·50	+6·83	·001
LAS	High	6	−2·00	7	−1·86	− ·14	n.s.
	Low	3	+ ·67	11	+1·10	− ·43	n.s.

Mention ought, perhaps, to be made of the fact that both HCA and LCA *S*s show a negative shift score, i.e., a decrease in the fear of death, under identical conditions. Thus when high and low levels of pre-experimental FDS are combined under the LAS condition, as in Table 8.1, HCA *S*s get a mean negative shift score of −1.11 while the mean FDS shift score for LCA *S*s is −.05. Similarly, it can be seen in Table 8.1 that, within the high level of pre-experimental FDS, but again under the LAS condition, HCA *S*s obtained a mean FDS shift score of −2.00 as compared to —1.06 for LCA *S*s. If we discount, as virtually negligible, the LCA shift score of −.05, the remaining three negative FDS shift scores seem best accounted for by the effects of statistical regression. Since the LAS condition arouses so little sexual feeling, it seems to permit the occurrence of the same sort of regression effects that are typically found among control groups: a drop in mean retest score for initially high-scoring *S*s and a rise in mean retest score for initially low-scoring *S*s. This is exactly what appears to have happened with initially high and low scoring HCA and LCA *S*s under the LAS conditions. Thus, both HCA and LCA *S*s who are high in pre-experimental FDS show negative mean FDS scores. On the other hand, both HCA and LCA *S*s who are low in pre-experimental FDS show positive shift scores under LAS conditions. Finally, HCA *S*s who tend, as we have indicated, to have high pre-experimental FDS scores as a consequence of the positive correlation between FDS and CA, also decrease in FDS under the LAS condition when the high and low levels of pre-experimental FDS are combined.

In order to test the possibility that results might be accounted for by a guilt reaction to infringement of moral values concerning the

TABLE 8.2. *Differences between HMS and LMS Ss in mean FDS shift scores under HAS and LAS conditions.*

	Strength of morality					
	HMS		LMS			
Strength of sexual arousal	*N*	Mean FDS shift	*N*	Mean FDS shift	Difference between means	*p*
HAS	15	+2·13	14	+·93	+1·20	n.s.
LAS	13	−1·08	14	+·22	−1·30	n.s.

sexual feelings aroused by the HAS, the mean FDS shift scores of the high and low MS *S*s were compared under both HAS and LAS conditions. The results of this analysis, presented in Table 8.2, indicate that, although there appears to be a slight tendency for *S*s high in MS to show higher FDS shift scores than *S*s low in MS, the difference is far from statistical significance. The possibility, then, that an infringement of moral values induced by the nudes caused an increase in fear of death is not supported.

It should be noted, finally, that our measure of the morality variable appears to be quite independent of the castration anxiety and fear of death measures. The product-moment correlation between pre-experimental FDS and pre-experimental MS was only −.034, while the correlation between CA and pre-experimental MS was also low and statistically insignificant (a phi coefficient of .105).

The results of the present experiment are interpreted as lending support to the validity of the Freudian concept of castration anxiety. Such an interpretation seems especially warranted since the plausible alternative explanation which we investigated failed to yield significant changes in the fear of death when *S*s were categorized in terms of their moral scruples against sexual behaviour. Since our pre-experimental measures of castration anxiety and morality were found to be quite independent of each other, we may conclude, with some confidence, that it was the arousal of castration anxiety rather than guilt feelings which produced the significant differences which we obtained.

Of course, nothing that was done here bears directly on the question of the etiology of castration anxiety. However, by demonstrating that sexually arousing stimuli exerted predicted and differential effects upon individuals with varying degrees of castration anxiety, we have provided circumstantial evidence which is consonant with Freud's emphasis on the significance of the sexual motive in the genesis of castration anxiety.

SUMMARY

The aim of this experiment was to test an hypothesis concerning the psychodynamic relationship between castration anxiety and the fear of death. Specifically, the hypothesis predicted that persons who have a high degree of castration anxiety (HCA) would show a greater increase in fear of death after the arousal of their sexual feelings than persons who have a low degree of castration anxiety (LCA).

Fifty-six male undergraduates of Yale College were assigned to two experimental conditions in a 'before-after' design which permitted the manipulation of two levels of sexual arousal. Before being exposed to one or the other of these manipulations, *S*s filled out booklets containing a scale designed to measure the fear of death (FDS), a questionnaire concerning moral standard of sexual behaviour (MS), and a measure of castration anxiety (CA).

High arousal of sexual feeling (HAS) was induced by showing the *S*s four pictures of nude females. The condition of low arousal of sexual feeling (LAS) consisted of showing *S*s four pictures of fashion models. Following the experimental manipulations, *S*s again filled out the original FDS. In addition, *S*s answered a questionnaire aimed at checking on the degree of sexual arousal which *S*s perceived in the experimental manipulations.

The results clearly confirmed the hypothesis: HCA *S*s showed a significantly greater increase in fear of death than LCA *S*s after being exposed to the sexually arousing stimuli of the HAS condition. There were no significant differences in mean FDS shift scores between HCA and LCA *S*s under the LAS condition. A post-experimental check of the difference in perceived arousal of sexual feelings revealed that *S*s perceived the HAS condition as significantly more arousing than the LAS condition. A plausible alternative explanation of the obtained results was investigated and rejected. Thus, it was found that *S*s who differed in the strength of their moral standards of sexual behaviour did not differ significantly in their mean FDS scores after being exposed to the HAS condition.

COMMENT

This is perhaps the most impressive study of any that we have discussed so far. It is truly experimental in the sense that attempts are made to manipulate variables rather than simply observe inter-correlations among them; we would agree that such studies provide a far more rigorous test of any theory than non-experimental studies and are more difficult to fault. The experiment has been widely discussed and acclaimed (e.g. Mahl, 1969) and is reprinted in at least one book of readings (Southwell & Merbaum, 1964). Kline

(1972) regards it as 'strong support for the Freudian concept of the castration complex' and maintains that the results 'can only be understood' in these terms.

It is particularly this last position that we wish to take issue with. The authors and most subsequent writers maintain that the study demonstrates a link between castration anxiety and the fear of death in that a significant increase in fear of death was observed in subjects classified as high in castration anxiety following sexual arousal. This hypothesis does seem logically derived from Freudian theory and the statistical analysis is satisfactory. As with many of the studies discussed previously, however, the value of the conclusions depends heavily upon the operational definitions of the concepts involved. In this study there are three major variables that required measurement: castration anxiety, fear of death, and sexual arousal. Let us consider how each of these was defined.

Castration anxiety was assessed by showing a cartoon from the Blacky Test depicting a blindfolded dog with a knife about to fall across its tail, and another dog looking on. Subjects responded in terms of descriptions of the degree of anxiety attributed to the onlooking dog, ranging from 'fairly detached' to 'deeply upsetting'. Perhaps this procedure could be *interpreted* as an index of castration anxiety, but for the moment let us adopt an eclectic, non-theoretical attitude, and make a guess as to what it measures most directly. In this case a personality dimension such as anxiety or emotionality (the pervading importance of which is well established; Eysenck, 1970) would seem the most likely possibility. There is, of course, no evidence that the Blacky picture in question actually taps this trait, but such an interpretation is far more straightforward than that of castration anxiety and does not involve complex theoretical assumptions such as symbolic equation of the dog's tail with the subject's genitals.

Fear of death was supposedly measured by a five-item questionnaire, with six response categories permitted for each item. Unfortunately, this scale would be expected to measure two other variables besides the actual content of the statements comprising it: (1) a tendency to agree with any statement (since the scale is not balanced for direction of scoring), and (2) a tendency to give extreme responses, e.g. 'strongly agree', rather than mild ones such as 'slightly agree'. These two effects can summate if there is any tendency for average responses to fall on one side of the neutral line. A full discussion of the problems involved in attitude scale construction may be found in Wilson (1973). For the present it is sufficient to note that the scale used by Sarnoff and Corwin might measure fear of death to some extent, but it almost certainly measures 'yea-saying' and extremeness response biases as well, and these in turn are known to reflect both personality traits and transient states.

Finally, there is the definition of sexual arousal. This variable was manipulated by presenting pictures of nude females and having subjects write about their reactions to them (versus the control condition in which fully clothed fashion models were shown). Such a procedure might well have had an effect upon the sexual arousal of the subjects, but it probably had several other effects in addition. One likely possibility is that showing the nude pictures served to induce a generally bold, masculine and informal set within the subject, allowing him to feel more relaxed and extravert in the experimental situation. Again, we have no way of verifying this hypothesis, but it is certainly no less likely than any of the assumptions based upon psychoanalytic theory that are integral to the logic of this experiment.

Now that we have considered some alternative interpretations of the variables that are involved in the experiment, do they permit us to offer an alternative explanation of the Sarnoff and Corwin finding? (Remember, according to Kline there is *no other way* of understanding their results.) Analysing the experiment in our terms, subjects were first assessed on a questionnaire measuring their decisiveness and confidence (the FD scale). Four weeks later, half of them (the HAS group) went through a procedure that induced them to feel more relaxed, informal and extravert in the experimental situation. They then filled out the confidence questionnaire again, and those that were high on trait anxiety (high CA scorers) showed the greatest gain in confidence since the first time the questionnaire was completed. In other words, high anxiety subjects are more affected by experimental procedures that induce relaxation than subjects who are already low on anxiety.

This interpretation sounds quite plausible to us, and certainly no more complicated than the Freudian theory that the experiment was set up to test. Admittedly it is an *ad hoc* explanation, but perhaps not an unreasonable one. As we have noted, of all the studies we have so far examined this one comes closest to offering some kind of support for a Freudian hypothesis; it merits an attempt at replication with better measuring instruments and an effort to control for the alternative hypothesis that we have described. Until such time it cannot be accepted as striking evidence for the Freudian position.

Before leaving this study by Sarnoff and Corwin, there is one other problem with the concept of castration anxiety that should be mentioned. Freud regards it as a *repressed* dynamic force operating at an *unconscious* level. But men are quite naturally concerned for the safety of their genitals because of their vulnerability; they are conscious of this concern and are quite able to report on it. Now suppose the Blacky Test or whatever is used to assess castration anxiety is picking up variations in *conscious* concern about the genitals, perhaps dependent on the importance and value attached to them by different males; it would follow that those who are most concerned about their equipment (i.e. those who value sex highly) are likely to be those who when reminded of their pleasure by viewing nude women become more distressed by the thought of their mortality (increase their scores on a fear of death scale). Here we have another alternative hypothesis involving no Freudian concepts, since castration anxiety cannot be claimed as Freudian unless it is demonstrated to be unconscious. This is probably the more important criticism of the psychoanalytic interpretation of the Sarnoff and Corwin finding, and one that will be seen to apply to nearly all studies of the male form of the castration complex.

REFERENCES

BLUM, G. S. (1949) A study of the psychoanalytic theory of psychosexual development. *Genet. Psychol. Monogr.*, **39**, 3-99.

ESMAN, A. (1954) A case of self-castration. *J. Nerv. Ment. Dis.*, **120**, 79-82.

EYSENCK, H. J. (1970) *The Structure of Human Personality*. London: Methuen.

FODOR, N. (1947) Varieties of castration. *Amer. Imago*, **2**, 32-48.

FREUD, S. (1949) Analysis of a phobia in a five-year-old boy. In S. FREUD, *Collected Papers*, Vol. III, pp. 149-295. London: Hogarth Press.

FRIEDMAN, S. M. (1952) An empirical study of the castration and Oedipus complexes. *Genet. Psychol. Monogr.*, **2**, 61-130.

KLINE, P. (1972) *Fact and Fantasy in Freudian Theory*. London: Methuen.

KOBLER, F. (1948) Description of an acute castration fear based on superstition. *Psychoanal. Rev.*, **35**, 285-9.

MAHL, G. F. (1969) *Psychological Conflict and Defence.* New York: Harcourt-Brace-Jovanovich.

ROTHENBERG, S. & BRENNER, A. B. (1955) The number 13 as a castration fantasy. *Psychoanal. Quart.*, **24**, 545-59.

SCHWARTZ, B. J. (1955) Measurement of castration anxiety and anxiety over loss of love. *J. Pers.*, **24**, 204-19.

—— (1956) An empirical test of two Freudian hypotheses concerning castration anxiety. *J. Pers.*, **24**, 318-27.

SOUTHWELL, E. A. & MERBAUM, M. (eds.) (1964) *Personality: Readings in Theory and Research.* Belmont, Calif.: Wadsworth.

STARCKE, A. (1921) The castration complex. *Int. J. Psychoanal.*, **2**, 179-201.

WILSON, G. D. (1973) *The Psychology of Conservatism.* London: Academic Press.

9

Calvin Hall and Robert L. Van de Castle (1965)[1]

An empirical investigation of the castration complex in dreams[2]

Journal of Personality, 33, 20-9

According to the classical theory of the castration complex as it was formulated by Freud (1925, 1931, 1933), the male is afraid of losing his penis (castration anxiety) and the female envies the male for having a penis (penis envy). One consequence of this envy is that she wants to deprive the male of his organ (castration wish).

The empirical work investigating this topic has generally produced results consistent with Freud's formulation. Hattendorf (1932) indicated that the second most frequent question asked of mothers by children in the 2- to 5-year-old group concerned the physical differences between the sexes. Horney (1932) reported that when a clinic doctor tried to induce boys and girls to insert a finger in a ball that had developed a split, significantly more boys than girls hesitated or refused to accede to this request. Using a doll play interview Conn (1940) noted that two-thirds of children who reported that they had seen the genitals of the opposite sex could not recall their attitude or feelings about the initial discovery and over one-third who could recall their attitude definitely felt something was wrong. On the basis of these results the author concludes (Conn, 1940, p. 754), 'It appears that the large majority of boys and girls responded to the first sight of genital differences with tranquil, unperturbed acceptance.' This conclusion was criticized by Levy (1940), who carried out repeated doll play interviews with children and concluded (p. 762), 'The typical response of the children in our culture, when they become aware of the primary difference in sex

[1]Institute of Dream Research.

[2]This investigation was supported by a USPHS research grant No. MH 06510 from the National Institute of Mental Health, USPHS.

anatomy, confirms the psychoanalyst's finding, namely, that castration anxiety is aroused in boys and a feeling of envy with destructive impulse toward the penis in girls.' In a widely quoted review of psychoanalytic studies by Sears (1943) a few years later he summed up the castration studies with the statement (p. 36), 'Freud seriously overestimated the frequency of the castration complex.' In a study of problem children, Huschka (1944) reported that 73 per cent of parents dealt with masturbation problems destructively and that the most common threat was that of genital injury. The normal children used by Friedman (1952) completed stories involving castration situations and the author interpreted his data as offering support for the commonness of castration anxiety, particularly in the case of boys.

The remaining studies used college students as subjects. Blum (1949) found significantly more responses to the Blacky Test indicative of castration anxiety among males than females. A method of scoring castration anxiety from TAT scores was developed by Schwartz (1955) who found (1956) that male homosexuals displayed significantly more castration anxiety than normal males and that males obtained higher castration anxiety scores than females. Using a multiple-choice question about the castration card of the Blacky, Sarnoff and Corwin (1959) reported that males with high castration scores showed significantly greater increase in fear of death than low castration males did after being exposed to sexually arousing stimuli.

The foregoing studies indicate that techniques designed to elicit unconscious material are generally successful in demonstrating the manifestations of the castration complex that would be predictable from Freudian theory. It should follow then, that since dreams have been characterized as 'the royal road to the unconscious', manifestations of the castration complex would be clearly discernible in dreams. The present study was undertaken to investigate whether differences in dream contents, presumably related to castration reactions, would appear between adult male and female dreamers.

The specific hypothesis tested in this investigation is that male dreamers will report more dreams expressive of castration anxiety than they will dreams involving castration wishes and penis envy while the pattern will be reversed for females, i.e., they will report more dreams containing expressions of castration wishes and penis envy than they will dreams containing castration anxiety.

METHOD

Subjects

A total of 120 college students divided into three groups of 20 males and 20 females each served as *S*s. Groups 1 and 2 were students in Hall's undergraduate class in personality at Western Reserve University during 1947 and 1948. The recording of nocturnal dreams was described to the students as a class project for which they would be given extra credit if they participated, but would not be penalized for not doing so. They were given opportunities to earn extra credit in other ways than recording dreams. Dreams were reported on a standard report form. These dreams have been published in *Primary Records in Psychology* (Barker & Kaplan, 1963), and Groups 1 and 2 consist of the first 40 of the 43 female series and the first 40 of the 44 male series reported therein.

Group 3 were students in Van de Castle's class in abnormal psychology at the University of Denver during 1962 and 1963. They were required to hand in an average of two dreams a week. Standard instructions similar to those on Hall's form were given. Students were allowed to turn in daydreams if they could recall no nocturnal dreams, but only nocturnal dreams were scored in this study.

Scoring for Castration Complex Indicators in Dreams

A scoring manual which sets forth the criteria for castration anxiety (CA), castration wish (CW), and penis envy (PE) in reported dreams was devised. These criteria were selected because either they directly reflect concern over castration or they represent displacements from one part of the body, i.e., the genitals, to another part of the body, e.g., the hand, or they make use of commonly recognized symbols for the male genitals, e.g., guns, knives, and pens. Copies of a revised version of the original manual (*Institute of Dream Research*, 1964) are available on request to the authors. A summary of the criteria follows.

Criteria for Castration Anxiety

1. Actual or threatened loss, removal, injury to or pain in a specific part of the dreamer's body; actual or threatened cutting, clawing, biting or stabbing of the dreamer's body as a whole or to any part of the dreamer's body; defect of a specified part of the

dreamer's body; some part of the dreamer's body is infantile, juvenile, or undersized.

2. Actual or threatened injury or damage to, loss of, or defect in an object or animal belonging to the dreamer or one that is in his possession in the dream.

3. Inability or difficulty of the dreamer in using his penis or an object that has phallic characteristics; inability or difficulty of the dreamer in placing an object in a receptacle.

4. A male dreams that he is a woman or changes into a woman, or has or acquires female secondary sex characteristics, or is wearing woman's clothes or accessories.

Criteria for Castration Wish

1. The criteria for castration wish are the same as those for castration anxiety except that they do not occur to the dreamer but to another person in his dream.

Criteria for Penis Envy

1. Acquisition *within* the dream by the dreamer of an object that has phallic characteristics; acquisition of a better penis or an impressive phallic object.

2. The dreamer envies or admires a man's physical characteristics or performance or possession that has phallic characteristics.

3. A female dreams that she is a man or changes into a man, or has acquired male secondary sex characteristics, or is wearing man's clothing or accessories which are not customarily worn by women.

Each dream was read and scored for each of these criteria. The maximum score was one point for each condition, even if several independent instances of the same condition occurred within the dream. It was possible, however, for the same dream to be scored for more than one condition, e.g., a dream could be given one point for CA and one point for PE.

After the writers had acquired practice in the use of the manual, a reliability study was made. 119 dreams of eight males and 123 dreams of eight females were scored independently by the writers. The scores were then compared. An agreement was counted if both judges scored the same condition, e.g. a castration anxiety, in the same dream or if both judges did not score a condition, e.g., penis envy, in the same dream. A disagreement was counted if one judge scored for a condition and the other judge did not score for the same condition in the same dream. The results are presented in Table 9.1.

TABLE 9.1. *Percentage of agreement between two scorers.*

Number Dreamers	Number Dreams	Castration Anxiety	Castration Wish	Penis Envy
8 males	119	87	94	96
8 females	123	89	94	93
16	242	88	94	94

Results

The number of dreams containing scorable elements for the three groups of *S*s is shown in Table 9.2. It will be noted that in every group the number of male dreams exceeds the number of female dreams for castration anxiety, while in every group the number of female dreams is higher than male dreams for both the castration wish and the penis envy categories.

TABLE 9.2. *Number of dreams showing castration anxiety (CA), castration wish (CW) and penis envy (PE) among college students.*

	Number of Dreams Analyzed		Number of Dreams Containing Castration Anxiety		Castration Wish		Penis Envy	
GROUP*	MALE	FEMALE	M	F	M	F	M	F
1	308	305	40	7	5	8	2	5
2	327	328	54	15	11	21	5	13
3	318	323	57	35	21	32	9	14
Total	953	956	151	57	37	61	16	32
Range (per dreamer)	7–24	10–21	0–8	0–4	0–4	0–6	0–2	0–3

*N = 20 male and 20 female dreamers for each group.

Since the distribution of scores for any category was markedly skewed with zero scores predominating for many individual dreamers, it was felt that the assumptions for any parametric statistic such as t could not be met. Statistical evaluation of the hypothesis was therefore made by use of the Chi-square technique. The unit of analysis was the *individual dreamer*. The analysis consisted of determining the number of male and female dreamers whose CA score exceeded the combined total of their CW and PE scores and the number of male and female dreamers whose combined CW and PE scores exceeded their CA score. Ties (10 male and 19 female) were evenly divided between these two groupings. The resulting 2 × 2 table is shown in Table 9.3.

TABLE 9.3. *Number of male and female dreamers with CA scores higher and lower than CW and PE scores.*

	CA more than CW and PE	CW and PE more than CA	Total
Number of male dreamers	48	12	60
Number of female dreamers	21·5	38·5	60
	69·5	50·5	120

$\chi^2 = 24$

The majority of male dreamers had higher CA scores while the majority of female dreamers had higher CW and PE scores. The hypothesis of this study was thus supported at a high level of statistical significance ($p < .001$).

Do each of the conditions, CW and PE, contribute substantially to the obtained difference? Table 9.2 reveals that each of these conditions appears in approximately twice as many female dreams as male dreams. To make sure that such a difference was not produced by a few atypical dreamers, a count was made of the number of women whose scores for each of these separate conditions exceeded that of their CA score. It was found that 20 women had CW scores higher than CA scores, whereas only 5 males scored in this direction, and that 12 women had PE scores higher than their CA scores whereas the same was true for only 1 male. The answer to the question raised earlier is that both CW and PE contribute substantially to the obtained difference.

To look at the sex differences from another viewpoint let us examine the relative freedom from castration anxiety in male and female dreamers. Exactly 50 per cent ($N=30$) of women in the present sample had zero CA scores whereas only 13 per cent ($N=8$) of males received zero CA scores. These additional analyses concur in supporting the hypothesis of this investigation, namely that manifestations of castration anxiety in dreams are more typical of males and manifestations of both castration wishes and penis envy are more typical of females.

DISCUSSION

Although the differences are clearcut in favour of the hypothesis, nonetheless there are many manifestations of castration wish and penis envy in men's dreams and many manifestations of castration anxiety in women. The male's wish to castrate others and his envy and admiration of another man's physical and sexual equipment are not difficult to understand. In view of the great amount of physical aggression that is expressed in men's dreams (Hall and Domhoff, 1963), and the amount of competition that men engage in during their waking life, perhaps it is not surprising that their dreams should contain castration wishes and penis envy. Moreover, these may be, as psychoanalytic theory claims, an archaic wish in the male to castrate the father which manifests itself in displaced ways in their dreams. But castration anxiety still takes precedence over these other themes in male dreams.

The amount of castration anxiety in female dreams is less easy, perhaps, to comprehend. Why should there be anxiety over losing something they do not have and never have had? The psychoanalytic explanation is that females unconsciously feel they once had the same genital organs as the male, and that they were taken from them. The menses are a constant reminder of this fantasied event. Accordingly, we would expect to find in their dreams expressions of this fantasied castration. Men dream of what might happen whereas women dream of what they think has happened. The fact that anxiety is usually stronger for an anticipated future event than for a realized past one would explain why men have more castration anxiety than women do.

It will be observed (Table 9.2) that more castration anxiety is expressed in the dreams of males (151 occurrences) than castration wish plus penis envy is in the dreams of females (93 occurrences). The explanation for this may be that the female displaces her penis envy in other ways than that of wishing to castrate others. Freud (1917) mentions two such displacements. He writes: 'In girls, the discovery of the penis gives rise to envy for it, which later changes into the wish for a man as the possessor of a penis. Even before this the wish for a penis has changed into a wish for a baby' (p. 132).

This suggested to us another testable hypothesis, namely, that more dreams of babies and of getting married should be reported by women than by men. Accordingly, we went through the 1909 dreams and scored them for the presence of weddings and babies. Females had 60 dreams in which weddings or preparations for weddings occurred: males had only 9 such dreams. Females had 85 dreams in which babies or very young children figured; males had 32 such dreams. These findings appear to confirm the hypothesis, although, of course, other explanations for women dreaming more than men do of weddings and babies may occur to the reader.

The subjects of this investigation were for the most part in their late teens and early twenties. What happens to manifestations of the castration complex in dreams with age? Relative to this question we would like to mention the findings obtained from analyzing 600 dreams collected from a man between the ages of 37 and 54. The 600 dreams were divided into six sets of 100 dreams each. Each dream was scored for castration anxiety, castration wish, and penis envy. The results are presented in Table 9.4. The incidence for each of the three categories does not vary to any great extent over the 17 years, nor do the averages differ noticeably from the averages for college men. In this one case, at least, castration anxiety appears to express itself at the same rate in dreams into the fifties.

TABLE 9.4. *Manifestations of the Castration Complex in the dreams of a middle-aged man.*

	Incidence per 100 dreams							Average for
	I	II	III	IV	V	VI	Average	College Men
Castration anxiety	14	18	13	15	10	17	14·5	15·8
Castration wish	4	3	2	5	8	5	4·5	3·9
Penis envy	2	1	2	0	1	2	1·3	1·7

In an earlier investigation by one of the writers (Hall, 1955), it was concluded that the dream of being attacked is not a manifestation of castration anxiety as suggested by the findings of Harris (1948) but represents the feminine attitudes of weakness, passivity, inferiority and masochism as formulated by Freud. The findings of the present study do not conflict with the earlier one because the criteria used for scoring castration anxiety were different from the criterion used for identifying the dream of being attacked. The dream of being attacked consists, for the most part, of attacks on or threats to the dreamer's *whole* body. In the present study, attacks upon the whole body are categorically excluded except for a small number of cases where the threat is one of cutting, clawing, biting, or stabbing. The damage or threat must be to a *specific part* of the body in order for it to be scored as castration anxiety. Moreover, the criteria used in the present investigation are much more extensive. They include damage to a possession of the dreamer, his difficulty in using phallic objects, and the feminization of a male.

Although the hypothesis of this investigation was derived from Freudian theory, and its confirmation therefore supports the theory, the results may be accounted for by other theoretical positions. For example, the greater incidence of injuries and accidents in male dreams may merely reflect the nature of the activities in which they engage in waking life as compared with the activities of women. It is believed that men engage in more dangerous activities and take more risks than women do. If this is the case it might be expected that their dreams would be in accord with their waking life experiences. On the other hand, if they do in fact take more chances and risk physical harm, this raises the question of why they do. It does not suffice, we feel, to say that they have adopted the role which 'society' has fashioned for them. Why has 'society' created such a role and why do boys acquiesce in being shaped to the role? *Ad hoc* explanations of findings, in any event, are not very satisfying.

SUMMARY

This study was undertaken to investigate whether sex differences would be found in the incidence of manifestations of castration anxiety (CA), castration wish (CW), and penis envy (PE) in dreams. Criteria for each of these three components of the castration complex were formulated on the basis of which a scoring manual was written.

It was hypothesized that male dreamers will report more dreams expressive of CA than they will dreams involving CW and PE whereas the pattern will be reversed for females, i.e., they will report more dreams containing expressions of CW and PE than they will dreams containing CA. The hypothesis was supported for three different groups of college students evenly divided as to sex, and the combined results for the 120 students were significant beyond the .001 level.

Additional data were also presented to show that many more women than men dream about babies and weddings and that the relative incidence of the various castration components remains quite stable throughout a long dream series spanning 17 years.

Although the results are congruent with Freudian theory, and to that extent add to the construct validity of the castration complex, it was recognized that alternative theoretical positions could be invoked to account for the findings of this investigation.

COMMENT

This study must rank among the most celebrated of empirical 'verifications' of Freudian theory. It is reprinted in Lindzey and Hall's *Theories of Personality: Primary Sources and Research* (1965), one of the criteria for selecting articles being that they 'should provide clear evidence relevant to a hypothesis explicitly derived from the relevant theory'. Kline (1972) describes it as 'impressive support for the Freudian concept of the castration complex, as indeed it is for psychoanalytic dream theory' (p. 113). The Hall and Van de Castle study is particularly important for Freudian theory because it is apparently the *only* empirical study that has been widely accepted as evidence for the penis envy concept. Kline's exhaustive review cites two other studies, those of Johnson (1966) and Landy (1967), but treats both as jokes. (It is not clear whether or not they were intended by their authors to be satirical.)

Basically, the study purports to show that the dreams of men include more events that indicate castration anxiety, while women's dreams are more suggestive of penis envy and castration anxiety. But there is an astonishing flaw in the methodolgy. Several of the criteria for scoring castration anxiety in dreams are so phrased that they could only logically apply to males (e.g. 'Inability or difficulty of the dreamer in using his penis . . .'; 'A male dreams that he is a woman or changes into a woman, or has or acquires female secondary sex characteristics, or is wearing women's clothes or accessories'). Quite apart from the fact that it is hard to see much connection between these activities and castration anxiety, they cannot be scored for females anyway – so it is not surprising that males obtained higher scores. Likewise, the criteria for scoring penis envy included: 'The dreamer envies or admires a man's physical characteristics'; 'A female dreams that she is a man or has acquired male secondary sex characteristics, or is wearing men's clothing or accessories'. *Since these dreams could not logically be scored for males, the 'discovery' of a greater number of 'penis envy dreams' in females is tautological.* On these grounds at least, we could discount the Hall and Van de Castle study as a test of the Freudian hypothesis.

Even if we were charitable or imperceptive enough to overlook this drastic flaw in procedure, the sex difference in dream content could still be explained more parsimoniously in terms of the characteristic activities and interests of men and women (see comment on Hall, 1963, above). The authors themselves admit that the greater incidence of injuries and accidents in male dreams (also interpreted as castration anxiety) might simply reflect the fact that men engage in more dangerous activities than women in waking life. As regards the dreams of women, how can we say that the appearance of phallic symbols indicates penis *envy* rather than penis *interest*? It may be that women want a penis *in* them, not *on* them. Hall and Van de Castle also found that women dream more about babies and weddings, interpreting this as a manifestation of 'displaced penis envy'. Might it not mean simply that women are more interested in these things than men?

Why *penis* envy anyway? Could this be male conceit on the part of Freud? A feminist version of Freudian theory with a central concept of 'cavity envy' would account just as well for the empirical 'evidence' provided by Hall and Van de Castle. The high incidence of castration themes in male dreams would then be interpreted as a reflection of their *castration wish*, while females would dream about phallic symbols because of their *penis anxiety* (the fear that some day they might grow a dreadful cancerous protruberance in their crutch like that which they saw on their brother during infancy). This theory is not seriously put up as an alternative explanation of the results of this study, but simply to illustrate the flexibility of Freudian-type theorizing and interpretation. The point is that Hall and Van de Castle have completely sidestepped the problem of explaining why it is that women allegedly dream about phallic objects because they *want* a penis, while men dream about injury to their genitals because they *don't want* to be castrated.

On the basis of these considerations we conclude that the Hall and Van de Castle study cannot be taken as providing support either for the castration complex or for the Freudian theory of dream interpretation.

REFERENCES

BARKER, R. & KAPLAN, B. (eds.) (1963) *Primary Records in Psychology*. Publication No. 2. Lawrence, Kansas: Univ. of Kansas Publications.

BLUM, G. S. (1949) A study of the psychoanalytic theory of psychosexual development. *Genet. Psychol. Monogr.*, **39**, 3-99.

CONN, J. H. (1940) Children's reactions to the discovery of genital differences. *Amer. J. Orthopsychiat.*, **10**, 747-54.

FREUD, S. (1917) On transformations of instinct as exemplified in anal erotism. In *The Standard Edition*, Vol. XVII, pp. 127-33. London: Hogarth Press, 1955.

—— (1925) Some physical consequences of the anatomical distinction between the sexes. In *The Standard Edition*, Vol. XIX, pp. 248-58. London: Hogarth Press, 1961.

—— (1931) Female sexuality. In *The Standard Edition*, Vol. XXI, pp. 225-43. London: Hogarth Press, 1961.

—— (1933) *A New Series of Introductory Lectures on Psychoanalysis*. Chapter 5, pp. 153-85. New York: Norton.

FRIEDMAN, S. M. (1952) An empirical study of the castration and Oedipus complexes. *Genet. Psychol. Monogr.*, **46**, 61-130.

HALL, C. S. (1955) The significance of the dream of being attacked. *J. Pers.*, **24**, 168-80.

HALL, C. & DOMHOFF, B. (1963) Aggression in dreams. *Internat. J. Soc. Psychiat.*, **9**, 259-67.

HARRIS, I. (1948) Observations concerning typical anxiety dreams. *Psychiatry*, **11**, 301-9.

HATTENDORF, K. W. (1932) A study of the questions of young children concerning sex. *J. Soc. Psychol.*, **3**, 37-65.

HORNEY, KAREN (1932) The dread of woman. *Internat. J. Psychoanal.*, **13**, 348-60.

HUSCHKA, MABEL (1944) The incidence and character of masturbation threats in a group of problem children. In S. S. TOMKINS (ed.), *Contemporary Psychopathology*. Cambridge, Mass.: Harvard Univ. Press.

INSTITUTE OF DREAM RESEARCH (1964) *A Manual for Scoring Castration Anxiety, Castration Wishes, and Penis Envy in Dreams.*

JOHNSON, G. B. (1966) Penis envy or pencil needing? *Psychol. Rep.*, **19**, 758.

KLINE, P. (1972) *Fact and Fantasy in Freudian Theory*. London: Methuen.

LANDY, E. E. (1967) Sex differences in some aspects of smoking behaviour. *Psychol. Rep.*, **20**, 578-80.

LEVY, D. M. (1940) 'Control-situation' studies of children's responses to the differences in genitalia. *Amer. J. Orthopsychiat.*, **10**, 755-62.

LINDZEY, G. & HALL, C. S. (1965) *Theories of Personality: Primary Sources and Research*. New York: Wiley.

SARNOFF, I. & CORWIN, S. B. (1959) Castration anxiety and the fear of death. *J. Pers.*, **27**, 374-85.

SCHWARTZ, B. J. (1955) Measurement of castration anxiety and anxiety over loss of love. *J. Pers.*, **24**, 204-19.

—— (1956) An empirical test of two Freudian hypotheses concerning castration anxiety. *J. Pers.*, **24**, 318-27.

SEARS, R. (1943) Survey of objective studies of psychoanalytic concepts. *Soc. Sci. Res. Coun., Bulletin*, 51.

PART THREE

Repression

10

David S. Holmes (1972) [1]

Repression or interference? [2] A further investigation

Journal of Personality and Social Psychology, 22, No. 2, 163-70

The experiment was carried out to determine whether the reduced recall usually observed in subjects after receiving ego-threatening information is due to repression or interference. Subjects learned a list of words, had their recall tested for the list, and then took a personality test in which the words were used as stimuli. Subjects were then given either ego-threatening, ego-enhancing, or neutral feedback. Following this, they were tested for recall again, debriefed, and tested for recall once more. Subjects receiving threatening and enhancing feedback performed alike and showed poorer recall on the post feedback test than the subjects receiving neutral feedback. Since the subjects in the threat and enhancement conditions performed the same in terms of the number and nature of the words forgotten and since there was no reason to expect repression in the enhancement condition, it was concluded that post-feedback recall decrements were due to interference.

The research strategy that has been most influential in offering support for the concept of repression was developed by Zeller (1950a). This approach has three major parts. First, experimental and control subjects learn and have their retention tested for a list of words. On this test, no differences are expected. Second, the experimental subjects are 'ego threatened' (subjects are forced to fail on another task or are given negative personality feedback), while control subjects are not threatened. Then both groups are given a second recall test for the words. Since it is assumed that the anxiety introduced by the threat procedure will generalize to the words because they were learned in the same situation, and since it is also

[1]Requests for reprints should be sent to David S. Holmes, Department of Psychology, University of Kansas, Lawrence, Kansas, 66044.

The author would like to thank B. Kent Houston for his help with the preparation of the manuscript and Roger H. Ratliff for his assistance with the data collection.

[2]This investigation was supported by United States Public Health Service Grant 1 RO1 MH20819-01.

assumed that this anxiety will result in repression, it is predicted that on the second recall test the performance of the experimental subjects will be below that of the control subjects. Third, in an attempt to 'lift the repression', the threat is eliminated (subjects are allowed to succeed or are debriefed), and the subjects are then given a third recall test on which it is predicted that there will be no differences in recall between the groups. Using this approach, numerous investigators have found results consistent with the predictions, and these results have been cited as empirical evidence for the existence of repression (Aborn, 1953; Flavell, 1955; Merrill, 1954; Penn, 1964; Truax, 1957; Worchell, 1955; Zeller, 1950b, 1951).

Recently, the interpretation of these findings as evidence for repression has been called into question by two investigations. D'Zurilla (1965) carried out post-experimental interviews with subjects who had participated in an experiment similar to the one discussed above and, contrary to what would be expected on the basis of repression, found that 62 per cent of the experimental subjects thought about things related to the threatening task, while only 24 per cent of the control subjects thought about things related to their task; that is, the experimental subjects attended to rather than avoided the threat. D'Zurilla went on to point out that the additional thoughts of the experimental subjects were irrelevant to the task of recalling the words, and he therefore speculated that the 'increase in amount of conflicting cognitive events could have reduced the efficiency of recall [p. 256]' in the experimental group. In other words, he suggested that the reduced recall following ego threat might be due to response competition rather than to repression.

Holmes and Schallow (1969) attempted to experimentally test the question of whether reduced recall following ego threat was due to repression or response competition. In addition to the groups that received ego-threatening (experimental) or no (control) feedback, these investigators employed a third group which was shown a neutral movie (interference). After the experimental manipulation (negative feedback, no feedback, interfering movie), all of the subjects were tested for their retention of some previously learned words. They were then debriefed and tested again for retention. Consistent with the predictions based on the interference theory, the investigators found that while there were no differences among the groups prior to the experimental manipulation, after the manipulation, the control group performed significantly better than either the ego-threat or interference groups and, of most importance, that there were no differences between the performance of the ego-threat or interference groups. After the debriefing, which redirected the subjects' attention to the words, the recall test again indicated no differences between any of the groups. In reviewing their results, Holmes and Schallow (1969) pointed out that:

> If only the curves of the control and ego-threat groups are considered, the results of the present study can be viewed as a replication of the earlier work in which it was concluded that the ego threat had resulted in repression. However, the fact that in the present study the performance of the interference group differed from the control group but did not differ from the ego-threat group suggests that previous interpretations of differences between ego-threat and control groups as being due to repression could be called into serious question . . . While it is impossible to prove the null hypothesis that the same process was operating in both the ego-threat and interference conditions, the inability to generate differential predictions which are supported by the data is certainly suggestive. It might, therefore, be that response competition rather than repression is responsible for the lowered recall performance found in the ego-threat condition of experiments of this type [pp. 150-1].

As the authors indicated, the fact that the interference and ego-threat groups performed in the same way does not necessarily prove that the same process was operating in both situations. This criticism is especially relevant since in their experiment the two hypothesized interferences were very different in origin and nature; that is, in the interference condition, the interference stemmed entirely from an extrinsic source (the movie) and was impersonal, while the hypothesized interference in the ego-threat condition was intrinsic to the individual (concerns about adjustment) and highly personal. These are important differences, and they increase the conceptual distance between the conditions that the authors wanted to suggest as equivalent. If the interference that was hypothesized to be present in the two conditions had been more similar in source and nature, the authors would have been in a better position to suggest that repression was actually due to interference and response competition.

The present experiment was carried out in an attempt to overcome the problems noted above. Similar to the earlier experiment, the subjects in the control condition were given neutral feedback, while the subjects in one experimental condition were given negative 'ego-threatening' personality feedback. In contrast to the previous work, however, in the second experimental group, an attempt was made to introduce interference by giving the subjects positive 'ego-enhancing' personality feedback.

In this experiment the only difference between the ego-threatening and interference conditions was the fact that in one case the feedback was ego threatening, while in the other it was ego enhancing. This difference is, of course, crucial for the different predictions stemming from the interference and the repression theories. Interference theory ignores the threat versus enhancing nature of the feedback and suggests that the same type of interference (thoughts about the feedback) would be elicited and, therefore, would affect recall in both experimental conditions. Consequently, this position would not predict a difference in recall performance between the two experimental groups. Furthermore, since it was expected that less interference would be elicited in the control condition than in either of the experimental conditions, interference theory would predict that after the experimental manipulation, the recall performance of the control subjects would be superior to that of the experimental subjects. On the other hand, repression theory emphasizes the influence of ego threat and predicts a reduced recall only for those subjects exposed to an ego threat. That is, the repression position would predict that the performances of the subjects in the control and ego-enhancement conditions would be similar and that the performance of the subjects in these conditions would be superior to that of subjects in the ego-threat condition. These are the differential predictions that were under investigation in the present experiment.

Interestingly enough, with regard to post-debriefing performance, both theories predict an improvement. In the case of interference theory, the improvement would stem from the fact that after being debriefed, the subjects would no longer be distracted by the thoughts and concerns elicited by the feedbacks, while according to repression theory the improvement would stem from a return of the repressed made possible by the elimination of the anxiety.

METHOD

Subjects

Subjects in this experiment were 36 women from introductory psychology classes at the University of Texas at Austin. Subjects were run in groups of two, and each subject was assigned to one of three conditions. During the experiment, each subject was seated in a chair facing a projection screen and was separated by a partition from the other subject. Attached to the arm of the subject's chair was a 'response panel' which contained one green signal light and four switches labelled A, B, C, and D. The experimenter sat behind the subjects at a screened-off control centre where he controlled the signal light and recorded which switches were thrown by the subjects.

Procedure

When the subjects arrived at the laboratory, they were assigned a seat and then told that the experiment would be run completely by a computer located in an adjoining room. The experimenter then threw a switch and took his place at the control centre. Throwing the switch activated a concealed tape recorder which was supposedly running in conjunction with the computer and which was used to present all of the instructions. The subjects were first presented with a list of 40 words that was read twice. It was pointed out that these words would be used in a later part of the experiment and that at this point the subjects should 'just listen to the words and become familiar with them'. The words that were presented were the same ones used earlier by Holmes and Schallow (1969, p. 147, Table 1). After the words had been read, the subjects were asked to write down as many of the words as they could remember on a word familiarity check form. Supposedly, this was done as a check on their familiarity with the words, but actually it provided the premanipulation measure of recall for the words. After 2 minutes, the forms were collected, and the tape-recorded instructions went on to explain that the experiment in which the subjects were participating was a test 'of a very sensitive and accurate test of personality . . . which can be used to predict future adjustment and performance in college women' and which was being adapted for use at the university. It was explained to the subjects that 'the famous Rorschach Psychodiagnostic Inkblots' would be projected on the screen one by one, and that while each blot was on the screen, four nouns would be read aloud to them. The task of each subject was to decide which of the four nouns best described the blot she was looking at and to indicate her choice by throwing the appropriate switch on her response panel. They were led to believe that this would register their responses in the computer, which would then score the responses and give each subject feedback concerning each of her responses. Feedback was provided via the light on the response panel which flashed on and off one, two or three times after the subject made each response. Each subject was told to count the flashes and record the number on the score sheet she had been given. The score sheets supposedly were going to be collected at the end of the session so that the members of the Psychology Department could evaluate the subjects' performance and determine whether the subjects 'should receive future attention of any kind'. Between recording their scores and being presented with the next inkblot, the subjects were told to use the number of flashes they had received as feedback after their preceding response to look up the meaning of that response in the computer code books that they had been given. Each computer code book contained three response interpretations for each blot; one ego enhancing, one ego threatening, and one neutral. Each interpretation was printed on a separate page, and the pages were official-looking computer printouts. Each interpretation page had a table on it identifying the blot and the number of flashes with which that interpretation was associated. Three different books were constructed so that the same number of flashes would result in three different feedbacks, depending on which book was being use. Consequently, in any one experimental session, the subjects in different conditions could be run despite the fact that the apparatus gave all subjects the same number of flashes for feedback. Subjects in the threat and enhancement conditions received negative or positive feedback after responding to Blots II, III, VI, VIII, and X. For example, after Blot VI, in the enhancement group, the subjects were informed that

> This response is indicative of outstanding leadership abilities. The leadership ability should enable this woman to assume positions of responsibility in large groups as well as in interpersonal relationships, and she should meet with considerable success.

After Blot X, they were informed that

> This response indicates that the individual is exceptionally well adjusted. This level of adjustment will enable her to function at a personal and academic level well above that of the average college student.

On the other hand, after Blot VI, the subjects in the threat group were informed that

> This response indicates the possibility that the individual has some underlying personality problems. Either at the present time or in the near future this underlying maladjustment could cause serious difficulties for this person in her interpersonal relations with friends and superiors.

After Blot X, they were informed that 'This response is suggestive of a high degree of pathology, and corrective steps must be considered.' After responding to these blots, the subjects in the neutral condition received feedback indicating that their response had no particular significance. Feedback to all subjects after responding to Blots IV, VII, and IX indicated that 'This response is consistent with previous responses thus confirming previous feedback. This response adds no new information.' Subjects were not given feedback after responding to the first blot since the computer supposedly did not yet have enough information.

It is important to note that the words offered as response possibilities for the Rorschach inkblots were the same as those presented on the list at the beginning of the experiment and for which recall was tested. In this way, threat was directly associated with the material that was to be recalled.

After the subjects had looked up the interpretation of their last response, the score sheets and the computer code books were collected, and then the subjects were given the second 2-minute recall test using a word familiarity check form. This provided the measure of the subjects' post-manipulation recall for the words. After this recall test, the tape-recorded voice of the experimenter completely debriefed the subjects concerning the experimental manipulations. The subjects were then given a final 2-minute recall test using a word familiarity check form, and this provided the post-debriefing recall measure.

In summary, the procedure was as follows: learning task for 40 words; pretreatment recall test for words (Test 1); Rorschach administration (previously learned 40 words as response alternatives) with subjects getting either ego-threatening, ego-enhancing, or neutral feedback; post-treatment recall test for words (Test 2); debriefing, post-debriefing recall tests for words (Test 3). It should be noted that the procedure was almost completely automated and that the subjects were simultaneously run in different conditions, therefore reducing or eliminating any subtle experimenter effects. The high degree of automation in addition to the large amount of bogus technical information that the subjects were given concerning the test, its scoring, and the built-in safeguards to assure the reliability and validity of the feedback served to make the deceptions very believable.

RESULTS

The manipulations used in this experiment were evidently quite credible since only one subject (enhancement condition) indicated

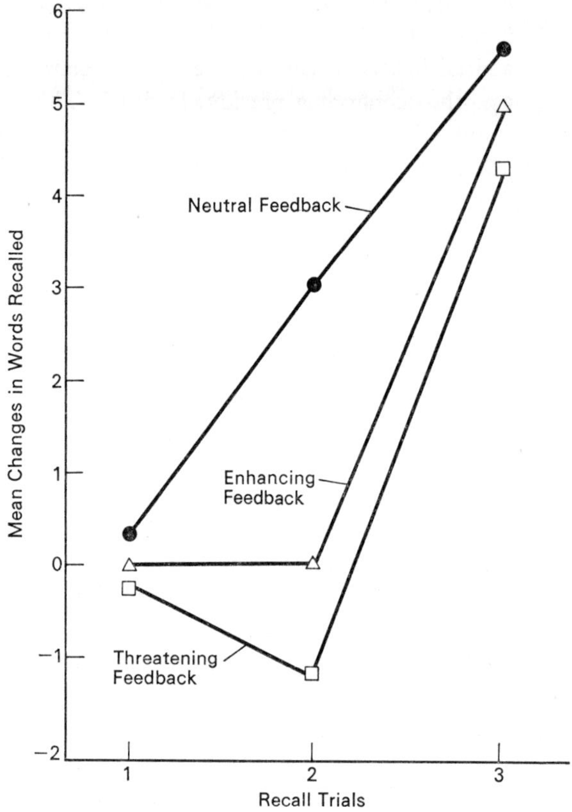

Figure 10.1. *Mean changes in words recalled by the subjects in the ego-threatening, ego-enhancing, and neutral feedback conditions. (Since change scores were plotted in this figure, all scores at Point* 1 *are actually* 0 *and were included only as a reference point.)*

that she did not believe the instructions. The data from this subject and those of one other subject in the enhancement condition who did not follow the instructions were not used in the analyses. The recall data are presented graphically in Figure 10.1.

Effect of Differential Feedback on Recall

A between-within analysis of variance comparing the recall performance of the three groups (neutral, enhancing, threatening) over the three trials (Recall Tests 1, 2, and 3) was carried out on the data. This analysis indicated that the groups effect was not significant (F=.97, df=2/31), that the trials effect was significant (F=37.94, df=2/62, p<.001), and that the Groups × Trials interaction approached significance (F=2.20, df=4/62, p=.079). The important question to be answered, however, was which of the two rival hypotheses (i.e., repression or interference) was best able to account for the patterning of results. The repression hypothesis predicted that on the second trial the neutral and the enhancement groups would perform alike and better than the threat group. On the other hand, the interference hypothesis predicted that on the second trial the neutral group would perform better than the threat and enhancement groups and that these latter two groups would perform alike. Neither the repression nor interference hypotheses predicted differences between any of the groups on Trials 1 (before manipulation) or 3 (after debriefing). In other words, the hypotheses differed concerning whether on Trial 2 the enhancement group would perform like the neutral group (repression hypothesis) or whether it would perform like the threat group (interference hypothesis). The following procedure was used to statistically evaluate the rival hypotheses. The sum of squares for the Groups × Trials interaction (with 4 degrees of freedom) was partitioned into two components. One component (with 1 degree of freedom) reflected the extent to which the obtained means were congruent with what was expected from the particular hypothesis in question, namely, interference or repression. The other component (with 3 degrees of freedom) was the remainder sum of squares for the interaction not accounted for by the predicted relationships (after Winer, 1962, p. 65). The results indicated that the component of the Groups × Trials interaction predicted by the interference hypothesis was significant at the .01 level of confidence (F=7.27, df=1/62), while the F for the remainder was less than one and not significant (F=.51 df=3/62). On the other hand, the component of the Groups × Trials interaction predicted by the repression hypothesis was significant at only the .05 level of confidence ($F=4.03$, $df=1/62$), while the F for the remainder was greater than one ($F=1.59$, $df=3/62$, $p<.25$). To decide how well data can be explained by a particular hypothesis, one should know how much of the data *can* be accounted for (the predicted component) as well as how much of the data *cannot* be accounted for (the remainder component). On both counts, the interference hypothesis was superior.[1]

That the performance of the groups conformed to what was expected by the interference hypothesis is further corroborated by the following subanalyses of the data. Between Recall Trials 1 and 2, the neutral group showed greater improvement in recall than either the enhancement or threat groups ($F=2.79$, $df=1/20$, $p=.107$; $F=18.84$, $df=1/22$, $p<.001$). Looked at in another way, the subjects in the neutral group improved in performance ($F=66.00$, $df=1/11$, $p<.001$), while those in the enhancement group remained the same, and those in the threat group deteriorated somewhat ($F=1.73$, $df=1/11$, $p=.213$). The fact that the subjects in the enhancement and threat groups performed in essentially the same manner and differed from the subjects in the neutral group could lead to the conclusion that feedback, irrespective of whether it was very positive or very negative, had the effect of interfering with recall performance, and that it was this interference rather than repression that resulted in the reduced level of recall.

One alternative hypothesis must be examined, however. It may be that the reduced recall on Trial 2 evidenced by the subjects in the threat group was due to repression, while the reduced recall on Trial 2 evidenced by the subjects in the enhancement group was due to interference. That is, while the resulting overall performances were the same, the underlying processes may have been different. If repression was the underlying process, it would be expected that the reduced recall in the threat group resulted from a large decrement in recall of *response words* used by the subjects (i.e., those that the subjects selected as responses) because these were the words directly associated with threatening feedback. It would also be expected that there would be only a minimal decrement in the recall of the words

[1] It should be noted that these two sets of comparisons are not orthogonal and that the only difference between the two components revolves around one mean. Therefore, in view of that and the fact that the component of the interaction predicted by interference was significant at the .01 level, it is not surprising that the component of the interaction predicted by repression was significant at the .05 level.

that were not used as responses (i.e., those that were not selected) because these were not associated with threatening feedback. On the other hand, if interference were the underlying process, it would be expected that the reduced recall in the threat group resulted from a recall decrement distributed across all of the words (i.e., those that were and were not selected as responses and, consequently, were and were not associated with threatening feedback) because interference would influence all words equally.

To test these alternative predictions, the proportions of response words recalled were compared across the three trials for the three groups. (Each subject's score was the number of her response words recalled on a trial divided by the total number of words that she recalled on that trial.) Data from the neutral and enhancement groups were used for comparison since it is clear that repression was not occurring in these groups. The mean proportions are presented in Table 10.1. Inspection and analysis of these data did not suggest that

TABLE 10.1. *Mean proportions of response words recalled.*

Group	Test 1	Test 2	Test 3
Neutral	24	32	34
Enhancement	25	35	33
Threat	23	35	34

on Test 2 the subjects in the threat group recalled proportionally fewer response words than did the subjects in the other groups ($F=.22$, $df=2/31$). Furthermore, a between-within analysis of variance comparing the three groups across the three tests did not reveal the interaction predicted on the basis of repression ($F=.25$, $df=4/62$); that is, the subjects in the threat group did not evidence a relative reduction in their recall of response words on Trial 2. With regard to this latter analysis, it might be noted that there was not a significant groups effect ($F=.92$, $df=2/31$), but there was a significant trials effect ($F=16.53$, $df=2/62$, $p<.001$) which was due to the fact that in each case after words were used as responses (i.e., between Trials 1 and 2), the degree to which they were recalled improved relative to non-response words—a finding that would be expected on the basis of the increased attention that they had received as a function of being used as responses. In summary of these analyses, it is clear that no evidence was found for the predictions based on the theory of repression, and it seems reasonable to conclude that the reduced recall in both the enhancement and threat groups was due to interference caused by thoughts elicited by the feedback.

Effect of Debriefing on Recall

A between-within analysis of variance comparing the performance of the three groups over the second and third recall trials revealed a strong trend in the direction of the predicted interaction ($F=2.21$, $df=2/31$, $p=.125$). Non-orthogonal analyses that were carried out to describe this interaction indicated that the subjects in the enhancement and threat groups evidenced about the same amount of improvement between the second and third trials ($F=.12$, $df=1/20$, $p=.725$), while both of these groups tended to show greater improvements in performance than did the neutral feedback group ($F=2.39$, $df=1/20$, $p=.135$; $F=3.58$, $df=1/22$, $p=.069$). Since the enhancement group evidenced the same amount of improvement as the threat group, and since there was no evidence that repression was occurring in the threat group on Trial 2, it does not seem justified to conclude that this improvement in performance was due to a 'return of the repressed', as it is usually interpreted. Rather, it seems that the general improvement in each of the three groups between Trials 2 and 3 was due to greater attention to the recall task after the debriefing which eliminated thoughts elicited by the previous manipulation and made the task more salient. The greater improvement in the threat and enhancement groups as compared to the neutral group occurred because the subjects in these groups were initially (Trial 2) more distracted and had lower levels of performance, and, therefore, the redirection of their attention had more impact both on their attention and on their subsequent performance. These findings are consistent with the interference explanation and inconsistent with the return-of-the-repressed explanation.

DISCUSSION

From the preceding results it seems clear that the presentation of salient feedback concerning the subject's personality interfered with recall performance on what seemed to the subject to be an unrelated task. Of most importance, however, is the fact that the effect was found regardless of whether the feedback was ego enhancing or ego threatening. The fact that ego-enhancing feedback had essentially the same effect as ego-threatening feedback raises serious questions concerning the interpretation used by many authors that the reduced recall after threatening feedback is due to repression. Similarly, it seems doubtful that the post-debriefing improvement in recall performance that has been noted by many investigators can be attributed to a return of the repressed. The conclusion that post-debriefing improvement cannot be attributed to a return of the repressed stems from the indication of the present experiment that repression was not occurring in the first place and from the finding that the same effect was noted in the ego-enhancing group in which there was no reason to expect repression, much less a return of the repressed.

The present results suggest that the recall decrements found in this experiment and in others of this type were due to problems with retrieval from long-term memory and that these problems were caused by attentional factors. More specifically, because the subjects were able to overcome the earlier recall deficit when their attention was focused on the critical material (i.e., after the debriefing), it must be concluded that the earlier recall deficit was due to poor retrieval of learned material stored in long-term memory. The poor retrieval apparently resulted from the subjects' attention to other (interfering) material. Interestingly enough, the attention-interference explanation is consistent with the results of Aborn (1953), who reported that when subjects were given a set to learn rather than incidental learning instructions, the recall decrement usually attributed to repression did not materialize. That is, when the subjects' set focused their attention on the critical material, there was no decrease in the recall, despite the presence of threat.

It should be noted that the present research is not the first instance in which the interference hypothesis has provided the most viable explanation for a performance deficit associated with personality factors. In their extensive reviews of the research on the performance deficit usually associated with schizophrenia, Buss and Lang (1965) and Lang and Buss (1965) concluded that interference was probably responsible for this deficit. It should be noted that these authors also pointed out that when the schizophrenics' attention and sets were properly focused and maintained, the deficit was eliminated. This effect is not dissimilar from the effect found in the present experiment when the subjects were debriefed and, as a result, had their attentions redirected. What is important here is not that interference impairs performance, because that effect has been known for a long time; what is important is the very strong possibility that the recall deficit that was previously thought to stem from repression is, in fact, a function of interference. This interpretation of the effects may find applicability beyond the research strategy considered in this paper.

It might be suggested that polarizing the question as 'repression *or* interference' is inappropriate and that it would be more constructive to conceive of interference as the process by which repression occurs. With regard to this, however, it should be pointed out that the concept of repression already implies a process, and that process is very different from the interference process. Most important in this regard, however, is the fact that the unconscious plays a crucial role in the process traditionally associated with the process of repression, while it plays no role whatsoever in the interference process discussed here. This difference would result in widely divergent prescriptions for dealing with material that has been 'repressed'. In view of the theoretical confusions and conflicting implications that would result from the synthesis of these concepts, it seems desirable to maintain a clear distinction between them.

In reviewing the threat and enhancing feedback conditions employed in this experiment, it is important to note that in both cases the feedbacks were highly personal and that in both cases the interference that was hypothesized to result from the feedbacks (thoughts about the feedbacks) was produced by the subjects themselves. By using conditions that were so similar, the conceptual distance between the conditions was reduced over what it was in the previous work (Holmes & Schallow, 1969), thus making it easier to suggest that the same process was operating in both conditions when the groups in these conditions evidenced similar performances. Despite this, however, it still must be pointed out that it is impossible to prove the null hypothesis, and, therefore, the fact that the threat and enhancement groups performed the same does not necessarily prove that repression as it is traditionally conceived of was not occurring in the threat group. On the other hand, of course, neither can it be proved that interference was not taking place in the threat group. In considering the alternatives, it seems to the present author that parsimony as well as the weight of experimental evidence is in favour of the interference explanation. Independent of what actually was or was not occurring, and apart from theoretical speculations generated by this research, it must definitely be concluded that because of the alternative explanations for the data, Zeller's (1950a) paradigm cannot be used to provide evidence for the concept of repression. This leaves the concept of repression in a precarious position with respect to the necessary experimental verification.

COMMENT

At this point we might have reprinted the classical study of Zeller (1950b) which first introduces an experimental paradigm that is widely supposed to demonstrate the Freudian concept of repression. Since the appearance of Zeller's work the paradigm has been used many times and frequently cited as evidence for the existence of repression. Instead we have chosen to reprint this recent study by Holmes which incorporates an important criticism of the Zeller paradigm, and, moreover, provides an experimental demonstration that the criticism is applicable.

Zeller had shown that subjects who are 'ego threatened' in some way (e.g. by negative personality feedback) have poorer verbal recall than controls who are not made anxious in this way. The interpretation of this finding was that anxiety induced by the threat procedure had generalized to the verbal material because it was learned in the same experimental situation, and as a result of this anxiety memory for the words was repressed. This study by Holmes tests the alternative hypothesis that the reduced recall following ego threat is due to response competition (interference) rather than repression. This hypothesis is confirmed by the finding that 'ego enhancing' feedback, which may be presumed to be distracting without being threatening, was equally detrimental to recall. These results suggest that 'the recall decrements found in this experiment and in others of this type were due to problems with retrieval from long-term memory and that these problems were caused by attentional factors'. According to Holmes 'this leaves the concept of repression in a precarious position with respect to the necessary experimental verification'.

Certainly we would agree with Holmes, that his finding indicates that none of the studies using Zeller's paradigm can be used as evidence for the concept of repression, and since the argument is fully detailed in the paper above there is no need for us to dwell on it further. There are, however, other approaches to the study of repression that are less obviously open to interpretation in terms of response competition. One such study that has been fairly widely acclaimed is that of Levinger and Clark (1961), to be discussed next. Kline (1972, p. 160) also notes the Holmes criticism of the Zeller paradigm, apparently without being aware that it had been anticipated in a number of papers (e.g. D'Zurilla, 1965; Holmes and Schallow, 1969), but in any case, he argues that 'experimentally induced anxiety is too trivial to form an analogue of Freudian repression'. What is necessary, according to Kline, is a design that makes use of repressions that have already developed as a result of the past experience of the subjects. The Levinger and Clark experiment fits this requirement also, and is the study of repression about which Kline is most enthusiastic.

REFERENCES

ABORN, M. (1953) The influence of experimentally induced failure on the retention of material acquired through set and incidental learning. *J. Exp. Psychol.*, **45**, 225-31.

BUSS, A. & LANG, P. (1965) Psychological deficit in schizophrenia: I. Affect, reinforcement, and concept attainment. *J. Abnorm. Psychol.*, **70**, 2-24.

D'ZURILLA, T. (1965) Recall efficiency and mediating cognitive events in 'experimental repression'. *J. Pers. Soc. Psychol.*, **3**, 253-6.

FLAVELL, J. (1955) Repression and the 'return of the repressed'. *J. Consult. Psychol.*, **19**, 441-3.

HOLMES, D. & SCHALLOW, J. (1969) Reduced recall after ego threat: Repression or response competition? *J. Pers. Soc. Psychol.*, **13**, 145-52.

KLINE, P. (1972) *Fact and Fantasy in Freudian Theory*. London: Methuen.

LANG, P. & BUSS, A. (1965) Psychological deficit in schizophrenia: II. Interference and activation. *J. Abnorm. Psychol.*, **70**, 77-106.

MERRILL, R. M. (1954) The effect of pre-experimental and experimental anxiety on recall efficiency. *J. Exp. Psychol.*, **48**, 167-72.

PENN, N. (1964) Experimental improvements on an analogue of repression paradigm. *Psychol. Record*, **14**, 185-96.

TRUAX, C. (1957) The repression response to implied failure as a function of the hysteria-psychasthenia index. *J. Abnorm. Soc. Psychol.*, **55**, 188-93.

WINER, B. (1962) *Statistical Principles in Experimental Design.* New York: McGraw-Hill.

WORCHELL, P. (1955) Anxiety and repression. *J. Abnorm. Soc. Psychol.*, **51**, 201-5.

ZELLER, A. (1950a) An experimental analogue of repression: I. Historical summary. *Psychol. Bull.*, **47**, 39-51.

—— (1950b) An experimental analogue of repression: II. The effect of individual failure and success on memory measured by re-learning. *J. Exp. Psychol.*, **40**, 411-22.

—— (1951) An experimental analogue of repression: II. The effect of induced failure and success on memory measured by recall. *J. Exp. Psychol.*, **42**, 32-8.

11

George Levinger[1] *and James Clark*[2] *(1961)*

Emotional factors in the forgetting of word associations[3]

Journal of Abnormal and Social Psychology, 62, No. 1, 99-105

Since the publication of Jung's pioneering studies on word association (1906), there has been a steadily increasing number of studies directed toward the possible relationship between emotional and cognitive variables. In the 1920s and 1930s, a major research effort was to demonstrate that emotion is one of the determinants of memory. Apparently, this effort was part of a more general attempt to examine the implications of statements by Freud, Jung, and other psychoanalytic writers. Rapaport (1942), Meltzer (1930), Zeller (1950), among others, have reviewed many of the studies which served either to support or to invalidate the above thesis, and these studies will not be reviewed here. It might be noted, however, that in recent years interest in the emotional determinants of memory has diminished, and attention has shifted to affective factors related to perception. One sign of this shift was Rapaport's decision in 1950 to republish 'unaltered' the 1942 edition of his book *Emotions and Memory*.

One might believe that this multitude of investigations would have led to some reasonably secure conclusions about the influence of emotional factors in the memory process. Yet this is not the case. For example, Bugelski's (1956) text on learning rejected the idea

[1]Western Reserve University.

[2]Michigan State University.

[3]The research reported here was done while the authors were at the University of Michigan. The study was supported, in part, by a grant (M-450) from the National Institute of Mental Health, United States Public Health Service, administered by E. S. Bordin. Portions of this paper were presented at the 1958 APA meetings in Washington, D.C.

The authors are indebted to R. S. Davidson, R. R. Bush, and H. B. Ranken for commenting on certain statistical issues.

that there is any evidence linking emotional factors to memory. Underwood, in a recent statement, refused to attach importance to the role of affect in forgetting until further research establishes a more 'reliable body of facts' (1957, p. 57). Even Rapaport (1942), after his rather sympathetic survey of the relevant literature, concluded that considerably more work is needed before one can understand the nature of such a relationship.

The present study grew out of various failures – by the first author and by other investigators (e.g., Grummon & Butler, 1953; Merrill, 1952) – to confirm the validity of a word association technique used by Keet (1948) for evoking the forgetting of 'traumatic' words. Keet had employed the Jung association method for trying to locate that word in the stimulus list which resulted in the most 'traumatic' response on the part of the subject (*S*). Having located such a word, Keet found that *S*s blocked in remembering it during a subsequent learning task, enabling Keet to introduce either of two experimental quasi-counselling methods for helping *S* to overcome his forgetting of the word.

After failing with 10 *S*s to replicate Keet's method for producing the supposed trauma, the first author tried a variation of his technique. Instead of asking *S*s merely to associate any word upon the second presentation of the stimulus list – which is the traditional procedure (e.g., Hull & Lugoff, 1921; Jung, 1906; Keet, 1948) – *S*s were asked to *remember* their first free association (the procedure used by Rapaport, Gill & Schafer, 1946). Responding to this, *S*s recalled the large majority of their previous associations, but forgot many of those which had an apparently emotional significance. For example, one *S* responded 'bad' to the stimulus word 'love', and later failed to remember this response. To develop this procedure for the purpose of setting up a laboratory analogue of a counselling session, though, it was necessary to demonstrate that the forgetting observed is indeed related to emotional factors.

The study reported here was conducted, therefore, to examine the general hypothesis that the forgetting of word associations is related positively to their emotional significance. In other words, it was expected that the more emotional the reaction to a stimulus, the less likely that the specific response would be recalled.

This hypothesis seems relevant to other research on affective factors in recall. Yet the only other study known to the writers that dealt with directly pertinent data is one by Rapaport, Gill and Schafer (1946). The writers reported that *S*s forgot their associations to traumatic stimulus words significantly more often than those given to non-traumatic words. In that study, however, the stimulus words were not equated for familiarity of usage, and also other variables may have accounted for the results. Thus, Laffal (1955) found that a large proportion of *S*s' variance in failures to reproduce associations, delayed association time, and other 'response faults' were attributable to the interference among mutually competing responses – which he labelled 'response entropy'.

METHOD

Subjects

The *S*s were female volunteers from an undergraduate course at the University of Michigan. Thirty-four participated in the main part of the experiment. They were seen singly and were administered the word association test and the recall test. Free associations, reaction times, and recall responses were obtained for all *S*s. Galvanic skin responses were secured from only 20 *S*s (the GSR apparatus was inoperative on a number of occasions).

About four months after their original testing, 27 *S*s[1] returned for retesting. These *S*s again gave their free associations to the original list, and rated each of the stimulus words for emotionality.

Procedure

Each *S* was scheduled for a one-hour individual appointment. When the GSR apparatus[2] was in order, one experimenter (*E*1) attached the GSR electrodes to the *S*'s left hand and forearm, fastened her hand into a wooden glove, and placed her arm in a comfortable position on a cushion. While *E*1 helped *S* relax, the other experimenter (*E*2) adjusted the apparatus and waited for the levelling of the skin resistance. *E*1 then gave the following instructions:

> The first part of this study has to do with people's reactions to different words. I am going to read you a list of words – one at a

[1]The *S*s were paid to come to the retest session. Of the seven *S*s who did not return, four were no longer on campus and the remaining three could not be scheduled for an appointment.

[2]The GSR apparatus was designed and built by D. Rigler (cf. his doctoral dissertation, 1957). A constant current of 40 microamperes was passed through *S*, and changes in resistance were measured. Clay disc electrodes were strapped to *S*'s forearm and hand, which was held immobile in a wooden glove.

> time. Each time I say a word, I want you to tell me the first word which comes to mind. So, for example, I might say the word 'table', and you might then think of the word 'chair'. In that case you would immediately say 'chair'. I want you to do this as quickly as possible, since I am going to time you. Do you have any questions?

The list of 60 words was read to *S*. Reaction times were recorded to tenths of seconds. Meanwhile, *E*2 recorded *S*'s GSR deflections which followed the presentation of each stimulus word. After each GSR deflection returned to the base point, *E*2 flashed a light concealed from *S*, and *E*1 could proceed to read the next stimulus word.

At the end of the 60 words, *E*1 asked *S* to recall the associations as follows:

> That was fine. Let's take a short break ... Now let's go on to the second part of the task. This time I am going to read you the same list of words. But this time, each time I say a word, I want you to *remember* the word you said the *last* time. So, for example, if I had said 'table' and you 'chair', this time you would try to remember 'chair', and say it as soon as you remember it. Do you understand?
>
> It may happen that you will not be able to remember a word. In that case, I want you to try to think of it and guess as close to the word as you can. If you do guess at a word, just tell me that you are guessing. Also, if you think you have forgotten a word and should remember it later on, be sure to tell me the word immediately.

Following these last instructions, the stimulus list was read once more and recall responses were noted.

The Word List

The word list is reproduced in Table 11.1. Varieties of word association lists have been used widely, ever since Jung's publication of his technique in 1906. Forty of the words in this list were selected from Hull and Lugoff's (1921) English version of Jung's list. Hull and Lugoff studied the reactions of 100 individuals to each of the 100 words in Jung's list. The stimulus words were compared according to heir tendency to elicit 'complex signs of emotional disturbance' – such as long reaction time, inability to make any response, misunderstanding of the stimulus word, etc.

TABLE II.I. *The list of stimulus words and the data.*

Stimulus Word	T-L[a] Count	Zero Recall	Mean GSR	Mean RT	Mean ER	Pop. Var.	Retest Var.
1. head[b]	AA	0	33·6	1·5	5·00	14	18
2. *man*	AA	3	20·8	1·5	5·81	16	7
3. frog	25	2	24·7	1·6	2·19	14	12
4. *conduct*	A	1	31·0	2·4	5·40	11	10
5. *truth*	AA	6	33·6	2·1	4·85	9	13
6. fur	A	0	37·4	2·0	3·27	11	12
7. *pity*	A	7	34·1	2·8	6·35	20	13
8. lake	AA	0	15·1	1·7	3·59	12	10
9. *deceive*	33	11	24·9	3·6	5·89	16	18
10. *weak*	A	6	22·8	1·9	5·31	9	5
11. ink	20	1	17·3	1·7	2·19	4	8
12. cold	AA	2	21·7	1·9	3·88	12	14
13. *fear*	AA	18	35·8	3·6	6·78	21	23
14. lamp	A	1	19·2	2·0	1·88	7	6
15. *dead*	AA	4	40·4	2·6	5·98	15	14
16. *power*	AA	7	39·5	2·1	5·44	16	14
17. hay	46	1	14·3	2·6	2·35	12	12
18. *mother*	AA	2	35·7	1·8	6·53	11	8
19. village	AA	0	16·4	1·8	4·37	10	5
20. wild	AA	3	37·7	3·5	5·50	26	20
21. *excel*	11	6	37·1	3·0	4·80	25	19
22. *love*	AA	9	34·6	2·1	6·80	12	11
23. sing	AA	6	26·2	2·0	4·93	18	14
24. *friendly*	AA	7	31·2	2·6	6·34	23	17
25. *strong*	AA	9	18·6	2·2	4·12	12	13
26. painting	45	1	42·3	2·2	5·59	19	16
27. *despise*	26	0	30·8	2·1	6·19	6	6
28. *compete*	11	6	24·4	3·0	5·61	16	16
29. month	AA	0	24·1	1·7	2·58	8	9
30. *bad*	AA	6	13·7	2·0	5·31	8	4
31. cow	A	0	19·3	1·8	1·92	9	15
32. new	AA	3	18·3	1·9	3·92	7	11
33. *angry*	A	14	14·9	2·2	6·80	16	16
34. tree	AA	1	15·8	1·8	2·70	15	15
35. *woman*	AA	0	14·7	1·7	6·00	5	6
36. mountain	AA	0	21·1	1·9	3·12	15	14
37. carrot	8	0	23·3	2·2	2·04	19	14
38. *hate*	A	12	21·4	2·3	6·90	10	13
39. long	AA	4	22·2	2·4	2·66	11	13
40. *ridicule*	9	1	30·8	2·4	6·09	19	15
41. *kiss*	AA	3	58·6	2·7	6·81	16	8
42. house	AA	6	15·4	2·1	4·62	13	4
43. *false*	A	9	22·0	2·0	5·80	12	11
44. window	AA	4	29·5	1·9	2·42	13	16

Stimulus Word	T-L[a] Count	Zero Recall	Mean GSR	Mean RT	Mean ER	Pop. Var.	Retest Var.
45. *father*	AA	1	14·6	1·5	6·17	4	4
46. door	AA	1	19·4	1·9	2·24	7	12
47. pencil	40	1	12·8	1·4	1·73	8	16
48. *sin*	A	9	45·1	3·1	6·53	15	18
49. *quarrel*	A	3	13·1	1·9	5·94	12	10
50. hunger	37	1	18·2	1·9	4·89	11	14
51. *marry*	AA	1	50·0	3·3	6·90	18	17
52. voyage	41	1	22·4	1·9	4·66	11	11
53. salt	AA	0	11·8	2·5	2·08	9	9
54. *damage*	32	5	14·4	2·3	4·59	22	17
55. bird	AA	1	21·1	1·8	3·12	16	19
56. *good*	AA	3	13·8	1·6	5·83	5	3
57. book	AA	1	19·3	1·5	4·39	11	16
58. *beating*	5	9	29·9	2·6	6·05	21	20
59. old	AA	7	14·1	1·8	4·55	14	12
60. big	AA	2	14·7	1·5	2·92	12	13

[a]T-L Count refers to the frequency of each word per million words in the English language, as reported by Thorndike and Lorge (1944). AA means more than 100 per million; A means more than 50 per million.

[b]Stimulus words printed in ordinary type were selected by *E*s as 'neutral', and italicized words were selected as 'emotional'.

The 30 neutral words in this study were selected from the least 'disturbing' 50 words of the Hull-Lugoff series. Ten of the emotional words were selected from the top half of the series, with some modifications of verbal form (e.g., from 'fearing' to 'fear'). Since the other words on the Hull-Lugoff list appeared too neutral, the remaining 20 stimuli were selected *a priori* to represent objects and activities that might produce some emotion in *S*. As shown in Table 11.1, the two sets of 30 words were approximately equal with regard to their frequency of usage, as reported by Thorndike and Lorge (1944).

Retest Procedure

About four months after the original test, the *S*s were contacted once again and offered remuneration for returning for another appointment. This time *S*s were scheduled in groups ranging in size from 2 to 14. The word list was administered again, with the same instructions as given during the first part of the previous procedure. *S*s wrote their associations into a 60-page booklet, being allowed 8 seconds between the presentation of one stimulous word and the next.

In the second part of the retest period, *S*s rated each of the stimulus words on several seven-point scales, including one which ranged from 'emotional' to 'unemotional'. Each *S* received a 60-page booklet containing the scales on every page. In giving the instructions, the *E* said that, even when it seemed difficult to rate a word on a scale, one had to make the best possible try and assign some rating. Each word was presented for 18 seconds.[1]

Indices

The following indices were constructed as measures of recall, of emotion, of response variability, and reaction time.

Recall. Responses on the recall test were classified into three categories: Total Recall, Zero Recall, Partial Recall. Total Recall refers to all answers which were identical to the *S*'s original association; Zero Recall refers either to no answer at all or to clearly incorrect ones; Partial Recall refers either to incorrect answers similar to the original response (e.g., 'cool' after 'cold', or 'trip' after 'journey') or to correct answers which occurred after *S* had already given an erroneous one. On the recall test, 85.8 per cent of the responses showed Total Recall, 11.1 per cent Zero Recall, and 3.0 per cent Partial Recall. All but one *S* forgot at least two associations, but none forgot more than 14.[2]

Emotion. Three criteria of emotion were employed in this study. The first was galvanic skin response. The GSR index consisted of changes in the *S*'s resistance while she gave each word association. All GSR deflections were converted to standard scores as ratios of the *S*'s base resistance, $\Delta R/R$ (see Woodworth & Schlosberg, 1955, p. 157). By this method, valid comparisons could be made among the responses for any given *S*.[3]

[1]Between the two retest tasks, two rather brief personality tests were administered in connection with some exploratory research.

[2]It is assumed that all failures by *S*s to repeat their initial response, when instructed to remember it on the second stimulus presentation, constituted inadequate retention. When these occurred, *S*s tried hard to recall the missing word; occasionally they would give a delayed correct response, and other times they would manage partial recall.

[3]When GSR scores were averaged across *S*s, an interesting finding emerged. For the 26 stimulus words which were identical in this study and Smith's study (1922), there was a moderately high correlation between the GSRs – rho = ·56. After adding four more words, presented in slightly different form in the two studies (e.g., 'beating' vs. 'beat'), rho increased to ·60. Such a correlation between results more than 25 years apart bolsters one's confidence in the potential stability of a GSR index.

The second index consisted of the *a priori* classification of the stimulus words by the *E*s as either 'emotional' or 'neutral'. The third index was the emotionality of the stimulus words as rated by the *S*s during the second testing session.

Response variability. Two indices were constructed pertaining to a response-competition explanation of forgetting. One was called Population Variability: the number of different responses by the 34 *S*s given to each stimulus word on the initial association test. The other was Retest Variability: the number of different responses given by the (retested) *S*s to each stimulus word in the two different administrations 4 months apart. In constructing these indices, it was assumed that the greater the number of different responses for a stimulus, the greater would be the potential competition (or interference) among alternative responses.

Reaction time. This variable was measured in tenths of seconds by *E*1, from the time he began to say the stimulus word to the beginning of *S*'s response.

HYPOTHESES AND RESULTS

Hypothesis 1

Associations that are subsequently forgotten have higher GSR deflections than those subsequently remembered. This hypothesis was supported. For each of the 20 *S*s for whom GSRs were available, the mean difference between scores on the Zero Recall and the Total Recall associations was computed. Although not all *S*s had higher average deflections during the former responses, the difference was significant at beyond the .05 level ($T=51$, $N=20$, two-tailed $p<.05$, by Wilcoxon's matched pair signed-rank test; cf. Wilcoxon, 1949).

Hypothesis 2

Associations to 'emotional' words, on the stimulus list selected by the *E*s, show greater forgetting than associations to 'neutral' words. This hypothesis received strong confirmation. Comparing each *S*'s number of Zero Recall associations for the emotional and neutral words, it was found that 31 *S*s forgot more of the former, 3 *S*s forgot an equal number of each, and none forgot more of the latter. (By sign test, this difference is significant far beyond the .001 level.) Of the total of 228 Zero Recall associations (cf. Table 11.1), more than 78 per cent were responses to stimuli initially classified as 'emotional'. For example, 18 *S*s – more than half – failed to recall their responses to 'fear', 14 and 9 did not recall their associations to 'angry' and 'love', respectively; but no one forgot on such neutral words as 'head', 'fur', 'lake'.

Hypothesis 3

Associations to words high on emotionality, as rated by the *S*s, show greater forgetting than those low on emotionality. This hypothesis also was confirmed beyond the .001 level of significance, by sign test. Twenty-eight *S*s had more Zero Recall for associations to stimuli that were above the median on emotionality, two for those given to stimuli below the median, while four *S*s forgot an equal number of associations to high and low emotional stimuli.

These findings may appear to demonstrate that the forgetting of word associations was indeed related to emotional factors. One cannot accept this conclusion, however, until one has examined the alternative explanation that the forgetting of such responses is determined by the degree of competition among alternative responses. Laffal's (1955) finding that 'response faults' on word association tests, long considered to be indicators of emotional disturbance, are highly correlated with 'response entropy', referring to the uncertainty that any single response is connected with the stimulus, is illustrative of this line of explanation. Our index of Zero Recall is one kind of response fault, although this index has been little used in previous studies.

Following this line of reasoning, we examined the relation between forgetting (Zero Recall) and the two indices of response competition (Population and Retest Variability). The relations were almost as high as in Hypotheses 2 and 3, and also significant beyond the .001 level. Twenty-six *S*s forgot more associations to stimuli with high Population Variability, and only three did the opposite. Twenty-four *S*s showed higher Zero Recall for responses to stimuli with high Retest Variability, and only six showed lower forgetting for such responses.

Thus, it was found that forgetting was almost equally related to the indices of emotional significance and those of response interference, although perhaps slightly more to the former indices. This finding led to a further exploration among the different response indices. It was asked: Can the forgetting of word associations be accounted for in terms of *either* emotional inhibition or response competition, or did *each* variable account for different parts of the outcome?

Whereas until now the findings have pertained to the 34 *individuals* in the sample, the following analysis was performed on the responses to the set of 60 *words* in the stimulus list. Since the distributions of most of the variables were rather skewed, the scores for each variable were transformed to a normal distribution (cf. Edwards, 1954, pp. 107-11).

Correlations among the variables are shown in Table 11.2.[1] It is evident that Zero Recall was correlated with all variables except GSR.

TABLE 11.2. *Intercorrelations among the response variables*[a]

Variable	Mean GSR	Mean RT	E–N[b]	Mean Emot.	Pop. Var.	Ret. Var.
Zero Recall	·16	·49	·55	·50	·38	·28
Mean GSR	—	·50	·28	·43	·45	·40
Mean Reaction Time		—	·36	·37	·58	·50
'Emotional-Neutral'			—	·76	·16	–·04
Mean Emotionality				—	·31	·09
Population Variability					—	·71
Retest Variability						—

[a] Correlations were by Pearson *r*, except for the use of point biserials for all correlations with the dichotomous 'emotional-neutral' variable.

[b] A positive correlation with the E – N variable means a positive relationship with the emotional end.

To explore these relationships further, some partial correlations were computed between Zero Recall and other variables, removing the effects of Population Variability and Retest Variability. Doing this, it was found that the relation between Zero Recall and Mean Emotionality, for example, was little changed. The partial correlations were .44 and .50, removing Population and Retest Variability, respectively.

[1]The following correlational analysis does not assume that the 60 words were a random sample of all possible words, since the words were selected to represent different points on an assumed continuum of emotionality. For this reason, the *statistical* significance of the correlations cannot be assessed. However, the correlations do have *substantive* significance, since they show the amount of variance in Zero Recall attributable to each variable.

The result demonstrated the apparent existence of two independent determinants of forgetting. It led to a more systematic examination of the correlational matrix – namely, a principal components factor analysis (cf. Hotelling, 1933). In the factor analysis, two main dimensions appear. Table 11.3 shows the results for Principal Axes I and II, and for the Rotated Axes I′ and II′. Factor I′ seems to represent the emotionality dimension, while Factor II′ shows response variability. The remaining three variables are located between these two dimensions. GSR and Reaction Time fall more toward the variability factor, while Zero Recall is clearly biased toward emotionality.

TABLE 11.3. *Factor loadings of response variables.*

Variable	Principal Axes		Rotated Axes	
	I	II	I′	II′
Zero Recall	·63	−·19	·59	·29
Mean GSR	·58	·15	·33	·50
Mean Reaction Time	·77	·12	·50	·60
'Emotional-Neutral'	·62	−·62	·86	−·03
Mean Emotionality	·75	−·46	·86	·18
Population Variability	·70	·46	·20	·81
Retest Variability	·55	·64	−·04	·84

Only two important factors were found. In locating the distribution of the remaining variance, a third factor was found most loaded with GSR (−.44) and Zero Recall (+.39), while all other loadings remained small.

It seems clear that the emotionality and the variability measures were relatively independent, while both were related to forgetting. What remains unknown is the nature of the relationships. The factor analysis does not justify the conclusion that forgetting is determined more by emotional factors, since it demonstrates only statistical and not casual connections. Yet statistical relations are a necessary condition for casual ones.

The findings lead one to conclude that the forgetting of word associations was a function of two independent factors – the emotion-arousing potentiality of the stimulus words and their tendency to evoke mutually competing responses. This conclusion seems similar to one reported by DeLucia and Stagner (1954) from a study of word recognition. They noted that word recognition time was clearly affected by '. . . two sets of determinants: frequency of usage and emotion-arousing value' (p. 309).

Before turning to a discussion of the results, some findings about frequency of word usage are presented. The frequency of usage of the 'emotional' and 'neutral' *stimulus words* was equal with reference to the Thorndike-Lorge word count, as mentioned earlier. When the varying frequency of these words was related to their tendency to evoke Zero Recall associations, no difference was found between high and low frequency stimuli (by median test, $X^2=0.27$; not significant).

Comparing the word frequencies of the Total Recall *associations* with those of the Zero Recall ones, it was found that the frequencies of the former were higher than those of the latter. It is possible, then, that the relatively greater unfamiliarity of certain associations may have played a part in *S*s' forgetting. Nevertheless, the difference between the two kinds of associations was substantively small: e.g., while 83 per cent of the remembered associations occurred 50 or more times per million words in the Thorndike-Lorge count, over 70 per cent of the forgotten associations fell in this same category. Thus, the frequency in the English language of the stimulus and response words did not appear to have an important effect on the occurrence of forgetting.

DISCUSSION

Three different indices of the emotional import of the stimulus words were found to be significantly related to *S*s' failure to recall their associations. Such forgetting was unrelated to the word frequency of the stimuli, and had little relation to the word frequency of the responses. What is the meaning of these results?

The findings have been considered in terms of two different explanations, which both focus on the strength of the association between stimulus and response. One is based on an hypothesis of response variability, which asserts that probability of recall depends on the slope of the response hierarchy, as inferred from the frequencies with which different responses have been associated to the stimulus in the past (cf. Osgood, 1953, pp. 550-1). The other explanation invokes the hypothesis that the more emotional the stimulus, the weaker the connection between it and the specific response by *S* in the association test. The validity of this hypothesis depends on the presumed existence of an 'emotional inhibition' process, operating at the moment when *S* makes the association.

The hypothesis of response variability bases its inferences on general population parameters, which suggest the probability of the occurrence and reoccurrence of various stimulus-response connections. The hypothesis of emotional inhibition does not contradict the validity of that approach, but focuses on more specific blocking or failures to recall. Since specific predictions are usually more erroneous than general ones, it is not surprising that little evidence for the validity of the emotional inhibition hypothesis has yet been found.

The present evidence leads us to propose that the two different explanations are supplementary, and not contradictory. Let us briefly review the data.

The finding that GSRs on the first presentation were higher for subsequently forgotten than for subsequently remembered associations is not central to this discussion. Actually GSR, assumed to be an index of emotional activation during the associative process, bore a higher relation to response variability than to stimulus emotionality.

On the other hand, as seen in the correlation analysis, the stimuli regarded as emotional by *E*s and *S*s evoked greater forgetting of associations than did those regarded as neutral. Furthermore, Zero Recall was found to be independently correlated with these indices of emotionality and with those of response variability – the former correlations being higher than the latter. Although the nature of the data prevents the assessment of their statistical significance, this exploratory analysis does raise certain questions for future studies.

First, to what extent is forgetting determined by emotionality? The results of this study merely demonstrate certain correlations between these variables. Yet, in the writers' opinion, they lend some support to the hypothesis that emotional factors can determine forgetting. It seems unlikely that an 'emotionless' theory of association can explain these findings.

Second, what is the relation between the emotional significance of stimulus words and the variability within response hierarchies? The present study found relatively low, but positive, correlations between these sets of variables. Yet it remains possible that emotional words in general tend to elicit more competition among alternative responses than do unemotional ones. And if this were so, why? The answer to such a question does not necessarily lie within the frame of a psychoanalytic repression model. On the other hand, it does not appear to be provided by more systematically supported theories of memory and forgetting.

SUMMARY

The study aimed to demonstrate that the forgetting of word associations is related positively to their emotional significance.

Thirty-four *S*s were administered a list of stimulus words, containing half 'emotional' and half 'neutral' words. *S*s gave free associations to the words, while measures of galvanic skin response and reaction time were obtained. Immediately thereafter, the words were presented again in the same order, and *S*s tried to recall their previous associations. Four months later, *S*s returned and again gave free associations to the same stimuli, and also rated the emotionality of each stimulus word.

It was found that *S*s showed significantly higher GSRs while giving associations which were later forgotten than while giving those which were later remembered. Also, stimulus words rated highly emotional by (*a*) the *E*s, and (*b*) the *S*s, were far more likely to elicit associations which were later forgotten than were those stimuli rated low on emotionality.

It was also found that stimulus words which evoked high variability in responses (*a*) among different *S*s, and (*b*) between tests for the same *S*s, were more likely to have their associations forgotten than those which had low variability in responses.

In a factor analysis of the correlations among different variables, it was discovered that emotionality and response variability were independently related to forgetting. It was proposed that the forgetting of word associations is a function of both emotional and non-emotional determinants.

COMMENT

Kline (1972, p. 164) goes as far as to say that 'this study . . . provides irrefutable evidence for the Freudian concept of repression'. Leaving aside the question whether the notion of 'irrefutable evidence' has any place in science (where at best we are dealing with theories and hypotheses which may for the time being account for a number of facts, but are almost certain to be overthrown by better theories and hypotheses), we may proceed in the conviction that this is the strongest card in Kline's pack, particularly in the area of repression, and that if this can be trumped, then the rest must be regarded as likely to be even easier to dispose of.

What, again, did Levinger and Clark do? They recorded associations, reaction times and GSRs to 30 emotive and 30 neutral words balanced for frequency. Subjects were then asked to repeat their associations. It was found that forgotten associations were accompanied by higher GSRs, that associations to emotive words were forgotten more than those to neutral words, and that associations to words which the subjects had rated high on emotionality were forgotten more than those to words rated low. A factor analysis was carried out to disprove the alternative hypothesis that forgetting was a function of response competition alone. Although this alternative was effectively eliminated, we would like to draw attention to another non-Freudian explanation that was not discounted.

These results are completely in line with predictions from Walker's (1958) theory of action decrement, and the experimental evidence of Kleinsmith and Kaplan (1963, 1964), Howarth and Eyesenck (1968), and others. In brief, this theory suggests that long-term remembering is determined by the transfer of learned material from the short-term memory, which consists of reverberating circuits in the cortex, to long-term memory, which consists of chemical engrams in the cells; this transfer is called consolidation, and is facilitated by cortical arousal. During consolidation the relevant cells are occupied and less available for reproduction, hence memory for material giving rise to strong arousal (emotional, etc.) is less well remembered. When consolidation is finished, however, e.g. after an hour to 24 hours, consolidation does not interfere any longer with reproduction, and now the arousal-producing material is better remembered. The studies already mentioned give ample proof of this relationship between poor memory in the short run, and emotionally and GSR production in certain words. *In the long run, however, this relationship is reversed.*

Levinger and Clark (1961) appear to have given their recall test immediately after the original word association test (they also gave another recall test after 4 months, but this does not seem to have been scored in relation to forgetting). It would follow that the results are exactly as predicted by the Walker hypothesis, and do not provide 'irrefutable evidence for the Freudian concept of repression'. It should be noted that the authors themselves claim no such thing; they merely claim that the results 'lend some support to the hypothesis that emotional factors can determine forgetting'. This statement is unexceptionable; Kline's interpretation is not.

It should be possible to arrange a crucial experiment to decide between the two theories in question, i.e. Freud's and Walker's: Until this is done no claims can be made for or against the theory of repression. However that might be, it is surprising that neither Levinger and Clark nor Kline thought of mentioning an alternative theory which has such strong experimental support, and which fits their data like a glove. Nothing can illustrate as well as this failure the divorce between experimental psychology and 'dynamic' personality theory; until 'dynamic' writers learn to pay attention to laboratory evidence relevant to their theories and concepts there is little hope of putting psychoanalysis on a scientific footing.

REFERENCES

BUGELSKI, B. R. (1956) *The Psychology of Learning*. New York: Holt.

DeLUCIA, J. J. & STAGNER, R. (1954) Emotional vs. frequency factors in word-recognition and association time. *J. Pers.*, **22**, 299-309.

EDWARDS, A. L. (1954) *Statistical Methods for the Behavioural Sciences*. New York: Rinehart.

GRUMMON, D. L. & BUTLER, J. M. (1953) Another failure to replicate Keet's study, 'Two verbal techniques in a miniature counseling situation'. *J. Abnorm. Soc. Psychol.*, **48**, 597.

HOTELLING, H. (1953) Analysis of a complex of statistical variables into principal components. *J. Ed. Psychol.*, **24**, 417-41, 498-520.

HOWARTH, E. & EYSENCK, H. J. (1968) Extraversion, arousal, and paired-associate recall. *J. Exp. Res. Pers.*, **3**, 114-16.

HULL, C. L. & LUGOFF, L. S. (1921) Complex signs in diagnostic free association. *J. Exp. Psychol.*, **4**, 111-36.

JUNG, C. G. (1906) *Diagnostiche Associationsstudien*, Part I. Leipzig: Barth.

KEET, C. D. (1948) Two verbal techniques in a miniature counseling situation. *Psychol. Monogr.*, **62** (7, Whole No. 294).

KLEINSMITH, L. J. & KAPLAN, S. (1963) Paired-associate learning as a function of arousal and interpolated interval. *J. Exp. Psychol.*, **65**, 190-3.

—— (1964) Interaction of arousal and recall interval in nonsense syllable paired-associate learning. *J. Exp. Psychol.*, **67**, 124-6.

KLINE, P. (1972) *Fact and Fantasy in Freudian Theory*. London: Methuen.

LAFFAL, J. (1955) Response faults in word association as a function of response entropy. *J. Abnorm. Soc. Psychol.*, **50**, 265-70.

MELTZER, H. (1930) The present status of experimental studies on the relationship of feeling to memory. *Psychol. Rev.*, **27**, 124-39.

MERRILL, R. M. (1952) On Keet's study, 'Two verbal techniques in a miniature counseling situation'. *J. Abnorm. Soc. Psychol.*, **47**, 722.

OSGOOD, C. E. (1953) *Method and Theory in Experimental Psychology*. New York: Oxford Univ. Press.

RAPAPORT, D. (1942) *Emotions and Memory*. Baltimore: Williams & Wilkins. (Reprinted New York: International University Press, 1950.)

RAPAPORT, D., GILL, M. & SCHAFER, R. (1946) *Diagnostic Psychological Testing*, Vol. II. Chicago, Ill.: Year Book Publishers.

RIGLER, D. (1957) Some determinants of therapist behaviour. Unpublished doctoral dissertation, Univ. of Michigan.

SMITH, W. W. (1922) *The Measurement of Emotion*. New York: Harcourt, Brace.

THORNDIKE, E. L. & LORGE, I. (1944) *The Teacher's Word Book of* 30,000 *Words*. New York: Teachers' College, Bureau of Publications.

UNDERWOOD, B. (1957) Interference and forgetting. *Psychol. Rev.*, **64**, 49-60.

WALKER, E. L. (1958) Action decrement and its relation to learning. *Psychol. Rev.*, **65**, 129-42.

WILCOXON, F. (1949) *Some Rapid Approximate Statistical Procedures*. New York: American Cyanamid Company.

WOODWORTH, R. S. & SCHLOSBERG, H. (1955) *Experimental Psychology*. (Rev. ed.) New York: Holt.

ZELLER, A. F. (1950) An experimental analogue of repression: I. Historical summary. *Psychol. Bull.*, **47**, 39-51.

12

Joseph Adelson and Joan Redmond (1958)

Personality differences in the capacity for verbal recall

Journal of Abnormal and Social Psychology, 57, 244-8

When we think of the topic 'psychoanalysis and memory' we are likely to bring to mind Freud's theory of repression; and we are also apt to think of that curious scatter of experiments – some of them knowing and clever, some of them innocent of understanding – which have striven to confirm or confute Freud's observations. Many of these studies concentrate on the stimulus: they ask whether a certain type of stimulus – 'disturbing', 'unpleasant' – can, by evoking anxiety, bring into play the ego's defences so as to inhibit or distort recall. Other studies centre on the experimental subject: by inducing a momentary state of distress, they seek to bring about some disturbance in recall.

Our research approaches psychoanalysis and memory from a somewhat different perspective. It focuses on the problem of individual differences in the *capacity* for recall. The topic is much neglected in an otherwise extensive tradition of research; there have been few studies of differences in recall capacity; and there appear to have been none that look to personality as a source of such differences. At a first glance, psychoanalytic theory seems to offer no explicit statement on the problem, but a closer examination yields this hypothesis: individuals fixated at the late anal phase (the so-called anal retentives) have a greater ability to recall verbal material than those fixated at the early anal phase (anal expulsives).

Surely a far-fetched idea; but it may gain plausibility if we take the retentive-expulsive dimension to specify, not psychosexual fixation points *per se*, but differing forms of ego organization.[1] To begin with the anal retentive: (*a*) He has developed fairly stable techniques for

[1]The discussion will follow a line of approach suggested by Fenichel (1945, pp. 295–300) and Rapaport (1951, pp. 622–5).

coping with aggressive impulses. The dominant defences are reaction-formation, undoing, and the various forms of isolation (including intellectualization). The isolation defences are especially relevant here: their use gives a systematic and orderly cast to the thought process; verbal stimuli can be effectively organized and codified; when counter cathexes are directed against affects, ideation proper remains undisturbed. (*b*) His defensive style is characterized by a peculiar absorption in words and concepts. As Fenichel puts it: 'He flees from the macrocosm of things to the microcosm of words' (1945, p. 295). Cathexes are directed toward language, ideas, the thinking process itself.

These processes occur among (indeed, partly define) the obsessional neuroses. In the severe obsessional personality, however, we generally find that cognitive functioning is seriously burdened by the strenuous demands of defence; among 'normal' retentives, cognitive style is in the obsessional direction – systematic and orderly – yet is spared the brittleness and rigidity, the vulnerability to breakthrough that we see among the clinically obsessional.

Far less is known about 'anal expulsive' normals, and so we must offer here a more hesitant formulation. We take it that in this group, too, character structure has developed out of the struggle between parent and child on the issue of aggression. The anal retentive tames his hostile drives by turning against them, or by isolation; the expulsive person shows a less thorough, less efficient regulation of these impulses. Aggression continues to be discharged, but in a muted, modified way, the dominant defences being aim-inhibition and displacement. The original aims – aggression and disorder – are, so to speak, blunted, and find a modulated continuation in messiness, rebelliousness, impulsiveness.

The intrapsychic system, then, shows a *relative* failure to neutralize aggressive drives or to bind them adequately through counter-cathexes. A persistent imbalance between impulses and defence produces sporadic inefficiencies in certain types of cognitive performances. Leakages of aggression elicit anxiety and so bring about momentary disruptions of attention and concentration.

We are now in a position to turn to the problem of recall. Among retentives, the use of isolation permits a heightening of attention to external stimuli; unwelcome impulses and effects, which would disturb attention, are warded off. Equally important, we find a tendency to hypercathect words, an increased altertness to them. In concert, these processes produce a peculiar efficiency in the apprehension of verbal stimuli. Expulsives, on the other hand, are characterized by defensive processes that lead to a decreased capacity for verbal recall; the manner of handling impulses and affects brings about momentary disturbances of attention and concentration.

METHOD

Subjects. The sample consisted of 61 college women, all of them first-year students at Bennington College.

The Criterion for Anality. The Blacky Test was used to determine the type of anal fixation. Several weeks prior to the experiment itself, the test had been administered on a group basis to all entering students at the college. An *S* was designated 'Expulsive' if she received a score of + + (very strong) or + (fairly strong) on Anal Expulsion, and a score of o on Anal Retention; the reverse was true for the scoring of retentiveness. *S*s receiving scores on both dimensions were not included An *S* was rated 'Neutral' if she received o scores on both dimensions. The experimental group was composed of 32 expulsives, 18 retentives, and 11 neutrals.

The Stimuli. Two prose passages were used, one with innocuous, the other with disturbing content. We wanted to determine whether the hypothesized differences in recall would be present only when the material was of a nature to evoke defences, or whether they would also be found with relatively neutral material.

a. 'Disturbing' passage. Here we wanted a passage which would be threatening enough to elicit defences, yet sufficiently decorous to permit its presentation to young ladies in a classroom setting. So we devised a passage which stated, rather crudely, Freud's theory of psychosexuality:

> Psychoanalysis is the creation of Sigmund Freud, who was born in 1856 and died in 1939. Beginning with the attempt to cure neurotic patients, Freud developed one of the most significant systems for understanding human behaviour. His psychology has had widespread influence to the extent that it has completely revised the previous understanding of human nature. At the centre of his system is the idea that early childhood experiences influence later personality. This is called the Theory of Psychosexual Development, the major features of which follows:
>
> During the first oral stage, the child receives intense pleasure sucking the mother's breast. There is a desire to eat everything

and resistance to being deprived of this pleasure when weaned.

During the second oral stage, intense pleasure is received through using the teeth to bite and devour, desiring to chew and gnaw at the mother, with fear of punishment in return.

During the anal stage, pleasure is obtained through retaining bowel movements and through eliminating them. The child resists being trained to be neat and clean, and would rather smear his faeces.

During the oedipal stage, the female child feels sexually attracted to her father, is jealous of her mother for possessing him, and wishes for the death or disappearance of her mother.

Between the third and fifth year, children experience intense pleasure through masturbation, by playing with their sexual organs. Along with this there is a strong fear of being caught and punished.

During this same period, female children become aware that they lack a penis. They feel inferior, believing that its absence is a punishment, and are jealous of the male's sexual organ.

Children sometimes feel intense hostility and jealousy toward a sibling. They feel that they are being neglected in favour of the other child, and wish for the sibling's death or disappearance.

b. 'Innocuous' passage. Here we wanted didactic, colourless prose, and so chose the following passage:

Undoubtedly the most famous brick house in seventeenth century New England was that built for Peter Sergeant in Boston. Sergeant, who had come to Boston in 1667, became a wealthy merchant and later served as a judge and a member of the Governor's Council. The land he bought on October 21, 1676, a large tract extending halfway from Washington to Tremont Street, included a fine garden and orchard, stable, and coach house. The big house which he built with brick walls about 2 feet thick, was completed in 1697. The Sergeant House was early accustomed to society. Governor and Lady Bellomont visited it for several months in 1697, and Sergeant's third wife, whom he married in 1707, was Lady Phips, widow of the former Governor Sir William Phips. After Sergeant's death in 1714 the mansion was purchased by the province (in 1716) to serve as a residence for the royal governors. It was thenceforth known as the Province House.

c. Scoring. Because of differences in the sentence structures of the two passages, we used a separate scoring system for each. The 'disturbing' passage had been written so as to permit its being scored by phrases, or thought units; *S* was given one point for each phrase precisely or substantially correct. In the scoring of the 'innocuous' passage, one point was given for each word (except for conjunctions and prepositions) correctly reproduced; dates and numbers accurately recalled were given two points. Since the scoring of the 'innocuous' passage was more or less mechanical, requiring only the counting of words, no study of inter-judge agreement seemed necessary. For the scoring of the 'disturbing' passage, scoring criteria were first established for each phrase; then a sample of the protocols was scored separately by two judges. Agreement between them was nearly complete and formal testing of interjudge agreement was therefore omitted.

Administration. The recall tasks were administered to five classes in freshmen literature which met at the same hour. The experimenter introduced the task in these words: 'Read these papers carefully twice. You will be asked questions on them later.' *S*s were then given the passages to read. The passages were printed on separate sheets of paper. The classes were allowed about ten minutes to read the material. The passages were then collected, writing paper distributed, and *S*s told: 'Now write down all you can remember about what you have just read.' This was a test of immediate recall. We were also interested in learning what differences, if any, would be present in delayed recall. One week later, the experimenters therefore returned to the classes and asked them to reproduce all they could now remember about the passages.

There were 78 *S*s in the five classes. All were included in the analysis, except those with Blacky scores on both anality dimensions and those who were absent from either or both of the class meetings when the recall testings were done.

RESULTS AND DISCUSSION

Anal Retention vs. Expulsion and Recall

In Table 12.1, we find the results for both passages and for immediate and delayed recall. Retentives show a significant superiority in reproduction of both types of material: their advantage persists over time.

We may gain a more graphic impression of the differences if we look at the data from the point of view of quartile extremes. For example, when we consider the distribution of scores for 'disturbing passage–immediate recall', we find that retentives, who make up 36 per cent of the total sample, contribute 69 per cent of the scores in the top quartile and only 9 per cent in the bottom quartile. Roughly equivalent distributions are found for the other passage and other testings.

TABLE 12.1. *Differences between expulsives and retentives in verbal recall. (Expulsives* N = 32; *retentives* N = 18).

Tests	Group	*M*	*SD*	*t*	*P*
Innocuous passage – Immediate recall	Expulsive	19·9	12·84	2·25	·05
	Retentive	28·3	12·08		
Innocuous passage – Delayed recall	Expulsive	9·9	6·00	2·60	·02
	Retentive	15·1	8·66		
Disturbing passage – Immediate recall[a]	Expulsive	21·6	9·59	2·68	·02
	Retentive	28·7	12·29		
Disturbing passage – Delayed recall[a]	Expulsive	11·1	5·92	3·66	·001
	Retentive	19·3	8·94		

[a] The mean scores for the disturbing passages refer to thought units.

We made no specific hypothesis about the neutral *S*s; however, we wanted to determine the recall performance of this group. If we take the *S*s to represent average functioning in recall, we would have some basis for judging whether the expulsive-retentive differences are due to the superior recall capacity of retentives, the inferior capacity of expulsives, or both. We found that for all four comparisons the neutral group is located midway between the other two. This finding suggests that both the retentive and expulsive may occupy extreme positions in recall performance.

Other Possible Sources of the Differences

a. Other psychosexual dimensions. We next considered whether differences in recall are associated exclusively with anality; could it be that anality is one of several psychosexual dimensions where we would find similar differences? To test this possibility, we looked for recall differences (both passages, both testings) on all of the other Blacky dimensions; that is, we compared the recall scores of high and low groups on Oral Sadism, Oral Eroticism, Oedipal Intensity, and so on; we also compared high and low groups on Total Pregenitality. Of 40 differences tested, only two were significant at the .05 level: the high group on Oedipal Intensity has better recall scores for the 'innocuous passage–delayed recall'; the low group on Ego Ideal has higher recall scores on 'disturbing passage–immediate recall'. These results (two of 40 at the .05 level) are what we would expect by chance alone.[1]

It is interesting to note that no Blacky group receives recall scores (on each of the four passage-testing comparisons) as high as those received by the retentives; and only one Blacky group has a mean recall score as low as those received by the expulsives.

b. Intellectual capacity. Another possible explanation of the results is that expulsives and retentives are intellectually unequal, and that the differences in recall performance are due to intellectual differences associated with the type of anal fixation. To check this, we compared the SAT scores (V and M) of both groups; these were available for most of our *S*s. For both V and M there are no significant differences between the groups; indeed, their means are almost identical.

Partial Replication

An unpublished study by Nahin (1953) supports some of these findings. Nahin's research was on a somewhat different topic, but a portion of her study duplicates some elements of the present one. The criterion for anality was the Blacky Test; *S*s were Bennington College freshmen. However, she used only a 'disturbing' prose passage (basically equivalent to the one reported here) and tested only for immediate recall. She found significant differences between expulsive and retentive *S*s.

Nonverbal Recall

What about the recall of nonverbal stimuli? Should we expect to find expulsive-retentive differences here as well? The question is relevant to some parts of the theory underlying this research. The retentive *S* is presumed to be sensitive to words, at least in some respects: he tends to reduce anxiety inherent in 'things' by capturing them verbally, by transposing them into the safer, more tractable realm of language: taming by naming, let us say. There develops, then, a peculiar efficiency in certain (though surely not all) verbal perform-

[1]The tables which report these and other results described here may be found in Redmond (1954).

ances, as this study has suggested. Now one might wonder whether this capacity is operative only when the stimuli are verbal (or can be made so by being 'named' or 'labelled'), or whether we are dealing with a more general disposition.

We cannot, unfortunately, provide a satisfactory answer to the question. Although we carried out a study of the recall of nonverbal stimuli, circumstances did not allow a precise enough duplication of the conditions of the verbal recall research. It is reported here briefly.[1]

A set of 20 abstract line drawings were developed. The pictures were simple enough in design to permit ready reproduction by the experimental *S*s, and were so drawn that they did not resemble common forms or objects; consequently, they could not be 'labelled'. In the experiment, the drawings were projected on a screen, one at a time, for 15 seconds. *S*s were students in a large lecture class at the University of Michigan, all of whom had earlier been tested for expulsion-retention. Except for slight and necessary changes in wording, the instructions were the same as in the verbal recall study. After the drawings had been exposed, the group were then asked to reproduce them. The reproductions were scored by a six-category scheme (e.g., perfect reproduction; one slight error, etc.). Male and female *S*s were treated separately, since they distribute differently on expulsion–retention; there were 33 female retentives and 22 expulsives, 21 male expulsives and 10 retentives. Expulsion-retention differences, within sex, were tested for each of the six scoring categories and for various combinations of categories. No significant differences were found; in fact, recall scores throughout are highly similar.

But the variations in experimental procedure are too marked to allow us to treat the two recall studies as comparable. In all likelihood, recall performances can be significantly influenced by differences in motivational conditions, experimental set, testing atmosphere, and so on. It seems the most judicious course to take the findings on nonverbal recall as, at best, suggestive.

Discussion

The study has demonstrated that under certain conditions we can obtain personality differences in verbal recall. Yet all of our experience in the area of personality and cognition warns us to caution in

[1]The authors are grateful to John Hirtzel for carrying out the analysis of the data.

generalizing the findings. The results may very well be tied to a particular set of experimental conditions: change the stimuli, in length or content; change the experimental instructions; change the method of testing recall, from reproduction to recognition, as an example; use a different sampling of *S*s; make any of these changes and, for all we know, the differences may fail to appear. Our understanding of the expulsion-retention variable and of the influence of personality on recall is still too uncertain to allow us to extrapolate the findings with any sense of confidence.

There are, then, a great many occasions for speculation offered by the research. The stimuli, the details of administration, the experimental atmosphere (especially the role of anxiety in producing the results) – each of these gives us an opportunity to reconsider the meaning of the experiment. But perhaps the most critical question to be raised concerns the expulsion-retention variable itself.

In formulating the central hypothesis of the research, we took the position that recall inferences are based on capacity differences: ambivalent motivation was assumed for both groups of *S*s. The assumption, however, is open to challenge: can we explain the findings equally well as arising from motivational differences between expulsives and retentives?

A considerable body of unpublished data makes this a highly credible alternative. Anal retentives, it appears, show a marked disposition towards compliance and conformity, especially so in the presence of authority; and expulsives are distinguished by an edgy, often sullen independence. Thus we can well imagine the retentives, solemn, *bürgerlich,* eager to do well, bending to the experimental task with dedication and gravity; and it is quite as easy to see the expulsives, sceptical or diffident and rebellious, giving the task only cursory attention.

There is, at this moment, no way of choosing between the motivational and cognitive interpretations of the findings; they are equally plausible. If the nonverbal recall experiment had been comparable to the earlier study, then we would have some reason for believing that motivational differences are not the source of the recall differences. (Even so, it could be argued that nonverbal stimuli do not engage motivation or interest to the same degree that words do.) As it is, the question must remain open, awaiting further research.

The position we take on this issue – motivation vs. capacity – will determine whether we view the recall differences as a function of differences in acquisition, or retention, or performance. If a motivational factor is involved we can regard it as influential at any or all points between stimulus presentation and reproduction. The contrast between eager and indifferent attitudes towards the task might operate in the amount of attention given the stimuli, or in the intention to retain what was learned, or in the degree of interest in reproducing the stimuli.

Our own approach is derived from the cognitive concepts of psychoanalytic theory, and so we interpret the findings as an outcome of variations in cognitive style. From this viewpoint, one is led to stress differences in the capacity for attention and concentration, which would operate with particular force during the process of acquisition. We would then see the experiment as a study of incidental learning, rather than retention or performance.

SUMMARY

It was hypothesized that 'anal retentive' individuals have a greater ability to recall verbal material than 'anal expulsive' subjects. The hypothesis was derived from an analysis of differences in ego organization between the two groups.

The subjects were 61 first-year college women. The criterion of 'anality' was the Blacky Test: there were 32 expulsives, 18 retentives, and 11 neutrals. Subjects were asked to read two prose passages, each of several hundred words. One passage discussed sexual and aggressive themes and was considered 'disturbing' in content; the other was an 'innocuous' description of colonial architecture. Subjects were asked to reproduce the passages immediately after presentation and again one week later.

Retentives showed a significant superiority over expulsives in the reproduction of both passages immediately and one week later. Neutrals scored midway between the two extreme groups on the four testings. There were no differences in intellectual capacity between retentives and expulsives as measured by the SAT., V and M. None of the other Blacky dimensions is associated with recall differences. The findings have been partially corroborated in another study. A study of the recall of nonverbal stimuli showed no differences between expulsives and retentives; since the research methods of this study differed in some possibly critical respect from the investigation of verbal recall, the findings are offered as suggestive rather than definitive.

COMMENT

This paper appears in the book of readings edited by Lindzey and Hall (1965) where it is described as 'a sophisticated extension of the work that has been done on the repression out of consciousness of threatening experiences'. The primary criterion for selection of empirical studies for that volume was that they 'should provide clear evidence relevant to a hypothesis explicitly derived from the relevant theory'. There is some disagreement, however, as to whether the study fits the bill; Kline (1972, p. 85) says that 'Adelson and Redmond are not clear as to how they derive their hypothesis from psychoanalytic theory'. The frequency with which different experts on psychoanalytic theory disagree as to what hypotheses may be derived from the theory does little to inspire confidence in its clarity; but we shall disregard this problem in the meantime and allow the authors the benefit of the doubt.

The hypothesis was that 'anal retentive' individuals would show better verbal recall than 'anal expulsives' because of differences in 'defensive style' between the two groups. The Blacky Test was used to assign 61 female students to retentive, expulsive, and neutral categories, and the retentive group was found to display superior recall of two prose passages (one 'disturbing' and one neutral) both immediately and one week later. Therefore, the Freudian theory concerning the two phases of anal fixation and their relationship to ego-defence styles was regarded as being supported.

This classic experiment is apparently carefully conducted and we have no reason to question the adequacy of the statistical analysis. Unfortunately though, it has not proved easy to replicate. A partial replication (Nahin, unpublished) is reported in the Adelson and Redmond paper itself, but the authors' own attempt to replicate it with nonverbal learning material (abstract line drawings) was completely unsuccessful. Pederson and Marlowe (1960) attempted a fairly direct replication of the study, to find that expulsives recalled 'disturbing' material better than retentives, whereas retentives tended to recall more innocuous material. Marcus (1963) found that retentives were superior to expulsives on recall of both verbal and nonverbal material, but only on a delayed recall test (not on immediate recall). Finally, Fisher and Keen (1972) replicated the Adelson and Redmond experiment using three different recall measures (paragraph recall, paired associates learning, and verbal retention in a group interaction situation) and failed to find any differences between expulsives and retentives, despite the fact that the latter group was significantly more intelligent. As they say: 'enough conflicting results question characteristic generalities . . . it is doubtful that this evidence will show statistical significance in subsequent efforts'.

The first criticism of this study, then, is that it has failed to obtain replication on several subsequent occasions. But supposing it had; could it then be regarded as good support for Freudian theory? As with several studies discussed previously, we would be inclined to question exactly what personality characteristic was being measured by the Blacky Test. If we can accept the description of the two character types provided by Adelson and Redmond, the 'retentive' tends to be obsessional, systematic, orderly, controlled, solemn, dedicated, and more concerned with words than things, whereas the 'expulsive' is messy, rebellious, impulsive, and easily distracted. Anyone at all familiar with trait theories of personality would immediately recognize this dichotomy as relating very closely to Eysenck's primary dimension of personality, introversion versus extraversion (Eysenck, 1970). This concept involves no assumptions about fixation at various levels of psychosexual development; in fact; its genetic basis has been clearly established (Eysenck, 1967). Furthermore, viewing the study in these terms points up the relevance of a whole new set of theoretical constructs and empirical findings.

Introverts, compared with extraverts, are hypothesized to be higher in cortical arousal, easier to condition, and less susceptible to the effects of reactive inhibition (e.g. distraction and fatigue). These differences account for their general tendency to be superior on tasks involving cortical processes, especially those that are boring or require a great deal of persistence; they would also account for the findings of Adelson and Redmond. Eysenck's theory, however, also takes account of the Yerkes-Dodson Law which suggests that there is an optimum level of arousal for the performance of any given task. Subjects who are high in arousal (introverts) tend to perform better on simple and innocuous tasks, whereas low-arousal subjects (extraverts) tend to perform relatively well on complex and arousing tasks (see Wilson, 1973). Here we have an explanation of the Pederson and

Marlowe finding that expulsives were better with 'disturbing' material and retentives better with innocuous material.

The studies of Kleinsmith and Kaplan (discussed above in the comment on Levinger and Clark) have shown that material learned under conditions of high arousal is poorly recalled in the short term but better recalled in the long term. Howarth and Eysenck (1968) demonstrated a similar interaction between personality and time of recall; compared with extraverts, introverts showed inferior verbal recall when tested immediately but superior recall on a delayed test, a finding that is consistent with Eysenck's theory that introverts show higher levels of cortical arousal than extraverts. Once again, if we identify the retentive-expulsive dimension with introversion-extraversion (and thus differential levels of arousal) then the findings of Marcus (1963) are readily understood. The interaction that he finds between personality and time of recall in determining verbal recall performance may be regarded as directly in line with the Howarth and Eysenck study.

The only finding in the present series that is not readily accommodated by Eysenck's theory is that of Fisher and Keen; in this case the results are completely negative and of course do not support the Freudian position either. It would be exaggerating to claim that these studies taken together provide striking support for Eysenck's theory of personality, but they are even less convincing as support for psychoanalytic theory, and it should be remembered that they were all set up specially to test or illustrate Freudian concepts rather than to compare the two approaches to personality.

REFERENCES

EYSENCK, H. J. (1967) *The Biological Basis of Personality.* New York: C. C. Thomas.

——(1970) *The Structure of Human Personality.* London: Methuen.

FENICHEL, O. (1945) *The Psychoanalytic Theory of Neurosis.* New York: Norton.

FISHER, D. F. & KEEN, S. L. (1972) Verbal recall as a function of personality characteristic. *J. Genet. Psychol.,* **120,** 83-92.

HOWARTH, E. & EYSENCK, H. J. (1968) Extraversion arousal and paired-associate recall. *J. Exper. Res. in Pers.,* **3,** 114-16.

KLINE, P. (1972) *Fact and Fantasy in Freudian Theory.* London: Methuen.

LINDZEY, G. & HALL, C. S. (1965) *Theories of Personality: Primary Sources and Research.* New York: Wiley.

MARCUS, M. M. (1963) The relation of personality structure to the capacity for memory retention. Unpublished Ph.D. thesis, Univ. of Pittsburgh.

NAHIN, BARBARA (1953) Psychosexuality and memory. Unpublished thesis, Bennington College, Vermont, Va.

PEDERSON, F. & MARLOWE, D. (1960) Capacity and motivational differences in verbal recall. *J. Clin. Psychol.*, **16**, 219-22.

RAPAPORT, D. (1951) *Organization and Pathology of Thought.* New York: Columbia Univ. Press.

REDMOND, JOAN (1954) Anality and memory. Unpublished thesis, Bennington College, Vermont, Va.

WILSON, G. D. (1973) Abnormalities of Motivation In H. J. EYSENCK (ed.), *Handbook of Abnormal Psyhcology* (2nd ed.), London: Pitman.

PART FOUR

Humour and Symbolism

13

Harry F. Gollob[1] and Jacob Levine[2] (1967)

Distraction as a factor in the enjoyment of aggressive humour[3]

Journal of Personality and Social Psychology, 5, No. 3, 386-72

Freud has argued that successful aggressive humour distracts a person so that he is not fully aware of the content of what he is laughing at. If a person focuses his attention on the fact that the humour expresses aggressive impulses, his inhibitions become mobilized and he is then relatively unable to enjoy the humour. Female Ss made humour ratings of cartoons before and after they had their attention focused on cartoon content by being asked to explain the joke. Although initially highest in humour, high-aggressive cartoons received significantly lower ratings on the post-test than either low-aggressive or nonsense cartoons.

Humour has long been recognized as a social force which plays an important part in our daily lives (Levine, 1968). Freud (1960) and others have emphasized the close relationship between the dynamics of humour appreciation and defensive processes more generally. Furthermore, Freud's (1960) work provides a useful theoretical framework which allows one to form many eminently testable hypotheses concerning the dynamics of humour appreciation. It is the purpose of this paper to describe an experimental investigation of one such hypothesis.

Freud (1960) has emphasized the importance of distinguishing between tendentious jokes, which serve some sexual or aggressive purpose, and innocent (non-tendentious) jokes, in which pleasure depends only on the mental activity associated with the joke technique (e.g. incongruity, play on words, representation by the opposite, etc.). Tendentious jokes make possible the expression and partial satisfaction of sexual or hostile impulses in the face of an obstacle which

[1]University of Michigan.

[2]West Haven Veterans' Administration Hospital, Connecticut.

[3]This article is a somewhat expanded version of a paper which was presented at the 1965 American Psychological Association Convention in Chicago.

opposes more direct expression of the impulse. Thus, tendentious jokes provide pleasure through both the joke technique (which is common to both innocent and tendentious jokes), and through providing partial satisfaction of impulses which would otherwise remain unexpressed and unsatisfied. When enjoying a tendentious joke, one does not ordinarily know what part of pleasure is due to the joke technique and what part is due to the underlying content. Freud (1960, pp. 150-3) felt that if a person becomes fully aware that a joke expresses unacceptable sexual or hostile impulses, his inhibitions (or awareness of external obstacles) become mobilized and he is then relatively unable to enjoy the joke. Thus Freud argues that in order for tendentious humour to be successful it *must* provide distraction so that the person does not immediately become fully aware of what he is laughing at. Probably the most important source of distraction which the joke provides is that which results from the 'innocent' aspects of the joke, that is, the pleasure and laughter which are derived from the joke technique itself.

In the present experiment subjects gave humour ratings of cartoons before and after they had their attention focused on the cartoon content by being asked to explain the joke. Freud's theoretical notions led to the hypothesis that cartoons depicting a high degree of interpersonal aggression, although selected to be the most humourous on the pre-test, would on the post-test be rated significantly less funny than either low-agressive or innocent cartoons.

METHOD

Selection of Cartoons

The cartoons used in this study were of three types: high interpersonal aggression, low interpersonal aggression, or nonsense. Nonsense (innocent) cartoons were defined for judges as 'cartoons which contain minimal drive content or anxiety arousing material'. From a large pool of cartoons we selected 40 cartoons depicting various degrees of interpersonal aggression and also selected 20 nonsense cartoons. Seven advanced graduate students in personality and clinical psychology then selected from this smaller pool cartoons whose *only* important theme was that of interpersonal aggression. They placed cartoons which they felt met the criterion for being nonsense cartoons in a separate pile. Each judge then sorted the aggressive cartoons which he had selected into five categories ranging from low- to high-aggressive content.

Six of the seven judges agreed on 30 cartoons whose *only* important theme was that of interpersonal aggression, and also agreed on 13 cartoons which could be considered nonsense (innocent) cartoons. On the basis of the judges' mean aggression ratings for the 30 aggressive cartoons, 8 of the 10 most aggressive and 8 of the 10 least aggressive cartoons were selected for use in the pre-test. Eight of the 13 nonsense cartoons were also selected for the pre-test.

Study I

Subjects were 14 female college students who participated in the study during a regular session of an introductory psychology course. The course instructor introduced the experimenter to the class and explained that the data were being collected for research purposes only and that neither he nor anyone else in the school would have access to the data. During all phases of the study, work done by subjects was anonymous, and instructions emphasized that the experimenter was interested only in the results of the group, as a whole. The 24 cartoons selected for the pre-test were presented in booklet form, with each subject receiving the cartoons in a different random order. Subjects were asked to rate each cartoon on an 8-point scale ranging from 'very funny' to 'not at all funny'. On the basis of these pre-test humour ratings four cartoons were selected which were high in aggressive content and had a mean humour rating which was slightly higher than the mean rating of the four low-aggressive cartoons and of the four nonsense cartoons which were selected. The 12 cartoons included in the final set are described in Table 13.1.

Ten days after the pre-test, during a regular class session, the same subjects completed the second part of the experiment. For each booklet, the order of presentation of the final set of 12 cartoons was randomly determined. Subjects were asked, for each cartoon in turn, to 'state what about the cartoon you think is funny, or is supposed to be funny. Describe as vividly as you can the intended point of the joke . . .'. Immediately after having considered a cartoon in this manner, subjects rated the cartoon on an 8-point scale according to how funny it seemed to them at the time. Subjects were allowed 30 minutes to complete this task. Finally, subjects rated each cartoon according to the intensity of 'interpersonal aggression' it portrayed. These aggressiveness ratings overwhelmingly supported our *a priori* division of the cartoons into nonsense (minimal aggression), low-aggression, and high-aggression categories.

TABLE 13.1. *Description of cartoons.*

High aggression

1. A rifle is rigged to shoot anyone who enters the room. A woman, looking toward the door, calmly and seductively calls out, 'It's not locked, honey.'

2. On a golf course, one golfer is choking another to death. A third golfer nonchalantly walks over and says to the aggressor, 'Pardon me, old man. Your grip's all wrong.'

3. A husband and wife are fighting viciously in the presence of two guests. The woman guest leans over and whispers to her husband, 'I've heard they don't get along very well.'

4. A pipe-smoking gentleman is calmly raking leaves around a tree to which is tied a big woman, presumably his wife. It looks as if he is going to burn her at the stake while doing his fall chores around the estate.

Low aggression

5. A floorwalker accompanied by a large, frowning, formidable-looking woman explains to the adjustment clerk that, 'The customer is always right, Benson. Misinformed perhaps, inexact, bull-headed, fickle, ignorant, even abominably stupid, but never wrong.'

6. A service-station attendant says, 'Oil's dirty,' as he casually wipes the oil dipstick on his customer's tie.

7. As they walk past a theatre marquee advertising the movie, *Monster from the Slimy Swamp*, a husband annoys his wife by saying, 'Look—your mother's name in lights!'

8. A man with a severe hangover slumps miserably in an easy chair while his angry wife plays a recording of him saying, 'What! Leave already? Why, it's only three o'clock—the night's young . . . !'

Nonsense

9. A crab with a black and white checkered pattern on its shell is standing by the kerb of a swanky hotel. A doorman nonchalantly motions to guide a guest toward the crab. The guest replies, 'I'm afraid you misunderstood. . . . I asked for a Checkered cab.'

10. Two tipplers coming home from a wild night on the town are gaily staggering up and down walls, as well as back and forth across the sidewalk and street.

11. While his surprised wife watches, a man paints his living-room by holding a paint roller against the wall as he rides back and forth on a bicycle.

12. A 'Robot Adding Machine' equipped with myriad dials and gauges is using an abacus to do its adding.

Due to the fact that the final set of cartoons was selected on the basis of pre-test ratings made by the *same* group of subjects who took the post-test, the results of Study I were affected to some degree by effects of statistical regression. However, the magnitude of possible effects of such regression was slight, and furthermore the pattern of means for the initial and final sets of cartoons was such that the overall effects of statistical regression *opposed* the predicted results.[1]

Study II

Study II was carried out about 3 months after the first study and is basically a replication of Study I. Subjects were 14 female college students fitting the same description as that given for subjects in Study I. The procedure used was essentially the same as in Study I, with the exception that the final set of 12 cartoons was presented in *both* the pre- and post-test. Thus statistical regression did not affect the results of Study II.

RESULTS

The results of Studies I and II are presented in Tables 13.2 and 13.3, respectively. Pre-and post-test humour ratings for the three cartoon types are given in the first two lines of each table, and the pre- minus post-test differences are shown on the third line of the tables. Although there are some large, unexplained differences between Tables 13.2 and 13.3, the *pattern* of means in both studies is very similar with respect to the hypotheses presently under investigation. Thus, in order to facilitate discussion, the results of the two

[1]Since cartoon selections were made *within* the three types of cartoons, it is statistical regression *within* cartoon types that we must consider. The mean funniness rating of the four high-aggression cartoons finally chosen for use in the post-test was *smaller* than the mean of the eight high-aggression cartoons used in the pre-test. The mean rating of the four selected low-aggression and the four selected nonsense cartoons, respectively, was *greater* than the rating for the eight low-aggressive and eight nonsense cartoons used in the pre-test. Thus, if only statistical regression within classes were operating, we would, upon retesting, expect the mean funniness rating for the high-aggression cartoons to *increase*, and the ratings for the low-aggression and nonsense cartoons to *decrease*. Thus, the predicted results of this study are *opposed*, rather than aided, by the effects of statistical regression within cartoon types.

TABLE 13.2. *Mean ratings of cartoon types in study I.*

	High aggressive	Low aggressive	Nonsense
Pre	5·55	5·21	5·16
Post	3·29	4·09	4·10
Difference	2·26	1·12	1·06

studies were averaged. The pre- and post-test means so obtained are plotted in Figure 13.1. Averaging the third line of Tables 13.2 and 13.3 yields the mean pre- minus post-test differences of 1.57, .67, and .47 for high-aggression, low-aggression, and nonsense cartoons, respectively. Thus, the greater the aggression content of the cartoons,

TABLE 13.3. *Mean ratings of cartoon types in study II.*

	High aggressive	Low aggressive	Nonsense
Pre	5·09	5·05	4·36
Post	4·21	4·83	4·48
Difference	·88	·22	− ·12

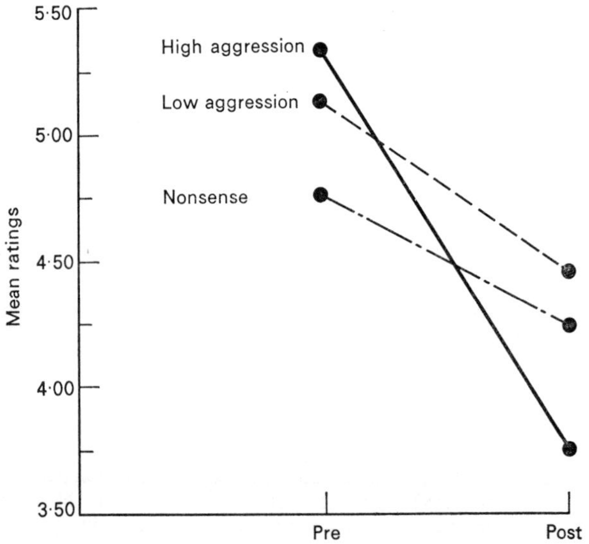

Figure 13.1. *Pre- and post-test humour ratings of cartoon types.*

the greater the decrease in the humour ratings between the pre- and post-test sessions (combined $p < .001$[1]). Furthermore, Figure 13.1 shows clearly that, as hypothesized, the high-aggressive cartoons, although rated funniest on the pre-test, received lower funniness ratings on the post-test than did either the low-aggressive (combined $p < .05$) or the nonsense cartoons (combined $p < .05$).

DISCUSSION

Although the results of the present study are consistent with Freud's theory of humour, it is incumbent upon us to briefly discuss some apparently plausible alternative explanations of the data. Perhaps the high-aggressive cartoons differed systematically from the low-aggressive and nonsense cartoons on some dimension other than amount of aggressiveness, and some process occurring along this dimension accounted for the results. We cannot rule out this possibility, but we do regard it as unlikely.

In studies of this type one quite naturally wonders about the role of demand characteristics (Orne, 1962). Subjects in each study were interviewed as a group about what they thought the experimenter was investigating. Although subjects felt the study was concerned in some way with aggression and humour, no subject seemed even obliquely aware of the possibility that we were interested in seeing whether the decrease in funniness from pre- to post-test was different for different types of cartoon content.

Another problem in interpreting the results of this study is related to the fact that differential pressures to give socially desirable responses may have existed in the pre- and post-test conditions. Thus, subjects' concern about what conclusions the experimenters would draw about them on the basis of their cartoon ratings may have been greater during the post-test than during the pre-test. If subjects' 'evaluation apprehension' (Rosenberg, 1965) was greater during the post-test it would be expected that the humour ratings of cartoons depicting highly aggressive, socially undesirable behaviours would decrease more than the ratings of cartoons depicting activities with a higher degree of social acceptability. The plausibility of this explanation of the results is weakened by the facts that all work was

[1]The significance tests used to obtain the 'combined *p* values' presented in this report were based on Stouffer's method (see Mosteller & Bush, 1954, p. 329) for combining the results of two separate investigations. Since *a priori* hypotheses are being tested, one-tailed *p* values are reported.

anonymous, subjects did not communicate with each other during the study, and subjects had no feedback about how others in the class were responding to particular cartoons. Thus, external social pressures to give socially desirable responses were minimal. To the extent that we actually were successful in minimizing subjects' real or imagined perception of such *external* social pressures, it seems reasonable to interpret the results in terms of *intrapsychic* defence processes.

It is notable that three of the four high-aggression items and two of the four low-aggression items are concerned with violence between spouses. It is interesting to inquire whether or not the results would hold up with equally aggressive content which is not as close to an area of so much probable conflict for the college girls in this study. Relevant to this point is the fact that the only 'non-marriage' high-aggression cartoon (2, which was rated least funny on the pre-test) decreased in its humour rating more than all but one (3) of the 'marriage' topic high-aggression cartoons. Furthermore, *every* high-aggression cartoon decreased more in humour than did any of the low-aggression cartoons.

Since much, if not most, aggressive humour is very obviously aggressive, a question may be raised as to whether or not we are assuming that the subjects in the present study were so naive that they were not aware without prompting that the cartoons were aggressive. It is important to remember that there are varying degrees of awareness. The main idea presented here is that people usually laugh at an aggressive joke or cartoon without thinking vividly and *explicitly* about the gory details of the aggression. If it does happen that a person becomes highly conscious of the fact that the humour expresses, and in a sense endorses, an extremely aggressive act, his inhibitions against being too aggressive become mobilized and he then perceives the cartoon as less humorous.

The present study attempted to mobilize subjects' inhibitions surrounding aggression by having them focus their attention on the aggressive content of the cartoons. Shortly following completion of the present study, Singer, Gollob and Levine (1966) conducted an analogous experiment in which control and inhibition conditions, respectively, were established by exposing male college subjects to artwork depicting either pleasant or brutally sadistic scenes. All subjects then made humour ratings of 12 cartoons depicting various degrees of interpersonal aggression. It was found that the aroused inhibitions interfered specifically with the appreciation of aggressive cartoons, with most interference occurring for cartoons highest in aggressive content. Thus, the study by Singer *et al.*, and the present study complement each other in providing experimental support for the notion that mobilization of strong inhibitions surrounding aggression interferes with the enjoyment of aggressive humour.

In conclusion, although we recognize that alternative explanations may account for the data obtained in this investigation, our positive results increase our subjective confidence in the heuristic and predictive usefulness of Freud's hypotheses concerning distraction as an important factor in the enjoyment of aggressive humour.

COMMENT

According to Kline (1972) the Freudian theory of humour is not an important part of psychoanalysis. 'It could be proven entirely false in every detail and the basic structure of Freudian theory could remain unshaken' (p. 194). In addition to this, Kline is generally not very impressed by the empirical studies on Freud's theory of humour that he reviews; the above paper by Gollob and Levine is apparently the one he regards as most favourable to the theory. 'The hypothesis that distraction is an important factor in the enjoyment of aggressive humour is certainly supported by these results' (p. 199). Although the Freudian theory of humour is apparently not central to psychoanalysis, and this particular study does not appear central to the Freudian theory of humour, we have chosen to comment on it because it is viewed by Kline as the most positive contribution to the area. It also appears in the recent volume of readings called *Motivation in Humour* edited by Jacob Levine (1969).

It is a truly experimental study in the sense that one variable at least (attention to the content of the joke) is deliberately manipulated. Unfortunately, a vital control is missing; all the subjects were asked to say what was funny about all the jokes between the pre-test and post-test, so there is no way of telling what changes might have taken place in the absence of this experimental treatment. Since it is well known that our reaction to a joke is heavily dependent upon whether or not we have heard it before, the omission of this control is nothing short of disastrous to the logic of the experiment and the conclusion drawn from it by the authors. On the basis of this criticism alone the experiment could be disregarded as evidence for any Freudian hypothesis.

Now suppose the experiment was repeated with adequate controls and the results still showed the same effect, i.e. a greater decrease in expressed enjoyment of aggressive humour relative to non-aggressive humour as a result of having subjects say what is funny about them. It would not be difficult to provide an explanation of this finding without drawing upon psychoanalytic concepts. The most obvious possibility is that drawing students' attention to the aggressive content of the jokes serves to engender a heightened sense of responsibility, and perhaps concern about how the psychologist might interpret their personality and motives on the basis of their responses to the humour test. After all, students as a group are known to have strong moral feelings relating to violence (cf. their attitudes to the Vietnam war). On the other hand, student values do not really deplore sexual interest and behaviour, so we might expect that the Gollob-Levine finding would not hold up if the aggressive content of the jokes was replaced with sexual content. That is what was found by Verinis (1970): 'Expectations were that those *S*s asked to analyse (sexual) cartoons for their point would show less enjoyment than those *S*s not asked to do this. These expectations were not supported.' (Note that Verinis did employ a 'non-analysing' control such as we said that Gollob and Levine should have used; so this negative finding of Verinis is of greater import than the previous result.)

Gollob and Levine attempt to cover themselves against the social desirability interpretation by pointing out that subjects worked anonymously. Thus they hoped that 'external social pressures to give socially desirable responses were minimal'. Nevertheless, they admit that 'evaluation apprehension' cannot be excluded as a possible explanation of their result; the differences could be due to motives influencing the conscious reporting of 'funniness', rather than humorous affect *per se*. Gollob and Levine also note that 'one quite naturally wonders about the role of demand characteristics' in determining the outcome of this experiment. Unfortunately, they do little to release us from this curiosity reporting only that *S*s were unaware of the true aims of the experiment. It would have been much more enlightening if they had told us what *S*s *did* think the experiment was about; this might have helped us to evaluate the feasibility of the social desirability hypothesis.

Towards the end of their discussion Gollob and Levine cite as support for the present study another study by Singer, Gollob and Levine (1967) in which 'inhibitions surrounding aggression were mobilized' by showing sadistic Goya etchings to the subjects. This treatment was found to interfere specifically with appreciation of aggressive humour in a manner similar to the study reprinted above. The argument sounds convincing until we realize that other authors have used an identical procedure for increasing the degree of drive arousal and consequently the enjoyment of humour in the drive-related area. Thus, for example, Strickland (1959) found that showing nude pictures to their *S*s increased rather than interfered with their appreciation of sexual jokes. It is a noteworthy reflection on the lack of preciseness of Freudian theory that this completely opposite result was also interpreted in terms of ego-defence mechanisms. What the psychoanalytic theory apparently needs is some means of predicting when arousal of a particular drive will decrease the liking for relevant jokes as a result of 'mobilized inhibitions' or facilitate enjoyment through 'tension relief'.

The most critical hypothesis that seems to us to derive logically from the Freudian theory of humour would be that of an inverse relation between overt (or experimentally aroused) aggressiveness and sexuality, and liking for aggressive and sexual jokes. (If the pleasure derived from a joke is due to the partial expression of a repressed wish, then the greater the degree of repression the more pleasure ought to be gained from the joke.) The majority of studies reprinted and cited by Levine (1969), however, appear to show disconfirmation of the Freudian theory; instead of the predicted inverse relation between drive arousal and enjoyment of relevant humour there is in most cases a direct relation. This agrees well with what might be regarded as the most likely candidate for an alternative theory, namely some form of trait theory; conservative, non-aggressive, introverted persons show these traits not only in their general behaviour and attitudes, but also in their evaluation of jokes, leaving liberal, aggressive, outgoing extraverts to enjoy sexual and aggressive jokes (Eysenck, 1947; Wilson & Patterson, 1969). This view bypasses the complex web of regression, insight and other 'dynamic' factors postulated by most of the writers represented in Levine's book. It is undoubtedly possible to manipulate these many ill-defined variables in such a way as to explain away (after the event) the embarrassing results reported; what is clear is that they do not enable one to predict the outcome of the experimental tests in anything like as clear a fashion as does the simple trait theory. Curiously enough, none of the authors seems to conclude that the theory tested is in fact wrong; disconfirmation seems to enhance the liking of Levine and his colleagues for the theory disconfirmed. Our conclusion would be that the currently available attempts to empirically confirm the Freudian theory of humour provide little comfort for that position, but rather, support a trait theory orientation, with humour preferences directly reflecting general personality characteristics and motive strengths.

REFERENCES

EYSENCK, H. J. (1947) *Dimensions of Personality*. London: Kegan-Paul.

FREUD, S. (1960) *Jokes and their Relation to the Unconscious*. Ed. and transl. by J. STRACHEY. (Orig. published 1905). New York: Norton.

KLINE, P. (1972) *Fact and Fantasy in Freudian Theory*. London: Methuen.

LEVINE, J. (1968) Humour. In *International Encyclopedia of the Social Sciences*. New York: Macmillan.

—— (ed.) (1969) *Motivation in Humor*. New York: Atherton.

MOSTELLER, F. & BUSH, R. R. (1954) Selected quantitative techniques. In G. LINDZEY (ed.), *Handbook of Social Psychology*, Vol. I, pp. 289-334. Reading, Mass.: Addison-Wesley.

ORNE, M. T. (1962) On the social psychology of the psychological experiment: With particular reference to demand characteristics and their implications. *Amer. Psychol.*, **17**, 776-83.

ROSENBERG, M. J. (1965) When dissonance fails: On eliminating evaluation apprehension from attitude measurement. *J. Pers. Soc. Psychol.*, **1**, 28-42.

SINGER, D. L., GOLLOB, H. F. & LEVINE, J. (1966) Inhibitions and the enjoyment of aggressive humor: An experimental investigation. Paper read at Eastern Psychological Association, New York, April 1966.

—— (1967) Mobilization of inhibitions and the enjoyment of aggressive humor. *J. Pers.*, **35**, 562-9.

STRICKLAND, J. F. (1959) The effect of motivation arousal on humor preferences. *J. Abnorm. Soc. Psychol.*, **59**, 278-81.

VERINIS, J. S. (1970) Inhibition of humor enjoyment: Effect of

sexual content and introversion-extraversion. *Psychol. Reports*, **26**, 167-70.
WILSON, G. D. & PATTERSON, J. R. (1969) Conservatism as a predictor of humour preferences. *J. Consult. Clin. Psychol.*, **33**, 271-4.

14

H. J. Eysenck[1] *and M. Soueif*[2] *(1972)*

An empirical test of the theory of sexual symbolism

Perceptual and Motor Skills, 35, 945-6

Summary: A theory was tested according to which rounded figures (female symbols) would be preferred by males, elongated figures (male symbols) by females. Preference judgments obtained from 451 male and 445 female students failed to bear out this prediction.

It has been known for a very long time that rounded shapes may represent the female genital organs and pointed shapes the male; this sexual symbolism was already explicitly recognized by the ancient Greek and Roman writers, and Eysenck (1972) has referred to medieval English writings discussing the priapic significance of church steeples and similar structures. For reasons unknown to us, this theory is often ascribed to Freud; thus Kline (1972), in a recent book on empirical tests of Freudian theories, states that: 'On the Freudian hypothesis that rounded shapes represent the female genital organs and pointed shapes the male, McElroy presented a 12-item test (each item consisting of one rounded and one pointed shape) to 380 boys and 399 girls . . . As predicted from the Freudian theory, males preferred female shapes and females preferred male shapes, a preference which increased with age' (p. 210). McElroy's (1954) study with Scottish children was followed by Jahoda's (1956) study of Ghanaian children, which gave rather similar results. There is thus some evidence for the proposition that penis-like shapes are preferred by females, vagina-like shapes by males, although the relevance of Freud to this interpretation (other than in the nature of a popularizer of widely known facts) is not clear. Kline accepts these data as evidence for the theory of symbolism, but it should be noted

[1]University of London.
[2]University of Cairo.

that, in addition, we have the hypothesis that males and females will prefer symbols referring to the other sex; only if both these hypotheses are true will the predicted cross-preference judgments actually be found. A negative result would be more likely to reflect on the second of these hypotheses, in view of the widespread acceptance, over several thousand years, of the symbolic nature of pointed and rounded shapes. This second hypothesis accepted by Kline and others is not actually stated by Freud; it may or may not represent the spirit of his theory.

A replication study was undertaken by us, using Egyptian students (451 male, 445 female; *M* age = 20 years) studying either fine arts or more general subjects on the arts side. Stimuli were chosen from Birkhoff's (1933) set of 90 polygons. Polygons 14, 71 and 75 were chosen as penis symbols; the first of these is elongated and pointed, and the two latter were found to have a high loading on a factor characterized by 'elongated projections' (Eysenck, 1968; Eysenck & Castle, 1970). Polygons 16 and 30 were chosen as female symbols because they were rounded, having high loadings on Eysenck's 'circle' factor. Polygons 32 and 63 were also chosen as female symbols, being oval or elliptical; in many ways an oval shape resembles the vagina better than does a circle, and such common terms as 'fig' (in Italian) to refer to the female sex organs suggest an oval rather than a round shape. All 90 polygons were administered to *S*s for rating on a 7-point scale, with 7 being the most liked, and 1 being the least liked category; the method of administration has been described elsewhere (Soueif & Eysenck, 1972).

Mean scores for the 7 polygons in question, as well as *SD*s and significance levels (*t* tests), are given in Table 14.1. It will be seen that the male symbols are significantly preferred by the males in every case, contrary to prediction. For the female symbols, two show no significant difference between males and females; of the other two, one is preferred by the men, the other by the women. Insofar as these data go, therefore, they do not support the theory attributed to Freud, and in good part support the opposite view (at least for the male symbols), i.e., that males (and possibly females) tend to prefer shapes symbolic of their own sex. We would be inclined to attribute little importance to the data one way or the other; even where differences are significant, they are quite small, and statistically significant only because of the large numbers of subjects employed. The (non-Freudian) theory of symbolism is not impugned by these results; we would suggest that for shapes of any kind to be symbolic

TABLE 14.1. *Mean ratings of polygons for men and women.*

Symbols		Men	Women	*P*
Male	14	2·54±1·82	2·28±1·66	·05
	71	3·05±1·84	2·45±1·61	·001
	75	4·26±1·74	3·91±1·78	·01
Female	16	3·36±1·84	3·62±1·85	·05
	30	2·38±1·59	2·48±1·57	n.s.
	32	3·53±1·85	3·42±1·83	n.s.
	63	3·24±1·76	2·78±1·70	·001

of sexual parts requires a special setting and that in the absence of such a setting (in the theatre, or at a party, etc.) shapes are not interpreted symbolically. We suggest that the whole notion of testing the theory of symbolism in this manner is mistaken, and that this mistake may indeed be attributed to the uncritical acceptance of Freudian notions of 'pan-sexuality' and unconscious mental processes.

COMMENT

This brief study is included because Kline (1972) and many others have used the hypotheses presented by McElroy (1954) and Jahoda (1956), and the facts adduced by them, to argue in favour of a Freudian theory of sexual symbolism. If this were acceptable, then the contradictory findings of this study and others (e.g. Bernard, 1972) would seem to disprove the Freudian theory. However, there are several reasons for disbelieving that Freudian theory is being tested at all. In the first place, the notion that the male and female sexual organs can be symbolized by pointed and round objects is of course too ancient to permit even a guess as to its origin; every literate society contains ample evidence that its members have habitually used sexual symbolism in art, in speech, in dramatic representation, etc. A test of this particular hypothesis would be irrelevant to Freud's contribution. In the second place, the alleged test of Freud's theory incorporates two assumptions which are at best doubtful, and which may be quite untrue. The first assumption is that males like better (in some sense) the symbolized female genitalia, while females like better (in some sense) the symbolized male genitalia.

The word 'like' here is rather indeterminate. Even leaving out the facts of homosexuality/lesbianism and narcissism (which may afflict a very large proportion of subjects), 'liking' may be understood in two senses. Males prefer to caress, fondle and kiss female genitals, while females prefer to caress, fondle and kiss male genitals; this no doubt is true in many cases. But equally, men 'like' their own genitals in the sense of valuing them highly, taking good care of them, being proud of them, and liking to exercise them; similarly women 'like' their own genitals, take a great interest in them, and in the pleasure they obtain from this source. When presented with symbolic representations of male and female genitals, it is open to the individual male or female subject to react with 'liking' in either of these ways; he may prefer the symbolic representation of his own type of genital, or he may prefer the symbolic representation of the opposite sex type of genital. There is nothing in Freud to help us in coming to any decision, and consequently no proper prediction can be made.

The second assumption which is being made is that potentially symbolic figures are always and under all circumstances regarded as symbolic. This is very unlikely, and it is not an assumption which is clearly derived from Freud. When a person is playing football, he is more likely to regard the football as an object to be kicked, rather than as a female sex symbol. When a soldier fires his gun at an enemy, he is more likely to consider the gun as a firearm than as a male sex symbol. Similarly, when asked for preference judgments, as in the experiment here described, it is not clear why the subject should make his judgments in terms of irrelevant symbols, rather than in terms of objective aesthetic factors. To assume that symbolic processes are *always* active and present is certainly an hypothesis which would require much evidence before being acceptable. It is, however, an assumption which must be made if we are to make any prediction about preference judgments of the kind here considered.

Our conclusion, then, would be that these studies do not in fact support or disprove Freudian theory, but that they are irrelevant to it. The notions underlying the use of preference judgments for the purpose of testing Freudian hypotheses are at first sight appealing, but on closer scrutiny must be regarded as fallacious.

REFERENCES

BERNARD, Y. (1972) Sex influence in aesthetic behaviour. *Percept. and Motor Skills*, **34**, 663-6.

BIRKHOFF, G. D. (1933) *Aesthetic Measure*. Cambridge, Mass.: Harvard Univ. Press.

EYSENCK, H. J. (1968) An experimental study of aesthetic preference for polygonal figures. *J. Gen. Psychol.*, **79**, 3-17.

—— (1972) *Psychology is about People*. New York: Library Press.

EYSENCK, H. J. & CASTLE, M. (1970) Training in art as a factor in the determination of preference judgments for polygons. *Brit. J. Psychol.*, **61**, 65-81.

JAHODA, G. (1956) Sex differences in preferences for shapes – a cross-cultural replication. *Brit. J. Psychol.*, **47**, 126-32.

KLINE, P. (1972) *Fact and Fantasy in Freudian Theory*. London: Methuen.

MCELROY, W. A. (1954) A sex difference in preferences for shapes. *Brit. J. Psychol.*, **45**, 209-16.

SOUEIF, M. & EYSENCK, H. J. (1972) Factors in the determination of preference judgments for polygonal figures. *Int. J. Psychol.*, **7**, 145-53.

PART FIVE

Psychosomatics

15

Marvin Stein[1] *and Perry Ottenberg*[2] *(1958)*

Role of odours in asthma[3]

Psychosomatic Medicine, 20, 60-5

Bronchial asthma may be considered as a symptom rather than a disease entity. Such a point of view emphasizes the varied aetiologic factors and the need for varied approaches to a clarification of its causes. The most thoroughly investigated aetiologic factor has been that of hypersensitivity which has been demonstrated, experimentally, as well as clinically, in humans and animals (Herxheimer, 1953; Neely, 1941; Ratner, 1953).

There are individuals with asthma, however, in whom no specific sensitivity to extrinsic factors can be demonstrated. Others in whom skin sensitivity exists do not always have symptoms when the test substances are inhaled, and at times symptoms may be present without exposure to the sensitizing substances.

Considerable evidence has been accumulated suggesting that psychological factors are of importance in the production and development of asthma. The relationship of emotional factors to asthma has been reviewed by authors such as Wittkower, Dunbar, French *et al.*, and more recently by Leigh. Much of the recent emphasis on the psychological genesis of asthma has been concerned with the view that the significant psychodynamic process in the asthmatic patient is the unconscious fear of the loss of the mother, and that the asthmatic attack is equivalent to a repressed cry.

Another aetiological approach to asthma has been the consideration of the role of odours. Some investigators (Brown & Colombo, 1954;

[1]Assistant Professor, Mental Health Career Investigator, National Institute of Health, United States Public Health Service.

[2]Instructor and Fellow of the American Fund for Psychiatry.

[3]Presented at the Annual Meeting of the American Psychosomatic Society, Atlantic City, N.J., 5 May 1957.

This investigation was supported in part by a grant from the van Ameringen-Haebler Corporation, New York.

Feinberg & Aries, 1932) have suggested that asthmatic attacks following the inhalation of odours are due to the particulate nature and the specific allergenic effects of the substance inhaled. In some cases this would seem to be true, but this observation does not fully explain the role of odours in the production of asthmatic attacks. This report will present some preliminary observations and considerations of the psychological role of odours in asthmatic patients.

METHOD

Two series of observations were made:

Part I

A series of 25 asthmatic patients interviewed by the authors. The patients were seen on the medical wards or in the outpatient allergy clinic of the Hospital of the University of Pennsylvania. This was a group of men and women, young and old, with asthma of recent onset or long duration. In each of the interviews, an attempt was made to determine if odours were related to the patients' asthma. In the initial inquiry, the patients were asked what they had noticed would precipitate an attack. If odours were not included, they were then asked specifically about the relation of odours to the onset of an asthmatic attack.

The responses obtained from the asthmatic patients were analyzed for the character of the odorous substances related to asthmatic attacks utilizing the psychosexual stages of development as the basis for the classification. Three judges were asked to independently classify these substances under one of the following three categories:

Food (*Oral*). Those statements referring to foods, cooking, and eating, and any activities related to these.

Cleanliness-Uncleanliness (*Anal*). Those statements referring to cleanliness, uncleanliness, bodily discharges, and any activities related to these.

Romance (*Genital*). Those statements referring to sex, romance, love, affection, and any activities related to these.

Part II

A series of 19 common odorous substances were presented in a standardized manner to a group of 20 apparently healthy subjects and to a group of 20 asthmatic subjects. Some of the asthmatic patients from the study in Part I were also included in this experiment. Examples of some of the odorous substances are cassia oil, benzaldehyde, cloves, cedarwood oil, rose oil, lavender oils, as well as synthetic reproducible preparations of faeces and sweat. The odorous substances were placed in small glass-topped bottles which were wrapped in aluminium foil to minimize the contamination of the exterior of the bottles with odours. The subjects were requested with each odour to close their eyes, to inhale twice, and to report everything that came to their mind. Adequate time was allowed between odours to avoid interference of adaptation.

A content analysis of the associations to the odours was made, using the previously described categories of Food, Cleanliness-Uncleanliness, and Romance. A fourth category, Blocking of Association, was added. This category included those reactions in which no association was offered. The associations were independently scored in one of the four categories by three judges.

RESULTS

Part I

Twenty-two of the 25 asthmatic patients who were interviewed stated that odours precipitated attacks. Of these 22 patients approximately 50 per cent of them specified odours in their descriptions of precipitating factors, whereas the others included odours only when specifically asked about the relation of asthmatic attacks and exposure to odours. A typical example is that of F. C., a 50-year-old woman who has had asthma for some 20 years. She stated, 'Odours bother me; with any disinfectant or cleaning agent I'll get asthma. It's funny – if someone is working for me and they are sweating, the smell makes me have an asthmatic attack. It always happens. Perfumes do it too.'

Another example is that of H. P., who associated to the inquiry about odours and asthma: 'Odours bother me greatly. Like pine – anything I use to clean a wooden floor. Like G... cleaning a hopper or sink, if it's too strong it makes me dry in the throat. A tar road chokes me up tight with gasping. I get a severe asthma attack with any paint odour. I suppose it's the turpentine odour in it. It is not as severe with an ironing smell, a damp, stuffy, choked-up smell. The odour with a steam iron or burning trash all bring an asthma attack in a hurry. When I turn on the gas oven, the odour chokes me up. My oven is clean. Odour cuts off my wind.'

TABLE 15.1. *Classification of odorous substances that precipitated asthmatic attacks.*

Category	Odour	Number	Total
Food	Bacon	2	3 (5%)
	Onion, garlic	1	
Cleanliness-Uncleanliness	Urine	1	45 (74%)
	Sweat	2	
	Faeces	2	
	Disinfectant	7	
	Bleach	3	
	Camphor	2	
	Dirty, musty	7	
	Smoke	6	
	Sulphur	5	
	Chemicals	2	
	Paint	5	
	Horses	2	
	Barn	1	
Romance	Perfume	10	13 (21%)
	Spring	2	
	Flowers	1	

An analysis of the classification of the odorous substances associated with the onset of an asthmatic attack revealed few odours directly related to foodstuffs (5 per cent), or of a romantic character (21 per cent). The majority of the substances mentioned (74 per cent) were classified under the heading Cleanliness-Uncleanliness (Table 15.1). The agreement of the judges was highly significant ($p<0.001$). Odours relating to dirt, disinfectants, paints, and effluvia frequently precipitated attacks. Of the subjects who associated odours with their asthma, 91 per cent included in their responses an odorous substance which was categorized as Cleanliness-Uncleanliness. Of interest is the relative absence of these substances in the usual history of allergy.

Furthermore, 55 per cent of the patients included an odour in only one category, 31 per cent in two categories, and 14 per cent in three categories. Of the patients who reported odours in only one category, 83 per cent of these odours were classified under the heading of Cleanliness-Uncleanliness. The romantic odours, by and large, were specified along with odours in the Cleanliness-Uncleanliness group. The food odours were mentioned only when odours of the other two groups were included in the replies.

Part II

Figure 15.1 presents a content analysis of the associative reactions to the odours utilizing the previously described categories. The responses are expressed as the mean number per category for the control and asthmatic groups. The judges' agreement in scoring these reactions was highly significant ($p<0.001$). It can be seen that for both groups the largest incidence of responses was in the Cleanliness-Uncleanliness category. There were no significant differences for the three previously mentioned categories. The asthmatic population, however, had a significantly greater ($p>0.01$) number of blocks of association per case than the apparently healthy group. The odours were presented in a random manner, and individuals who blocked had previously perceived odours and continued with responses immediately following the blocking. The blocks were presented essentially as two kinds of association disturbances. In one type the subject would state that he could not smell the odour, or it was faint, and in the other type the subject perceived the odour but reported no association. The apparently healthy group had a mean of 0.65 of the former type of blocks per case and the asthmatic group had a mean of 1.45 per case. This difference was significant at the 5 per cent level. There was no significant difference between the two groups for the other type of blocking of associations.

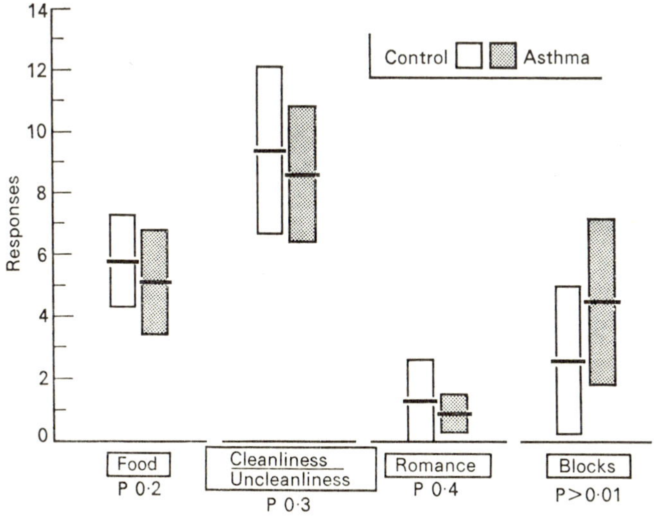

Figure 15.1. Content analysis of associative reactions to odours. The responses are expressed as the mean < one standard deviation.

DISCUSSION

There have been several recent reports (Brown & Colombo, 1954; Feinberg & Aries, 1932; Hoersch, 1943) in which the role of odours in the aetiology of asthma has been considered. These have been primarily concerned with the odour of foods. The attacks following the inhalation of odours are attributed to the particulate nature and specific allergenic effects of the substances. Tests for skin sensitivity to odorous substances are often negative, but this may be due to the small size of the particles. This explanation does not fully account for the role of odours in the production of asthmatic attacks, and neglects the psychological meaning of odours. The great emotional significance of odours for the asthmatic is strongly suggested by the significant number of associative disturbances which they gave in response to odours in this study.

A number of investigators (Deutsch, 1939; Dunbar, 1938; Treuting & Ripley, 1940) have reported that asthmatic patients undergoing psychotherapy or psychoanalytic treatment frequently show a great interest in the sense of smell. Federn (1913) reported the psychoanalysis of a case of bronchial asthma which was characterized by a predominance of olfactory associations. French *et al.* (1941) gave the account of a dream of an asthmatic patient in which 'he urinated upon a hot stove in a box car as he saw two inspectors approaching and then ran away to watch with glee how they would choke up with the bed smell.'

These clinical findings may be secondary reactions to the fear of odours causing an attack; however, they may also represent essential manifestations of the psychophysiological processes in asthma.

We have found that odorous substances in the category of Cleanliness-Uncleanliness play an important part in the life of the asthmatic patient. Odours relating to dirt, disinfectants, paints, and effluvia frequently precipitate attacks. Jamieson (1947) made a similar observation in his report of the case of a 27-year-old housewife who had a cough and wheeze whenever she was washing diapers or changing wet diapers. The attack came on after 2 minutes and persisted a half hour. Whenever there was stool in the diaper the asthma was more severe. The odour of heavy perspiration led to somewhat similar attacks. These attacks of dyspnea, coughing, and wheezing also occurred if there was flatus without urine or stool. Limburger cheese, skunk cabbage, or the putrid smell of rotting seaweed also produced a tightening in the chest with wheezing. Sniffing a dry diaper gave her no trouble, whereas a wet, uriniferous diaper produced a typical paroxysm. Jamieson demonstrated that the attacks were due to the odour of the ethereal sulphates, indol and skatol, which are the end products of protein metabolism.

Several of our patients reported experiences similar to Jamieson's case. The smell of strong urine, the odour associated with cleaning the hopper or sink, and the 'locker room smell' produced attacks. Although urine, faeces, sweat, cleaning agents, paints, and perfumes may be physical irritants related to the phenomenon of 'physical allergy' (Peshkin, 1951), from the point of view of this report these evocative odours may also have psychological meaning to the asthmatic patient.

The psychological role of odours in asthma may be related to childhood experiences and unresolved conflicts. Stein, Ottenberg, and Roulet have studied the development of olfactory attitudes and have found that adult olfactory preferences are related to childhood patterns. From a position of early childhood acceptance of the odours of faeces or sweat, children showed increasing dislike reactions (Fig. 15.2). The significant shift in affective olfactory judgments occurred at age 5 to 6, and the hypothesis was presented that the development of adult olfactory preferences is greatly influenced by infantile sexual strivings, as well as by toilet training.

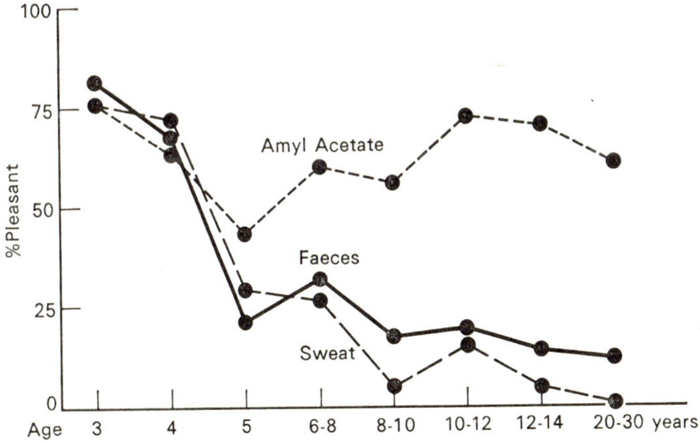

Figure 15.2. The development of olfactory attitudes. The responses are expressed as percentage of pleasant reactions in each of the age groups.

The childhood experiences and infantile conflicts of the patients in the present study cannot be ascertained clearly from the data reported herein, although the nature of the odorous substances associated with the onset of attacks suggests that it may be related to the phase of development concerned with excretory functions. The odorous substances which precipitated attacks in the present study were primarily anal derivatives and have been previously described under the heading Cleanliness-Uncleanliness. A fair percentage of our subjects related odours of a romantic nature to the onset of attacks; however, by and large, these were included along with anal odours. The special relation to and overlapping of the anal phase of psychosexual development with the genital phase makes it even more difficult to further delineate the conflict.

Fenichel (1945) has stressed the pregenital character of asthma with all the features of an increased anal-sadistic orientation. It also has been suggested by Bacon (1956) that asthma is related to attempts to ward off fantasied noxious attacks which have a strong anal olfactory component. The frequent use of 'perceptual blocking' in which the asthmatic denies even the presence of an odour may be considered as an attempt to avoid stimulation of conflict areas.

Integrated with the formation of olfactory attitudes, there are many physiological responses which also aid in the avoidance of olfactory stimulation. There are subtle movements and postures of the mouth and nose which derive directly from rejective reflexes having to do with food and odours that are disagreeable (Bull, 1944; Darwin, 1955). These reflexes consist essentially of movements of the nostrils in the presence of disagreeable odours and serve as a mechanical effort to exclude them.

The deeper respiratory functions often participate in reactions which involve the nose. When the mucosa of the nasopharynx is stimulated by strong odours, foreign bodies, or dust, there is a prompt generalized bronchiolar constriction (Hoff & Breckenridge, 1951; Rall, Bilbert & Trump, 1945). This reflex is in part dependent upon receptors in the nasopharynx which fire centrally via the trigeminus and vagus, and has the clear biological purpose of denying further access of the irritating agents to the deeper ramifications of the lungs. The hypothesis is presented that asthma in some patients is related to this respiratory reflex and that the attack is a means of physiologically defending against the activation by odours of unresolved childhood conflicts.

The overdetermination of odours in asthma may be related not only to childhood experiences and unresolved conflicts, but to genetic or constitutional factors involving the olfactory and respiratory systems. Preliminary investigation reveals that there may be quantitative variations in the respiratory response to odours. There may also be quantitative differences in the sensory thresholds of olfaction. Further consideration and investigation of the psychological role of odours in asthma are required.

SUMMARY

1. The psychological role of odours in the aetiology of asthma has been considered.

2. A series of 25 asthmatic patients were interviewed in an attempt to determine if odours were related to the patients' asthma. Twenty-two of the 25 patients stated that odours precipitated asthmatic attacks. An analysis of the character of the odours revealed that these odours were for the most part anal derivatives.

3. A series of 19 common odorous substances were presented in a standardized manner to a group of apparently healthy subjects and to a group of asthmatic patients. The subjects were requested to report everything that came to mind. The asthmatic subjects had significantly more blocking of associations.

4. These observations have been discussed in relation to childhood experiences and unresolved conflicts. The infantile conflict could not be clearly ascertained from the data reported, although the nature of the odours associated with attacks suggest that it may be related to the anal phase of psychosexual development.

5. It has been suggested that the frequent use by asthmatic patients of a 'perceptual' type of blocking of associations to odours may be considered as an attempt to avoid stimulation of unresolved infantile conflicts.

6. A respiratory reflex has been described which has the purpose of denying further access of odours to the lungs. The hypothesis has been presented that in some patients the asthma attack is a means of physiologically defending against the activation by odours of unresolved childhood conflicts.

7. Further investigation is required of the psychological role of odours in asthma. This must include not only consideration of childhood experiences, but genetic and constitutional factors which involve the olfactory and respiratory systems.

COMMENT

The psychoanalytic hypothesis supposedly tested by this experiment is that asthmatic attacks represent 'a means of physiologically defending against the activation by odours of unresolved childhood conflicts'. Two approaches were adopted by the authors: First, they gathered information about the types of odours that provoked attacks in asthmatics and were able to classify 74 per cent of these as 'anal derivative'. Second, they recorded free associations of asthmatics and healthy controls to a variety of odours and found that the asthmatics showed more 'blocking of associations' than controls. Kline (1972, p. 283) agrees with the authors that this study 'supports the psychoanalytic anal aetiology of asthmatics'. We shall discuss the two findings in turn.

It is difficult to know how to criticize the first of Stein and Ottenberg's findings because it is not easy to see in what way it is supposed to constitute evidence for the anal aetiology of asthma. The smells said by asthmatics to be implicated in their attacks were classified three ways: those connected with *food* (bacon, onion and garlic), those connected with *romance* (perfume, spring, flowers) and those concerned with *cleanliness-uncleanliness* (including dirty and musty smells, disinfectant, sulphur, smoke, paint, horses, etc.). Then suddenly comes the 'logical' leap that ensures support for psychoanalytic theory – these three groups of odours are called 'oral', 'genital' and 'anal' respectively, and since 74 per cent of them fall into the latter category the entire Freudian theory about the significance of toilet training experiences in childhood, etc. is held to be supported. It does not seem to have occurred to the authors that their 'anal' category was considerably broader than the other two categories put together in terms of the odours encompassed or that the 74 per cent of smells falling into this category have dirty associations and are much more *unpleasant* than food odours and perfumes to the vast majority of non-asthmatic people. Only two out of 45 of this category were anal in the literal sense (i.e. the smell of faeces); the connection of the anus with smoke, bleach, paint, camphor, etc. seems to us very tenuous.

In short, Stein and Ottenberg have apparently demonstrated that the odours which evoke asthmatic attacks tend to be those which most healthy people would regard as unpleasant. In fact, in many cases we might expect on evolutionary grounds that these smells would produce a biological aversion reaction. Since the symptoms of asthma involve a constriction of air passages it is not unreasonable to interpret them as representing an attempt to avoid taking in smells that are particularly offensive to the individual. We cannot see what this finding has to do with either the anus or 'unresolved childhood conflicts'; to us it seems to fit the physiological (hypersensitivity) theory of asthma very well but is quite irrelevant to the Freudian hypothesis.

The second finding reported in this paper was that, compared to healthy controls, asthmatics showed more 'blocking of associations' to a variety of odours. We are told little about what constituted a 'blocked association' except that this category 'included those reactions in which no association was offered'. The significance of the difference in number of blocked associations between asthmatics and controls is given both in the text and Figure 15.1 as ($p > .01$); this is a somewhat unconventional significance level and we can only assume that they meant ($p < .01$). There seems little need to dwell at length on this finding; we will list three objections to its interpretation as evidence favouring the Freudian position, any one of which would be alone sufficient to disregard it:

1. On the Freudian hypothesis the significantly greater amount of blocking should have occurred only on the 'anal' odour category. No evidence is presented that this was the case; in fact, examination of Figure 15.1 suggests that the difference between the asthmatic and control groups was distributed across all three categories of smells equally.

2. If we are to accept that blocking of associations is a valid measure of emotionality (an implicit assumption in this study) then it seems to us self-evident that odours, insofar as they are implicated in the onset of asthmatic attacks, will tend to be more threatening to asthmatics than controls. After all, the symptoms of asthma are presumably quite unpleasant; why should we be surprised if patients show signs of emotionality when exposed to stimuli that are likely to precipitate an attack?

3. Even if the above point is not regarded as sufficient to explain the connection between asthma and emotional responses to smells, there would still be no need to fall back upon an explanation in

terms of toilet training and childhood conflicts. Eysenck (1967) has presented a great deal of evidence relating to a general factor of neuroticism which is very largely inherited and accounts for the intercorrelations among a variety of neurotic symptoms. This personality factor would quite readily explain the connection between asthmatic symptoms and emotionality as measured by associative blocking.

We conclude that this study by Stein and Ottenberg has failed to provide any support for the psychoanalytic view of asthma. Only by exceptionally woolly generalization and sometimes even sheer imagination is it possible to see these results as relevant to anal eroticism and 'unresolved childhood conflicts'. In fact, no evidence is presented that would enable us to discount the hypersensitivity (allergy) theory of asthma. The fact that 'there are individuals with asthma . . . in whom no specific sensitivity to extrinsic factors can be demonstrated' does not necessitate the addition of psychosomatic explanations. This is akin to arguing that heavenly bodies beyond the range of today's telescopes are probably cuboid rather than spheroid. At present the simplest hypothesis is that asthma results from hypersensitivity to specific substances some of which can be identified and some not; certainly the findings presented in this study do not enable us to reject this hypothesis.

REFERENCES

BACON, C. L. (1956) The role of aggression in the asthmatic attack. *Psychoanal. Quart.*, **25**, 309.

BROWN, E. A. & COLOMBO, N. J. (1954) The asthmagenic effect of odors, smells and fumes. *Ann. Allergy*, **12**, 14.

BULL, N. (1944) The olfactory drive in dislike. *J. Psychol.*, **17**, 3.

DARWIN, C. (1955) *Expression of the Emotions in Man and Animal.* New York: Philosophical Library.

DEUTSCH, F. (1939) The associative anamnesis. *Psychoanal. Quart.*, **8**, 354.

DUNBAR, H. F. (1938) Psychoanalytic notes relating to syndromes of asthma and hay fever. *Psychoanal. Quart.*, **7**, 25.

EYSENCK, H. J. (1967) *The Biological Basis of Personality.* New York: C. C. Thomas.

FEDERN, P. (1913) Beispiel von Libidoverschiebung waerhrend der Kur. *Int. Ztschr. f. Ärztliche Psa.*, **1**, 303.

FEINBERG, S. M. & ARIES, P. L. (1932) Asthma from food odors. *J.A.M.A.*, **98**, 2280.

FENICHEL, O. (1945) *The Psychoanalytic Theory of Neurosis.* New York: Norton.

FRENCH, T. M. *et al.* (1941) Psychogenic factors in bronchial asthma. *Psychosom. Med.*, Monograph 4, National Research Council, Washington, D.C.

HERXHEIMER, H. (1953) Induced asthma in humans. *Internat. Arch. Allergy*, **3**, 192.

HOERSCH, A. J. (1943) Allergy to food odors. *J. Allergy*, **14**, 335.

HOFF, H. E. & BRECKENRIDGE, G. C. (1951) The physiology of respiration. In H. A. ABRAMSON (ed.), *The Treatment of Asthma.* Baltimore, Md.: Williams & Wilkins.

JAMIESON, H. C. (1947) Asthma due to the odor of urine, feces, and sweat. *Ann. Allergy*, **5**, 234.

KLINE, P. (1972) *Fact and Fantasy in Freudian Theory.* London: Methuen.

LEIGH, D. (1953) Allergy and the psychiatrist. *Internat. Arch. Allergy*, **4**, 227.

NEELY, F. L. (1941) Experimental asthma. *J. Lab. and Clin. Med.*, **27**, 319.

PESHKIN, M. M. (1951) Critical evaluation of diagnostic tests for sensitization. In H. A. ABRAMSON (ed.), *The Treatment of Asthma.* Baltimore, Md.: Williams & Wilkins.

RALL, J. E., BILBERT, N. C. & TRUMP, R. (1945) Certain aspects of the bronchial reflexes obtained by stimulation of the nasopharynx. *J. Lab. and Clin. Med.*, **30**, 953.

RATNER, B. (1953) Individual differences in guinea pigs in the development of experimental asthma. *Tr. New York Acad. Sci.*, **15**, 77.

STEIN, M., OTTENBERG, B. P. & ROULET, N. In preparation.

TREUTING, T. F. & RIPLEY, H. S. (1940) Life situation, emotion, and bronchial asthma. *J. Nerv. Ment. Dis.*, **108**, 380.

WITTKOWER, E. (1935) Studies on the influence of emotions on the functions of organs, *J. Ment. Sci.*, **81**, 533.

16

Howard M. Wolowitz[1] *and*
Samuel Wagonfeld[2] *(1968)*

Oral derivatives in the food preferences of peptic ulcer patients: An experimental test of Alexander's psychoanalytic hypothesis[3]

The Journal of Nervous and Mental Disease, 146, No. 1, 18-23

Psychoanalytic investigators have long been aware of the significance of habits involving the mouth as an index of one's relative involvement with two basic types of oral pleasure – oral aggression and oral passivity. In 1924 Glover noted:

> . . . all gratifications are capable of distinction in accordance with the satisfaction of active or passive aims: they stamp respectively the biter or the sucker. Study the mouthpieces of pipes, the stub ends of pencils, observe the reactions of your friends to hard and soft foods, the degree of incorporation of the soup spoon, or the noisy sucking in of soup and you will be able to hazard a guess as to instinct modification after birth which may require the deepest analysis to bring home to the individual (p. 154).

On the basis of intensive clinical observation theoreticians have related a number of personality characteristics to the two positions of preferred oral gratification (Abraham, 1953; Erikson, 1950; Freud, 1938; Fromm, 1947; Glover, 1924; Jones, 1923). A factor analytic investigation by Goldman-Eisler (1956) experimentally confirmed the expectation that these oral personality traits tend to cluster and are related to reported early oral experiences.

In his novel, *Pictures from an Institution*, Randall Jarrell (1954) perceptively illustrated the relationship between food preferences and particular personality traits originally suggested by Glover. In his

[1]Department of Psychology, University of Michigan.
[2]Department of Psychiatry, University of Colorado Medical Center.
[3]The authors are indebted to the permission and encouragement of Dr Arthur French and Dr Robert Bolt of the Gastro-Intestinal Clinic of the University of Michigan to carry out this study.

portrait of Gertrude, 'most terrifying of female novelists', as an independent, unloving and unloved, hard, hatchet-wielding satirist of a progressive woman's college, Jarrell observed:

> Gertrude didn't eat much, and Sidney [her husband] has accustomed himself to not eating much. There were many things she couldn't eat and more that she wouldn't eat: all her childhood aversions had persisted, and she joined to them the unwomanly but thinly feminine trait of being able to get along on crackers, a sucked lemon, and the last lettuce-leaf in the back of the vegetable drawer of the refrigerator.
>
> She especially disliked most Southern foods; she said in her rough way, 'Grits! I'd as soon eat boiled grubworms as grits,' but then her face paled at the thought of the grubworms, and she wished she had spoken like a lady. Mashed potatoes, oatmeal, boiled or poached eggs, almost all soft bland foods were repulsive to her. The foods she liked were clear green independent stand-offish foods: she belonged to our Age of Salads. There was something faintly nauseating to her about the thought of chewing – or, worse still, of eating something so soft that it didn't need to be chewed (p. 206).

Jarrell's depiction throughout the novel is clearly one of an oral sadistic person whose food preferences and aversions express her bitter, angry, independent and alienated position.

Utilizing these observations and insights, Wolowitz (1964) constructed a forced choice food preference inventory (FPI) based on the following considerations: a number of basic food characteristics afford differential opportunity for oral passive (sucking) *vs.* oral aggressive (biting) gratification. Thus we might expect oral passive persons to prefer the former of each of the following food characteristics and oral aggressive persons to prefer the latter; soft *vs.* hard, liquid *vs.* solid, sweet *vs.* bitter, sour *vs.* salty, wet *vs.* dry, bland *vs.* seasoned, thick *vs.* thin, rich *vs.* light. The early diets of infants emphasize the former of these bipolar characteristics; hence oral passive fixation should result in a regressive longing for these earlier experienced gratifications.

Consequently, a number of food choices were paired which forced the subject to choose between an alternative which stressed an oral passive *vs.* an oral aggressive gratification such as the following: peanut butter *vs.* peanut brittle, mashed potatoes *vs.* french fried potatoes, sweet apple *vs.* sour apple, canned or stewed fruit *vs.* fresh fruit, creamed corn *vs.* niblets, cooked carrots *vs.* raw carrots, applesauce *vs.* fresh raw apple, ripe fresh fruit *vs.* unripe fresh fruit, soft rolls *vs.* hard rolls, heavy cream *vs.* light cream.

In the early studies these food choices were pretested and subjected to an item analysis leading to the construction of a pool of item alternatives which had satisfactory internal consistency reflected in split-half reliability estimates (Wolowitz, 1964). The validity of the instrument as a measure of oral derivatives was established by demonstrating that male alcoholics choose oral passive alternatives significantly more often (60.5 per cent of the choices) than a control group of male non-alcoholics (43.7 per cent of their choices) and by demonstrating that there was a significant correlation ($r=0.41$) between scores on the food inventory and scores on the Goldman-Eisler personality trait questionnaire for all subjects.

This success with the FPI suggested the possibility of experimentally testing another psychoanalytic hypothesis concerning the role of oral needs in certain forms of psychopathology. In particular Alexander (1950) hypothesized that the frustration of intense cravings for oral passive gratifications which have been frustrated either through a defensive need to reaction form against them or because of the lack of external gratification play a significant aetiological role in the formation of peptic ulcers. The suggested mediating mechanism consisted of a chronic over-mobilization of certain physiological reactions, most notably hypersecretion of gastric acid (HCl), in anticipation of oral gratifications.

Previous investigation of the role of food choices in peptic ulcer patients (Von Wirdum & Weber, 1961) followed past efforts of psychologists who focused on the general degree of aversiveness to food as an index of maladjustment (Altus, 1949; Gough, 1946; Smith *et al.*, 1955; Wallen, 1945) or on the actual and imagined role of certain food offenders in causing gastric distress in the diet (Koch & Donaldson, 1964). None of these studies, however, could be considered a test of the role of oral needs in peptic ulcer as hypothesized by Alexander.

One of the the dangers inherent in experimental attempts to test psychoanalytic hypotheses is ignoring other specific parameters of importance (Rapaport, 1960). In the present context the postulated defences against the open recognition of oral passive craving represents such a relevant parameter. The FPI, however, was designed to index oral strivings at an unconscious derivative level. When questioned intensively, naive subjects are not able to ascertain correctly the purpose of the inventory – indeed, some get angry for having to engage in what they perceive as a meaningless task.

On the basis of Alexander's hypothesis it was expected that patients with gastric ulcers would obtain significantly higher oral passivity scores on the FPI than a comparable control group.

The initial test of this hypothesis (Wolowitz, 1965) involved administering an expanded 103-item FPI, with a comparable split-half reliability (r=0.75), to a group of 20 male patients hospitalized for peptic ulcer and 23 hospitalized psychiatric controls. All patients were obtained from a Veterans Administration Hospital population. Both groups were comparable in respect to age, education, religion, social class, marital status, birthplace and geographical residence. The mean score of the ulcer patients was 60.1 (58.3 per cent oral passive choices) while the mean score of the control group was 50.7 (49.2 per cent oral passive choices). This difference was significant ($p<.005$) and therefore confirmed the hypothesis.

These results may, however, be questioned on several counts. The difference between the groups may be due to the fact that the controls consisted of psychiatric patients who may be especially oral aggressive. Another possibility is that the presence of intense gastric distress of any kind results in a preference for oral passive foods because of either a cultural stereotype or a real relationship between ease of digestibility and oral passive foods (e.g., the 'chicken soup' cure). Still another possibility is that the occupancy of a dependent role such as that of patient induces a regression to a more passive position expressed in a preference for oral passive food choices as demonstrated in some research (Raike, 1966; Wolowitz, 1965). In this connection it is possible that, although the psychiatric controls also occupied the role of patient, the ulcer patient status is perceived as even more dependent than the status of psychiatric patient.

To contend with these potential objections it was deemed necessary to obtain a more comparable control group of patients who like the ulcer patients also suffered from gastro-intestinal distress but who were free of peptic ulcers. It was decided to omit patients with the diagnosis of ulcerative colitis since the aetiology of this syndrome is somewhat ambiguous from the psychodynamic viewpoint, with theorists having emphasized both oral and anal conflicts.

PROCEDURE

The first 100 consecutive patients (50 males and 50 females) admitted to the outpatients gastro-intestinal clinic of the University of Michigan Hospital for gastro-intestinal symptoms who were assigned a definite diagnosis other than ulcerative colitis were included in the study.

The patients were given a 103-item FPI and asked a few questions about their status in regard to variables such as education, occupation, religion, when their file information was incomplete. They were told simply that the FPI was part of a study of some possible relationship between food preference and various disorders.

The standard instructions accompanying the FPI emphasized that the subject *had* to choose one of the two alternatives offered in each item solely on the basis of which was more preferred *regardless* of other considerations such as which was thought to be healthiest or which was actually part of the current diet. This was intended to minimize the role of extraneous determinants of food choices other than affective preference. The subject was allowed to indicate no choice only when he was unfamiliar with one or both item choices. This almost never occurred.

The patients were not informed of the detailed purpose of the experiment, and the investigators did not have any chance to influence their responses since the inventory was objective and self-administering and all choices were immediately recorded on IBM answer sheets. The FPI was scored for the number of oral passive alternatives endorsed of the 103 total possible.

RESULTS

Of the pool of 100 patients the experimental group consisted of 38 patients diagnosed as having a peptic ulcer while the control group was composed of the remaining 62 patients whose distribution of diagnoses is indicated in Table 16.1.

The patients' diagnoses were reexamined two months after the termination of the study from their medical records to insure their stability. Only patients whose diagnosis remained the same and was supported by X-ray evidence were included in the sample of ulcer patients.

The characteristics of the two groups of patients on the control variables are reported in Table 16.2. With the exception of age there were no significant differences (*i.e.*, $p < .05$) between the groups. The ulcer group tended to be somewhat older, significantly, than the non-ulcer group and to have a slightly greater (but not significant) ratio of males to females. However, there was no significant relationship between age and FPI scores ($r=0.04$, $p>.05$, NS) nor between sex and FPI in either the ulcer group (male mean=60.8, $t=0.45$, $p>.05$, NS) or the non-ulcer group (male mean=54.6, female mean =49.6, $t=1.89$, $p>.05$, NS).

TABLE 16.1. *Distribution of diagnoses of the non-ulcer control group.*

Diagnosis	Frequency
Gastro-intestinal bleeding	1
Ileocolitis	1
Scleroderma	1
Viral gastritis	1
Functional constipation	1
Chronic gastritis	1
Edema	1
Multiple sclerosis	1
Hyperthyroid	1
Polycystic kidney	1
Diverticulitis	1
Urticaria	1
Syncope	1
Gastro-intestinal injuries (auto accident)	1
Pancreatitis	2
Diabetes mellitus	2
Esophageal spasm	2
Gastro-intestinal bleeding (haemorrhoids)	2
Cancer	3
Nontropical sprue	3
No gastro-intestinal disease	3
Hiatus hernia	6
Chronic regional enteritis	8
Functional bowel disorder	17
Total	62

Table 16.3 depicts the means and variances of both groups on the FPI. The differences between the groups is significant ($p<.001$) in the direction predicted by Alexander's hypothesis. The ulcer patients endorsed 58.1 per cent of the oral passive choices (mean=59.9 of 103 items) while the non-ulcer patients endorsed only 50.1 (mean=51.6 of 103 items). These respective percentages of endorsement are comparable to the previously reported percentages obtained with the group of male alcoholics (60.5 per cent) and their controls (43.7 per cent) as well as with the initial group of Veterans Administration

Hospital ulcer patients (58.3 per cent) and their psychiatric controls (49.2 per cent).

TABLE 16.2. *Control variable characteristics of ulcer and non-ulcer patients.*

Variable	Ulcer Patients	Non-ulcer Patients	Significance of the Difference
Religion			
Protestant	63%	70%	$\chi^2 = 0{\cdot}44$, 2 df
Catholic	22%	18%	$p > {\cdot}05$ NS
Other	15%	12%	
Birthplace			
Midwest	60%	72%	$\chi^2 = 4{\cdot}01$, 3 df
South	10%	16%	$p > {\cdot}05$ NS
East or West Coast	14%	5%	
Foreign	16%	7%	
Marital status			
Married	84%	66%	$\chi^2 = 0{\cdot}04$, 1 df
Single or divorced	16%	34%	$p > {\cdot}05$ NS
Race			
White	100%	90%	$\chi^2 = 2{\cdot}52$, 1 df
Negro	0%	10%	$p > {\cdot}05$ NS
Education			
Mean	10·8	12·2	CR = 1·71
σ^2	12·7	10·3	$p > {\cdot}05$ NS
Age			
Mean	49·6	41·5	CR = 2·7
σ^2	217·7	183·9	$p > {\cdot}01$
Percentage pounds over (+) or under (−) weight			
Mean	−4·0	−3·3	CR = 0·21
σ^2	263·7	230·6	$p > {\cdot}05$ NS
Occupational status (of husband if married)			
Professional	18%	20%	$\chi^2 = 1{\cdot}02$, 3 df
White collar (semi- and unskilled)	26%	22%	$p > {\cdot}05$ NS
Blue collar (skilled)	24%	18%	
Blue collar (semi- and unskilled)	32%	40%	
Sex			
Male	65%	40%	$\chi^2 = 0{\cdot}61$, 1 df
Female	35%	60%	$p > {\cdot}05$ NS

TABLE 16.3. *Comparison of the scores of ulcer and non-ulcer patients on the FPI.*

Criterion Group	Food Preference Inventory Score (103 Items)			
	N	Mean	SD	C.R.
Ulcer patients	38	59·9	9·6	
Non-ulcer patients	62	51·6	10·4	4·01, $p <$ ·001, 1 tail

The results of this experiment confirmed the prediction that ulcer patients would endorse a greater number of oral passive food choices than the controls. Previous possible objections raised in connection with the initial experiment on ulcer patients and psychiatric controls no longer seem applicable. Since the psychiatric controls endorse oral passive choices as frequently as any of the other control groups, the difference could not have been due to their greater oral aggressiveness. Moreover, the similar percentage of oral passive choices endorsed by all control groups and the similar percentage endorsed by the various experimental groups across varied settings lend a greater degree of confidence in the stability of the results.

The possibility that the ulcer patients endorse a greater percentage of oral passive choices either because of an actual or imagined relationship between oral passive food qualities and ease of digestibility is now precluded since the control group consisted of patients with gastro-intestinal distress. This control also rules out the possibility that greater regression to oral passivity was induced by more dependency involved in being a gastro-intestinal patient than in being a psychiatric patient.

The results of this experiment support Alexander's contention, based on clinical observations, that oral passive needs are significantly higher in peptic ulcer patients. These findings cannot be accounted for solely by the presence of gastro-intestinal symptoms. The results indicate that oral passive needs play a significant though perhaps not exclusive role in the aetiology of peptic ulcer.

SUMMARY

The purpose of this study was to subject to experimental test a prediction based on Alexander's clinically derived hypothesis that oral passive wishes play an important role in peptic ulcer.

Previous research using the food preference inventory (FPI) as a measure of the presence of oral passive and oral aggressive derivatives found that ulcer patients have significantly greater oral passive wishes than a control group of psychiatric patients. These results, however, were questioned as a possible artifact of the use of psychiatric patients in particular as controls. Consequently it was decided to obtain a comparable control group of non-ulcer patients with gastro-intestinal problems.

One hundred (100) patients were obtained at an outpatient gastro-intestinal clinic who were assigned definite diagnoses, excepting ulcerative colitis. Thirty-eight patients with a diagnosis of peptic ulcer formed the experimental group while 62 patients with other diagnoses constituted the control group.

All patients were given a forced choice food preference inventory with standard instructions. In addition, information was obtained for all subjects on extraneous but possibly confounding variables such as age, education, marital status. In accordance with Alexander's hypothesis, it was predicted that the ulcer group would have a more oral passive mean score on the FPI (i.e., higher) than the non-ulcer control group.

As predicted, the ulcer group's mean oral passive score was significantly higher ($p<.001$) than the non-ulcer group, thereby supporting Alexander's contention that oral passive psychological needs play an important role in the aetiology of peptic ulcer. There were no significant differences between the groups on any of the extraneous control variables, with the exception of age (the ulcer group's mean age was 8.1 years greater), which itself, however, had no significant relationship to FPI scores.

Since the control group in this study, unlike that in a previous study, was just like the experimental group with the exception of the presence of an ulcer and the differences between the groups remained comparable to that of the previous study, it was concluded that Alexander's contention is strongly supported.

COMMENT

Kline (1972, p. 289) concludes from a review of all the studies of peptic ulcer and ulcerative colitis that 'the evidence does not confirm psychoanalytic theory, except for the studies of Wolowitz using a food preference inventory'. According to Kline, 'these studies by Wolowitz, especially the second by Wolowitz and Wagonfeld (1968), must be held to confirm the psychoanalytic theory of peptic ulcer'. This study, then, would seem the obvious one to consider in connection with the Freudian theory of ulcers.

The hypothesis supposedly tested is attributed to Alexander rather than Freud himself, nevertheless it falls within the general area of psychoanalytic theorizing. 'The frustration of intense cravings for oral passive gratifications which have been frustrated either through a defensive need to reaction form against them or because of the lack of external gratification play a significant aetiological role in the formation of peptic ulcers.' Wolowitz and Wagonfeld compared 38 peptic ulcer patients with 62 non-ulcer gastro-intestinal patients on a food preference questionnaire and found that the former group obtained a higher 'oral passive' score, i.e. they chose soft, liquid, sweet, sour, bland, thick and rich food (oral passive preferences) rather than hard, solid, bitter, salty, dry, seasoned, thin and light foods (oral aggressive preferences). This result was held to support Alexander's hypothesis. We might speculate that if the results had come out the opposite way Alexander's hypothesis would still have been held to be supported since his clause about the 'defensive need to reaction form' allows the hypothesis to accomodate any outcome (cf. our comment on the Scodel, 1957, paper).

Can we suggest a reasonable alternative explanation for the results as they actually turned out? The most obvious possibility, of course, is that the 'passive' foods (soft, liquid, sweet, non-spicy, etc.) are preferred by ulcer patients because they are easier to digest and less irritating to the stomach than the 'aggressive' foods (hard, solid, bitter, seasoned, etc.). Wolowitz and Wagonfeld apparently hope that they are covered against this objection by their use of a control group suffering from other types of gastro-intestinal disorder, therefore a great deal rests on the adequacy of this control. Inspection of Table 16.1, which lists the diagnoses included in the control group, however, suggests that many of them could be classified as acute or traumatic compared to ulcers which are characteristically chronic and constitutional. Disorders such as hiatus hernia, cancer, and auto accident injuries are unlikely to have troubled the patient over such a long period that they would have led to a modification of food preferences, whereas ulcers tend to develop slowly over a long period of time before necessitating surgery – time enough, perhaps, for adaptive changes in food selection to occur either spontaneously or on medical advice.

If a psychosomatic explanation is regarded as necessary at all, then a far simpler one than Alexander's is available. If ulcers are partly due to anxiety interfering with the production of gastric juices via autonomic nervous system connections, then foods that are soft, sweet, rich, etc. would be more effective as reducers of anxiety through reciprocal inhibition (see Wolpe, 1958). This explanation is complementary rather than opposed to the one above, but again involves no psychoanalytic assumptions concerning oral gratification and fixation in early childhood or reaction formations against these fixations.

Before closing the list of alternative explanations, we must point out that all Wolowitz and Wagonfeld have actually demonstrated is a relationship between ulcers and food preferences; psychologists should not need reminding that this tells us nothing about the direction of cause and effect. Perhaps the food preferences are directly implicated in the aetiology of ulcers in that our biochemical constitution is partly influenced by the chemicals that we take into our body in the form of food? Perhaps both ulcers and food preferences reflect some third variable such as neuroticism or social class? The first hypothesis that we suggested above seems to us the most plausible and parsimonious, but the results presented by Wolowitz and Wagonfeld do not really permit us to decide among any of these alternatives.

REFERENCES

ABRAHAM, K. (1953) The influence of oral erotism on character-formation. In *Selected Papers on Psychoanalysis*, pp. 393-406. New York: Basic Books.

ALEXANDER, F. (1950) *Psychosomatic Medicine*. New York: Norton.

ALTUS, W. D. (1949) Adjustment and food aversions among Army illiterates. *J. Consult. Psychol.*, **13**, 429-32.

ERIKSON, E. H. (1950) *Childhood and Society*. New York: Norton.

FREUD, S. (1938) Three contributions to the theory of sex. In *The Basic Writings of Sigmund Freud*, pp. 553-629. New York: Random House.

FROMM, E. (1947) *Man for Himself*. New York: Rinehart.

GLOVER, E. (1924) The significance of the mouth in psychoanalysis. *Brit. J. Med. Psychol.*, **4**, 134-55.

GOLDMAN-EISLER, F. (1956) Breastfeeding and character-formation. In C. KLUCKHOHN, H. A. MURRAY & D. M. SCHNEIDER (eds.), *Personality in Nature, Society and Culture*, pp. 146-84. New York: Knopf.

GOUGH, H. G. (1946) An additional study of food aversions. *J. Abnorm. Soc. Psychol.*, **41**, 86-8.

JARRELL, R. (1954) *Pictures from an Institution*. London: Faber & Faber.

JONES, E. (1923) The God complex. In *Essays in Applied Psychoanalysis*, pp. 244-65. London: International Psychoanalytic Press.

KLINE, P. (1972) *Fact and Fantasy in Freudian Theory*. London: Methuen.

KOCH, J. P. & DONALDSON, R. M. (1964) A survey of food intolerances in hospitalized patients. *New England J. Med.*, **271**, 657-60.

RAIKE, J. P. (1966) Preferred oral modalities as a function of induced self-concept. Unpublished honours thesis. Ann Arbor: Univ. of Michigan.

RAPAPORT, D. (1960) The structure of psychoanalytic theory. *Psychol. Issues*, **2**, 1.

SMITH, W. I., POWELL, E. K. & ROSS, S. (1955) Manifest anxiety and food aversions. *J. Abnorm. Soc. Psychol.*, **50**, 101-4.

WALLEN, R. (1945) Food aversions in normal and neurotic males. *J. Abnorm. Soc. Psychol.*, **40**, 77-81.

VON WIRDUM, P. & WEBER, A. (1961) The occurrence of food preferences and aversions in groups of patients with peptic ulcer, asthma and neurosis. *J. Psychosom. Res.*, **5**, 280-6.

WOLOWITZ, H. M. (1964) Food preferences as an index of orality. *J. Abnorm. Soc. Psychol.*, **69**, 650-4.

—— (1965) Self-concept, role and psychosexual oral position. Unpublished manuscript.

—— (1967) Oral involvement in peptic ulcer. *J. Consult. Psychol.*, **31**, 418-19.

WOLPE, J. (1958) *Psychotherapy by Reciprocal Inhibition*. Stanford, Calif.: Stanford Univ. Press.

17
Yizhar Eylon (1967)[1]

Birth events, appendicitis and appendectomy[2]

British Journal of Medical Psychology, 40, 317-32

Freud (1905), in describing the case of Dora, was probably the first to relate appendicitis to birth fantasies. When 17 years old this patient suffered a sudden attack of appendicitis. A year later, in the autumn of 1900, Dora was under analysis with Freud. It was discovered then that the earlier illness occurred nine months after an episode in which she received improper proposals from a married man. She had been caring for this man's children (by his real wife) and had secret hopes that he would marry her. Freud concluded that 'Her supposed attack of appendicitis had thus enabled the patient . . . to realize a fantasy of childbirth' (p. 103).

Almost two decades later Stoddart (1922) reported the case of a male patient undergoing psychotherapy who one day told his analyst that he had swallowed a grape pip and was afraid it might give him appendicitis. Analysis of this fear revealed that the patient's concept of the appendix was 'that of a tube leading into a hollow cavity' (p. 45). Appendicitis was considered a distension of this cavity, which might be caused by the swallowed grape pip. Stoddart points out that a grape seed could 'germinate into life'. Seed is a symbolic equivalent to semen. The distension of the cavity would therefore be akin to a pregnancy.

Groddeck (1923) interpreted an attack of appendicitis in a male as a wish to be a woman in order to be able, ultimately, to bear a child. According to him, this wish is demonstrated through many somatic symptoms and appendicitis is only one of the several possibilities (pp. 15-19).

[1]University of Alberta, Edmonton, Alberta, Canada.

[2]This paper is based on a thesis submitted to the University of Alberta in partial fulfilment of the requirements for the M.A. degree.

These ideas were not pursued further. Indeed, psychosomatic medicine has not devoted much attention to the problem of appendicitis. The books of such authorities in psychosomatic medicine as Alexander (1950), Alexander & French (1948), Grinker & Robbins (1953), the Liefs (1963), and Wittkower & Cleghorn (1954) do not contain any references to appendicitis. On the other hand, in her compendium of psychosomatic literature, Dunbar (1954) reviews a few papers dealing with psychological factors in appendicitis. While it is pointed out that psychogenic factors are of importance in this illness, they are not defined and no reference is made to birth. Furthermore, the main subject of discussion is pseudoappendicitis. Continuing this focus, Dunbar (1955) describes the case of an analyst whose patient underwent an appendectomy. Shortly afterwards, following some emotional upsets, the analyst himself was stricken with severe abdominal pains which were exactly like those experienced during an attack of appendicitis. He was reluctant to submit to an operation and 'began to think of what might have caused his pains'. Upon his discovery of various possible gains from illness at that particular time, the abdominal pains subsided. Subsequent medical examination confirmed 'that there was nothing wrong with his appendix' (pp. 49-50).

In like vein Weiss & English (1957) deal briefly with the case of a patient who, beginning with appendectomy, had a series of abdominal operations in quick succession. The patient was diagnosed as suffering from 'chronic appendicitis'.

In this context it is of interest to present the opinions of prominent pathologists: Robbins (1962) writes that 'True chronic inflammation of the appendix is rare' and unequivocal differential diagnosis uncertain (p. 702); moreover, Boyd (1961) states that 'it is doubtful if there is such an entity as chronic appendicitis' (p. 761).

It can be seen, then, that psychosomatic medicine has rarely dealt with appendicitis, and whenever it has done so the main concern has been with what might be called 'functional appendicitis'; that is, with those patients whose appendices, upon removal, are found to be normal in subsequent laboratory examination. This problem has aroused considerable interest among physicians in general.

In reference to which categories of patients are most prone to have normal appendices removed, Lee (1961) studied a large sample of patients in the British National Health Service hospitals during the year 1956-7. All cases considered had 'appendicitis' as their principal diagnosis when they left the hospital. Lee found that for males the highest frequency of appendicitis occurs at age 12, for females at age 17. The other finding was that the ratio of females to male cases of appendicitis at age 15-24 varied between 1.6:8–1.8:1 (years 1955-7). In the period 1931-5 it was 1.8:1, i.e. no change in the ratio over the years. The histological data were not available, but Lee feels that in young females some 'appendicitis' cases are not due to inflammation of the appendix.

Harding (1962) examined 1300 appendices removed surgically over a period of seven years beginning in 1955. He found that in the sample as a whole there were 39.6 per cent normal appendices, but the percentage of normal appendices varied between different age-sex groups. The highest percentage was found among females 11-20 years old – 62.0 per cent; among the males in the same age group the percentage was only 24.6. The author advances two hypotheses as explanation for so many diagnostic errors in young females: (*a*) the symptoms are derived from the ovary; (*b*) psychological reasons.

More recent studies (Ingram, Evans & Oppenheim, 1965; Meyer, Unger & Slaughter, 1964) attempted to find a relationship between 'normal appendectomies' and psychological factors operating in such patients.

The Ingram research studied 118 female patients (age 15-35) whose final diagnosis on admission was 'appendicitis' or 'pain in the right iliac fossa – cause unknown'. The figure represents all the female patients with the above diagnoses admitted to one surgical unit in a British hospital during a period of four years. Ninety-one patients were actually operated on, fifty-six of these were found to have normal appendices. The social history of each patient was obtained by a social worker in one interview and the Cornell Medical Index was administered to all the patients. A follow-up interview was carried out 1-3 years after the initial investigation. Some could not be met again personally and the information was obtained by letter from the patient herself or from other sources. The result of the operation was defined as 'satisfactory' if the patient was cured of her abdominal pain and had no new complaints. It was deemed unsatisfactory if there were recurrence of the abdominal pain and/or additional complaints of psychosomatic symptoms.

The investigators found that in the group operated on, women who had normal appendices removed had significantly more emotional problems than women with diseased appendices. Results of the follow-up, in which 112 of the 118 patients were traced, showed: (*a*) satisfactory outcomes were much more likely after the removal of a diseased appendix; (*b*) there was an association between emotional problems and an unsatisfactory outcome at time of follow-up. The authors, explaining these data, conjecture that when the appendix is normal the origin of the pain may be the right colon.

Meyer and his colleagues (1964) included in their initial sample 533 patients in an American hospital operated upon for the primary diagnosis of appendicitis during the years 1949-51. According to the pathologists' diagnosis 144 were excluded from the sample since it was doubtful whether the appendix was the cause of symptoms. This left a sample of 389 patients in whom, according to the pathologists' diagnosis, (*a*) the appendix was surely the cause of symptoms or (*b*) surely was not the cause of symptoms. The hospital records of all these patients were reviewed.

The view may be taken that the cases in category (*b*) were diagnostic errors and probably the majority suffered from other illness that caused the symptoms of appendicitis (e.g. ovarian cyst, mesenteric adenitis, etc.).

There were 173 female patients in the sample. The type of hospital service was selected as an index of economic class: ward service was construed as an indicator of lower economic class, semi-private and private services as an indicator of higher economic class. Of these females 103 were in the age range 10-29 years: 46 of them were located for a health interview conducted by a psychiatric social worker 9-12 years after the appendectomy, information on 19 additional females was obtained by questionnaire, leaving 38 on whom information could not be obtained.

The researchers found that the female patients between the ages of 10 and 29 had a higher proportion of normal appendices removed than the male patients of the same age. In other age-groups a significant difference between the sexes was not present. It was also found that the young female patient who had a normal appendix removed had more illness in the ten years following appendectomy than one who had a pathological appendix removed. Finally, among all the females (173 patients) there was a significantly larger proportion of normal appendices removed from patients in the higher economic class as compared with the patients from the lower economic class.

In the last decade only one author has pointed out that there exists a possibility of a relationship between birth fantasies and appendicitis. Inman (1958, 1962) cited a few cases of appendicitis in which the illness could be related to birth fantasies. In the majority of cases there existed a temporal proximity between the appendicitis and a birth of a baby or a wedding in the psychological vicinity of the afflicted person. Following Inman's thinking it is reasonable to assume that there is some event in real life that gives rise to birth fantasies, which initiate acute pain in the right iliac fossa, leading to the diagnosis of acute appendicitis and appendectomy. The most plausible events related to birth fantasies would be, in all likelihood, childbirth, forthcoming childbirth, or wedding among people who are psychologically close to the patient. The following hypothetical chain becomes obvious: a birth event (childbirth, forthcoming childbirth, or wedding); birth fantasies; pain in the right iliac fossa; diagnosis of acute appendicitis; appendectomy.

Inman's suppositions were based on perceptive observations, distributed over a period of time. Owing to the circumstances within which his thinking emerged a pathologist's findings could not be included in his work and the number of cases described is limited. Nonetheless, worthwhile testable hypotheses may be derived from his ideas.

The present study will test the following hypotheses:

(1) The proportion of appendectomies among surgery patients who have a birth event in their personal history (BE group) will be significantly higher than the proportion of appendectomies among surgery patients who do not have a birth event in their personal history (NBE group).

(2) The proportion of normal appendices will be higher in appendectomies following birth events than in appendectomies not following birth events.

(3) In the group of young females the proportion of appendectomies in the BE group will be higher than in any other group of surgery patients formed on the basis of sex and age.

(4) In the group of females with high socioeconomic status (high SES) the proportion of appendectomies in the BE group will be higher than in any other group of surgery patients formed on the basis of sex and SES.

METHOD

Subjects. The sample used in this study was composed of seventy patients who underwent an operation at the Royal Alexandra Hospital in Edmonton between 1 October 1965 and 6 January 1966. There were two groups: appendectomy and matched cases.

Appendectomy group. In order to minimize the influence of the diagnostic error of the operating surgeon, it was decided to include in the appendectomy group only those patients whose pre-operative and post-operative diagnoses were both appendicitis.

All patients meeting this requirement, 15 years of age or older, and who underwent an appendectomy in the hospital between 1 October 1965 and 23 December 1965 were potential subjects. There were 49 such patients in the hospital. However, only 35 have been included in the study and interviewed (AI group). Fourteen patients were not interviewed (ANI group), although they were potential subjects. The reasons for not interviewing them were: 5 patients were discharged from the hospital earlier than expected; for 5 patients the attending physician's permission to interview his patient could not be secured; 1 patient was a deaf-mute; 1 patient did not speak English; for 1 patient an answer from the attending physician was not obtained before the patient's discharge from the hospital; and 1 patient refused to be interviewed. There were 21 males and 14 females in the AI group. The ANI group was composed of 6 males and 8 females.

Matched cases group. This group (MC) (see Table 17.1) was selected from among all the patients who underwent an operation other than appendectomy in the hospital during the same period of time as the AI group. However, the following categories of patients were *a priori* excluded from this group: patients undergoing surgery following accident or fracture (because these injuries are often externally imposed), tonsillectomy patients (because usually they leave the hospital before they can speak freely), and children below 15 years (because there were no children in the AI group). Matched cases, paired according to sex and age to cases in the AI group, were selected from the remaining pool of the surgery patients. There were 21 males and 14 females in the MC group.

Selection of the subjects. Between 1 October 1965 and 23 December 1965 the records of the operating room of the hospital were checked daily. Whenever a case that could be included in the AI group was found, the records for that day were scrutinized for a matched case to be included in the MC group. The cases were matched to AI patients according to sex and age. Any patient of the same sex, up to two years younger or older than the AI case to be matched, was considered. If more than one potential matched case was found on a particular day, the selection was determined by tossing a die. If potential matched cases could not be found on the same day, the records were searched during the following days, until at least one potential matched case was found. Whenever the selected matched case was not available for interviewing, another patient was selected in one of two ways: (1) from among the potential matched cases operated on the same day but rejected following the tossing of the die; (2) if cases were not available from the same day, the operating-room records were searched during the following days, until at least one matched case was found. For this reason the intake of MC patients continued until 6 January 1966.

TABLE 17.1. *Summary of operations performed on the MC group patients.*

Type of operation	No. of cases
Haemorrhoidectomy	3
Submucous resection (in one case accompanied by nasal polypectomy)	3
Bilateral internasal antrostomy	1
Cholecystectomy (in some cases accompanied by cholangiogram or incidental appendectomy)	4
Excision of pilonidal sinus	3
Excision of tumour, right wrist, with application of plaster cast (slab) and excision of naevus on navel	1
Repair of anal fissure	1
Unilateral vein ligation and stripping, left leg	1
Incision and drainage of ischio-rectal abscess	1
Removal of foreign body from jejunum	1
Discectomy, lumbar 5, sacral 1	1
Submucous resection, bilateral intranasal antrostomy, and right myringotomy	1
Hysterectomy (accompanied by salpingectomy, oophorectomy or incidental appendectomy)	3
Bilateral Goldens operation, first and fifth toes	1
Excision of ovarian cyst (accompanied by incidental appendectomy)	2
Incision and drainage of left elbow (following cellulitis)	1
Excision or resection of ingrown toenail	2
Left tympanoplasty	1
Incision and drainage of right femur and aspiration of right knee	1
Repair of pectus excavatum	1
Right oophorectomy	1
Transurethral resection of bladder tumour	1
Total	35

After the selection of a potential subject, the head nurse on his ward was asked to request permission of the attending physician to interview the patient. Following the physician's approval the patient was asked to participate in the study, and if he agreed he was interviewed. If a potential AI subject could not be interviewed, his matched case was not included in the study.

Procedure. The subjects were interviewed in the hospital a few days after the operation, but not earlier than on the second post-operative day. The interview was conducted in a room in which only the subject and the interviewer were present. After the ward nurse had introduced the interviewer to the patient and left the room, the reasons for the visit were briefly explained and the enquiry commenced forthwith. The interview was structured, based on an open-ended questionnaire. The same basic questionnaire was used for all the subjects included in the sample. At the end of the study the reports of the pathologist were checked for each interviewed subject in the AI group to find out whether the removed appendix was pathological or normal.

The questionnaire. The introductory remarks and the questionnaire were formulated in such a way as not to reveal the purpose of the study to the interviewee. At the beginning of the interview the subject was told only that a study was being conducted among the patients in the hospital and that he was invited to participate. Those participating in the study were assured of strict confidentiality and anonymity in possible reporting of the results. The questionnaire contained 63 open-ended questions; of these 6 pertained to births, pregnancies and adoptions in the family; 6 to births, pregnancies and adoptions among friends, neighbours and distant relatives; 2 questions dealt with weddings and other celebrations. The 14 questions dealing directly with the subject of inquiry were interspersed among other questions; question no. 20 being the first one dealing with birth. The remaining 49 questions dealt with the medical history of the patient; illness among family members, friends, and neighbours; patient's social life and recreation a short time before the admission to the hospital; identifying data (date of birth, marital status, etc.); sociometric choices; and factors which were defined as determining socioeconomic status (SES) – that is, education, income, and occupation.

Construction of SES indices. Three factors were considered as determining the SES of a subject: education, income, and occupation. All the factors had equal weight. On each factor a person could receive 1-3 points, the values of the three factors were summed up and the result considered as indicating the SES level of this person. Table 17.2 describes the assignment of points on each factor.

TABLE 17.2. *Assignment of points for education, income, and occupation.*

	Points		
Factor	1	2	3
Education	0 – 9 years	10 – 12 years	13 + years
Income	Less than $5000 per year	$5000 – $10,000 per year	More than $10,000 per year
Occupation	Labourers – any level of skill (including farm hands)	Clerical, sales, technicians, farmers, small businessmen	Professional, managerial, large businessmen and proprietors

The total number of points for an individual could vary between 3 and 9. Subjects receiving 3-4 points were considered as having low SES, 5-7 points medium SES, 8-9 points high SES.

If a subject was still attending a high school, the occupation and the education of his father were considered; if he was attending an educational institution of a level higher than a high school, the occupation of his father, but his own education, were considered. If a subject was a housewife, the occupation of her husband was considered.

The information about the education, income, and occupation was obtained from each subject during the interview. Whenever doubt has arisen as to the classification of a particular occupation, Hollingshead's (1957) index was consulted.

Example: Suppose that a subject was a truck driver, had completed 11 years of schooling, and the gross income of his family was $6000 per year. He received one point on the occupational scale, two points on the educational scale, and two points on the income scale. His total number of points was five, accordingly his SES was defined as 'medium'.

Definition of birth event. In terms of time this concept was defined as within one month before or after the operation. By persons involved, it included parents of the subject, spouse, siblings, children, aunts, uncles, first cousins and the five psychologically closest people not already listed. The five psychologically closest people were determined on the basis of sociometric choices given by the subject during the interview. The birth event was denoted as an actual birth of a baby, a pregnancy, and a wedding at which the subject was present.

Assignment to experimental groups. The study group (BE) was composed of all those subjects whose interview data revealed a birth event as defined above in their background. The control group (NBE) was composed of all those subjects whose interview data did not reveal a birth event. As can be seen from the diagram (Table 17.3), subjects from both AI and MC groups have been included either in the BE or NBE groups.

TABLE 17.3. *Summary of group names by abbreviation, description, and source (see text for complete details).*

Abbreviation	Description	Source
AI	Appendectomy patients who were interviewed	All appendectomy patients in hospital during the study period (except those included in the ANI group)
ANI	Appendectomy patients who were not interviewed	Appendectomy patients that could not be interviewed
MC	Matched cases	Selected from among surgery patients (other than appendectomy) in hospital during the study period
BE	Following the interview a birth event was found in the personal history	Drawn from both AI and MC groups
NBE	Following the interview a birth event was not found in the personal history	Drawn from both AI and MC groups

RESULTS

Preliminary considerations

Because almost 30 per cent of the potential subjects have not been included in the study, there existed the possibility of some kind of bias. Therefore, the sex distribution, the mean age, and the proportions of normal appendices of the AI and ANI groups were compared. The sex and age data were obtained from the operating-room records, the condition of the removed appendix from the pathologist's report. Other data on the ANI group were not available.

The sex distribution of both groups is presented in Table 17.4. The test of significance of the difference between proportions yielded a result of $z < 1$. The mean age of the AI group was 28.34 years, and the mean age of the ANI group was 30.00 years; a t-test of the difference between means yielded a result of $t < 1$. The proportion of normal appendices in the AI group was 0.11, in the ANI group this proportion was 0.29; a test of significance of the difference between proportions yielded a value $z = 1.04$ ($P > 0.20$). On the basis of these findings it was concluded that on those characteristics compared the ANI group did not differ significantly from the AI group.

TABLE 17.4. *Distribution of males and females in the AI and ANI groups.*

Group	Male	Female	Total
AI	21	14	35
ANI	6	8	14
Total	27	22	49

When matched cases for patients in the AI group were selected, a leeway of 2 years in either direction was allowed. The mean ages of the AI group (28.34 years) and of the MC group (28.66 years) were compared, yielding a value of $t < 1$. As mentioned above, the sex distribution in both groups was identical.

Test of the hypotheses

As can be seen from Table 17.5, a very small number of subjects could be assigned to the BE group according to the original definition of birth event. The test of significance of the difference between proportions yielded a result of $z < 1$.

Because psychologically important persons and the time of the birth event were defined arbitrarily, a decision was made to redefine these variables. Analysis of the interview questionnaires revealed that in the majority of the cases the most important people for the subject were members of the family, sociometric choices beyond the family circle being given usually only when explicitly requested. Therefore only family members (as originally defined) were left in the category of 'persons involved in the birth event'. On the other hand, when asked about recent or forthcoming births the subjects mentioned events in the remote past and months ahead. However, subjects did not mention expected births beyond six months ahead. It seemed reasonable therefore to impose a six-month time limit upon births in the past and the same time limit upon weddings. The new definition of a birth event, involving changes in time and persons, arrived at on the basis of the data, is as follows: (*a*) time – within six months before or after the operation; (*b*) persons involved – parents of the subject, spouse, siblings, children, aunts, uncles, first cousins; (*c*) birth event – retained as defined originally, i.e. birth of a baby, expected birth, and a wedding at which the subject was present.

TABLE 17.5. *Distribution of appendectomies and other operations in the BE and NBE groups (the groups defined according to the original specifications).*

	TYPE OF OPERATION		
Group	Append-ectomy	Other	Total
BE	5	3	8
NBE	30	32	62
Total	35	35	70

The subjects were assigned to the BE and NBE groups according to the new definition and the data were reanalysed. The results henceforth presented are based on the new definition of the groups and all tests of significance are two-tailed.

TABLE 17.6. *Distribution of appendectomies and other operations in the BE and NBE groups.*

	TYPE OF OPERATION		
Group	Append-ectomy	Other	Total
BE	17	5	22
NBE	18	30	48
Total	35	35	70

The data presented in Table 17.6 support the first hypothesis. The test of significance of the difference between proportions yielded a result of $z=2.83$ ($P<0.005$). There was a significant association between appendectomy and a birth event. An association between other operations and birth event did not exist.

Table 17.7 shows that the proportions of normal appendices were virtually the same in both groups. Therefore, the second hypothesis of this study has to be rejected.

TABLE 17.7. *Distribution of pathological and normal appendices in the BE and NBE groups.*

	CONDITION OF APPENDIX		
Group	Pathological	Normal	Total
BE	15	2	17
NBE	16	2	18
Total	31	4	35

For the purpose of testing the third hypothesis, 'young females' were defined as females aged 15-29 on the day of the operation. Table 17.8 shows that among young females the proportion of appendectomies in the BE group was 0.67, while in the rest of the sample it was 0.81. The results are in the opposite direction to that predicted. The third hypothesis has to be rejected.

TABLE 17.8. *Distribution of appendectomies and other operations in the BE and NBE groups among young females and in the rest of the sample.*

	YOUNG FEMALES			REST OF THE SAMPLE			
Group	Appendectomy	Other	Total	Appendectomy	Other	Total	Grand total
BE	4	2	6	13	3	16	22
NBE	3	6	9	15	24	39	48
Total	7	8	15	28	27	55	70

The group of females with high socioeconomic status (high SES) was very small, therefore it was combined with the group of females with medium SES. The combined group is termed as having 'upper

SES'. In Table 17.9 it is found that among upper SES females the proportion of appendectomies in the BE group was 0.60, while in the rest of the sample it was 0.82. The results were in the opposite direction to the predicted one. The conclusion is that the fourth hypothesis has to be rejected.

TABLE 17.9. *Distribution of appendectomies and other operations in the BE and NBE groups among females with upper SES and in the rest of the sample.*

	UPPER SES FEMALES			REST OF THE SAMPLE			
Group	Append-ectomy	Other	Total	Append-ectomy	Other	Total	Grand total
BE	3	2	5	14	3	17	22
NBE	6	8	14	12	22	34	48
Total	9	10	19	26	25	51	70

Additional findings

Information on subjects' sex, age, SES, marital status, and being or not being a parent was available. The sample was broken down according to the values of these variables and statistical analysis of the data carried out.

Table 17.10 shows that the sex variable was not an important factor. Among the males the difference between the proportions of appendectomies in the BE and NBE groups was 0.350; among the females the difference was 0.467. The difference between the differences was 0.117 and this value was not significant ($z < 1$).

TABLE 17.10. *Distribution of appendectomies and other operations in the BE and NBE groups among males and females.*

	MALES			FEMALES			
Group	Append-ectomy	Other	Total	Append-ectomy	Other	Total	Grand total
BE	9	3	12	8	2	10	22
NBE	12	18	30	6	12	18	48
Total	21	21	42	14	14	28	70

The breakdown of the sample according to age, type of operation, and assignment to the experimental groups is presented in Table 17.11. Among the younger subjects the difference between the proportions of appendectomies in the BE and NBE groups was 0.430; in the older group this difference was 0.398. Comparison of the differences yielded a result of $z < 1$.

TABLE 17.11. *Distribution of appendectomies and other operations in the BE and NBE groups among younger and older subjects.*

	15 – 29 YEARS			30+ YEARS			
Group	Append-ectomy	Other	Total	Append-ectomy	Other	Total	Grand total
BE	12	4	16	5	1	6	22
NBE	8	17	25	10	13	23	48
Total	20	21	41	15	14	29	70

The group of subjects with high SES was very small (nine cases only). For this reason, it was combined with the group of subjects with medium SES; the combined group is termed as having 'upper SES'. The data presented in Table 17.12 show that in the low SES group the difference between the proportions of appendectomies in the BE and NBE groups was 0.706; in the upper SES group the difference was 0.196. Comparison of the differences yielded a value of $z = 1.93$ ($P < 0.06$). This result did not meet the usual rule of thumb requirement that the level of probability should be 5 per cent. Nonetheless, considering the smallness of the sample, the result seems to indicate that the association between birth events and appendectomies was much stronger in the lower than in the upper social classes. This finding will be discussed later, as if it had met the usual requirement for level of significance.

TABLE 17.12. *Distribution of appendectomies and other operations in the BE and NBE groups among subjects with low SES and upper SES.*

	LOW SES			UPPER SES			
Group	Append-ectomy	Other	Total	Append-ectomy	Other	Total	Grand total
BE	9	0	9	8	5	13	22
NBE	5	12	17	13	18	31	48
Total	14	12	26	21	23	44	70

The sample did not include widowed persons. Four subjects who were either divorced or separated were included with the subjects in the 'unmarried' group. Among the married subjects the difference between the proportions of appendectomies in the BE and NBE groups was 0.585; among the unmarried subjects the difference was 0.187. Comparison of the differences yielded a value of $z = 1.53$ ($P < 0.13$). The result was not significant at the 5 per cent level. On the other hand, computation of Tschuprow's T yielded the following results: for the married group $T = 0.25$; for the unmarried group $T = 0.01$. This seems to denote that the association between birth events and appendectomies was stronger among the married than among the unmarried subjects.

TABLE 17.13. *Distribution of appendectomies and other operations in the BE and NBE groups among married and unmarried subjects.*

	MARRIED			UNMARRIED			
Group	Append-ectomy	Other	Total	Append-ectomy	Other	Total	Grand total
BE	11	2	13	6	3	9	22
NBE	6	17	23	12	13	25	48
Total	17	19	36	18	16	34	70

As shown in Table 17.14, among the parents the difference between the proportions of appendectomies in the BE and NBE groups was 0.465; among the non-parents the difference was 0.297. The difference between the differences was 0.168 and this result was not significant ($z < 1$).

TABLE 17.14. *Distribution of appendectomies and other operations in the BE and NBE groups among parents and non-parents.*

	PARENTS			NON-PARENTS			
Group	Append-ectomy	Other	Total	Append-ectomy	Other	Total	Grand total
BE	11	2	13	6	3	9	22
NBE	8	13	21	10	17	27	48
Total	19	15	34	16	20	36	70

DISCUSSION

The main hypothesis

The data presented lend strong support to the first hypothesis of this study. When surgery patients are divided into two groups – the appendectomies and other operations – appendectomies follow birth events more frequently than the other operations combined. The strength of association does not seem to depend on sex or age factors (Tables 17.10 and 17.11).

An important view of psychosomatic disease and emotion in general is the Papez-MacLean theory. This theory, as developed by MacLean (1949), considers the limbic system (sometimes termed 'rhinencephalon') as the centre of emotion. Furthermore, it is pointed out that there are many strong connexions between the limbic system and the centres of the autonomic nervous system as contrasted with difficulty in demonstrating pathways between the neocortex and the hypothalamus. This suggests the dominance of the limbic system in the realm of visceral activity. Consequently, MacLean refers to the limbic system as the 'visceral brain', to distinguish it from the neocortex ('word brain') which controls the body musculature and subserves the function of the intellect.

The topographical position of the limbic system in the brain seems to enable it to associate many unrelated phenomena. 'This region of the brain appears to be so strategically situated as to be able to correlate every form of internal and external perception. In other words, the possibility exists in this region for bringing into association not only oral and visceral sensations, but also impressions from the sex organs, body wall, eye, and ear' (MacLean, 1949, p. 351). MacLean goes on to emphasize that 'in contrast to the neopallium, the rhinencephalon has many and strong connections with the hypothalamus for discharging its impressions'. To put it somewhat differently, the phylogenetically older part of the brain (the limbic system) is capable of associating different stimuli, but is incapable of analysing them. 'Considered in the light of Freudian psychology, the visceral brain would have many of the attributes of the unconscious' (p. 348).

The strong support lent to this theory by subsequent experimental work enabled Morgan (1965) to state: 'The Papez-MacLean theory is now much more than a theory. It is a general description of what experiment has established, namely, that the limbic system is the central system in emotion' (p. 312).

It is now possible to see the implications of this theory for the explanation of the dynamics of psychosomatic disorders. MacLean (1949) says:

> It should be remarked that one of the striking observations regarding the patient with psychosomatic illness is his apparent intellectual inability to verbalize his emotional feelings . . . In the psychosomatic patient it would almost seem there was little direct exchange between the visceral brain and the word brain, and that emotional feelings built up in the hippocampal formation, instead of being relayed to the intellect for evaluation, found immediate expression through autonomic centres. In other words, emotional feelings, instead of finding expression and discharge in the symbolic use of words and appropriate behaviour, might be conceived as being translated into a kind of 'organ language' (p. 350).

The original problem remains to be explained. Birth is preceded by a sexual intercourse. In Western culture birth *per se* is not considered a taboo subject. By contrast, sexual intercourse is a taboo subject. It is understandable that once a person has learned 'where babies come from' the two subjects of birth and sexual intercourse become inseparable. Consciously a person may be preoccupied with thoughts about birth, pregnancy, or a new baby, but unconsciously he is preoccupied with sexual fantasies. Following this association, conscious and unconscious birth fantasies occur. The first kind is perfectly acceptable to society and the inner moral censor, the second kind is abhorrent to both society and the inner moral censor. It can be assumed with confidence that whenever the second type of fantasy emerges (and it likely follows the conscious preoccupation with birth), feelings of guilt arise as well. The feelings of guilt remain unconscious and, of course, their source remains unconscious. These feelings are 'stored' in the limbic system and never reach the neocortex. The psychic tension is not discharged through verbal or other behaviour, controlled by the neocortex, but downward through the limbic system, using 'organ language'. The vermiform appendix, being a part of the viscera and controlled by the autonomic nervous system, is well fitted to express 'organ language'.

There is one type of sexual intercourse which is fully sanctioned in Western culture; that between husband and wife. Sexual fantasies concerning one's spouse do not usually cause feelings of guilt. If the foregoing explanation is valid, wives should not have appeared among persons whose birth event preceded the appendectomy. There were six married males undergoing appendectomy in the BE group; two of them mentioned their wives as persons associated with birth events. In both cases the pregnancy preceded the marriage: one married when his bride was in the sixth month of pregnancy; the second, while only 17 years old, was already a father of a two-and-a-half months old baby. In this case also the marriage was probably contracted to sanction the pregnancy (the date of marriage was not obtained).[1] In both instances, then, strong feelings of guilt might have arisen.

An attempt may be made now to explain the puzzling phenomenon of very low frequency of appendicitis during the first two years of life (Longino, Holder & Gross, 1958). Two complementary hypotheses may be advanced: (*a*) the young child's vocabulary is very limited, he cannot understand notifications about birth events; (*b*) the mechanism of repression is not yet established at this early age; when psychic tension accumulates in the nervous system it can be relayed to the neocortex and discharged behaviourally rather than somatized. The reason the vermiform appendix is selected as the site of the lesion remains an open question.

It could be maintained that appendicitis is akin to pseudocyesis. However, the data presented by Bivin & Klinger (1937) seem to refute this assumption. These authors review 444 cases of pseudocyesis described in the literature during the period 1685-1935, and appendicitis is never associated with pseudocyesis. It is hardly likely, in any case, that diagnostician would confuse pseudocyesis and appendicitis.

Another possible explanation of this finding, congruent with Groddeck's (1923) hypothesis, is that the birth event gives rise to a birth wish, which is expressed through appendectomy (symbolic delivery). If this is so, then among childless people there should be a stronger association between birth events and appendectomies than among parents. This supposition, however, is not supported by the data represented in Table 17.14.

At this present writing, little more than speculation may be advanced toward more acceptable explanations: (*a*) it is possible that not only the appendix is affected following birth events (Inman, 1958, 1962, 1965), (*b*) there might be a familial predisposition

[1] Considering the age of his baby, it is of interest to note that this patient succumbed to appendicitis almost exactly a year after having the intercourse with his future wife which led to her out-of-wedlock pregnancy.

(constitutional or other) toward the same type of illness[1] (Adler, 1929), (*c*) the appendix is situated in the pelvic region. These hypotheses need not be considered mutually exclusive.

The remaining hypotheses

The second hypothesis of this study stated that the proportion of normal appendices will be higher in appendectomies following birth events than in appendectomies not following birth events. This hypothesis was rejected. It was based on the findings of the Ingram research (1965), where it was reported that patients who had normal appendices removed exhibited more emotional problems than patients who had pathological appendices removed. The implicit assumption behind this hypothesis was that birth events (and birth fantasies), being psychogenic factors, represent emotional problems and are associated with functional illness. However, the Ingram sample did not exclude all those patients who had a post-operative diagnosis other than 'appendicitis'. In other words, all the diagnostic errors of the surgeons were included in the sample. This fact explains, perhaps, why Ingram found more health complaints after the removal of normal as contrasted with that of pathological appendix. The Meyer group (1964) also reported more illness under similar circumstances. On the other hand, in the present study the possibility of diagnostic error was greatly reduced by excluding from the sample all those patients who did not have a post-operative diagnosis of 'appendicitis'. The present sample represents a different population and, as might be expected, the results are different.

The third and the fourth hypotheses had the same implicit assumption behind them and were an attempt to replicate the findings of Meyer, Unger & Slaughter (1964). Again, the population studied was different in the present investigation. The Meyer, like that of the Ingram work, included all appendectomy patients in the sample and this explains the rejection of these hypotheses. An additional reason for rejection of the fourth hypothesis may be the great difference between definitions of SES used by the Meyer and present study.

An important conclusion may be reached following the acceptance of the first, and rejection of the second, third and fourth hypotheses;

[1] Sixty per cent of the appendectomy patients included in the sample reported that at least one of their parents or siblings also underwent appendectomy.

namely, psychogenic factors appear to operate in the genesis of appendicitis with an organic basis.

Additional findings

The SES factor appeared to be a notably important determinant of the strength of association between birth events and appendectomies (Table 17.12). Differential patterns of behaviour may possibly contribute to the observed difference in the strength of the association between birth events and appendectomies across the social classes.

It has been found that members of the lower social class very frequently have relatives, outside their immediate households, living in the same community (Pineo, 1964). By way of contrast, members of the middle and upper classes are often isolated geographically from their kinship groups (Seely, Sim & Loosley, 1964). In these classes young people leave the communities in which they have grown, bringing with them to the new place only their nuclear families. The geographical isolation is also a social isolation (Seeley *et al.*, 1964). The ties with the kinship group are weak, the psychological importance of the non-nuclear part of the family becomes marginal.

Differential patterns of social activities are another factor which may be considered in this context. Members of the middle and upper classes generally join formal associations and frequently more than one (Komarovsky, 1946). On the other hand, members of the lower social class rarely join formal associations, and if they do, often remain inactive. In this class the leisure time is spent in informal groups composed predominantly of relatives (Dotson, 1951); the social activities are restricted to the kinship group. Family celebrations and other familial events figure prominently against this background; they probably attain more importance in the lower than in any other social class.

These two patterns of life may be contrasted: in the lower class the family unit is embedded in an extended kinship system and the family's social activities are limited to it. In the upper classes the family unit is isolated geographically and socially from its kinship group. Birth events in the non-nuclear part of the family probably lose much of their psychological impact in the upper social classes as compared to the lower class.

Finally, there exists a possibility that because of the differences in modes of communication (Schatzman & Strauss, 1955) members of the lower social class tend to verbalize their emotions less. Following socially unacceptable fantasies, the discharge (direct or indirect) of feelings of guilt through verbal behaviour is not as readily available to them as to the members of middle and upper classes.

It was also found that there was a stronger association between birth events and appendectomies in the group of married than in the group of unmarried subjects (Table 17.13). This finding should be related to the fact that the marriage ceremony frees the couple to anticipate parenthood; unmarried persons, according to existing social mores, should not plan to have children. Therefore, married people probably pay more attention to birth events and these are apt to attain more prominence in their psychological world.

Suggestions for further research

The most challenging question to be submitted to future research is whether the morbid influence of a birth event is restricted to the appendicitis-appendectomy sequence, or whether there are some other diseases as much related to birth events.

Another interesting problem is the length of time elapsing between a birth event and the onset of illness. A closely related problem is whether an attack of appendicitis is temporally associated with the actual date of birth (or wedding), or with the date on which the future patient learned about the birth (or his participation in the wedding).

In this study birth fantasies were related to a birth event actually taking place in real life. However, as seen in the case of Dora (Freud, 1905), birth fantasies can be related to an imagined birth event as well. Furthermore, birth fantasies might possibly arise without being preceded by a birth event (real or imagined). Future research will probably attempt to discover the circumstances upon which birth fantasies may appear.

Finally, a cross-cultural research should be conducted to ascertain whether the association between birth events and the appendicitis-appendectomy sequence can be found in non-Western cultures, or if it is a culturally restricted phenomenon.

SUMMARY

Two groups of surgery patients were interviewed in hospital a few days after operation in order to find out whether there was a birth event (BE) preceding their admission to the hospital. One group consisted of thirty-five patients undergoing appendectomy, following a primary diagnosis of appendicitis; the second group was composed of thirty-five patients matched according to age and sex to the appendectomy patients and undergoing a variety of other operations in the same hospital and at the same time. A significant association between BE and appendectomy was found; the association between BE and other operations did not exist. Certain psychosocial variables were found to affect the strength of association between BE and appendectomy. The results were discussed with reference to the Papez-MacLean theory of psychosomatic disease and findings presented in sociological literature.

ACKNOWLEDGEMENTS

It is my pleasure to acknowledge my gratitude to Dr D. Spearman, thesis supervisor, who has guided this project through its many stages, offered many stimulating suggestions, and has greatly improved the style of the final report. Dr J. Guild sponsored the research at the hospital, helped in the final formulation of the questionnaire and contributed many valuable suggestions concerning interviewing in a clinical setting. I am also indebted to Dr W. Rozeboom and Dr S. Weisz. Finally, I would like to thank all those physicians, nurses, and patients at the Royal Alexandra Hospital who co-operated in this research.

COMMENT

The hypothesis that Eylon is attempting to investigate in this study is that 'some event in real life gives rise to birth fantasies which initiate acute pain in the right iliac fossa, leading to the diagnosis of acute appendicitis and appendectomy'. Comparing a group of appendectomy patients with a matched group of other surgical cases, he finds a significantly greater number of 'birth events' in the recent histories of the experimental group. Birth events included actual births, pregnancies in close relatives and weddings attended by the patient himself. According to Kline (1972, p. 291): 'the main finding, that birth events were related to appendectomy as distinct from other surgical operations, suggests strongly that psychogenic factors influence appendicitis. This is striking support for the Freudian claim. It is difficult to think of any other theory that could predict such results'. This then, is the third and last study in the area of psychosomatics that is considered to provide good evidence for psychoanalytic theory; let us examine the claim.

First, it is necessary to point out that the positive result Kline calls the 'main finding' does not correspond to the central hypothesis stated above. Implicit in this hypothesis is the expectation that 'the proportion of normal appendices will be higher in appendectomies following birth events than in appendectomies not following birth events'; i.e. post-operative pathological examination of the appendices after removal should reveal a connection between birth events and *pseudoappendicitis* rather than genuine appendicitis. Eylon's results do not support this hypothesis.

Another hypothesis tested by Eylon, that could also be regarded as more critical to Freudian theory than the general connection between birth events and appendicitis, was that the association between birth events and appendicitis should be particularly strong for *young females* since they are presumably more susceptible to birth fantasies than other groups. In this case the results were in the opposite direction to the prediction.

We are left, then, with one relatively peripheral positive result to explain, that of a general association between appendectomies and birth events. Even here, it is noteworthy that with the criteria that Eylon initially set for defining birth events no significant connection with appendectomies was detected. Only by restricting the 'five psychologically closest people' to relatives of the patient and resetting the time limit from one month to *six* months before or after the operation was it possible to obtain a significant difference in the direction predicted by the hypothesis. Eylon deserves some credit for honesty when he admits that this new definition of the birth event was 'arrived at on the basis of the data', though it is a very dubious tactic from the scientific point of view.

But suppose this finding is a real one (i.e. able to be replicated), is it in fact so very difficult to think of a non-Freudian explanation for it? As with the previous study by Wolowitz and Wagonfeld, everything depends upon the appropriateness of the control group. If we can point to any differences between the two groups of patients other than the fact that one received diagnoses of appendicitis and the other not, then the logic of the study as a test of psychoanalytic theory breaks down. As it happens, such a difference is easily identified. Appendicitis is characteristically an extremely *acute* disease; it appears suddenly in otherwise normal, fit and healthy individuals, requiring immediate surgery which is usually accomplished with a minimum of complication and a recovery time of seldom more than a few days. It is most unlikely to prevent a person attending a wedding several months before or afterwards. On the other hand, many of the conditions included in the control group could be regarded as *chronic* and likely to give a great deal of pain and discomfort for long periods before and after surgery, often to the extent that it would be impossible to pursue a normal social life. Eylon may simply have shown that appendectomy patients lead an active social life relative to other surgical cases and are seldom prevented from attending weddings as a result of ill health. (Even if the actual conditions of the control patients listed in Table 17.1 would not themselves interfere with social appearances, most medical experts would agree that they are more likely to be correlated with generalized ill health than appendicitis.)

Finally, we must comment on Eylon's extraordinary attempt to explain 'the puzzling phenomenon of very low frequency of appendicitis during the first two years of life'. He suggests two hypotheses: '(*a*) the young child's vocabulary is very limited, he cannot understand notifications about birth events; (*b*) the mechanism of repression is not yet established at this early age; when psychic tension accumulates in the nervous system it can be relayed to the neocortex and discharged behaviourally rather than somatized'. Apparently because of his strongly pro-Freudian predisposition Eylon has not considered the possibility that appendicitis is not often diagnosed in young children because diagnosis is dependent upon exact localization of the pain by the patient, which of course is more difficult to obtain from a preverbal infant.

REFERENCES

ADLER, A. (1929) *Problems of Neurosis*. London: Kegan Paul, Trench, Trubner and Co.

ALEXANDER, F. (1950) *Psychosomatic Medicine*. New York: Norton.

ALEXANDER, F., FRENCH, T. M., *et al.* (1948) *Studies in Psychosomatic Medicine*. New York: Ronald Press.

BIVIN, G. D. & KLINGER, M. P. (1937) *Pseudocyesis*. Bloomington, Ind.: Principia Press.

BOYD, W. (1961) *Textbook of Pathology*, 7th ed. Philadelphia, Pa.: Lea and Febiger.

DOTSON, F. (1951) Patterns of voluntary association among urban working-class families. *Am. Sociol. Rev.*, **16**, 687-93.

DUNBAR, H. F. (1954) *Emotions and Bodily Changes*, 4th ed. New York: Columbia Univ. Press.

—— (1955) *Mind and Body: Psychosomatic Medicine*, 2nd ed. New York: Random House.

FREUD, S. (1905) *Fragment of an Analysis of a Case of Hysteria*. The standard edition of the complete psychological works of Sigmund Freud, vol. VII, 7-122. London: Hogarth Press, 1953.

GRINKER, R. R. & ROBBINS, F. P. (1953) *Psychosomatic Case-Book*. New York: Blakiston Company.

GRODDECK, G. W. (1923) *The Book of the It*. New York: Random House, 1961.

HARDING, H. E. (1962) A notable source of error in the diagnosis of appendicitis. *Brit. Med. J.*, II, 1028-9.

HOLLINGSHEAD, A. B. (1957) Two-factor index of social position. New Haven, Conn. Unpublished manuscript distributed by the author.

INGRAM, P. W., EVANS, G. & OPPENHEIM, A. N. (1965) Right iliac fossa pain in young women; with appendix on the Cornell Medical Index Health Questionnaire. *Brit. Med. J.*, II, 149-51.

INMAN, W. S. (1958) Clinical thought-reading. *Int. J. Psychoanal.*, **39**, 386-96.

—— (1962) Ophthalmic adventure: a story of frustration and organic disease. *Brit. J. Med. Psychol.*, **35**, 299-309.

—— (1965) Emotional factors in diseases of the cornea. *Brit. J. Med. Psychol.*, **38**, 277-87.

KLINE, P. (1972) *Fact and Fantasy in Freudian Theory*. London: Methuen.

KOMAROVSKY, M. (1946) The voluntary associations of urban dwellers. *Am. Sociol. Rev.*, **11**, 686-98.

LEE, J. A. H. (1961) 'Appendicitis' in young women. *Lancet*, II, 815-17.

LIEF, H. I., LIEF, V. F. & LIEF, N. R. (eds.) (1963) *The Psychological Basis of Medical Practice*. New York: Harper & Row.

LONGINO, L. A., HOLDER, T. M. & GROSS, R. E. (1958) Appendicitis in childhood. *Pediatrics*, **22**, 238-46.

MACLEAN, P. D. (1949) Psychosomatic disease and the 'visceral brain'. *Psychosom. Med.*, **11**, 338-53.

MEYER, E., UNGER, H. T. & SLAUGHTER, R. (1964) Investigation of a psychosocial hypothesis in appendectomies. *Psychosom. Med.*, **26**, 671-81.

MORGAN, C. T. (1965) *Physiological Psychology*, 3rd ed. New York: McGraw-Hill.

PINEO, P. (1964) The extended family in a working-class area of Hamilton. In B. R. BLISHEN, F. E. JONES, K. D. NAEGELE & J. PORTER (eds.) *Canadian Society: Sociological Perspectives*, rev. ed., pp. 135-45. Toronto: Macmillan.

ROBBINS, S. L. (1962) *Textbook of Pathology*, 2nd. ed. Philadelphia, Pa.: W. B. Saunders.

SCHATZMAN, L. & STRAUSS, A. (1955) Social class and modes of communication. *Am. J. Sociol.*, **60**, 329-38.

SEELEY, J. R., SIM, R. A. & LOOSLEY, E. (1964) Family and socialization in an upper class community. In B. R. BLISHEN, F. E. JONES, K. D. NAEGELE & J. PORTER (eds.), *Canadian Society: Sociological Perspectives*, rev. ed., pp. 103-34. Toronto: Macmillan.

STODDART, W. H. B. (1922) A symbolism of appendicitis. *Int. J. Psychoanal.*, **3**, 45.

WEISS, E. & ENGLISH, O. S. (1957) *Psychosomatic Medicine*, 3rd ed. Philadelphia, Pa.: W. B. Saunders.

WITTKOWER, E. D. & CLEGHORN, R. A. (eds.) (1954) *Recent Developments in Psychosomatic Medicine*. Philadelphia, Pa.: J. P. Lippincott.

PART SIX

Neurosis, Psychosis and Psychotherapy

18

Harold S. Zamansky (1958)[1]

An investigation of the psychoanalytic theory of paranoid delusions[2]

Journal of Personality, 26, 410-25

The purpose of the present study was to investigate, using an objective, partially validated technique, the psychoanalytic hypothesis that people who suffer from paranoid delusions have strong but unacceptable homosexual urges. In addition, an attempt was made to study the nature of these impulses and of the defences erected against them.

The psychoanalytic explanation of the dynamics involved in the development of paranoid delusions is that these delusions serve as defensive measures to enable the patient to handle a strong conflict over powerful but unconscious homosexual strivings. What happens is that the proposition 'I (a man) love him' is converted by reaction formation into 'I hate him'. As further insurance that the homosexual wish will not become conscious, this second proposition is transformed, by means of projection, into 'He hates me' (Freud, 1950b). One should find, then, that persons with paranoid delusions have strong homosexual wishes, but that these wishes are not permitted existence on a conscious level. Psychoanalysts generally (Fenichel, 1945, p. 435) have felt that this formulation applies not only to pure paranoia, but also to cases of the paranoid type of schizophrenia.

[1]Harvard University.

[2]This paper is based upon a portion of a dissertation submitted to the Department of Social Relations, Harvard University, in partial fulfilment of the requirements for the degree of Doctor of Philosophy in Clinical Psychology. The writer is greatly indebted to Dr Gardner Lindzey, who was principal advisor for this study and who was always liberal with advice, suggestions, and encouragement. In addition, the writer is grateful to Professor Henry A. Murray, who helped clarify a number of theoretical aspects of this experiment, and to Dr Norman Livson, University of California at Berkeley, who was especially helpful during the developmental phases of the study.

In the five decades since this formulation by Freud, his views have been supported by many psychoanalysts (Ferenczi, 1950; Payne, 1913-14, 1915; Shockley, 1913-14). Other analysts, while agreeing that the paranoid individual is characterized by powerful but unconscious homosexual conflicts, have suggested that homosexuality itself serves a defensive function in the development of the psychosis and is not the primary aetiological factor (Hendrick, 1939; Knight, 1940; Numberg, 1938; Thorner, 1949). Knight (1940), for example, pointed out that the strong homosexual wish of the male paranoid is, in actuality, a very intense and desperate attempt to neutralize and erotize a tremendous unconscious hate directed toward the father. The very powerful need to keep the homosexual urges from awareness is based not on cultural pressures which prohibit the expression of these urges, but on the fact that the least approach to the object arouses intense anxieties that both the object and the patient will be destroyed by the hostility in the patient and the consequent hostility aroused in the object. These theoretical positions were based on and supported by observations made by psychoanalysts in the usual analytic situation with their patients. The question must be raised, however, as to whether the setting of analytic therapy constitutes an adequate observational situation for the testing of an hypothesis. Psychoanalysts have at times been accused of finding in their patients the material they set out to find. Few attempts, for example, have been made by psychoanalysts to compare their findings with a suitable control group.

On the other hand, other investigators have attempted to test the psychoanalytic hypothesis using techniques other than the usual analytic interview and have varied widely in the degree to which their findings supported Freud's conclusions. The studies of Aronson (1953), Gardner (1931), Musiker (1952), and Norman (1948) were generally supportive. On the other hand, investigations such as those of Klein and Horowitz (1949) and Miller (1941) indicated that an intimate relation between paranoid delusions and homosexuality could be demonstrated for only a relatively small percentage of the cases studied.

Because of the conflicting and sometimes ambiguous results of the studies in this area and because of the lack of proper controls in many of them, it seems that the psychoanalytic hypotheses concerning paranoid delusions have yet to be adequately confirmed.

THE PRESENT STUDY

The necessity for obtaining a measurable expression of a need despite powerful forces which act constantly to inhibit its manifestation presented the most difficult practical problem in this study. In developing the technique employed in the present investigation, we began with the assumption that homosexuality is a function of a greater than usual attraction toward members of one's own sex and/or an active rejection of members of the opposite sex. From this it follows that if an individual with strong homosexual urges is placed in a situation in which there is an equal opportunity for attraction to either a member of his own sex or of the opposite sex, he should manifest by his behaviour (if the task is appropriately disguised) a greater attraction to the member of his own sex, and a lesser attraction to the opposite sex, than would the heterosexually oriented person.

More specifically, given an appropriately disguised task, it was expected that if a series of pairs of pictures, each pair consisting of a picture of a man and of a woman, were shown, one pair at a time, to a man with strong homosexual needs, he would spend a larger proportion of the total exposure time looking at the male member of the pairs than would a person with less or none of these needs.

Given the further assumption that paranoid individuals are characacterized by strong homosexual needs, the following hypotheses seemed reasonable:

Hypothesis 1: Men with paranoid delusions, when compared to men without these delusions, will manifest a greater attraction to males than to females.

Hypothesis 2: Paranoid men will manifest a greater avoidance of homosexually threatening stimuli than will non-paranoid men.

Hypothesis 3: Paranoid men, when compared with non-paranoid men, will express a greater preference for women and a lesser one for men as this expression becomes more explicit or conscious.

Hypothesis 4: Paranoid men, when compared with non-paranoid men, will manifest a greater attraction to males than to neutral (non-human) objects.

Hypothesis 5: Paranoid men will manifest a greater avoidance of women than will non-paranoid men.

The picture-pairs technique employed in the present study to test these propositions is based on the assumption that a person will manifest a preference for (or a rejection of) a particular kind of erotic object by looking more (or less) at it than at another kind of object. An initial attempt to validate this technique (Zamansky, 1956), using groups of normal and overt-homosexual males, suggested that it may be considered a valid reflector of object choice.

METHOD

Subjects

In the present study, two groups of *S*s, all patients at the Boston State Hospital, were used. The experimental group consisted of 20 males, most of whom were formally diagnosed as either paranoid condition or dementia praecox, paranoid type, in all of whom the dominant clinical symptom consisted of delusions of persecution, of reference, or of grandeur. These *S*s (as well as the controls) were selected on the basis of their psychiatrist's recommendation and of a thorough study by the writer of the individual case histories. The experimental *S*s ranged in age from 23 to 45 years, with a mean of 30 years. The range of the duration of their present hospitalization was from one month to two years, seven months, and averaged 13 months. Sixteen of the 20 *S*s had had a formal education consisting of some years of high school or better; 12 were or had been married. Twelve *S*s had been engaged in skilled or highly skilled occupations, while eight had been working at relatively nonskilled jobs such as shipper and shoe worker.

The 20 control patients were selected with a view to their being as similar to the experimental *S*s as possible, with the exception of the presence of a dominant paranoid picture. All of the control patients were formally diagnosed as belonging to one of the subtypes of dementia praecox other than the paranoid type. Their age ranged from 19 to 42 years and averaged 33 years. They had been hospitalized from two months to two years, nine months, with a mean of 18 months. Eighteen *S*s had had some high school education or better; only two had ever been married. Thirteen had been engaged in skilled or highly skilled occupations.

Experimental Measure

In the measure of latent homosexuality, 24 pairs of cards, each 9 × 12 inches, were used. On each card was pasted a picture cut from a popular magazine. The pictures were exhibited, a pair at a time, in a specially designed tachistoscope-like viewing apparatus, which permitted the undetected observation of the *S*'s eye movements by an *E* seated at the other end of the apparatus. Three push-button-controlled timers, operated by *E*, recorded the total exposure time as well as the *S*'s male-side and female-side fixation times for each pair of cards. The observation and timing were done for all the *S*s by the writer. To insure against the *E*'s learning the location of any particular picture, the left-right order of the cards was randomly changed after every three or four *S*s.

Psychoanalytic theory states that though strong homosexual impulses are present in people with persecutory delusions, there are also ego defences to prevent the emergence of these impulses into awareness. Thus, it is necessary in a technique of this sort that the *S*s be as unaware as possible of the fact that they are exercising some selection regarding which picture in each pair they look at for a longer period of time. For this reason, the instructions to the *S* indicated that the experiment was a study of the perception of differences in size. He was told that he was to look carefully at each pair of pictures in the viewing apparatus and tell the *E* which member of the pair was larger, that is, which picture had the greater overall surface area. In actuality, both pictures in any one pair, with the exception of three pairs of neutral pictures (i.e., pictures without people, usually landscapes of some sort), were identical in area, although their shapes usually differed. The *S* was allowed to look at each pair of pictures until he felt ready to make a judgment of size. Thus, the exposure of time of each pair was left entirely up to the *S*s.

As has been stated, 24 pairs of pictures were used in the experiment. Of these, six pairs consisted of a picture of a man and of a woman in ordinary dress and position, and three pairs of two or more men and two or more women. Since the task was disguised, it was expected that, if the psychoanalytic formulation is correct, the experimental *S*s would spend a greater proportion of the exposure time looking at the male member of each pair of pictures than would the control *S*s (Hypothesis 1).

In addition to testing for a preponderance of homosexual tendencies in paranoid over non-paranoid persons, an attempt was also made to obtain a manifestation of the strong defensive measures which are said to come into play whenever the emergence of these impulses into consciousness is threatened. For this purpose, two measures were used: (*a*) Included in the 24 pairs of pictures were four pairs of male-female pictures in which the men were pictured in poses which would appear threatening to a person attempting to ward off unconscious homosexual impulses (e.g., two men kissing, two men dressed in towels in a locker room with one man resting his hand upon the other's thigh). The pictures of the females in these pairs were in ordinary pose, not intended to be threatening. In the case of these four pairs of pictures, it was expected that the experimental *S*s would fixate less on the male and longer on the female member of each pair in an effort to avoid the threatening male pictures (Hypothesis 2). (*b*) After all the pictures had been presented once, the entire series was shown again, and this time the *S* was asked to state which picture of each pair he found more appealing – which appeared to attract him more. It was expected in the case of the paranoid *S* that, since the matter of preference was now presented to him on a much more conscious level, his defences would manifest themselves in such a way that he would select significantly fewer pictures of males than he had favoured by his fixation in the first part of the experiment (Hypothesis 3).

Besides investigating the presence of homosexual urges and defences against them in paranoid individuals, some attention was devoted to the question of whether this homosexuality consists primarily of an attraction to men or a rejection of women. For this purpose, four pairs were included in the 24 pairs of pictures which consisted of a picture of a man and a neutral picture (one without any people), as well as four pairs which consisted of a picture of a woman and a neutral picture. It was considered that an attraction to males would be implied if an *S* fixated longer than did the control *S*s on the male cards of the male-neutral pairs. Similarly, an avoidance of women would be implied if he looked longer than the control *S*s at the neutral pictures of the female-neutral pairs (Hypotheses 4 and 5).

Finally, three pairs were included in which both pictures were neutral ones. These were used to lessen the chance that the *S*s would become suspicious that it was their reactions to people that *E* was primarily concerned with. The order of the five different kinds of pairs was systematically varied throughout the entire series of 24. Table 18.1 summarizes the kinds of pictures used.

All the pictures of people (men, women, and threatening men) used in this study were selected from a group of about 175 photographs. The final selections were made from the ratings of five judges (advanced graduate students in clinical psychology). These judges were asked to rate all the male pictures along a four-point scale, in terms of the amount of threat they would have for a person defending against latent homosexual tendencies if he were shown the pictures in the context of performing an intellectual task. The pictures of women were rated according to the degree of threat they would have for a male *S* who is severely threatened by women as sexual objects. From these ratings, only those pictures upon which all five judges agreed closely were selected for inclusion in the experiment. The threatening male pictures were selected from those given a high rating on the threat continuum. The ordinary-pose male pictures (used in the male-female and male-neutral pairs) were taken from those rated as low in threat value. All of the female pictures were taken from the low end of the threat scale. The agreement of the five judges with one another on the threat value of the pictures finally selected to be used in the test was better than 90 per cent.

TABLE 18.1. *Description of picture-pairs.*

Kinds of pairs	Number of such pairs
Male-female	9
Male-neutral	4
Female-neutral	4
Threatening male-female	4
Neutral-neutral	3
Total	24

Scoring procedure

In the case of the nine male-female pairs of pictures, all the scores were expressed as the number of seconds spent looking at the male pictures minus the number of seconds spent looking at the female pictures. Such a score was obtained for each *S* on each pair of pictures. Then these scores were averaged (divided by nine) for each *S* across all male-female pairs. Finally, these individual mean scores were averaged (divided by 20) for each group of *S*s. Thus the final score (Mean Attraction Score) expresses in seconds the mean excess amount of time spent looking at the male pictures in the nine male-female pairs by all 20 *S*s in any one group. This same general procedure was also followed in arriving at the Mean Attraction Score for the other types of picture pairs. In the four threatening male-female pairs, the four male-neutral pairs, and the four female-neutral pairs, the original scores were expressed as the number of seconds spent looking at the threatening male, ordinary male, and female cards, respectively, minus the time devoted to the female, neutral, and neutral cards respectively.

Comparison of Groups

The performances of the experimental and control groups on any series of picture-pairs (such as male-female and female-neutral) were compared by calculating the significance of the difference between the Mean Attraction Score earned by each group for that particular set of cards. The usual formula for the significance of differences between the means of two independent samples was used. Since the direction of differences was predicted in advance in the hypotheses, all statistical results reported were based on one-tail tests of significance.

Since the individual Attraction Scores for the two groups of *S*s were in some cases not normally distributed, the results yielded by the *t* tests were checked against comparisons of the experimental and control groups by means of the Mann-Whitney test (and, in the case of Hypothesis 3, the Wilcoxon matched pairs test), a non-parametric measure which is independent of assumptions about the shape of the population distribution (Mosteller & Bush, 1954, pp. 314-17).

RESULTS

Hypothesis 1: Men with paranoid delusions, when compared to men without these delusions, will manifest a greater attraction to males than to females. The results summarized in Table 18.2 reveal that the paranoid *S*s tended, on the average, to look 1.49 seconds longer at pictures of men in the nine male-female pairs. The score of −.70 for the non-paranoid schizophrenics indicates that these *S*s averaged .70 seconds longer looking at the pictures of women. The difference between these two scores is significant at beyond the .001 level. The corresponding median scores for experimental and control groups were 1.47 and −1.03 seconds respectively, and the Mann-Whitney test of the difference between the two groups was also significant at less than the .001 level ($z=4.37$). These results lend strong experimental support to psychoanalytic formulations and to frequent clinical reports that paranoid delusions are usually accompanied by homosexual tendencies.

TABLE 18.2. *Mean attraction scores (M.A.S.) and significance levels.*

	TYPES OF PICTURE-PAIRS				
	Male-female	Threatening male-female	Male-neutral	Female-neutral	Neutral-neutral
M.A.S.: Experimental group	1·49	1·41	·56	−2·02	−·28
M.A.S.: Control group	−·70	·85	−·90	−·88	−·88
t	5·34**	·98	2·18*	1·46	1·28

$^{*}p < \cdot 05$ $^{**}p < \cdot 001$

Hypothesis 2: Paranoid men will manifest a greater avoidance of homosexually threatening stimuli than will non-paranoid men. This is one of the two measures by which it was attempted to obtain a manifestation of the defensive mechanisms which are said to prevent the homosexual impulses from entering awareness. It was expected that in the case of the four pairs containing the threatening male pictures, the experimental *S*s would look less at the male and longer at the female pictures than would the control *S*s. The second column of Table 18.2 shows that there was no significant difference between the Mean Attraction Scores of the two groups, i.e., the two groups did not differ in the proportion of time spent looking at the threatening male cards; thus, the prediction was not supported. Two possible reasons for this are that, (*a*) contrary to analytic theory, the paranoid person does not have a strong need to keep homosexually threatening material from awareness and (*b*) the threatening stimuli used in the experiment were, in fact, not sufficiently threatening to call forth an explicit avoidance reaction. While the data provide no definitive basis for choosing between these hypotheses, it will be seen from the discussion of Hypothesis 3, which follows, that the first of these explanations is highly untenable.

Hypothesis 3: Paranoid men, when compared with non-paranoid men, will express a greater preference for women and a lesser one for men as this expression becomes more explicit or conscious. The second technique employed in attempting to obtain a manifestation of the paranoid's defences against the awareness of homosexual impulses was to compare his selection of female pictures, as indicated by the amount of time he spent looking at them in preference to male pictures, with his selection when asked explicitly to specify 'Which do you prefer?' The evaluation of Hypothesis 3 was based on the nine pairs of male-female pictures. Table 18.3 reports the results of comparisons for the experimental and control *S*s. The figures in the first two rows of this table are group means and are based on raw scores which indicate the number of female pictures preferred by each *S* (either by verbal selection or by a longer fixation time than for the corresponding male picture) in the nine male-female pairs. Since each group was compared with itself, the calculation of *t* was based on the usual formula for the significance of differences between the means of two equated samples.

TABLE 18.3. *Verbal preference vs. preference by fixation.*

	Experimental group	Control group
Verbal preference	5·75	5·80
Fixation preference	2·80	5·60
t	4·40**	·27

$^{**}p < ·001$

As Table 18.3 indicates, when the paranoid *S*s were asked to state which picture they preferred, they selected a significantly greater number of women (and so, of course, fewer men) than they did when their preference was assessed by determining which picture they tended to look at longer (a much less explicit process). As a matter of fact, the mean of their verbal choices was almost identical with that of the control group. On the other hand, the control *S*s displayed no meaningful difference between the number of male and female pictures selected by verbal choice and by fixation preference. A non-parametric analysis of these data, using Wilcoxon's matched pairs test, yielded similar results.

These results support the hypothesis that, when measured by a disguised technique, men suffering from paranoid delusions indicate a higher preference for males than do men without paranoid delusions; however, when the question of their choice is made more explicit, and so more conscious, defensive forces are set into motion which lower the expressed preference for males and cause this preference to approximate that of persons who do not suffer from paranoid delusions.

Hypothesis 4: Paranoid men, when compared with non-paranoid men, will manifest a greater attraction to males than to neutral (non-human) objects.

Hypothesis 5: Paranoid men will manifest a greater avoidance of women than will non-paranoid men. The present study has corroborated the psychoanalytic contention that men with strong paranoid delusions may be characterized by more powerful homosexual urges than those who are relatively free of these delusions. One may ask further, however, whether this homosexuality is characterized by a primary attraction to men as sexual objects or whether it reflects principally a reaction to a rejection of women. As Knight pointed out (1940, p. 150), Freud's theory did not attempt to analyze the forerunners of the proposition, 'I love him'. In the present experiment an attempt was made to explore this question by the inclusion of four pairs of male-neutral and female-neutral pictures in the series of stimulus cards. The third column of Table 18.2 indicates that the experimental *S*s showed a preference for the pictures of males (in the male-neutral pairs) that was significantly greater than that of the control group. On the other hand (fourth column, Table 18.2), while there was some tendency ($t=1.46$) for the experimental *S*s to reject the female pictures (in the female-neutral pairs) more than did the controls, this difference was not statistically significant. Similar results were obtained from an analysis of these data by means of the Mann-Whitney test: a statistically significant ($z=1.97$) preference by the experimental *S*s for the male pictures and a trend ($z=-1.34$) toward avoidance of the female pictures. While these results fail to support Hypothesis 5 at an adequate level of statistical significance, the trend noted in the data suggests that the null hypothesis should be accepted with caution.

With this caution in mind, the present evidence indicates that the male paranoid is characterized by a strong attraction to men, without necessarily rejecting women as sexual objects.

The neutral-neutral picture pairs

The last column of Table 18.2 indicates that the experimental and control groups were not significantly differentiated by the three pairs in which neither picture was of a person. Since these pairs were included only to prevent the *S*s guessing the central focus of the experiment, no significant difference between the two groups was expected here.

DISCUSSION

The present experiment has corroborated the hypothesis that men with paranoid delusions are characterized by stronger homosexual needs than men who do not suffer from these delusions. The results of the attempt to demonstrate the presence of defensive measures that function to prevent these needs from entering the persons' cognitive field have been somewhat more equivocal. A comparison between the experimental and control groups' performance on the threatening male-female pictures yielded non-significant differences.

More conclusive evidence comes from the second technique employed to demonstrate defences against awareness of homosexuality. Here the results indicated that when the purpose of the test was disguised, the paranoid's choice of males was significantly greater than that of the non-paranoid, *but* when the matter of his selection was made more explicit and, presumably, more conscious, his choices of males approximated those of the non-paranoid in the same situation. From these results it appears that when homosexual impulses threaten to approach consciousness, the ego fulfils its protective function by bringing about a reorganization of cognitive forces so that, at least on a superficial level, the paranoid individual functions vis-à-vis objects of opposite sex in a manner approximating that of the non-paranoid person. It may be that in this suggestion lies one explanation of the discrepant findings of investigators in this area, i.e., it is likely that researchers have varied in the extent to which their techniques have evoked a defensive reaction in their *S*s which tended to obscure their results. It is, perhaps, no coincidence that the greatest experimental support of the psychoanalytic hypothesis has come from those studies which made use of projective techniques. These techniques have the advantage of permitting the *S* to give evidence of certain needs without his being aware that he is doing so.

Though the present experiment has demonstrated a greater degree of homosexuality in men with paranoid delusions than in non-paranoid individuals, these results tell us nothing about the role which homosexuality plays in the development of these delusions. Is it, as Freud believed, the primary aetiological factor, or is it merely a link in a chain of psychodynamic factors leading eventually to the development of delusions? The present experiment was not designed to answer this question directly. Nevertheless, it is possible to make a number of inferences from the pattern of the results.

These inferences are based upon a consideration of the nature of the paranoid's homosexual attraction. The results of the present experiment indicated that the experimental *S*s displayed a clear-cut preference for male figures (male-neutral pictures). On the other hand, the data did not demonstrate conclusively that the male paranoid tends to avoid female figures. If one assumes, then, that paranoid men are characterized by an attraction to males without necessarily expressing a rejection of women, the following reasoning seems appropriate:

Freud, in his discussion of homosexuality, listed a number of possible aetiological factors (1950a, p. 241 ff.). Most of these suggest that the (male) individual turns to men as sexual objects as the result of severe anxiety incurred at the idea of relations with women. For example, the individual may not be able to tolerate the absence of the penis in his love objects, or he may fear castration by the female sex organ, or he may feel required to reject women because of his father's wrath. In all of these cases a rejection of women as sexual objects precedes the development of an attraction to men.

In this same paper, however, Freud went on to mention yet another origin of homosexuality. He pointed out that powerful aggressive impulses that could culminate in death-wishes directed against male siblings might, 'under the influence of training', yield to repression and transformation, so that 'the rivals of the earlier period became the first homosexual love-objects'. Here, then, is an instance in which homosexuality may involve an attraction to men without being based on a prior rejection of women. Freud commented (1950a, p. 243) that this pattern 'led only to homosexual attitudes, which . . . did not involve a horror of women'. He was, however, careful to emphasize that this pattern might be typical only of homosexuals; he felt that, '. . . it is a complete contrast to the development of persecutory paranoia, in which the person who has before been loved becomes the hated persecutor, whereas here [in homosexuality] the hated rivals are transformed into love objects' (p. 242).

Knight (1940), however, suggested that the paranoid's homosexuality is actually a defence against powerful aggressive wishes toward male figures. In this, Knight has, in a sense, applied to the homosexuality of the paranoid one of Freud's explanations of general homosexuality and has thus presented an integrated theory of paranoid dynamics, one that takes into account more recent developments in psychoanalysis. It should be noted, however, that while both writers were dealing with the management of intense hostility toward male figures, Knight's focus was upon the figure of the father, while Freud's was upon male siblings.

If one considers, in the present experiment, that the paranoid patients were characterized by an attraction to males without at the same time manifesting a rejection of women, such a pattern would be consistent with what one would expect if the homosexual attraction were a function of intense hostile feelings directed toward male figures. It is suggested, therefore, that the results of the present experiment support the view of paranoia presented by Knight, namely, that the person with paranoid delusions is indeed characterized by strong homosexual impulses, but that these impulses themselves serve a defensive function, that of helping to neutralize and erotize powerful hostile wishes against male figures.

It is of interest here that in another study by the writer (Zamansky, 1956) in which the performances of male overt-homosexuals and normal controls were compared on the set of picture-pairs employed in the present experiment, the homosexuals manifested *both* an attraction to male figures and a rejection of female figures, although the latter was not so clearly demonstrated as the former. While a comparison of the two experiments is not entirely justifiable because the *S*s in the present study were somewhat older and of lower educational and socioeconomic status than the overt-homosexuals, it is, nevertheless, tempting to speculate that the homosexuality which is characteristic of the overt-homosexual may, in some degree, be of a different psychodynamic origin than that involved in the development of paranoid delusions. In contrast to the paranoid individual, the overt-homosexual's choice of male objects appears to be, at least in part, a function of his inability to tolerate the anxiety aroused by erotic relations with women.

This way of accounting for the data is highly speculative and needs testing by further experiments. It does, however, lead to hypotheses that might serve as the basis for these experiments. One would expect, for example, that overt-homosexuals would have less unconscious hostility toward men, or would be better able to handle their conscious aggressive feelings toward them, than would people with paranoid delusions. Again, one would expect overt-homosexuals to be more sensitive to anxieties of castration by women and to regard them more as threatening figures.

The question of 'choice of symptom' has always baffled students of psychopathology. In the area of the present experiment, theorists have been embarrassed by the question of why, given strong homosexual impulses, one person develops paranoid delusions and another becomes an overt-homosexual. Perhaps the answer lies in different origins of the homosexual attraction. The person whose homosexuality serves as a defence against strong hostile wishes dares not risk intimate contact with other men. Therefore, there is a great need for him to develop a means of avoiding this, such as projecting his homosexual impulses away from himself or transforming them into another emotional guise. The person, however, in whose homosexuality a hatred for members of the same sex plays a less important role has less of an intrapsychic need to deny it and can afford to give direct expression to his homosexual impulses in his behaviour.

SUMMARY

In this study an attempt was made to investigate the psychoanalytic theory that paranoid delusions are developed in an attempt to cope with powerful but unconscious homosexual urges. In addition, some aspects of the nature of these urges and of the defences erected against them were studied. Two matched groups of *S*s were used: a group of 20 hospitalized psychotic males (mostly diagnosed dementia praecox, paranoid type) in whom paranoid delusions were a dominant symptom, and 20 hospitalized schizophrenic males in whom paranoid symptoms were absent. The experimental technique provided for a measure of object choice as the difference in time spent looking at pictures of different kinds of (human) objects.

The following hypotheses were tested:

1. Men with paranoid delusions, when compared to men without these delusions, will manifest a greater attraction to males than to females.

2. Paranoid men will manifest a greater avoidance of homosexually threatening stimuli than will non-paranoid men.

3. Paranoid men, when compared with non-paranoid men, will express a greater preference for women and a lesser one for men as this expression becomes more explicit or conscious.

4. Paranoid men, when compared with non-paranoid men, will manifest a greater attraction to males than to neutral (non-human) objects.

5. Paranoid men will manifest a greater avoidance of women than will non-paranoid men.

The results of the experiment supported the first, third, and fourth hypotheses at a statistically significant level. The paranoid *S*s spent a significantly greater amount of time than did the non-paranoids in looking at the pictures of men in the male-female pairs and in the male-neutral pairs. When asked to express verbally their preference for pictures of men or of women, the paranoid *S*s selected significantly fewer men than they had chosen by the less explicit fixation-time technique. A similar difference was not manifested by the control *S*s.

These findings support the following conclusions:

1. Men with paranoid delusions tend to have stronger homosexual impulses than male psychotics who are relatively free from these delusions.

2. Men with paranoid delusions tend to avoid explicit or direct manifestations of homosexual object preference.

3. The homosexuality of paranoid men tends to be characterized by a primary attraction toward men as sexual objects, and not necessarily by an avoidance of women.

The results of the present experiment also permit the following inferences which are, however, merely speculations at the present stage of investigation:

1. The homosexuality of the male paranoid appears as an intermediary process in the development of his delusions, rather than being the primary aetiological agent.

2. One of the defensive functions which the homosexuality of the male paranoid serves is to help neutralize and erotize powerful aggressive wishes directed toward male figures.

COMMENT

As noted by Kline (1972, p. 269) this is 'probably the best known objective investigation into homosexuality and paranoia'. His enthusiasm for the study is almost boundless: 'The experimental technique was clever and the derivation of the hypotheses from the psychoanalytic theory subtle yet precise . . . The fact that paranoids fixated longer on the male pictures than did controls is impressive evidence that homosexuality is implicated in paranoia, especially since homosexuals have been shown thus to fixate . . . No other theory could predict such a finding.' If this is true then Freud has at last been found to have made a genuine contribution to modern psychology, especially since Zamansky's experiment has been essentially replicated at least once (Watson, 1965). We have chosen to reprint and comment upon the original Zamansky experiment because it is now regarded as a classical study, e.g. it is reproduced in the Lindzey and Hall (1965) collection of primary sources in personality theory and research. The comments that we make about this study will be seen to have relevance to Watson's replication which is also cited by Kline as 'powerful support' for Freudian theory.

Before pointing out what is wrong with these studies, it is interesting to note the origins of the psychoanalytic theory of paranoia. The theory derived from Freud's analysis of the case of a notorious German judge called Dr Schreber (1911); actually he never met the patient but based his interpretation on a reading of Schreber's autobiography. Thereafter it became the opinion of both Freud (1915, 1950b) and Ferenczi (1914, 1922, 1950) that all cases of paranoia and paranoid schizophrenia involved repressed homosexual desires and the defence mechanism of projection. This tendency to arrive at an entire theory by generalization from ideas emerging from the analysis of one particular case seems quite characteristic of the thinking of Freud. In the previous paper we saw that the psychoanalytic theory of appendicitis was derived from an analysis of the case of Dora (1905). In the paper by Wolpe and Rachman which follows we discover that the psychoanalytic theory of phobias and the notion of the castration complex arose out of the case of 'Little Hans', who once again was hardly ever seen by Freud himself (the case material being provided by the boy's father, an ardent supporter of Freud's).

When a global theory is generated on the basis of a single case it is reasonable to ask to what extent the theory is supported by using the same technique (clinical observation) on larger samples of patients. A recent study by Rossi, Delmonte and Terracciano (1971) set out to examine this question, and the conclusion was that 'the data, examined from the clinical-statistical point of view, do not support the analytical theory . . . The frequency of homosexual elements does not appear to be high in paranoid syndromes compared with other forms of schizophrenia'. This finding held not only for overt-homosexual tendencies but also for clinical assessments of 'unconscious homosexuality' based upon psychoanalytic formulations. *A priori* then, the case for Freud's hypothesis concerning the aetiology of paranoia does not look good. Nevertheless, there remains an outside possibility that his observations based on one patient he had never examined in person were in some way more insightful than those of Rossi *et al.* based on a sample of 100 assorted schizophrenics, so we will now consider Zamansky's experimental study.

Zamansky presents two positive findings: (1) Paranoids spent more time looking at pictures of men than non-paranoid schizophrenics when given the option of looking at women or non-human objects. (2) Relative to non-paranoids, the paranoids expressed a greater preference for the pictures of women. No doubt Freudian theory could explain these results (we have argued that it can 'explain' *any* results), but is it true, as Kline says, that 'no other theory could predict such a finding'? In fact, we do not need any theory to predict these results. One of the most outstanding features of paranoid illness is a tendency to be cagey, suspicious and sensitive to threat; given these traits the Zamansky findings follow logically. Paranoids would be expected to be more alert to men in the environment than either women or non-human objects simply because men offer a greater threat. There is no justification for assuming that homosexual attraction to men is the only reason for looking at them. Following exposure to pictures of homosexual encounters such as men kissing, however, the paranoids would be alert to the possibility that the 'shrink' is trying to label them as homosexual and would therefore be cautious about expressing preferences for male pictures. Meanwhile, the regular schizophrenics, who are typically more thought-disordered than paranoids, would be responding to the task in their usual erratic and unsystematic way.

Zamansky had validated his picture-preference test by showing previously that it did discriminate overt-homosexuals from normal men. This was a necessary but hopelessly insufficient precaution. The fact that an experimental procedure can be a measure of homosexuality under some circumstances does not preclude the possibility that it measures something else as well. The vital control that is missing from Zamansky's study, and Watson's replication, is the use of *other forms of threat* not involving homosexuality, e.g. pictures of electrical apparatus such as might be used for aversion therapy, or flying saucers carrying sexless space monsters. We would predict that the paranoids would show greater sensitivity to threats of this kind as well. In short, the paranoid's reaction to homosexual situations can be viewed as consistent with, and a part of, his general suspiciousness and vigilance in relation to threatening stimuli. Not only does this trait theory view involve fewer theoretical assumptions than the psychoanalytic theory, it is of much broader predictive value.

REFERENCES

ARONSON, M. L. (1953) A study of the Freudian theory of paranoia by means of the Blacky Pictures. *J. Proj. Tech.*, **17**, 3-19.

FENICHEL, O. (1945) *The Psychoanalytic Theory of Neurosis.* New York: Norton.

FERENCZI, S. (1914) Some clinical observations on paranoia and paraphrenia. In *First Contribution to Psychoanalysis*, p. 282. London: Hogarth Press and I.P.A., 1952.

—— (1922) Paranoia. In *Problems and Methods of Psychoanalysis*, p. 212. London: Hogarth Press and I.P.A., 1955.

—— (1950) On the part played by homosexuality in the pathogenesis of paranoia. In *Sex in Psychoanalysis.* New York: Basic Books.

FREUD, S. (1915) A case of paranoia running counter to the psychoanalytic theory of the disease. In *Complete Psychoanalytic Works*, Vol. 14. London: Hogarth Press and I.P.A., 1964.

—— (1950a) Certain neurotic mechanisms in jealousy, paranoia and homosexuality. In *Collected Papers,* Vol. II. London: Hogarth Press.

—— (1950b) Psychoanalytic notes upon an autobiographical account of a case of paranoia (dementia paranoides). In *Collected Papers,* Vol. III. London: Hogarth Press.

GARDNER, G. E. (1931) Evidences of homosexuality in one hundred and twenty unanalyzed cases with paranoid content. *Psychoanal. Rev.*, **13**, 57-62.

HENDRICK, I. (1939) The contributions of psychoanalysis to the study of psychoses. *J. Amer. Med. Ass.*, **113**, 918-24.

KLEIN, HENRIETTE R. & HOROWITZ, W. A. (1949) Psychosexual factors in the paranoid phenomena. *Amer. J. Psychiat.*, **105**, 697-701.

KLINE, P. (1972) *Fact and Fantasy in Freudian Theory*. London: Methuen.

KNIGHT, R. P. (1940) The relationship of latent homosexuality to the mechanism of paranoid delusions. *Bull. Menninger Clinic*, **4**, 149-59.

LINDZEY, G. & HALL, C. S. (eds.) (1965) *Theories of Personality: Primary Sources and Research.* New York: Wiley.

MILLER, C. W. (1941) The paranoid syndrome. *Arch. Neurol. Psychiat.*, **45**, 953-63.

MOSTELLER, F. & BUSH, R. R. (1954) Selected quantitative techniques. In G. LINDZEY (ed.), *Handbook of Social Psychology*, pp. 289-334. Cambridge, Mass.: Addison-Wesley.

MUSIKER, H. R. (1952) Sex identification and other aspects of the personality of the male paranoid schizophrenic. Unpublished doctoral dissertation, Boston Univ.

NORMAN, J. P. (1948) Evidence and clinical significance of homosexuality in 100 unanalyzed cases of dementia praecox. *J. Nerv. Ment. Dis.*, **107**, 484-9.

NUNBERG, H. (1938) Homosexuality, magic and aggression. *Int. J. Psychoanal.*, **19**, 1-16.

PAYNE, C. R. (1913-14) Some Freudian contributions to the paranoia problem. *Psychoanal. Rev.*, **1**, 76-83, 187-202, 308-21, 445-51.

—— (1915) Some Freudian contributions to the paranoia problem (continued). *Psychoanal. Rev.*, **2**, 93-101, 200-2.

ROSSI, R., DELMONTE, P. & TERRACCIANO, P. (1971) The problem of the relationship between homosexuality and schizophrenia. *Arch. Sex. Behav.*, **1**, 357-62.

SHOCKLEY, F. M. (1913-14) The role of homosexuality in the genesis of paranoid conditions. *Psychoanal. Rev.*, **1**, 431-8.

THORNER, H. A. (1949) Notes on a case of male homosexuality. *Int. J. Psychoanal.*, **30**, 31-47.

WATSON, C. G. (1965) A test of the relationship between repressed homosexuality and paranoid mechanisms. *J. Clin. Psychol.*, **21**, 380-4.

ZAMANSKY, H. S. (1956) A technique for assessing homosexual tendencies. *J. Pers.*, **24**, 436-48.

19

Joseph Wolpe[1] *and Stanley Rachman*[2] *(1960)*

Psychoanalytic 'evidence': A critique based on Freud's case of Little Hans[3]

The Journal of Nervous and Mental Disease, 130, No. 8, 135-48

Beginning with Wohlgemuth's trenchant monograph (1923), the factual and logical bases of psychoanalytic theory have been the subject of a considerable number of criticisms. These have generally been dismissed by psychoanalysts, at least party on the ground that the critics are oblivious of the 'wealth of detail' provided by the individual case. One way to examine the soundness of the analysts' position is to study fully-reported cases that they themselves regard as having contributed significantly to their theories. We have undertaken to do this, and have chosen as our subject matter one of Freud's most famous cases, given in such detail that the events of a few months occupy 140 pages of the *Collected Papers.*

In 1909, Freud published 'The Analysis of a Phobia in a Five-year-old Boy' (1950). This case is commonly referred to as 'The case of Little Hans'. Ernest Jones, in his biography of Freud, points out that it was 'the first published account of a child analysis' (Jones, 1955, p. 289), and states that 'the brilliant success of child analysis' since then was 'indeed inaugurated by the study of this very case' (p. 292). The case also has special significance in the development of psychoanalytic theory because Freud believed himself to have found in it 'a more direct and less roundabout proof' of some fundamental psychoanalytic theorems (p. 150). In particular, he thought that it provided a direct demonstration of the essential role of sexual urges in the development of phobias. He felt his position to have been

[1]Department of Neurology and Psychiatry, University of Virginia School of Medicine, Charlottesville, Virginia.

[2]Institute of Psychiatry, Maudsley Hospital, London.

[3]The writers are indebted to Stella Wolpe for some critical observations that led to the writing of this paper.

greatly strengthened by this case and two generations of analysts have referred to the evidence of Little Hans as a basic substantiation of psychoanalytic theories (e.g., Fenichel, 1945; Glover, 1956; Hendrick, 1939). As an example, Glover (1956, p. 76) may be quoted.

> In its time the analysis of Little Hans was a remarkable achievement and the story of the analysis constitutes one of the most valued records in psychoanalytical archives. Our concepts of phobia formation, of the positive Oedipus complex, of ambivalence, castration anxiety and repression, to mention but a few, were greatly reinforced and amplified as the result of this analysis.

In this paper we shall re-examine this case history and assess the evidence presented. We shall show that although there are manifestations of sexual behaviour on the part of Hans, there is no scientifically acceptable evidence showing any connection between this behaviour and the child's phobia for horses; that the assertion of such connection is pure assumption; that the elaborate discussions that follow from it are pure speculation; and that the case affords no factual support for any of the concepts listed by Glover above. Our examination of this case exposes in considerable detail patterns of thinking and attitudes to evidence that are well-nigh universal among psychoanalysts. It suggests the need for more careful scrutiny of the bases of psychoanalytic 'discoveries' than has been customary; and we hope it will prompt psychologists to make similar critical examinations of basic psychoanalytic writings.

The case material on which Freud's analysis is based was collected by Little Hans's father, who kept Freud informed of developments by regular written reports. The father also had several consultations with Freud concerning Little Hans's phobia. During the analysis, Freud himself saw the little boy only once.

The following are the most relevant facts noted of Hans's earlier life. At the age of three, he showed 'a quite peculiarly lively interest in that portion of his body which he used to describe as his widdler'. When he was three and a half, his mother found him with his hand to his penis. She threatened him in these words, 'If you do that, I shall send for Dr A. to cut off your widdler. And then what will you widdle with?' Hans replied, 'With my bottom.' Numerous further remarks concerning widdlers in animals and humans were made by Hans between the ages of three and four, including questions directed at his mother and father asking them if they also had widdlers. Freud attaches importance to the following exchange between Hans and his mother. Hans was 'looking on intently while his mother undressed'.

Mother: 'What are you staring like that for?'
Hans: 'I was only looking to see if you'd got a widdler, too.'
Mother: 'Of course. Didn't you know that?'
Hans: 'No, I thought you were so big you'd have a widdler like a horse.'

When Hans was three and a half his sister was born. The baby was delivered at home and Hans heard his mother 'coughing', observed the appearance of the doctor and was called into the bedroom after the birth. Hans was initially 'very jealous of the new arrival' but within six months his jealousy faded and was replaced by 'brotherly affection'. When Hans was four he discovered a seven-year-old girl in the neighbourhood and spent many hours awaiting her return from school. The father commented that 'the violence with which this "long-range love" came over him was to be explained by his having no play-fellows of either sex'. At this period also, 'he was constantly putting his arms round' his visiting boy cousin, aged five, and was once heard saying, 'I *am* so fond of you' when giving his cousin 'one of these tender embraces'. Freud speaks of this as the 'first trace of homosexuality'.

At the age of four and a half, Hans went with his parents to Gmunden for the summer holidays. On holiday Hans had numerous playmates including Mariedl, a fourteen-year-old girl. One evening Hans said 'I want Mariedl to sleep with me'. Freud says that Hans's wish was an expression of his desire to have Mariedl as part of his family. Hans's parents occasionally took him into their bed and Freud claims that, 'there can be no doubt that lying beside them had aroused erotic feelings in him;[1] so that his wish to sleep with Mariedl had an erotic sense as well'.

Another incident during the summer holidays is given considerable importance by Freud, who refers to it as Hans's attempt to seduce his mother. It must be quoted here in full.

'Hans, four and a quarter.[2] This morning Hans was given his usual daily bath by his mother and afterwards dried and powdered.

[1]This is nothing but surmise – yet Freud asserts 'there can be no doubt' about it.

[2]Earlier his age during the summer holidays is given as four and a half. Unfortunately, there is no direct statement as to the length of the holiday.

As his mother was powdering round his penis and taking care not to touch it, Hans said 'Why don't you put your finger there?'
Mother: 'Because that'd be piggish.'
Hans: 'What's that? Piggish? Why?'
Mother: 'Because it's not proper.'
Hans (laughing): 'But it's great fun.'

Another occurrence prior to the onset of his phobia was that when Hans, aged four and a half, laughed while watching his sister being bathed and was asked why he was laughing, he replied, 'I'm laughing at Hanna's widdler.' 'Why?' 'Because her widdler's so lovely.' The father's comment is, 'Of course his answer was a disingenuous one. In reality her widdler seemed to him funny. Moreover, this is the first time he has recognized in this way the distinction between male and female genitals instead of denying it'.

In early January 1908, the father wrote to Freud that Hans had developed 'a nervous disorder'. The symptoms he reported were: fear of going into the streets; depression in the evening, and a fear that a horse would bite him in the street. Hans's father suggested that 'the ground was prepared by sexual over-excitation due to his mother's tenderness' and that the fear of the horse 'seems somehow to be connected with his having been frightened by a large penis'. The first signs appeared on January 7, when Hans was being taken to the park by his nursemaid as usual. He started crying and said he wanted to 'coax' (caress) with his mother. At home 'he was asked why he had refused to go any further and had cried, but he would not say'. The following day, after hesitation and crying, he went out with his mother. Returning home Hans said ('after much internal struggling'), '*I was afraid a horse would bite me*' (original italics). As on the previous day, Hans showed fear in the evening and asked to be 'coaxed'. He is also reported as saying, 'I know I shall have to go for a walk again tomorrow,' and 'The horse'll come into the room.' On the same day he was asked by his mother if he put his hand to his widdler. He replied in the affirmative. The following day his mother warned him to refrain from doing this.

At this point in the narrative, Freud provided an interpretation of Hans's behaviour and consequently arranged with the boy's father 'that he should tell the boy that all this nonsense about horses was a piece of nonsense and nothing more. The truth was, his father was to say, that he was very fond of his mother and wanted to be taken into her bed. The reason he was afraid of horses now was that he had taken so much interest in their widdlers.' Freud also suggested giving Hans some sexual enlightenment and telling him that females 'had no widdler at all'.[1]

'After Hans had been enlightened there followed a fairly quiet period.' After an attack of influenza which kept him in bed for two weeks, the phobia got worse. He then had his tonsils out and was indoors for a further week. The phobia became 'very much worse'.

During March 1908, after his physical illnesses had been cured, Hans apparently had many talks with his father about the phobia. On March 1, his father again told Hans that horses do not bite. Hans replied that white horses bite and related that while at Gmunden he had heard and seen Lizzi (a playmate) being warned by her father to avoid a white horse lest it bite. The father said to Lizzi, *'Don't put your finger to the white horse'* (original italics). Hans's father's reply to this account given by his son was, 'I say, it strikes me it isn't a horse you mean, but a widdler, that one mustn't put one's hand to.' Hans answered, 'But a widdler doesn't bite.' The father: 'Perhaps it does, though.' Hans then 'went on eagerly to try to prove to me that it was a white horse'. The following day, in answer to a remark of his father's, Hans said that his phobia was 'so bad because I still put my hand to my widdler every night'. Freud remarks here that, 'Doctor and patient, father and son, were therefore at one in ascribing the chief share in the pathogenesis of Hans's present condition to his habit of onanism.' He implies that this unanimity is significant, quite disregarding the father's indoctrination of Hans the previous day.[2]

On March 13, the father told Hans that his fear would disappear if he stopped putting his hand to his widdler. Hans replied, 'But I don't put my hand to my widdler any more.' Father: 'But you still want to.' Hans agreed, 'Yes, I do.' His father suggested that he should sleep in a sack to prevent him from wanting to touch his widdler. Hans accepted this view and on the following day was much less afraid of horses.

Two days later the father again told Hans that girls and women have no widdlers. 'Mummy has none, Anna has none and so on.' Hans asked how they managed to widdle and was told 'They don't

[1]Incidentally contradicting what Hans's mother had told him earlier (p. 319).

[2]The mere fact that Hans repeats an interpretation he has heard from his father is regarded by Freud as demonstrating the accuracy of the interpretation; even though the child's spontaneous responses noted earlier in the paragraph point clearly in the opposite direction.

have widdlers like yours. Haven't you noticed already when Hannah was being given her bath.' On March 17 Hans reported a phantasy in which he saw his mother naked. On the basis of this phantasy and the conversation related above, Freud concluded that Hans had not accepted the enlightenment given by his father. Freud says, 'He regretted that it should be so, and stuck to his former view in phantasy. He may also perhaps have had his reasons for refusing to believe his father at first.' Discussing this matter subsequently, Freud says that the 'enlightenment' given a short time before to the effect that women really do not possess a widdler was bound to have a shattering effect upon his self-confidence and to have aroused his castration complex. For this reason he resisted the information, and for this reason it had no therapeutic effect.[1]

For reasons of space we shall recount the subsequent events in very brief form. On a visit to the Zoo Hans expressed fear of the giraffe, elephant and all large animals. Hans's father said to him, 'Do you know why you're afraid of big animals? Big animals have big widdlers and you're really afraid of big widdlers.' This was denied by the boy.

The next event of prominence was a dream (or phantasy) reported by Hans. 'In the night there was a big giraffe in the room and a crumpled one; and the big one called out because I took the crumpled one away from it. Then it stopped calling out; and then I sat down on the top of the crumpled one.'

After talking to the boy the father reported to Freud that this dream was 'a matrimonial scene transposed into giraffe life. He was seized in the night with a longing for his mother, for her caresses, for her genital organ, and came into the room for that reason. The whole thing is a continuation of his fear of horses.' The father infers that the dream is related to Hans's habit of occasionally getting into his parents' bed in the face of his father's disapproval. Freud's addition to 'the father's penetrating observation' is that sitting down on the crumpled giraffe means taking possession of his mother. Confirmation of this dream interpretation is claimed by reference to an incident which occurred the next day. The father wrote that on

[1]It is pertinent at this point to suggest that Hans 'resisted' this enlightenment because his mother had told him quite the opposite and his observations of his sister's widdler had not been contradicted. When he was four, Hans had observed that his sister's widdler was 'still quite small' (p. 155). When he was four and a half, again while watching his sister being bathed, he observed that she had 'a lovely widdler' (p. 164). On neither occasion was he contradicted.

leaving the house with Hans he said to his wife, 'Goodbye, big giraffe.' 'Why giraffe?' asked Hans. 'Mummy's the big giraffe,' replied the father. 'Oh, yes,' said Hans, 'and Hanna's[2] the crumpled giraffe, isn't she?' The father's account continues, 'In the train I explained the giraffe phantasy to him, upon which he said "Yes, that's right," And when I said to him that I was the big giraffe and that its long neck reminded him of a widdler, he said "Mummy has a neck like a giraffe too. I saw when she was washing her white neck".'

On March 30, the boy had a short consultation with Freud who reports that despite all the enlightenment given to Hans, the fear of horses continued undiminished. Hans explained that he was especially bothered 'by what horses wear in front of their eyes and the black round their mouths'. This latter detail Freud interpreted as meaning a moustache. 'I asked him whether he meant a moustache,' and then, 'disclosed to him that he was afraid of his father precisely because he was so fond of his mother'. Freud pointed out that this was a groundless fear. On April 2, the father was able to report 'the first real improvement'. The next day Hans, in answer to his father's inquiry, explained that he came into his father's bed when he was frightened. In the next few days further details of Hans's fear were elaborated. He told his father that he was most scared of horses with 'a thing on their mouths,' that he was scared lest the horses fall, and that he was most scared of horse-drawn buses.

Hans: 'I'm most afraid too when a bus comes along.'

Father: 'Why? Because it's so big?'

Hans: 'No. Because once a horse in a bus fell.'

Father: 'When?'

Hans then recounted such an incident. This was later confirmed by his mother.

Father: 'What did you think when the horse fell down?'

Hans: 'Now it will always be like this. All horses in buses'll fall down.'

Father: 'In all buses?'

Hans: 'Yes. And in furniture vans too. Not often in furniture vans.'

Father: 'You had your nonsense already at that time?'

[1]Hans's baby sister, *not* his mother. Again, the more spontaneous response directly contradicts Freud's interpretation. Thus Freud's subsequent comment that Hans only confirmed the interpretation of the two giraffes as his father and mother and not the sexual symbolism, transgresses the facts.

Hans: '*No* (italics added). I only got it then. When the horse in the bus fell down, it gave me such a fright really: That was when I got the nonsense.'

The father adds that, 'all of this was confirmed by my wife, as well as the fact that *the anxiety broke out immediately afterwards*' (italics added).

Hans's father continued probing for a meaning of the black thing around the horses' mouths. Hans said it looked like a muzzle but his father had never seen such a horse 'although Hans asseverates that such horses do exist'.[1] He continues, 'I suspect that some part of the horse's bridle really reminded him of a moustache and that after I alluded to this the fear disappeared.' A day later Hans observing his father stripped to the waist said, 'Daddy you are lovely! You're so white.'

Father: 'Yes. Like a white horse.'

Hans: 'The only black thing's your moustache. Or perhaps it's a black muzzle.'[2]

Further details about the horse that fell were also elicited from Hans. He said there were actually two horses pulling the bus and that they were both black and 'very big and fat'. Hans's father again asked about the boy's thoughts when the horse fell.

Father: 'When the horse fell down, did you think of your daddy?'[3]

Hans: 'Perhaps. Yes. It's possible.'

For several days after these talks about horses Hans's interests, as indicated by the father's reports, 'centred upon lumf (faeces) and widdle, but we cannot tell why'. Freud comments that at this point 'the analysis began to be obscure and uncertain'.

On April 11 Hans related this phantasy. 'I was in the bath[4] and then the plumber came and unscrewed it.[5] Then he took a big borer and stuck it into my stomach.' Hans's father translated this phantasy

[1]Six days later (p. 211) the father reports, 'I was at last able to establish the fact that it was a horse with a leather muzzle'.

[2]A good example of the success of indoctrination.

[3]One of many leading questions, the positive answer to which of course proves nothing. It is worth noticing how the same question, differently phrased, elicits contrasting answers from Hans. When asked earlier what he thought of when the horse fell, Hans replied that he thought it would always happen in future.

[4]'Hans's mother gives him his bath' (Father's note).

[5]'To take it away to be repaired' (Father's note).

as follows: 'I was in bed with Mamma. Then Pappa came and drove me away. With his big penis he pushed me out of my place by Mamma.'

The remainder of the case history material, until Hans's recovery from the phobia early in May, is concerned with the lumf theme and Hans's feelings towards his parents and sister. It can be stated immediately that as corroboration for Freud's theories all of this remaining material is unsatisfactory. For the most part it consists of the father expounding theories to a boy who occasionally agrees and occasionally disagrees. The following two examples (pp. 209 and 214) illustrate the nature of most of this latter information.

Hans and his father were discussing the boy's slight fear of falling when in the big bath.

Father: 'But Mamma bathes you in it. Are you afraid of Mamma dropping you in the water?'

Hans: 'I am afraid of her letting go and my head going in.'

Father: 'But you know Mummy's fond of you and won't let you go.'

Hans: 'I only just thought it.'

Father: 'Why?'

Hans: 'I don't know at all.'

Father: 'Perhaps it was because you'd been naughty and thought she didn't love you any more?'[1]

Hans: 'Yes.'

Father: 'When you were watching Mummy giving Hanna her bath perhaps you wished she would let go of her so that Hanna should fall in?'[1]

Hans: 'Yes.'

On the following day the father asks, 'Are you fond of Hanna?'

Hans: 'Oh, yes, very fond.'

Father: 'Would you rather that Hanna weren't alive or that she were?'

Hans: 'I'd rather she weren't alive.'

In response to close, direct questioning Hans voiced several complaints about his sister. Then his father proceeded again:

[1]Leading question.

Father: 'If you'd rather she weren't alive, you can't be fond of her, at all.'

Hans: (assenting[1]) 'Hm, well.'

Father: 'That's why you thought when Mummy was giving her her bath if only she'd let go, Hanna would fall in the water . . .'

Hans: (taking me up) '. . . and die.'

Father: 'and then you'd be alone with Mummy. A good boy doesn't wish that sort of thing, though.'

On April 24, the following conversation was recorded.

Father: 'It seems to me that, all the same, you do wish Mummy would have a baby.'

Hans: 'But I don't want it to happen.'

Father: 'But you wish for it?'

Hans: 'Oh, yes, *wish*.'[2]

Father: 'Do you know why you wish for it? It's because you'd like to be Daddy.'

Hans: 'Yes. How does it work?'

Father: 'You'd like to be Daddy and married to Mummy; you'd like to be as big as me and have a moustache; and you'd like Mummy to have a baby.'

Hans: 'And Daddy, when I'm married I'll have only one if I want to, when I'm married to Mummy, and if I don't want a baby, God won't want it either when I'm married.'

Father: 'Would you like to be married to Mummy?'

Hans: 'Oh yes.'

THE VALUE OF THE EVIDENCE

Before proceeding to Freud's interpretation of the case, let us examine the value of the evidence presented. First, there is the matter of selection of the material. The greatest attention is naturally paid to material related to psychoanalytic theory and there is a tendency to ignore other facts. The father and mother, we are told by Freud, 'were both among my closest adherents'. Hans himself was constantly encouraged, directly and indirectly, to relate material of relevance to the psychoanalytic doctrine.

[1]A very questionable affirmation.

[2]Original italics suggest a significance that is unwarranted, for the child has been manoeuvred into giving an answer contradicting his original one. Note the induced 'evidence' as the conversation continues.

Second, we must assess the value to be placed on the testimony of the father and of Hans. The father's account of Hans's behaviour is in several instances suspect. For example, he twice presents his own interpretations of Hans's remarks as observed facts. This is the father's report of a conversation with Hans about the birth of his sister Hanna.

Father: 'What did Hanna look like?'
Hans (hypocritically): 'All white and lovely. So pretty.'

On another occasion, despite several clear statements by Hans of his affection for his sister (and also the voicing of complaints about her screaming), the father said to Hans, 'If you'd rather she weren't alive, you can't be fond of her at all.' Hans (assenting): 'Hm . . . well.' (See above).

The comment in parentheses in each of these two extracts is presented as observed fact. A third example has also been quoted above. When Hans observes that Hanna's widdler is 'so lovely' the father states that this is a 'disingenuous' reply and that 'in reality her widdler seemed to him funny'. Distortions of this kind are common in the father's reports.

Hans's testimony is for many reasons unreliable. Apart from the numerous lies which he told in the last few weeks of his phobia, Hans gave many inconsistent and occasionally conflicting reports. Most important of all, much of what purports to be Hans's views and feelings is simply the father speaking. Freud himself admits this but attempts to gloss over it. He says, 'It is true that during the analysis Hans had to be told many things which he could not say himself, that he had to be presented with thoughts which he had so far shown no signs of possessing and that his attention had to be turned in the direction from which his father was expecting something to come. This detracts from the evidential value of the analysis but the procedure is the same in every case. For a psychoanalysis is not an impartial scientific investigation but a therapeutic measure' (p. 246).[1] To sum this matter up, Hans's testimony is subject not only to 'mere suggestion' but contains much material that is not his testimony at all!

From the above discussion it is clear that the 'facts of the case'

[1]Nevertheless, both the theory and practice of psychoanalysis are built on these 'not . . . impartial scientific investigations'. For Freud to admit this weakness has some merit, but the admission is neither a substitute for evidence nor a good reason for accepting conclusions without evidence.

need to be treated with considerable caution and in our own interpretation of Hans's behaviour we will attempt to make use only of the testimony of direct observation.

FREUD'S INTERPRETATION

Freud's interpretation of Hans's phobia is that the boy's Oedipal conflicts formed the basis of the illness which 'burst out' when he underwent 'a time of privation and the intensified sexual excitement'. Freud says,

> These were tendencies in Hans which had already been suppressed and which, so far as we can tell, had never been able to find uninhibited expression: hostile and jealous feelings against his father, and sadistic impulses (premonitions, as it were, of copulation) towards his mother. These early suppressions may perhaps have gone to form the predisposition for his subsequent illness. These aggressive propensities of Hans's found no outlet, and as soon as there came a time of privation and of intensified sexual excitement, they tried to break their way out with reinforced strength. It was then that the battle which we call his 'phobia' burst out (pp. 279-80).

This is the familiar Oedipal theory, according to which Hans wished to replace his father 'whom he could not help hating as a rival' and then complete the act by 'taking possession of his mother'. Freud refers for confirmation to the following. 'Another symptomatic act, happening as though by accident, involved a confession that he had wished his father dead; for, just at the moment that his father was talking of his death-wish Hans let a horse that he was playing with fall down – knocked it over, in fact' (p. 272). Freud claims that, 'Hans was really a little Oedipus who wanted to have his father "out of the way" to get rid of him, so that he might be alone with his handsome mother and sleep with her' (p. 253). The predisposition to illness provided by the Oedipal conflicts are supposed to have formed the basis for 'the transformation of his libidinal longing into anxiety'. During the summer prior to the onset of the phobia, Hans had experienced 'moods of mingled longing and apprehension' and had also been taken into his mother's bed on occasions. Freud says,

> We may assume that since then Hans had been in a state of intensified sexual excitement, the object of which was his mother. The

> intensity of this excitement was shown by his two attempts at seducing his mother (the second of which occurred just before the outbreak of his anxiety); and he found an incidental channel of discharge for it by masturbating . . . Whether the sudden exchange of this excitement into anxiety took place spontaneously, or as a result of his mother's rejection of his advances, or owing to the accidental revival of earlier impressions by the 'exciting cause' of his illness . . . this we cannot decide. The fact remains that his sexual excitement suddenly changed into anxiety (p. 260).[1]

Hans, we are told, 'transposed from his father on to the horses'. At his sole interview with Hans, Freud told him 'that he was afraid of his father because he himself nourished jealous and hostile wishes against him'. Freud says of this, 'In telling him this, I had partly interpreted his fear of horses for him: the horse must be his father – whom he had good internal reasons for fearing' (p. 264). Freud claims that Hans's fear of the black things on the horses' mouths and the things in front of their eyes was based on moustaches and eyeglasses and had been 'directly transposed from his father on to the horses'.[2] The horses 'had been shown to represent his father'.

Freud interprets the agoraphobic element of Hans's phobia thus.

> The content of his phobia was such as to impose a very great measure of restriction upon his freedom of movement, and that was its purpose . . . After all, Hans's phobia of horses was an obstacle to his going into the street, and could serve as a means of allowing him to stay at home with his beloved mother.[3] In this way, therefore, his affection for his mother triumphantly achieved its aim (p. 280).

Freud interprets the disappearance of the phobia as being due to the resolution by Hans of his Oedipal conflicts by 'promoting him (the father) to a marriage with Hans's grandmother . . . instead of killing him'. This final interpretation is based on the following conversation between Hans and his father.

On April 30, Hans was playing with his imaginary children.

[1]Thus a theoretical statement, beginning with 'We may assume' ends up as a 'fact'. The only fact is that the assumed sexual excitement is assumed to have changed into anxiety.

[2]But in fact the child was thinking of a muzzle (see above).

[3]It should be noted, however, that Hans's horse phobia and general agoraphobia were present even when he went out with his mother (p. 167).

Father: 'Hullo, are your children still alive? You know quite well a boy can't have any children.'

Hans: 'I know. I was their Mummy before, *now I'm their Daddy*' (original italics).

Father: 'And who's the children's Mummy?'

Hans: 'Why, Mummy, and you're their *Grandaddy* (original italics).'

Father: 'So then you'd like to be as big as me, and be married to Mummy, and then you'd like her to have children.'

Hans: 'Yes, that's what I'd like, and then my Lainz Grandmamma' (paternal side) 'will be their Grannie.'

CRITIQUE OF FREUD'S CONCLUSIONS

It is our contention that Freud's view of this case is not supported by the data, either in its particulars or as a whole. The major points that he regards as demonstrated are these: (1) Hans had a sexual desire for his mother, (2) he hated and feared his father and wished to kill him, (3) his sexual excitement and desire for his mother were transformed into anxiety, (4) his fear of horses was symbolic of his fear of his father, (5) the purpose of the illness was to keep near his mother and finally (6) his phobia disappeared because he resolved his Oedipus complex.

Let us examine each of these points.

(1) That Hans derived satisfaction from his mother and enjoyed her presence we will not even attempt to dispute. But nowhere is there any evidence of his wish to copulate with her. Yet Freud says that, 'if matters had lain entirely in my hands . . . I should have confirmed his instinctive premonitions, by telling him of the existence of the vagina and of copulation' (see p. 286). The 'instinctive premonitions' are referred to as though a matter of fact, though no evidence of their existence is given.

The only seduction incident described (see above) indicates that on *that particular occasion* Hans desired contact of a sexual nature with his mother, albeit a sexual contact of a simple, primitive type. This is not adequate evidence on which to base the claim that Hans had an Oedipus complex which implies a sexual desire for the mother, a wish to possess her and to replace the father. The most that can be claimed for this 'attempted seduction' is that it provides a small degree of support for the assumption that Hans had a desire for sexual stimulation by some other person (it will be recalled that he often masturbated). Even if it is assumed that stimulation provided by his mother was especially desired, the two other features of an Oedipus complex (a wish to possess the mother and replace the father) are not demonstrated by the facts of the case.

(2) Never having expressed either fear or hatred of his father, Hans was told by Freud that he possessed these emotions. On subsequent occasions Hans denied the existence of these feelings when questioned by his father. Eventually, he said 'Yes' to a statement of this kind by his father. This simple affirmative obtained after considerable pressure on the part of the father and Freud is accepted as the true state of affairs and all Hans's denials are ignored. The 'symptomatic act' of knocking over the toy horse is taken as further evidence of Hans's aggression towards his father. There are three assumptions underlying this 'interpreted fact' – first, that the horse represents Hans's father; second, that the knocking over of the horse is not accidental; and third, that this act indicates a wish for the removal of whatever the horse symbolized.

Hans consistently denied the relationship between the horse and his father. He was, he said, afraid of horses. The mysterious black around the horses' mouths and the things on their eyes were later discovered by the father to be the horses' muzzles and blinkers. This discovery undermines the suggestion (made by Freud) that they were transposed moustaches and eye-glasses. There is no other evidence that the horses represented Hans's father. The assumption that the knocking over of the toy horse was meaningful in that it was prompted by an unconscious motive is, like most similar examples, a moot point. Freud himself (1938) does not state that *all* errors are provoked by unconscious motives and in this sense 'deliberate'. This is understandable for it is easy to compile numerous instances of errors which can be accounted for in other, simpler terms[1] without recourse to unconscious motivation or indeed motivation of any kind. Despite an examination of the literature we are unable to find a categorical statement regarding the frequency of 'deliberate errors'. Furthermore, we do not know how to recognize them when they do occur. In the absence of positive criteria the decision that Hans's knocking over of the toy horse was a 'deliberate error' is arbitrary.

As there is nothing to sustain the first two assumptions made by Freud in interpreting this 'symptomatic act', the third assumption (that this act indicated a wish for his father's death) is untenable;

[1] See for example the experiments on learning and habit interference (McGeoch & Irion, 1952; Woodworth & Schlosberg, 1955).

and it must be reiterated that there is no independent evidence that the boy feared or hated his father.

(3) Freud's third claim is that Hans's sexual excitement and desire for his mother were transformed into anxiety. This claim is based on the assertion that 'theoretical considerations require that what is today the object of a phobia must at one time in the past have been the source of a high degree of pleasure' (p. 201). Certainly such a transformation is not displayed by the facts presented. As stated above, there is no evidence that Hans sexually desired his mother. There is also no evidence of any change in his attitude to her before the onset of the phobia. Even though there is some evidence that horses were to some extent previously a source of pleasure, in general the view that phobic objects must have been the source of former pleasure is amply contradicted by experimental evidence. Apart from the numerous experiments on phobias in animals which disprove this contention (Gantt, 1944; Liddell, 1944; Woodward, 1959), the demonstrations of Watson and Rayner (1920) and Jones (1924) have clearly shown how phobias may be induced in children by a simple conditioning process. The rat and rabbit used as the conditioned stimuli in these demonstrations can hardly be regarded as sources of 'a high degree of pleasure', and the same applies to the generalized stimulus of cotton wool.

(4) The assertion that Hans's horse phobia symbolized a fear of his father has already been criticized. The assumed relationship between the father and the horse is unsupported and appears to have arisen as a result of the father's strange failure to believe that by the 'black around their mouths' Hans meant the horses' muzzles.

(5) The fifth claim is that the purpose of Hans's phobia was to keep him near his mother. Aside from the questionable view that neurotic disturbances occur for a purpose, this interpretation fails to account for the fact that Hans experienced anxiety even when he was out walking *with his mother*.

(6) Finally, we are told that the phobia disappeared as a result of Hans's resolution of his Oedipal conflicts. As we have attempted to show, there is no adequate evidence that Hans had an Oedipus complex. In addition, the claim that this assumed complex was resolved is based on a single conversation between Hans and his father (see above). This conversation is a blatant example of what Freud himself refers to as Hans having to 'be told many things he could not say himself, that he had to be presented with thoughts which he had so far *shown* no signs of possessing, and that his

attention had to be turned in the direction that his father was expecting something to come' (p. 246).

There is also no satisfactory evidence that the 'insights' that were incessantly brought to the boy's attention had any therapeutic value. Reference to the facts of the case shows only occasional coincidences between interpretations and changes in the child's phobic reactions. For example, 'a quiet period' early followed the father's statement that the fear of horses was a 'piece of nonsense' and that Hans really wanted to be taken into his mother's bed. But soon afterwards, when Hans became ill, the phobia was worse than ever. Later, having had many talks without effect, the father notes that on March 13 Hans, after agreeing that he still *wanted* to play with his widdler, was 'much less afraid of horses'. On March 15, however, he was frightened of horses, after the information that females have no widdlers (though he had previously been told the opposite by his mother). Freud asserts that Hans resisted this piece of enlightenment because it aroused castration fears, and therefore no therapeutic success was to be observed. The 'first real improvement' of April 2 is attributed to the 'moustache enlightenment' of March 30 (later proved erroneous), the boy having been told that he was 'afraid of his father precisely because he was so fond of his mother'. On April 7, though Hans was constantly improving, Freud commented that the situation was 'decidedly obscure' and that 'the analysis was making little progress'.[1]

Such sparse and tenuous data do not begin to justify the attribution of Hans's recovery to the bringing to consciousness of various unacceptable unconscious repressed wishes. In fact, Freud bases his conclusions entirely on deductions from his theory. Hans's latter improvement appears to have been smooth and gradual and unaffected by the interpretations. In general, Freud infers relationships in a scientifically inadmissible manner: if the enlightenment or interpretations given to Hans are followed by behavioural improvements, then they are automatically accepted as valid. If they are not followed by improvement we are told the patient has not accepted them, and not that they are invalid. Discussing the failure of these early enlightenments, Freud says that in any event therapeutic success is not the primary aim of the analysis,[2] thus sidetracking the

[1]By Freud's admission Hans was improving despite the absence of progress in the analysis.

[2]But elsewhere (p. 246) he says that a psychoanalysis is a therapeutic measure and not a scientific investigation!

issue; and he is not deflected from claiming an improvement to be due to an interpretation even when the latter is erroneous, e.g., the moustache interpretation.

No systematic follow-up of the case is provided. However, fourteen years after the completion of the analysis, Freud interviewed Hans, who 'declared that he was perfectly well and suffered from no troubles or inhibitions' (!). He also said that he had successfully undergone the ordeal of his parents' divorce. Hans reported that he could not remember anything about his childhood phobia. Freud remarks that this is 'particularly remarkable'. The analysis itself 'had been overtaken by amnesia!'

AN ALTERNATIVE VIEW OF HANS'S PHOBIA

In case it should be argued that, unsatisfactory as it is, Freud's explanation is the only available one, we shall show how Hans's phobia can be understood in terms of learning theory, in the theoretical framework provided by Wolpe (1950). This approach is largely Hullian in character and the clinical applications are based on experimental findings.

In brief, phobias are regarded as conditioned anxiety (fear) reactions. Any 'neutral' stimulus, simple or complex, that happens to make an impact on an individual at about the time that a fear reaction is evoked acquires the ability to evoke fear subsequently. If the fear at the original conditioning situation is of high intensity or if the conditioning is many times repeated the conditioned fear will show the persistence that is characteristic of *neurotic* fear; and there will be generalization of fear reactions to stimuli resembling the conditioned stimulus.

Hans, we are told, was a sensitive child who 'was never unmoved if someone wept in his presence' and long before the phobia developed became 'uneasy on seeing the horses in the merry-go-round being beaten' (p. 254). It is our contention that the incident to which Freud refers as merely the exciting cause of Hans's phobia was in fact the cause of the entire disorder. Hans actually says, 'No. I only got it [the phobia] then. When the horse in the bus fell down, it gave me such a fright, really! That was when I got the nonsense' (p. 192). The father says, 'All of this was confirmed by my wife, as well as the fact that the anxiety broke out immediately afterwards' (p. 193). The evidence obtained in studies on experimental neuroses in animals (e.g., Wolpe, 1958) and the studies by Watson and Rayner (1920), Jones (1924) and Woodward (1959) on phobias in children indicate that it is quite possible for one experience to induce a phobia.

In addition, the father was able to report two other unpleasant incidents which Hans had experienced with horses prior to the onset of the phobia. It is likely that these experiences had sensitized Hans to horses or, in other words, he had already been partially conditioned to fear horses. These incidents both occurred at Gmunden. The first was the warning given by the father of Hans's friend to avoid the horse lest it bite, and the second when another of Hans's friends injured himself (and bled) while they were playing horses.

Just as the little boy Albert (in Watson's classic demonstration, Watson & Rayner, 1920) reacted with anxiety not only to the original conditioned stimulus, the white rat, but to other similar stimuli such as furry objects, cotton wool and so on; Hans reacted anxiously to horses, horse-drawn buses, vans and features of horses, such as their blinkers and muzzles. In fact he showed fear of a wide range of generalized stimuli. The accident which provoked the phobia involved two horses drawing a bus and Hans stated that he was more afraid of large carts, vans or buses than small carts. As one would expect, the less close a phobic stimulus was to that of the original incident the less disturbing Hans found it. Furthermore, the last aspect of the phobia to disappear was Hans's fear of large vans or buses. There is ample experimental evidence that when responses to generalized stimuli undergo extinction, responses to other stimuli in the continuum are the less diminished the more closely they resemble the original conditional stimulus.

Hans's recovery from the phobia may be explained on conditioning principles in a number of possible ways, but the actual mechanism that operated cannot be identified, since the child's father was not concerned with the kind of information that would be of interest to us. It is well known that especially in children many phobias decline and disappear over a few weeks or months. The reason for this appears to be that in the ordinary course of life generalized phobic stimuli may evoke anxiety responses weak enough to be inhibited by other emotional responses simultaneously aroused in the individual. Perhaps this process was the true source of Little Hans's recovery. The interpretations may have been irrelevant, or may even have retarded recovery by adding new threats and new fears to those already present. But since Hans does not seem to have been greatly upset by the interpretations, it is perhaps more likely that the therapy was actively helpful, for phobic stimuli were again and again presented to the child in a variety of emotional contexts that may have inhibited the anxiety and in consequence diminished its habit strength. The *gradualness* of Hans's recovery is consonant with an explanation of this kind (Wolpe, 1958).

CONCLUSIONS

The chief conclusion to be derived from our survey of the case of Little Hans is that it does not provide anything resembling direct proof of psychoanalytic theorems. We have combed Freud's account for evidence that would be acceptable in the court of science, and have found none. In attempting to give a balanced summary of the case we have excluded a vast number of interpretations but have tried not to omit any material facts. Such facts, and they alone, could have supported Freud's theories. For example, if it had been observed after Gmunden that Hans had become fearful of his father, and that upon the development of the horse phobia the fear of the father had disappeared, this could reasonably have been regarded as presumptive of a displacement of fear from father to horse. This is quite different from observing a horse phobia and then asserting that it must be a displaced father-fear without ever having obtained any direct evidence of the latter; for then that which needs to be demonstrated is presupposed. To say that the father-fear was repressed is equally no substitute for evidence of it.

Freud fully believed that he had obtained in Little Hans a direct confirmation of his theories, for he speaks towards the end of 'the infantile complexes that were revealed behind Hans's phobia' (p. 287). It seems clear that although he wanted to be scientific Freud was surprisingly naive regarding the requirements of scientific evidence. Infantile complexes were not *revealed* (demonstrated) behind Hans's phobia: They were merely hypothesized.

It is remarkable that countless psychoanalysts have paid homage to the case of Little Hans, without being offended by its glaring inadequacies. We shall not here attempt to explain this, except to point to one probable major influence – a tacit belief among analysts that Freud possessed a kind of unerring insight that absolved him from the obligation to obey rules applicable to ordinary men. For example, Glover (1952), speaking of other analysts who arrogate to themselves the right Freud claimed to subject his material to 'a touch of revision', says, 'No doubt when someone of Freud's calibre appears in our midst he will be freely accorded . . . this privilege.' To accord such a privilege to anyone is to violate the spirit of science.

It may of course be argued that some of the conclusions of Little Hans are no longer held and that there is now other evidence for other of the conclusions; but there is no evidence that in general psychoanalytic conclusions are based on any better logic than that used by Freud in respect of Little Hans. Certainly no analyst has ever pointed to the failings of this account or disowned its reasoning, and it has continued to be regarded as one of the foundation stones on which psychoanalytic theory was built.

SUMMARY

The main facts of the case of Little Hans are presented and it is shown that Freud's claim of 'a more direct and less roundabout proof' of certain of his theories is not justified by the evidence presented. No confirmation by direct observation is obtained for any psychoanalytic theorem, though psychoanalysts have believed the contrary for 50 years. The demonstrations claimed are really interpretations that are treated as facts. This is a common practice and should be checked, for it has been a great encumbrance to the development of a science of psychiatry.

COMMENT

At first sight, the reader may be somewhat surprised to see a single case report presented here in a book on the *experimental* study of Freudian concepts; many critics have pointed out that Freud relied to an undue extent on single case histories for his proof, rather than comparing experimental and control groups. Freud's reliance on evidence 'from the couch' has been much maligned; yet there are good reasons for accepting such studies as that of Little Hans as proper experimental studies, at least potentially. Pavlov, whose work is universally acknowledged as experimental and properly scientific, usually adduces records from individual animals as proof in his books, and Skinner, whose claim to the status of experimental psychologist will hardly be gainsaid, has done likewise with his rats and pigeons –

indeed, his book with Ferster (1957) consists of little else but such individual records, each constituting a single case study. There is here a conflict of attitude between those who seek for statistical control of variables, and look for statistical evidence of significance, and those who seek to control variables experimentally to such an extent that the effects of experimental manipulation stand out clearly. This dispute has often led to denigration of those not of the particular author's persuasion, but there seems to be little point to such discussion – both methods are clearly within the tradition of science, and both have their place, depending on the precise problem to be investigated. Quite generally, Claude Bernard was among the first to point out that in medicine each patient is a separate research problem, and that diagnosis and treatment constitute steps in the endeavour to solve this problem; successful treatment suggests that the solution has been found. In clinical psychology, Shapiro (1964, 1966, 1967, 1969) has strongly argued the case for the 'single case experiment', along similar lines. Freud, then, is not alone in his belief that the single case can be regarded as an experimental test-bed.

The essence of an experiment is the production of effect A by manipulation of variable B, in a predicted and invariant manner (A=(f) B). Consider two individual experiments of the 'single case' type which have been described in the literature (Eysenck, 1965). One concerns a man whose asthmatic attacks could be terminated or avoided by turning the picture of his mother-in-law to the wall; this was taken to verify the hypothesis that it was the emotional upset produced by the mother-in-law which set off the attack. In the other study a man was impotent with his wife in their bedroom, but not elsewhere; it was found that he had once received a savage beating-up by the blacksmith husband of a woman with whom he was having an affair. This beating-up was the UCS; the wallpaper pattern in the blacksmith's bedroom constituted the CS, and as it happened the wallpaper in the impotent husband's bedroom was similar to the CS. Removal of the wallpaper restored his potency. These single cases demonstrate experimental manipulation (turning over of the picture; change of wallpaper) resulting in a predicted change in behaviour (cessation of asthmatic attack; return of potency).

It would not in our view be reasonable to deny that specific hypotheses had been stated in each case, and had been verified by a strict application of the experimental method. The question that arises is whether such one-to-one correspondence can be found in the type of case history offered by Freud; does recovery from neurosis follow in any predictable manner upon manipulation of the patient instigated by the analyst? Are there alternative hypotheses which would explain the facts equally well, or better, than those considered by Freud? It seems to us that it would be quite unfair to Freud and psychoanalysis to exclude the type of evidence on which he placed greatest stress, on the arbitrary grounds that this evidence relied on single case reports. What is required, however, is to look at these case reports with a critical eye, to discover whether they do in fact provide the kind of experimental evidence which Freud believes they furnish. It is for this purpose that we have here reprinted a well-known enquiry into Freud's famous study of Little Hans, a study which is often said to mark the beginning of child analysis.

It would have been possible to reprint Freud's paper itself, and then make the sort of comments here made by Wolpe and Rachman; we have preferred to print the Wolpe and Rachman paper itself, for two reasons. In the first place, the Freud paper is rather long, and so well known that to reprint it would seem a task of supererogation. In the second place, Wolpe and Rachman have done the job of criticism better than we could have done, and there seemed little point in paraphrasing their account. Readers will see for themselves just how much reliance can be placed on Freud's preferred method of proof, and how easy it is to put up alternative theories to the psychoanalytic one offered by Freud. The alternative theory here given follows directly from the laboratory-based framework of modern conditioning theory; there is no need to invoke mysterious unconscious forces, or to browbeat the little boy into agreeing to interpretations which he clearly rejects. We can explain all the factual material in Freud's account by reference to well-known facts and principles, and indeed we can go farther than Freud in this respect and explain the refusal of Little Hans to accept the far-fetched theories of his father.

It might be a good exercise for the reader to look at other famous single-case histories, as told by Freud, and try to fit these into an alternative conditioning model; we believe that nothing could be more instructive than to try for oneself what Freud should have done, but never did – to construct and consider alternative theories to the psychoanalytic. We have tried to supplement the various experimental papers in this book by pointing out such possible alternative hypotheses in relation to the studies there reported, most of which follow Freud in leaving such alternative hypotheses out of consideration. It is particularly revealing that the same technique can be used even in the very heart of Freud's kingdom, namely the single-case history, and that it can be done with such devastating success as here in the case of Little Hans. We hope and trust that in future psychoanalysts reporting single-case histories will attempt to evaluate their own account by comparing predictions made therefrom with predictions made from alternative theories; only by following such a salutary practice are we likely to be able to weigh one set of theories against another.

REFERENCES

EYSENCK, H. J. (1965) *Fact and Fiction in Psychology*. London: Penguin.

FENICHEL, O. (1945) *The Psychoanalytic Theory of Neurosis*. New York: Norton.

FERSTER, C. B. & SKINNER, B. F. (1957) *Schedules of Reinforcement*. New York: Appleton-Century-Crofts.

FREUD, S. (1938) *Psychopathology of Everyday Life*. Harmondsworth: Pelican Books.

—— (1950) *Collected Papers*, Vol. III. London: Hogarth Press.

GANTT, W. H. (1944) *Experimental Basis for Neurotic Behaviour*. New York: Hoeber.

GLOVER, E. (1952) Research methods in psychoanalysis. *Int. J. Psychoanal.*, **33**, 403-9.

—— (1956) *On the Early Development of Mind*. New York: International Universities Press.

HENDRICK, I. (1939) *Facts and Theories of Psychoanalysis*. New York: Knopf.

JONES, E. (1965) *Sigmund Freud: Life and Work*, Vol. 2. London: Hogarth Press.

JONES, M. C. (1924) Elimination of children's fears. *J. Exp. Psychol.*, *7*, 382-90.

LIDDELL, H. S. (1944) Conditioned reflex method and experimental neurosis. In J. MCV. HUNT (ed.) *Personality and the Behaviour Disorders*. New York: Ronald Press.

MCGEOGH, J. & IRION, A. (1952) *The Psychology of Human Learning*. New York: Longmans.

SHAPIRO, M. B. (1964) The single case in psychological research: A reply. *J. Psychosom. Res.*, **8**, 283-91.

—— (1966) The single case in clinical-psychological research. *J. Gen. Psychol.*, **74**, 3-23.

—— (1967) Clinical psychology as an applied science. *Brit. J. Psychiat.*, **113**, 1039-42.

—— (1969) A clinically orientated strategy in individual-centred research. *Brit. J. Soc. and Clin. Psychol.*, **8**, 240-91.

WATSON, J. B. & RAYNER, P. (1920) Conditioned emotional reactions. *J. Exp. Psychol.*, **3**, 1-14.

WOHLGEMUTH, A. (1923) *A Critical Examination of Psycho-analysis*. London: Allen & Unwin.

WOLPE, J. (1958) *Psychotherapy by Reciprocal Inhibition*. Stanford, Calif.: Stanford Univ. Press.

WOODWARD, J. (1959) Emotional disturbances of burned children. *Brit. Med. J.*, **1**, 1009-13.

WOODWORTH, R. & SCHLOSBERG, H. (1955) *Experimental Psychology*. London: Methuen.

20

S. B. G. Eysenck (1956)[1]

Neurosis and Psychosis: An experimental analysis[2]

Journal of Mental Science, 102, No. 428, 517-29

The problem we are concerned with is the relationship between neurosis and psychosis. It is well known psychiatrically that many patients tend to be what are called 'mixed' states, meaning that the diagnostic classification is doubtful. Patients complaining of physical symptoms, such as sleeplessness, heart palpitations, and other signs of autonomic inbalance, accompanied by anxiety or phobias, and who seem well reality-oriented, are not hallucinated or deluded and do not show any cognitive deterioration, are classed as neurotics. Psychotics, on the other hand, are generally deluded and hallucinated, are poorly reality-oriented, tend to show signs of cognitive deterioration, but have an absence of the physical symptoms so characteristic of neurotic disorders.

Unfortunately, these sorts of syndromes are 'classical' or 'textbook' cases only rarely encountered clinically. They are very much the 'pure' type of neurotic and psychotic, and shown these, practically no psychiatrist would hesitate in his diagnosis. The confusion arises when, as is so often the case, patients present a 'mixed' picture, complaining of symptoms from each category. This is especially the case with 'early' neurotics or psychotics, because as time goes on, one or other of the disorders often appears to become dominant and one apparently displaces the other or is superimposed upon it.

Now in observing these 'mixed' cases as they appear clinically, two equally feasible interpretations can be posited, each compatible with psychiatric experience. Either neuroses and psychoses differ in degree of severity of illness only, or both disorders are present simultan-

[1]Institute of Psychiatry, Maudsley Hospital, University of London.

[2]This article is based upon a dissertation submitted in partial fulfilment of the requirements for the Ph.D. degree at the University of London.

eously. On examining the first possibility, the explanation of the phenomenon of the 'mixed' case is that neurotics, as they get more neurotic, in other words, as their illness progresses and becomes more severe, develop more and more psychotic symptoms, which finally displace the original ones. If a psychotic should improve he goes through the neurotic stage back to normality. The interpretation suggests that the two main mental disorders are measurable along one continuum, with normals, neurotics and psychotics separated from each other only in degree of severity of their symptoms. It is a continuum believed by psychoanalysts to be one of 'psychosexual regression', in which psychotics are most regressed, neurotics less so, and normals not at all. A 'mixed' case is, therefore, one in which the patient finds himself in 'transit', as it were, from one category to another; if he is becoming more severely ill he may already be showing psychotic symptoms, while still retaining some neurotic ones, and conversely if he should be recovering from a psychosis, he might have to show some neurotic symptoms en route to normality.

The other possible explanation for the undoubted presence of symptoms from both disorders in the same patient is that both disorders may in fact be present. If a patient is suffering from cancer and deafness he will show both syndromes simultaneously but there is no reason to suppose that therefore poor hearing develops into cancer. Similarly, it may be that neurotics are also psychotic sometimes, or vice versa, without there being any need for one disorder to develop into the other. This hypothesis, then, would suggest that the problem is a two-dimensional one, in which neuroticism and psychoticism are separate axes and independent of each other. Both possibilities are reasonable, logical, and consistent, but both cannot be simultaneously true.

The older school of psychiatry believed that neurosis and psychosis were separate disorders that could be present in one and the same individual simultaneously. More modern opinion, in particular the analytical school, holds that the only difference between the two major mental states is in degree of severity. Equally eminent authorities in the mental health field can be found to support either of the hypotheses. Myerson (1936), though not in agreement with the concept of regression, expressed the view that: 'Neuroses span the bridge between . . . normal mental states and certain psychotic states.' He expressed the standpoint of this side very succinctly in the following paragraph:

> I formally introduce the concept of neuropsychoses. The neuropsychosis comes in being by an intensification of the symptomatology of the neuroses. Unreality becomes that falsification of reality called delusion. The sense of being deficient becomes unworthiness, sin, and punishment. The change in bodily sensation passes from the stage of severe hypochondriasis to the somatic delusion. This development can be traced in many cases. It can be noted as a variable and reversible process, appearing or receding, as the patient gets worse or as he get better.

Finally, he believes that: 'the anxiety neurosis may and does become an anxiety psychosis, which, I believe, is the proper definition of involutional melancholia.' Rather than neuroses giving place to psychoses, however, one might argue that one diagnosis is replaced by another as the more dominant disorder manifests itself. Lewis (1949) put forward the view that

> Neurotic persons suffering from depression or excessive fatigue suddenly commit suicide. Such are undoubtedly psychoses from the beginning or at least it is not possible that one type of psychiatric disorder changes into another. To assume that such a change occurs or is possible we must have much more supporting evidence, as such a concept does violence to established biological laws.

Two facts have been established for us. The first is that neuroticism is not a state which is distinct from the normal, but that all stages of it are represented along a continuum (Eysenck, 1947, 1952a). There is only an arbitrary line of demarcation to one side of which people are called 'normal' and to the other side of which they are considered neurotic enough to be sent to hospital. The second is that the same arguments hold for psychoticism (Eysenck, 1952a, 1952b). We know, then, that neuroticism denotes a continuum from the normal to the extreme neurotic, and similarly that psychoticism denotes a continuum from the normal to the extreme psychotic. Our problem is to conduct an experimental study to decide between two equally feasible hypotheses regarding the relationship between these two continua. It would seem an important theoretical matter, quite apart from the practical importance of improving the psychiatric classificatory system with a view to applying the appropriate treatment to each case.

Eysenck (1952a) has discussed the question of the relation between normal neurotic, and psychotic groups, and has compiled a series of diagrams in which mean scores for the three groups, normal, psychotic, and neurotic, were plotted, one test on each exis. They all gave a 'triangular' pattern rather than a linear one, thus confirming the opinion of the Kraepelinian school, who considered the major psychiatric groups to differ by more than just degree of severity. De (1953), in a factorial study of the Word Association test, found similar results. Freeman (1951), using the Character Interpretation test, obtained results also favouring the 'two-dimensional' approach. Lubin (1951) used normal, neurotic and psychotic groups and gave them four sub-tests of the U.S.E.S. Manual Dexterity test. He analysed the data using canonical variate analysis and concluded that two dimensions were required to account for the distributions of scores made by the subjects in the three groups. Eysenck (1955), in a similar study using more diversified tests, came to the same conclusion. Finally, Trouton and Maxwell (1956), in a factorial study of symptom ratings on almost a thousand male patients, obtained two clear orthogonal factors which they identified as neuroticism and psychoticism respectively.

Evidence from different sources, using different types of tests and different methods of analysis, therefore, tends to support the two-dimensional rather than the one-dimensional point of view. However, the results cannot be regarded as definitive in view of the small numbers employed in some of the researches listed, and doubts as to the adequacy of the statistical methods in others. In particular, general factorial methods lack the final stage required for the solution of this problem, which is an estimate of the significance of the factors obtained. It seemed worth while, therefore, to carry out a large-scale study using a type of statistical analysis which permitted of an exact assessment of significance.

POPULATION

In order to get our results as clearly defined as possible it was not only necessary to get well diagnosed patient groups, but also to be somewhat careful in our choice of the normal control group. Ideally one would like a control group composed of individuals not suffering from mental disorders of any kind. But since neuroticism and psychoticism are each present to some extent in everybody, we were obliged to content ourselves with the criterion that none of the subjects should ever have been interviewed by a psychiatrist, except when army selection procedures of some kind necessitated it: none of the individuals were to have sought psychiatric help. Our control group was composed of four sub-groups, two male and two female. The male groups were both from the army. One came from the Royal Army Educational Corps, whose 30 members were all intelligent and stable individuals; most of them had received extensive educational training which enabled them to try for a commission in the army. Their ages ranged from 18 to 39 years. The other group of 29 subjects from the Royal Artillery re-allocation depot, was composed mostly of volunteers rather than National Service men, and turned out to be of low intelligence and poor stability. Their ages ranged from 18 to 45 years. The female groups were 29 student nurses from King's College Hospital and 35 student occupational therapists from the Maudsley Hospital, both of whom were of average intelligence (or above) and made stable and co-operative impressions. Their ages ranged from 19 to 33 years.

TABLE 20.1. *t and F ratio results for the age variable.*

	n	m	v	F	Per cent level
Controls	123	22·244	20·727	82·588	0·1
Neurotics	53	30·019	61·557		
Psychotics	51	38·804	162·961		

Controls and psychotics $t = 12{\cdot}632$ (significant at the 0·1 per cent level)
Controls and neurotics $t = 6{\cdot}012$ (significant at the 0·1 per cent level)
Neurotics and psychotics $t = 5{\cdot}690$ (significant at the 0·1 per cent level)

The patient groups consisted of in-patients of the Maudsley and Bethlem Royal Hospitals. Their ages ranged from 16 to 49 years for the 24 male neurotics, of whom 8 were hysterics and 16 anxiety states; from 19 to 50 years for the 31 female neurotics, of whom 7 were hysterics and 24 anxiety states; from 15 to 48 years for the 13 male schizophrenics; from 17 to 49 years for the 15 female schizophrenics; from 33 to 57 years for the 12 male psychotic depressives, and from 24 to 64 years for the 15 female psychotic depressives. There were, altogether, 55 psychotics and 55 neurotics, but as in isolated cases not all the tests were completed by each subject the numbers varied a little from group to group as indicated in the tables, 53 and 51 subjects respectively having scores for all the tests.

We tried to test only patients whose diagnoses were predominantly neurotic or psychotic so that as few 'mixed' cases were seen as possible. Also, patients with certain physical disabilities were excluded because loss of a hand, for example, would have made tests such as manual dexterity impossible. Finally, we had to insist on subjects being British, or at least having a very good command of the English language so that they would not be at an unfair disadvantage on the Word Association test.

A rough matching for sex was achieved between the groups, but age and intelligence provided significant differences between the groups (Tables 20.1 and 20.2).

TABLE 20.2. *F ratio results for the intelligence variable.*

	n	m	v	F	Per cent level
Controls	123	14·886	21·626	34·578	0·1
Neurotics	55	11·927	29·180		
Psychotics	55	8·255	27·045		

TABLE 20.3. *Correlations with age.*

	Controls	Neurotics	Psychotics
Expressive movements	0·121	0·326*	0·211
Manual dexterity	−0·275*	−0·099	−0·111
P.G.R.	−0·099	−0·086	−0·451**
Static ataxia	−0·068	−0·051	0·145
Maudsley Medical Questionnaire	0·113	0·238	0·105
Word association	0·022	0·071	0·037
	n = 123	n = 53	n = 51

SIGNIFICANCE LEVELS

	(n−2) d.f.	5%	1%
Controls	121	0·177	0·232
Neurotics	51	0·271	0·351
Psychotics	49	0·276	0·358

*$p < \cdot 05$ **$p < \cdot 01$

Fortunately correlations between the tests used and the two variables are very low throughout (Tables 20.3 and 20.4), only 8 out of 36 being significant, and then usually for one of the groups only. For no test are correlations significant for all three groups. It is unlikely, therefore, that age and intelligence could have accounted for the major results reported below.

TABLE 20.4. *Correlations with intelligence.*

	Controls	Neurotics	Psychotics
Expressive movements	−0·044	−0·153	−0·159
Manual dexterity	0·150	0·321*	0·383**
P.G.R.	0·184*	0·120	0·226
Static ataxia	0·110	−0·022	0·102
Maudsley Medical Questionnaire	−0·282**	−0·339*	−0·270
Word association	0·134	−0·144	−0·072
	n = 123	n = 53	n = 51

$^{*}p < \cdot 05$ $^{**}p < \cdot 01$ (Significance levels as in Table 20.3).

Even if it were possible to regard intelligence as a unitary trait it would be very difficult to choose groups equated for intelligence or to partial out its effects from the data, because there would still be great practical difficulties to overcome. Furneaux (1952) has reported on the series of Nufferno tests that have been developed which gave a hint of the complexity of the concept of intelligence. He has shown that there are at least three main independent determinants of success in conventional intelligence tests: speed (the time taken to complete the items successfully solved), continuance (the persistence or length of time an individual will keep on trying for a solution), and error (the error checking mechanism or the ability to realize that an error has been made at all). These very interesting findings suggest that the intelligence 'level' is a composite score of three independent components which must be measured separately to get a true estimate of the weak and strong aspects of an individual's score. Clearly, two of the three components of intelligence are not themselves cognitive faculties, and orectic influences may be of considerable importance. This is an especially serious point when dealing with abnormal groups because the relation among these variables may be different within the groups. Therefore it would be quite impossible to partial out the effect of 'intelligence', because intelligence, as measured by any of our more usual tests, is not in fact a unitary variable at all. In other words, if we partialled out the effect of these three variables in some arbitrary combination we might remove an orectic pattern vital to the disorder under investigation (Eysenck, 1953).

Having decided, then, not to partial out intelligence, the alternative procedure was adopted of only using tests showing relatively low correlations with intelligence, as conventionally measured. This does by no means solve this very difficult problem, but ensures that even on conventional grounds our results are acceptable. We used a short test of intelligence and correlated the results with individual tests for each group. We used part of the Shipley-Hartford test of deterioration for our test of intelligence because it was short, timed, and gave us the intelligence level of each individual at the time of testing rather than that before his breakdown. (The abstractive ability part of the test was used, this being the part which is supposed to measure the deterioration as distinct from the vocabulary part which is learned before the illness and is presumed to be retained.)

DESCRIPTION OF TESTS

Sixteen tests were administered to each subject, these being given in two sessions of approximately an hour and a half each. On analysing the data, six tests were chosen on which to perform a Discriminant Function analysis. The rationale for selecting these particular tests was based on a number of considerations. Primarily they were required to have an F ratio which was significant at a very high level, so that the differentiation between the groups could not have been due to chance errors. Since a large number of scores were in this category other considerations now entered into our choice. The tests seem to fall into several groupings with respect to mental functions, and we used those that differed most from each other, i.e. tests of autonomic imbalance, motor control, a questionnaire, etc. Furthermore, we chose only one score from each test, so that there was complete experimental independence between the scores. The distributions were required to be normal, and finally, only those scores were used which had very low correlations with age and intelligence (Tables 20.3 and 20.4).

The six scores concerned were:

The Amplitude Score on the Waves Test (Eysenck, 1952b)

In this test subjects are presented with a sheet of paper with a V marked in each corner; two of these are vertical and the other two horizontal. The instructions are for the subject to trace over the first V shape, then close his eyes and continue to draw a series of six similar V shapes along the page. Each set of waves is covered by the experimenter before the subject opens his eyes to draw the next set, so that size exaggerations are not seen until the test is at an end. The score we chose was the average amplitude over all four sets of waves.

The Total Score on the U.S.E.S. Manual Dexterity Test (Eysenck, 1952a)

This total score was the sum of four sub-tests which the subjects performed. The first involved placing pegs from the top half of a board to the lower half with both hands, the second required that each peg be turned over, with one hand only, and replaced in the same hole. The third and fourth parts involved finger rather than manual dexterity, and required the subject to assemble, and in the second case dis-assemble, washers and pegs on a small board.

Percentage Change Score on the Psychogalvanic Reflex Test

The subjects were asked to lie on a couch for a 'test of relaxation', and had dry electrodes strapped to their palms. They were left to relax for the first fifteen minutes, and a series of stimuli were then applied. They were asked to hold their breath and were then requested to answer more questions from the Maudsley Medical Questionnaire, which they had previously encountered while doing another test. The 'threat' effect of this request provided us with a change score from which a high F ratio was obtained between the groups. Since the scores were not normally distributed, a square root transformation was used to stabilize the variance. Details regarding this test and conditions of testing are given elsewhere (Eysenck, 1956).

Maximum Backward Sway Score (in Square Root Units) on the Static Ataxia Test

Both Body Sway and Static Ataxia (Eysenck, 1947) gave surprisingly good differentiations between the groups on backward sway. The score chosen is a measure of the maximum distance a subject swayed backwards during the 30 seconds duration of the Static Ataxia test. In this test a string is attached to the subject's clothing and runs back to a marker on a kymograph, thus enabling us to obtain a continuous record of the path the subject traversed during the thirty seconds of the test. The units in which our results are given are not in actual distances swayed, but in the corresponding distances covered in the records of the kymograph, and furthermore, these were also transformed into square roots (as were the PGR scores) in order to normalize variances. (In this test subjects are told to stand as still as they can and to keep their eyes shut.) For details see Eysenck (1947).

The Total 'Abnormal' Responses Score on the Maudsley Medical Questionnaire

This questionnaire (Eysenck, 1952a) comprises a series of items listing symptoms such as 'Do you suffer from sleeplessness?' The score was simply the number of items a subject endorsed. The questionnaire was given in two parts, one during the Luria test and the other during the PGR test.

Synonyms Score on the Word Association Test

A list of thirty words was shown to the subject, one at a time, and he was required to 'give the first word that comes into your mind'. The subject simultaneously manipulated the hand plates of the Luria test, but the score we used here was concerned only with his actual responses to the stimulus words. We took a series of scores, but selected the 'number of synonyms given' score for our final analysis.

RESULTS

Waves.[1] *Table 20.5*

We have included with our own results some which were obtained by Eysenck (1952a, b) using a neurotic population in one case and a psychotic one in the other. These results seem remarkably similar and bear out our findings that this is a very good test of psychoticism. Psychotics, it seems, exaggerate the amplitude (as well as the wave-length) of the waves they draw blindfolded, to a much greater extent than do the other groups.

[1]Means, variances, and F ratios are given throughout, as well as comparative data from previous studies where available.

TABLE 20.5.

WAVES

Average amplitude:

	Controls		Neurotics		Psychotics		Per cent level of
	m	v	m	v	m	v	F
This study	21·825	12·574	23·711	20·188	26·647	35·213	0·1
Eysenck 1952	22·38	14·58	—	—	26·70	30·78	0·1
Eysenck 1952a	25·08	25·96	25·15	32·15	—	—	N.S.

Average wavelength:

	Controls		Neurotics		Psychotics		Per cent level of
	m	v	m	v	m	v	F
This study	88·664	465·543	100·480	570·456	110·178	823·664	0·1
Eysenck 1952b	89·29	440·90	—	—	108·92	963·17	0·1
Eysenck 1952a	100·17	509·30	95·87	640·80	—	—	N.S.

	C	N	P
This study	n = 123	n = 55	n = 55
Eysenck 1952b	n = 100	n = —	n = 100
Eysenck 1952a	n = 172	n = 76	n = —

Total Score (Manual Dexterity). Table 20.6

This is another test in which control groups are best, psychotics worst, and neurotics in between. However, it may be possible here that the manual dexterity of these groups is slowed down for different reasons. Psychotics may be slow because of their mental retardation, while neurotics are more likely to be negatively affected through their anxiety which causes hand tremors, etc. Scores are given for subtests M, N, O, P as well as for Total Performance.

'Threat' Score (Psychogalvanic Reflex). Table 20.7

This score shows psychotics to have a markedly lower reactivity to the 'threat' stimulus than either of the other groups. They were found to have a substantially lower resistance than the other groups on all scores of the PGR whether during the rest period or under the influence of stimuli (Eysenck, 1956).

TABLE 20.6. *U.S.E.S. test of manual dexterity.*

	Control		Neurotic		Psychotic			Per cent
	m	v	m	v	m	v	F	level
M	75·447	44·216	72·618	67·537	66·545	128·215	21·695	0·1
N	88·593	104·637	86·745	73·823	77·982	160·166	19·765	0·1
O	27·756	24·153	25·291	19·803	21·055	28·978	35·306	0·1
P	25·650	10·393	23·945	10·015	21·800	15·793	24·828	0·1
T	217·390	395·256	208·600	333·689	186·727	799·795	37·573	0·1
		n = 123		n = 55		n = 55		

TABLE 20.7. *Psychogalvanic reflex: 'Threat' score before the Maudsley Medical Questionnaire Stimulus. (Percentage change in resistance units.) (Square root transformation.)*

	n	m	v	F	Per cent level
Controls	123	0·184	0·022	7·381	0·1
Neurotics	54	0·160	0·024		
Psychotics	51	0·095	0·017		

Backward Sway Score (Static Ataxia). Table 20.8

It will be seen that on this test psychotics have a tendency to sway backwards far more than do the other groups. A similar finding was reported by Williams (1932) for the body-sway suggestibility test; it is interesting to note that the obvious explanation of Williams's finding in terms of the alleged 'negativism' of schizophrenics can hardly be held to apply here since no suggestion is, of course, made during the static ataxia part of the test.

TABLE 20.8. *Static ataxia: maximum backward sway. (Square root transformation and Kymographic conversion.)*

	n	m	v	F	Per cent level
Controls	123	0·288	0·143	9·920	0·1
Neurotics	55	0·339	0·139		
Psychotics	55	0·598	0·342		

Abnormal Responses (Maudsley Medical Questionnaire). Table 20.9

These results, which agree well with other studies (Eysenck, 1947, 1952a) for neurotic groups, show psychotics to have a slightly lower score than neurotics.

TABLE 20.9. *Maudsley Medical Questionnaire: Number of 'Abnormal' responses.*

	n	m	v	F	Per cent level
Controls	123	10·114	32·167	65·583	0·1
Neurotics	55	20·527	39·921		
Psychotics	52	18·192	52·903		

Synonyms Score (Word Association Test). Table 20.10

These figures suggest that normals are less likely to respond with synonyms than are the abnormal groups. Unfortunately, it was not possible to compare our results (including all the other scores we took on the word association test) with those of De (1953), because his interest lay primarily in the comparison of the responses to emotional as compared with responses to neutral words.

TABLE 20.10. *Word association: Synonyms.*

	n	m	v	F	Per cent level
Controls	123	4·480	5·989	7·810	0·1
Neurotics	55	6·618	22·426		
Psychotics	55	6·164	23·436		

STATISTICAL TREATMENT

By using the statistical method known as Discriminant Function analysis it was hoped to throw some light on the problem of dimensionality in the mental health field.

An analysis of variance was performed to find the six most suitable scores for the Discriminant Function analysis. This latter method of analysis for more than two groups has been developed (largely) by Rao (1948b) and was studied carefully by Lubin (1950, 1951). Lubin used psychiatric groups similar to our own to demonstrate the statistical method involved, but his main interest lay in the technique rather than in the psychological results obtained.

Discriminant Function analysis involved the calculation of several matrices. First the total product-sum matrix (G) was computed for the six variables, and then the between groups product-sum matrix (B), the difference between these giving us the within groups product-sum matrix (W). We then followed Lubin's (1950) method of maximizing the square of the correlation ratio given by

$$R^2 = \left(\frac{\text{deviance between groups}}{\text{total deviance}}\right)$$

In essence, the problem is this: it is required to find the set of weights to use to derive a composite score from the six tests for each subject which will maximize the square of the correlation ratio (R^2) between that composite variate and the groups. Hence, if we take $R^2 = u'Bu/u'\ Gu$, we arrive at the equation $(G-^1B—R^2I)u=O$. (Where G = total product-sum matrix, B = between groups product-sum matrix, u is the column vector of weights, and u′ is its transpose, I=unit diagonal matrix.) The values of R^2 which satisfy this equation are the latent roots of the non-symmetric matrix $G-^1B$, each root having a corresponding latent vector u.

To obtain $G-^1B$ involves calculating the inverse of the matrix G and post-multiplying it by B. This results in a non-symmetric matrix from which the latent roots and vectors are extracted using an iterative method for non-symmetric matrices described by Maxwell (unpub. manuscript). As expected, only two latent roots were found as the rank of $G-^1B$ is always one less than the number of tests or the number of groups, whichever is the smaller.

Having obtained the two latent roots these were tested for significance using Bartlett's chi-squared test for the significance of the canonical roots: $X^2 = -\left(N-1-\frac{q+c}{2}\right)\log_e(1-\lambda)$, where λ is the root whose significance is being tested, q = number of tests, c = the number of groups and N = number of people. Since the sum of the diagonal entries of the matrix $G-^1B$ is equal to the sum of the latent roots, the percentage of the total variance accounted for by each of the roots can be calculated (Table 20.11). It will be seen that both roots are significant at the 0.1 per cent level. Thus the results of this research strongly support the hypothesis that neuroticism and psychoticism are two independent dimensions. It is impossible to account for the test responses of our three groups in terms of one dimension only. This does not imply, of course, that additional dimensions might not be required for a more adequate description of mental abnormality. If the neurotic and psychotic groups were to be broken down into sub-groups (i.e. hysterics, psychopaths, anxiety states, reactive depressions, obsessionals, manic depressives, and schizophrenics, etc.), and larger numbers of appropriate tests were employed, it is very likely that further dimensions, such as extraversion-introversion, would emerge. The number of dimensions found in an analysis of this type is limited but not determined by the number of groups and tests used.

TABLE 20.11. *Latent vectors.*

		X_1	X_2
1.	Expressive movements	−0·450,045	−0·116,244
2.	Manual dexterity	1·000,000	1·000,000
3.	P.G.R.	0·015,541	0·072,806
4.	Static ataxia	−0·272,682	−0·316,893
5.	Maudsley Medical Questionnaire	−0·774,271	0·394,398
6.	Word association	−0·217,552	0·125,206

Latent Roots

$\lambda_1 = 0{\cdot}437{,}605$; $\lambda_2 = 0{\cdot}172{,}877$; $\lambda_1+\lambda_2 = 0{\cdot}610{,}482$

Diagonal entries of matrix $G^{-1}B = 0{\cdot}610{,}484$

Hence λ_1 is 71·7 *per cent* of the variance and λ_2 is 28·3 *per cent.*

Significance of the Roots

$$X^2 = -\left(N-1-\frac{q+c}{2}\right)\log_e(1-\lambda)$$

$R_1^2 = \lambda_1 : X^2 = 127{\cdot}507$ which is significant at the 0·1 per cent level.
$R_2^2 = \lambda_2 : X^2 = 42{\cdot}026$ which is significant at the 0·1 per cent level.
Total λ_1 and $\lambda_2 : X^2 = 169{\cdot}533$ which is significant at the 0·1 per cent level.

As a final step, scores were computed for each subject on both canonical variates, and the percentage misclassification in each group calculated using a Rao quadratic discriminant function. The method is lengthy but the principle is quite straightforward. The latent vectors gave two sets of weights to apply to the scores, so that two measures could be calculated for each subject, one for each canonical variate. These scores Y_1 and Y_2 were found by multiplying the score of a subject on the tests by the appropriate weights, and summing them over the six tests. Having thus found a composite score for each person on both canonical variates, his position with respect to each axis was plotted, and these co-ordinates were then used in Rao quadratic discriminant function analysis.

TABLE 20.12. *Test score diagnosis.*

	Psychiatric Diagnosis			
	Controls	Neurotics	Psychotics	Totals
Psychotics	2	5	23	30
Neurotics	12	29	11	52
Controls	109	19	17	145
Totals	123	53	51	227

This implies the use of a formula to ascertain the likelihood of a subject belonging to each group. In Figure 20.1 each subject was given a position (Y_1 and Y_2 co-ordinates), using crosses to denote controls, dots to denote neurotics, and triangles to denote psychotics. To find the best line of demarcation between the groups, the likelihood scores for borderline cases of the three groups were found, the first lines of demarcation being judged by eye. The likelihood (L_{ij}) of the ith persons belonging to the jth group is given by the equation (Lubin, 1950):

$$L_{ij} = 2\log_e(n_j) - \log_e|c_j| - d_{ij}c_j^{-1}d_{ji}$$

where n_j = number of people in the jth group,

c_j = covariance matrix for that group,

d_{ij} = a(1×2) vector giving the deviations of the ith subjects' scores from the mean scores for the group concerned.

The borderline cases, of whom there were some thirty, each had their likelihood scores calculated from the formula above, one for

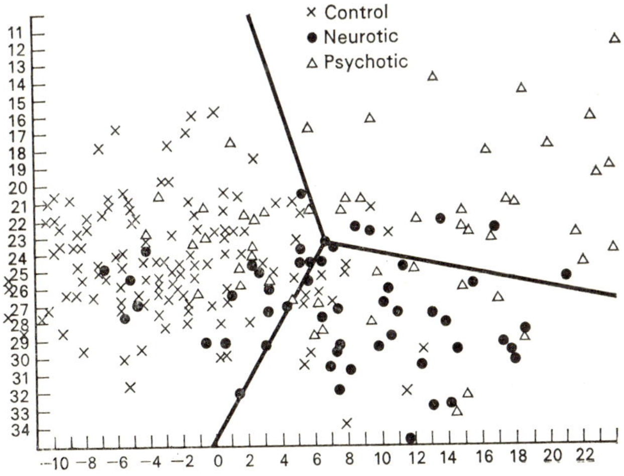

Figure 20.1.

each of the groups irrespective of that to which he was allocated by diagnosis. The best lines of demarcation were thus found.

In this way it was possible to re-classify the subjects according to their calculated likelihood scores, and the results of this appear in Table 20.12. From these figures it will be seen that 29 per cent of the subjects were misclassified. Furthermore, if another line is drawn (by eye), in order to find the amount of misclassification between neurotics and psychotics (i.e. leaving out the rather large control group), the misclassification between them is only 21 per cent.

These misclassifications, however, may well be due largely to errors in the criterion, that is to say, psychiatric diagnosis, rather than to the test allocation. Evidence regarding the unreliability of psychiatric diagnosis has been reviewed by Eysenck (1952a), who later (personal communication) found, when following up psychiatric diagnoses on certain subjects whose test results indicated a different diagnosis, that these had been changed in many cases, independently, to agree with the test results.

Apart from misdiagnoses between the two mentally disturbed groups, the composition of all 'normal' groups is of course somewhat suspect. Fraser (1947) has shown that in an unselected normal group some 10 per cent showed signs of severe psychiatric disabilities but had not yet resorted to psychiatric help, with a further 20 per cent showing mild psychiatric disabilities. Consequently, a fixed proportion of control group subjects would be expected to be 'misclassified'; they might be 'normal' in that they had not been seen by a psychiatrist, yet their test results correctly place them into the neurotic or psychotic categories.

With this argument in mind, separate plots were made for each of the four groups constituting our complete control group. It seemed likely from previous work (Eysenck, 1952a), from common knowledge and observation, that the R.A. Army group, which came from re-allocation units, would contain a larger proportion of psychiatrically abnormal members than would the other groups. The separate plots show that the R.A. Army had 7 out of 29 (or 24 per cent) misclassified; the King's College Nurses group had 3 out of 29 (or 10 per cent) misclassified; the R.A.E.C. group had 3 out of 30 (or 10 per cent) misclassified; and the Occupational Therapists had only 1 out of 35 (or 3 per cent) misclassified. Clearly, then, if the criteria of diagnoses were improved the percentage of misclassifications might be considerably lower.

SUMMARY

Our problem was to determine whether neuroticism was differentiated from psychoticism qualitatively or quantitatively. The first step was to choose a battery of tests that appeared suitable from the literature; that is to say, tests which were previously found to be good differentiators of neurotic from normal groups, and psychotic from normal groups respectively.

Having chosen sixteen such tests, these were administered to three main groups of subjects; 123 normal controls, 55 neurotics, and 55 psychotics. An analysis of variance was performed on the data to ascertain which of the test scores were the best differentiators. Six scores were chosen for the Discriminant Function analysis, largely on the basis of their high F ratios and their low correlations with age and intelligence. This Discriminant Function analysis was undertaken to ascertain whether the three groups, normal, psychotic, neurotic, could be described in terms of one dimension (one significant latent root only), or whether two dimensions would be required (two significant roots). Since we obtained *two* highly significant latent roots from our data, we conclude that two dimensions are needed to describe the differences of neurotics and psychotics from normal people.

A composite likelihood score was calculated from the set of weights (latent vectors) obtained from the canonical variate analysis, and these were plotted in the two-dimensional space with the variates Y_1 and Y_2 as the co-ordinates. The misclassification rate obtained on the basis of a redistribution of diagnoses according to test results was *29 per cent*, a figure which fell to *21 per cent* when the abnormal groups alone were considered.

ACKNOWLEDGEMENTS

The writer is indebted to the Bethlem Royal Hospital and the Maudsley Hospital Research Committee for a grant which made this study possible.

Thanks are due to Professor H. J. Eysenck for his many helpful suggestions and his willingness to discuss queries at all times, to Mr A. E. Maxwell for his patient help over the statistical treatment of the data, and to Professor P. E. Vernon for guidance throughout the research.

Finally, the help should be acknowledged of the doctors and nurses of the Maudsley and Bethlem Royal Hospitals for selecting suitable patients for testing; and also of all the subjects who so willingly underwent the testing procedure.

COMMENT

This study is concerned with a problem which is central to an understanding of the nature of mental disorder, and one in which Freudian theory appears to give a clear answer which is essentially different to the answer given by orthodox psychiatry. The problem relates to the respective relations between normality, psychosis and neurosis. On the Freudian hypothesis, we are dealing with a one-dimensional progression (Fig. C.1), while on the psychiatric hypothesis we are dealing with a two-dimensional framework (Fig. C.2). The argument is presented *in extenso* in Eysenck (1955); it derives essentially from Freud's notion of libidinal regression – the amount of regression determining whether the patient has a neurotic breakdown (moderate regression) or a psychotic episode (considerable regression). There are no qualitative differences involved, and consequently only one dimension is required to indicate the positions of typical normal, neurotic and psychotic groups. On orthodox psychiatric theories, psychosis is qualitatively different from neurosis, and consequently two independent dimensions are required to accommodate the three groups. The study here reprinted demonstrates clearly that the Freudian theory is not in accord with the outcome of the experiment undertaken; statistical tests indicate that *two* dimensions are required to account for the differential performance of the three groups involved.

This study has been replicated (Eysenck, 1955) on three groups of 20 normal, neurotic and psychotic subjects; four objective laboratory tests were used in the study. Fig. C.3 shows the outcome of the discrimination analysis, which again produced two clearly significant roots; Table C.1 shows the number of misclassifications when using the results of the tests to allocate subjects to the three groups. It is interesting to note that two neurotics, marked A and B in Fig. C.3, were placed by their test scores right in the centre of the psychotic cluster. Both were readmitted to the hospital later on, and both had

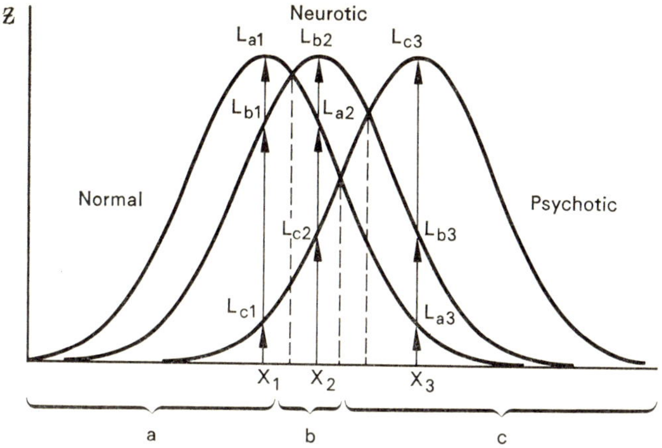

Figure C.1. *One-dimensional hypothesis of personality organization.*

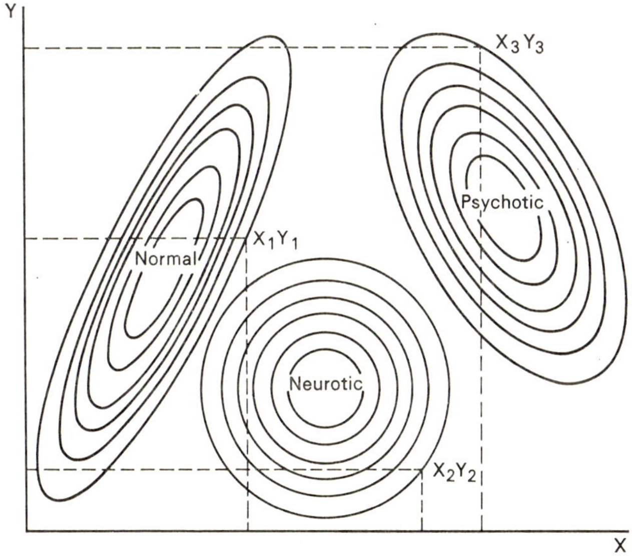

Figure C.2. *Two-dimensional hypothesis of personality organization.*

their diagnosis changed from neurotic to psychotic – 'schizophrenia' in the one case, 'paranoia' in the other. (This change was of course quite independent of the test result, which was not known to the psychiatrist making the diagnosis.) In part, therefore, errors in allocation may be due to errors in diagnosis.

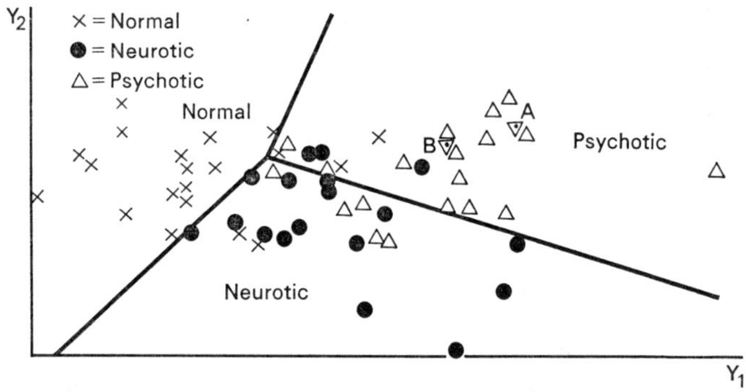

Figure C.3. *Variate scores and group segregation using visually fitted lines.*

TABLE C.1. *Classification by visually-fitted discriminant lines based on test scores compared with classification based on psychiatric diagnosis.*

	test			
Diagnosis	C	N	P	Total
Control	15	2	3	20
Neurotic	0	15	5	20
Psychotic	0	5	15	20
				60

Regression is a vital concept in Freud's theory, and its failure to predict correctly the dimensionality of the space occupied by the test performances of the groups investigated is therefore a serious one. Objection may be made to the use of the particular tests used, as not having any connection with Freudian theory, but such an objection would in our opinion be misconceived. If a general theory places three groups along a single continuum, then it would be expected that any test which significantly discriminates between at least two of these groups (and is therefore relevant to the distinction between them) would order the groups along the single dimension hypothesized. Failure to do so clearly favours the opposite theory, and lends credence to those who postulate a two-dimensional framework. It is of course true that the experimental and mathematical procedures here used are quite alien to the sort of work that is typically done by psychoanalysts in connection with their own practice, but this does not constitute a criticism. In science, a far-ranging theory is often tested and elaborated along lines which the author did not and could not foresee; a good example is atomic theory and Avogadro's number. Estimates of this number, and attempts to prove the physical existence of atoms and molecules, were made along a large number of independent lines – Brownian movement, gas viscosity, black-body radiation, etc. It is not necessary that the test of a theory should be along the accustomed paths; it is merely required that the test should logically follow from the theory. It is suggested that in this case the test does follow logically from the theory, and that consequently the failure of the outcome to agree with the prediction must be damaging to the theory.

REFERENCES

DE, B. (1953) A study of the validity of the word association technique for the differentiation of normal and abnormal persons. Ph.D. thesis, Univ. of London.

EYSENCK, H. J. (1947) *Dimensions of Personality*. London: Kegan Paul.

—— (1952a) *The Scientific Study of Personality*. London: Routledge & Kegan Paul.

—— (1952b) Schizothymia-cyclothymia as a dimension of personality. II. Experimental. *J. Pers.*, **20**, 345-84.

—— (1953) La rapidité du fonctionnement mental comme mesure de l'anomalie mentale. *Rev. Psychol. Appl.*, **3**, No. 4, 367-77.

—— (1955) Psychiatric diagnosis as a psychological and statistical problem. *Psychol. Rep.*, **1**, 3-17.

—— (1956) An experimental study of psychogalvanic reflex responses of normal, neurotic and psychotic subjects. *J. Psychosom. Res.*, **1**, 258-72.

FRASER, R. (1947) *The Incidence of Neurosis among Factory Workers*. London: H.M.S.O.

FREEMAN, F. (1951) An experimental study of projection among normal and abnormal groups in a structural situation. Ph.D. thesis, Univ. of London.

FURNEAUX, W. D. (1952) Some speed, error and difficulty relationships within a problem-solving situation. *Nature*, **170**, 37.

LEWIS, NOLAN D. C. (1949) Criteria for early differential diagnosis of psychoneurosis and schizophrenia. *Amer. J. Psychother.*, **3**, 4-18.

LUBIN, A. (1950) Linear and non-linear discriminating functions. *Brit. J. Psychol. (Statist.)*, **3**, 90-103.

—— (1951) Some contributions to the testing of psychological hypotheses by means of statistical multivariate analysis. Ph.D. thesis, Univ. of London.

MAXWELL, A. E. (unpub. ms.) Latent roots and vectors of matrices not axisymmetric.

MYERSON, A. (1936) Neuroses and psychoses. *Amer. J. Psychiat.*, **93**, 263-301.

RAO, C. R. (1948a) The utilisation of multiple measurements in problems of biological classification. *J. Roy. Stat. Soc.*, B.10, 159-93.

—— (1948b) Tests of significance in multivariate analysis. *Biomet.*, **35**, 58-79.

TROUTON, D. S. & MAXWELL, A. E. (1956) The relation between neurosis and psychosis. A factor analytic study of 819 neurotics and psychotics. *J. Ment. Sci.*, **102**, 1-21.

WILLIAMS, G. W. (1932) A study of the responses of three psychotic groups to a test of suggestibility. *J. Gen. Psychol.*, 7, 302-9.

21

H. J. Eysenck (1952)[1]

The effects of psychotherapy: An evaluation

Journal of Consulting Psychology, XVI, No. 5, 319-24

The recommendation of the Committee on Training in Clinical Psychology of the American Psychological Association regarding the training of clinical psychologists in the field of psychotherapy has been criticized by the writer in a series of papers (Eysenck, 1949, 1950a, 1950b). Of the arguments presented in favour of the policy advocated by the Committee, the most cogent one is perhaps that which refers to the social need for the skills possessed by the psychotherapist. In view of the importance of the issues involved, it seemed worth while to examine the evidence relating to the actual effects of psychotherapy, in an attempt to seek clarification on a point of fact.

BASE LINE AND UNIT OF MEASUREMENT

In the only previous attempt to carry out such an evaluation, Landis has pointed out that 'before any sort of measurement can be made, it is necessary to establish a base line and a common unit of measure. The only unit of measure available is the report made by the physician stating that the patient has recovered, is much improved, is improved or unimproved. This unit is probably as satisfactory as any type of human subjective judgment, partaking of both the good and bad points of such judgments' (1938, p. 156). For a unit Landis suggests 'that of expressing therapeutic results in terms of the number of patients recovered or improved per 100 cases admitted to the hospital'. As an alternative, he suggests 'the statement of therapeutic outcome for some given group of patients during some stated interval of time'.

Landis realized quite clearly that in order to evaluate the effective-

[1]Institute of Psychiatry, Maudsley Hospital, University of London.

ness of any form of therapy, data from a control group of non-treated patients would be required in order to compare the effects of therapy with the spontaneous remission rate. In the absence of anything better, he used the amelioration rate in state mental hospitals for patients diagnosed under the heading of 'neuroses'. As he points out:

> There are several objections to the use of the consolidated amelioration rate . . . of the . . . state hospitals . . . as a base rate for spontaneous recovery. The fact that psychoneurotic cases are not usually committed to state hospitals unless in a very bad condition; the relatively small number of voluntary patients in the group; the fact that such patients do get some degree of psychotherapy especially in the reception hospitals; and the probably quite different economic, educational, and social status of the State Hospital group compared to the patients reported from each of the other hospitals – all argue against the acceptance of [this] figure . . . as a truly satisfactory base line, but in the absence of any other better figure this must serve (1938, p. 168).

Actually the various figures quoted by Landis agree very well. The percentage of neurotic patients discharged annually as recovered or improved from New York state hospitals is 70 (for the years 1925-34); for the United States as a whole it is 68 (for the years 1926-33). The percentage of neurotics discharged as recovered or improved within one year of admission is 66 for the United States (1933) and 68 for New York (1914). The consolidated amelioration rate of New York state hospitals, 1917-34, is 72 per cent. As this is the figure chosen by Landis, we may accept it in preference to the other very similar ones quoted. By and large, we may thus say that of severe neurotics receiving in the main custodial care, and very little if any psychotherapy, over two-thirds recovered or improved to a considerable extent. 'Although this is not, strictly speaking, a basic figure for "spontaneous" recovery, still any therapeutic method must show an appreciably greater size than this to be seriously considered' (1938, p. 160).

Another estimate of the required 'base line' is provided by Denker:

> Five hundred consecutive disability claims due to psychoneurosis, treated by general practitioners throughout the country, and not by accredited specialists or sanatoria, were reviewed. All types of neurosis were included, and no attempt made to differentiate the

neurasthenic, anxiety, compulsive, hysteric, or other states, but the greatest care was taken to eliminate the true psychotic or organic lesions which in the early stages of illness so often simulate neurosis. These cases were taken consecutively from the files of the Equitable Life Assurance Society of the United States, were from all parts of the country, and all had been ill of a neurosis for at least three months before claims were submitted. They, therefore, could be fairly called 'severe', since they had been totally disabled for at least a three months' period, and rendered unable to carry on with any 'occupation for remuneration or profit' for at least that time (1946, p. 2164).

These patients were regularly seen and treated by their own physicians with sedatives, tonics, suggestion, and reassurance, but in no case was any attempt made at anything but this most superficial type of 'psychotherapy' which has always been the stock-in-trade of the general practitioner. Repeated statements, every three months or so by their physicians, as well as independent investigations by the insurance company, confirmed the fact that these people actually were not engaged in productive work during the period of their illness. During their disablement, these cases received disability benefits. As Denker points out, 'It is appreciated that this fact of disability income may have actually prolonged the total period of disability and acted as a barrier to incentive for recovery. One would, therefore, not expect the therapeutic results in such a group of cases to be as favourable as in other groups where the economic factor might act as an important spur in helping the sick patient adjust to his neurotic conflict and illness' (1946, p. 2165).

The cases were all followed up for at least a five-year period, and often as long as ten years after the period of disability had begun. The criteria of 'recovery' used by Denker were as follows: (*a*) return to work, and ability to carry on well in economic adjustments for at least a five-year period; (*b*) complaint of no further or very slight difficulties; (*c*) making of successful social adjustments. Using these criteria, which are very similar to those usually used by psychiatrists, Denker found that 45 per cent of the patients recovered after one year, another 27 per cent after two years, making 72 per cent in all. Another 10 per cent, 5 per cent, and 4 per cent recovered during the third, fourth, and fifth years, respectively, making a total of 90 per cent recoveries after five years.

This sample contrasts in many ways with that used by Landis.

The cases on which Denker reports were probably not quite as severe as those summarized by Landis: they were all voluntary, non-hospitalized patients, and came from a much higher socioeconomic stratum. The majority of Denker's patients were clerical workers, executives, teachers, and professional men. In spite of these differences, the recovery figures for the two samples are almost identical. The most suitable figure to choose from those given by Denker is probably that for the two-year recovery rate, as follow-up studies seldom go beyond two years and the higher figures for three-, four-, and five-year follow-up would overestimate the efficiency of this 'base line' procedure. Using, therefore, the two-year recovery figure of 72 per cent, we find that Denker's figure agrees exactly with that given by Landis. We may, therefore, conclude with some confidence that our estimate of some two-thirds of severe neurotics showing recovery or considerable improvement without the benefit of systematic psychotherapy is not likely to be very far out.

EFFECTS OF PSYCHOTHERAPY

We may now turn to the effects of psychotherapeutic treatment. The results of nineteen studies reported in the literature, covering over seven thousand cases, and dealing with both psychoanalytic and eclectic types of treatment, are quoted in detail in Table 21.1. An attempt has been made to report results under the four headings: (*a*) Cured, or much improved; (*b*) Improved; (*c*) Slightly improved; (*d*) Not improved, died, discontinued treatment, etc. It was usually easy to reduce additional categories given by some writers to these basic four; some writers give only two or three categories, and in those cases it was, of course, impossible to subdivide further, and the figures for combined categories are given.[1] A slight degree of subjectivity enters into this procedure, but it is doubtful if it has caused much distortion. A somewhat greater degree of subjectivity is probably implied in the writer's judgment as to which disorders and diagnoses should be considered to fall under the heading of 'neurosis'. Schizophrenic, manic-depressive, and paranoid states have been excluded; organ neuroses, psychopathic states, and character disturbances have been included. The number of cases where there was genuine doubt is probably too small to make much change in the final figures, regardless of how they are allocated.

[1]In one or two cases where patients who improved or improved slightly were combined by the original author, the total figure has been divided equally between the two categories.

TABLE 21.1. *Summary of reports of the results of psychotherapy.*

	N	Cured; much improved	Improved	Slightly improved	Not improved; died; left treatment	% Cured; much improved; improved
(A) PSYCHOANALYTIC						
1. Fenichel (1920–30, pp. 28–40)	484	104	84	99	197	39
2. Kessel & Hyman (1933)	34	16	5	4	9	62
3. Jones (1926–36, pp. 12–14)	59	20	8	28	3	47
4. Alexander (1932–7, pp. 30–43)	141	28	42	23	48	50
5. Knight (1941)	42	8	20	7	7	67
All cases:	760	335		425		44%
(B) ECLECTIC						
1. Huddleson (1927)	200	19	74	80	27	46
2. Matz (1929)	775	10	310	310	145	41
3. Maudsley Hospital Report (1931)	1721	288	900	533		69
4. Maudsley Hospital Report (1935)	1711	371	765	575		64
5. Neustatter (1935)	46	9	14	8	15	50
6. Luff & Garrod (1935)	500	140	135	26	199	55
7. Luff & Garrod (1935)	210	38	84	54	34	68
8. Ross (1936)	1089	547	306	236		77
9. Yaskin (1936)	100	29	29	42		58
10. Curran (1937)	83	51			32	61
11. Masserman & Carmichael (1938)	50	7	20	5	18	54
12. Carmichael & Masserman (1939)	77	16	25	14	22	53
13. Schilder (1939)	35	11	11	6	7	63
14. Hamilton & Wall (1941)	100	32	34	17	17	66
15. Hamilton *et al.* (1942)	100	48	5	17	32	51
16. Landis (1938)	119	40	47	32		73
17. Institute of Med. Psychol. (quoted Neustatter)	270	58	132	55	25	70
18. Wilder (1945)	54	3	24	16	11	50
19. Miles *et al.* (1951)	53	13	18	13	9	58
All cases:	7293	4661		2632		64%

A number of studies have been excluded because of such factors as excessive inadequacy of follow-up, partial duplication of cases with others included in our table, failure to indicate type of treatment used, and other reasons which made the results useless from our point of view. Papers thus rejected are those by Thorley & Craske (1950), Bennett & Semrad (1936), H. I. Harris (1939), Hardcastle (1934), A. Harris (1938), Jacobson and Wright (1942), Friess & Nelson (1942), Comroe (1963), Wenger (1934), Orbison (1925), Coon & Raymond (1940), Denker (1937), and Bond & Braceland (1937). Their inclusion would not have altered our conclusions to any considerable degree, although, as Miles *et al.* point out: 'When the various studies are compared in terms of thoroughness, careful planning, strictness of criteria and objectivity, there is often an inverse correlation between these factors and the percentage of successful results reported' (1951, p. 88).

Certain difficulties have arisen from the inability of some writers to make their column figures agree with their totals, or to calculate percentages accurately. Again, the writer has exercised his judgment as to which figures to accept. In certain cases, writers have given figures of cases where there was a recurrence of the disorder after apparent cure or improvement, without indicating how many patients were affected in these two groups respectively. All recurrences of this kind have been subtracted from the 'cured' and 'improved' totals, taking half from each. The total number of cases involved in all these adjustments is quite small. Another investigator making all decisions exactly in the opposite direction to the present writer's would hardly alter the final percentage figures by more than 1 or 2 per cent.

We may now turn to the figures as presented. Patients treated by means of psychoanalysis improve to the extent of 44 per cent; patients treated eclectically improve to the extent of 64 per cent; patients treated only custodially or by general practitioners improve to the extent of 72 per cent. There thus appears to be an inverse correlation between recovery and psychotherapy; the more psychotherapy, the smaller the recovery rate. This conclusion requires certain qualifications.

In our tabulation of psychoanalytic results, we have classed those who stopped treatment together with those not improved. This appears to be reasonable; a patient who fails to finish his treatment, and is not improved, is surely a therapeutic failure. The same rule has been followed with the data summarized under 'eclectic' treatment, except when the patient who did not finish treatment was definitely classified as 'improved' by the therapist. However, in view of the peculiarities of Freudian procedures it may appear to some readers to be more just to class those cases separately, and deal only with the percentage of completed treatments which are successful. Approximately one-third of the psychoanalytic patients listed broke off treatment, so that the percentage of successful treatments of patients who finished their course must be put at approximately 66 per cent. It would appear, then, that when we discount the risk the patient runs of stopping treatment altogether, his chances of improvement under psychoanalysis are approximately equal to his chances of improvement under eclectic treatment, and slightly worse than his chances under a general practitioner or custodial treatment.

Two further points require clarification: (*a*) Are patients in our 'control' groups (Landis and Denker) as seriously ill as those in our 'experimental' groups? (*b*) Are standards of recovery perhaps less stringent in our 'control' than in our 'experimental' groups? It is difficult to answer these questions definitely, in view of the great divergence of opinion between psychiatrists. From a close scrutiny of the literature it appears that the 'control' patients were probably at least as seriously ill as the 'experimental' patients, and possibly more so. As regards standards of recovery, those in Denker's study are as stringent as most of those used by psychoanalysts and eclectic psychiatrists, but those used by the State Hospitals whose figures Landis quotes are very probably more lenient. In the absence of agreed standards of severity of illness, or of extent of recovery, it is not possible to go further.

In general, certain conclusions are possible from these data. They fail to prove that psychotherapy, Freudian or otherwise, facilitates the recovery of neurotic patients. They show that roughly two-thirds of a group of neurotic patients will recover or improve to a marked extent within about two years of the onset of their illness, whether they are treated by means of psychotherapy or not. This figure appears to be remarkably stable from one investigation to another, regardless of type of patient treated, standard of recovery employed or method of therapy used. From the point of view of the neurotic, these figures are encouraging; from the point of view of the psychotherapist, they can hardly be called very favourable to his claims.

The figures quoted do not necessarily disprove the possibility of therapeutic effectiveness. There are obvious shortcomings in any actuarial comparison and these shortcomings are particularly serious when there is so little agreement among psychiatrists relating even to the most fundamental concepts and definitions. Definite proof would require a special investigation, carefully planned and methodologically more adequate than these *ad hoc* comparisons. But even the much more modest conclusions that the figures fail to show any favourable effects of psychotherapy should give pause to those who would wish to give an important part in the training of clinical psychologists to a skill the existence and effectiveness of which is still unsupported by any scientifically acceptable evidence.

These results and conclusions will no doubt contradict the strong feeling of usefulness and therapeutic success which many psychiatrists and clinical psychologists hold. While it is true that subjective feelings of this type have no place in science, they are likely to prevent an easy acceptance of the general argument presented here. This contradiction between objective fact and subjective certainty has been remarked on in other connections by Kelly and Fiske, who found that

> One aspect of our findings is most disconcerting to us: the inverse relationship between the confidence of staff members at the time of making a prediction and the measured validity of that prediction. Why is it, for example, that our staff members tended to make their best predictions at a time when they subjectively felt relatively unacquainted with the candidate, when they had constructed no systematic picture of his personality structure? Or conversely, why is it that with increasing confidence in clinical judgment . . . we find decreasing validities of predictions? (1950, p. 406).

In the absence of agreement between fact and belief, there is urgent need for a decrease in the strength of belief, and for an increase in the number of facts available. Until such facts as may be discovered in a process of rigorous analysis support the prevalent belief in therapeutic effectiveness of psychological treatment, it seems premature to insist on the inclusion of training in such treatment in the curriculum of the clinical psychologist.

SUMMARY

A survey was made of reports on the improvement of neurotic patients after psychotherapy, and the results compared with the best available estimates of recovery without benefit of such therapy. The figures fail to support the hypothesis that psychotherapy facilitates recovery from neurotic disorder. In view of the many difficulties attending such actuarial comparisons, no further conclusions could be derived from the data whose shortcomings highlight the necessity of properly planned and executed experimental studies into this important field.

COMMENT

The paper here reprinted raises an important question, or better still a series of questions; only some of these are relevant to our main problem. When the paper was originally published, it was almost universally assumed that psychoanalytic therapy was successful in the great majority of cases in 'curing' the particular disorder from which the patient was suffering. It was further universally assumed that *only* psychoanalytic therapy could succeed in doing so; mere 'symptom treatment', however successful it might be in the short run, was decried as inevitably leading to relapse and symptom substitution. The paper was written to challenge these beliefs, by pointing out that there was no evidence to support them; its result was very much like that of the child in the story of the Emperor's New Clothes, who called out: 'But he hasn't got any clothes on!' Many critics wrote and argued in opposition to the main conclusion, i.e. the absence of proper evidence for the success of Freudian therapy (e.g. Rosenzweig, 1954; Luborsky, 1954; DeCharms *et al.*, 1954; Duhrssen & Jorswieck, 1962) and the author wrote a number of replies (e.g. Eysenck, 1954, 1955, 1964a, 1964b). A long and sometimes bitter argument ensued, but informed psychoanalysts never in fact claimed that the missing evidence did exist. Thus Glover (1952) had already pointed out that

> the absence of statistics of therapeutic results, in particular the absence of information regarding failures, introduces grave possibilities of error. Unless we know with some precision the exact therapeutic limitations of psychoanalysis in different groups of mental disorder, we run the risk of providing new theories to explain away failure . . . But we can scarcely expect frankness so long as we foster the tradition that a recommended analysis followed *secundum artem* ought automatically to succeed . . . It is,

> moreover, a tradition which encourages the interminable analysis, and with the interminable analysis both clinical and theoretical perspectives go by the board.

And of course Freud himself had become more and more pessimistic about the practical success of psychotherapy; he was increasingly inclined to regard psychoanalysis as a method for exploring the mind, having no therapeutic effects.

The burden of the paper was to draw attention to the fact that what evidence there was about the effectiveness of psychotherapy and psychoanalysis was nugatory; no claims were made that the studies quoted *proved* psychoanalysis to be ineffective and useless. In view of the poor quality of the evidence such far-reaching claims would obviously have been quite out of place; yet most critics of the paper wrote as if this had in fact been the claim made, and pointed out the defects of the studies quoted. Such criticism of these studies is of course quite justified, but leaves the main conclusion unaltered; if this is all the evidence there is, and if this evidence is as poor as the critics say, then *a fortiori* it follows that there is no evidence to support the claims of therapeutic effectiveness for psychoanalysis. Since then, much more evidence has come forth, and reviews in book form have been published by Eysenck (1966; this is accompanied by comments and criticisms by well over a dozen well-known psychiatrists and psychologists) and by Rachman (1971).

Rachman's very carefully documented and argued book will undoubtedly become the standard source on this topic, and it is interesting to note that his conclusion is if anything more far-reaching than Eysenck's; the verdict is changing from *unproven* to a rather more definite assumption that when so many studies, some of them much better designed than those reviewed by Eysenck, and furnished with control groups, fail to show any superiority over spontaneous remission, then we must come nearer and nearer to the conclusion that psychoanalysis simply does not affect psychiatric disorders in a curative fashion. It is always difficult, and may be impossible, to prove a negative conclusion, but this is not really necessary; the evidence is completely congruent with a view that *if psychoanalysis has any effects over and above spontaneous remission, these cannot be large or important, if they exist at all.* For all intents and purposes, psychoanalysis has been shown to have little if any effect on neurotic or psychotic disorders; this conclusion is not absolute, i.e. it is subject to reconsideration should new evidence be brought up, but it is based on a large body of remarkably consistent results from many different sources. Certainly there is no hypothesis in experimental psychology which would still be maintained by any serious worker if so much negative evidence were available to contradict it; the reader is advised to consult Rachman's book to see just how strong the evidence is, and how weak are the arguments put forward against it.

We must now turn away from the simple demonstration that Freudian psychoanalysis is not a useful or effective method of therapy (interesting though that may be) and consider the facts against the background of the experimental testing of Freudian hypotheses. It is often argued, rather defensively, that Freudian therapy and Freudian theory are two different things, and that the success or failure of the former cannot be used to bolster or infirm the latter. This argument is difficult to accept. Freudian therapy was deduced, along theoretical lines, from Freudian theory; text books like Fenichel's (1945) leave little doubt about this structural congruence. It is only necessary to consider the alternative view, in order to reject it; this would state that Freudian theory did not logically lead to Freudian therapy, but that the system of therapy grew up independently of Freudian theory, did not influence, and was not in turn influenced by, Freudian theory, and had in fact no close connection with it. This is not the impression given by Freud's own writings, or by those of his followers.

Freud himself states quite explicity that 'starting out from the mechanism of cure, it now becomes possible to construct quite definite ideas of the origin of the illness'. Further, 'it is only experiences in childhood that explain susceptibility to later traumas' since '. . . it is only by uncovering these almost invariably forgotten memory traces and making them conscious that we acquire the power to get rid of these symptoms' (Freud, 1962, pp. 48 and 71). Thus we are told quite categorically that (1) the curative treatment is primary, leading to the elaboration of the causal theory; (2) uncovering childhood experiences enables us to effect cures (which are here defined as the removal of symptoms), and (3) it is only by this uncovering that such cures are to be achieved. Quite the contrary; there appears to be a very close and intimate connection between theory and therapy, with changes in the one followed immediately by changes in the other. Furthermore, Freudians have always argued quite explicitly that it follows from Freudian theory that 'symptom-orientated' therapies should result in relapse and symptom-substitution; early exponents of behaviour therapy were often criticized on these grounds.

How can such criticisms be made if there is no connection between theory and therapy? The truth would appear to be that there is a direct, hypothetico-deductive connection between the two, with the theory generating hypotheses about treatment, and treatment furnishing results which are interpreted within the confines of the original theory. Freud often argued that psychoanalytic insights received their proof 'on the couch'; in other words, he explicitly stated that theories find confirmation in what happens during treatment. How can such a claim be made, if at the same time it is argued that the failure of treatment is in no way connected with a similar failure of theory? It is noteworthy that this argument only became popular *after* the failure of psychoanalysis as a treatment technique became apparent; previous to that the superstitious success of treatment had often been adduced as proof of the correctness of the theory. We feel that the older argument is the more correct one; had Freudian treatment actually worked, this would indeed have been a powerful argument in favour of Freudian theory. Furthermore, anyone denying this would have been considered as arguing against an overwhelmingly strong proof of the theory in question. It seems perfectly permissible to turn this argument around and state that the failure of Freudian therapy clearly invalidates Freudian theory, at least in so far as this predicts success for such therapy.

While prior to the publication of this article psychoanalysts tended to claim that their (assumed) success in treatment validated Freud's theory, the (apparent) failure of treatment has since led to a change of argument. It is now more and more frequently said by psychoanalysts that their treatment does not cure the patient, but rather (1) enables him or her to live more peacefully with their symptoms, and (2) makes them better persons in some unspecified way (Rachman, 1971). These claims too have not been proved experimentally, so that it is impossible to say whether they are true or not; their rather indefinite nature makes it doubtful if any proper experimental check is in fact possible. But however that might be, they are certainly different from the claims made by Freud and his early followers, as deduced from his general theory; according to the original deductions made, therapy should do much more than simply leave the symptoms untouched, and merely make them more easily bearable. A patient who is impotent wishes to be relieved from his impotence, not become 'a better person', and he does not wish to become better adjusted to his impotence. An obsessional-compulsive patient wishes to be relieved of his obsessive thoughts and compulsive habits, a phobic of his phobias, an anxiety neurotic of his anxieties. Psychoanalysis flourished because it held out the hope that these things would come about, and the many confident claims that psychoanalysis, and only psychoanalysis, could bring such hopes to fruition contributed considerably to its wide acceptance. This being the state of affairs at present, we are faced with a choice.

It is possible to argue that the early psychoanalysts were right in stating that psychoanalytic theories led, through a fairly rigorous chain of deductions, to psychoanalytic methods of treatment, and that it could be deduced, from these premises, that psychotherapy should be (reasonably) successful in removing symptoms as well as the complexes supposed to underlie these symptoms. In so far as we adopt this view, we are able to controvert those who argue that Freudian theories are untestable; a clear and convincing test is in fact possible. When this test is carried out, i.e. by comparing the successes and failures of Freudian psychotherapy with the successes and failures of 'no treatment' or non-analytic treatment groups, the deduction from Freudian theory is fairly decisively invalidated. It is possible to argue about the details of many of these studies; the paper here reprinted already drew attention to many shortcomings, and Rachman's (1971) more recent survey bears witness to the fact that the majority of studies are still rather poor in design and execution (with some notable exceptions). It is of course open to Freudians to carry out further studies, better designed and controlled, in the hope that these would produce better results (from their point of view). But judging the evidence here and now, one cannot but conclude that the hypothesis is infirmed. This failure to confirm is of particular importance in view of the fact that the deductions which led to the elaboration of Freudian therapy made use of a large number of the hypotheses which make up Freudian theory; in other words, we are not just testing one or other of many hypotheses, any one of which might be disproved without too much damage to the overall theory. We are testing a vital deduction central to the whole edifice; if this is disproved, little remains.

The alternative to this argument would be to abandon the original argument, and state instead that Freudian methods of therapy are not deduced from Freudian theory, and are indeed independent of it. Or it might be said that success of Freudian therapy cannot be deduced from Freudian theory. If either of these arguments were to be advanced, we would have to conclude that Popper, Kuhn and the other philosophers who argued that Freudian theories are untestable are right; it is not possible in science to change one's deductions from a theory because these are disproved. One has to change the theory. (An exception would be if everyone had in fact made the wrong deductions, and had suddenly seen the error of their ways. It can hardly be suggested that this is so in this case; in any case, such widespread logical error would lead one to distrust a theory which was so unclear and imprecise as to make such erroneous deductions possible.) The results of the studies surveyed in this paper are therefore of considerable importance for the experimental testing of Freudian theories; they force us to conclude either that these have been decisively disproved, or else that they are not testable, and hence not scientific in any proper sense of that term. This is an important conclusion.

Another, equally important, argument is implicit in the results reported in the paper, and verified by many other writers summarized by Rachman (1971). We are now referring to the undoubted effectiveness of 'no psychiatric treatment', i.e. the phenomenon of spontaneous remission. Freud's position on this point is quite clear; indeed, it goes well beyond spontaneous remission. He regarded neurotic disorders as being generated by 'complexes' acquired in early childhood; it was these complexes which provided the energy which sustained the symptoms the patient complained about, and without complete eradication of these complexes no treatment could succeed. Symptom treatment was useless, leading to relapse or symptom substitution. No treatment (i.e. absence of proper psychoanalytic or psychiatric treatment) could not possibly affect the underlying complexes, and hence could do nothing to ameliorate the neurotic disorder. Hence we have here another crucial test of Freudian hypotheses, a test which goes straight to the centre of Freud's thinking about neurosis. And here again the evidence is very strongly counter to deduction from theory (Eysenck, 1963a; Rachman, 1971). Spontaneous remission is just about the best-documented, most clear-cut, and most reliable fact in the whole history of neurotic illness; Freud's failure to predict its existence, and in fact his theory's insistence on the impossibility of spontaneous remission, are very strong arguments against the adequacy or truth of that theory. The failure of relapse and of symptom substitution to occur after spontaneous remission is another crucial feature of this argument (Eysenck, 1963b); these were confidently predicted by psychoanalysts on the basis of Freud's theory to occur after any type of symptomatic treatment, or no treatment, yet the evidence is quite conclusive that in fact they do not occur with any frequency at all (Rachman, 1971).

The argument can be widened by adding the fact that behaviour therapy has been found to be extremely effective with many different types of neurotic disorders (Eysenck & Rachman, 1965; Eysenck & Beech, 1971). Yet behaviour therapy is clearly and avowedly symptomatic; according to Freud's theory no long-term success should be possible. The predicted relapses and symptom substitutions have obstinately refused to occur, and this failure poses considerable difficulties for any Freudian theory of neurosis. How can we explain, along Freudian lines, the very successful treatment of severely ill obsessive-compulsive patients, many of whom had previously failed to respond to psychotherapy (Hodgson, Rachman & Marks, 1972)? We would have to explain both their very quick and lawful response to the 'flooding' technique used, and their failure to develop the consequences (relapse and symptom substitution) so confidently predicted by Freudian psychotherapists. Here again we are faced with the same choice as in the case of the proven inadequacy of Freudian psychoanalysis. We can say that Freud's theory makes a clear prediction, thus controverting his critics who maintain that no such clear predictions occur in his writings; if we accept this view, then we must also conclude that his theory has been disproved.

The alternative would be to say that all those who made this sort of deduction from Freudian theory were in fact wrong, and that other deductions, more in line with reality, should have been made. This is the point made by Weitzman (1967) in a very interesting paper. He refers to a distinction drawn by Freud (1936) with respect to the repressed instinctual impulses. Freud wants us to distinguish 'between the two possibilities that, on the one hand, the old desire now operates only through its descendants, the symptoms, to which it has transformed all its cathectic energy, or on the other hand, that the desire itself persists in addition . . . There is much in the phenomena of both the morbid and the normal life of the psyche which seems to demand the raising of such questions. In my study of the breakdown of the Oedipus complex, I became mindful of the distinction between mere repression and the true disappearance of an old desire or impulse' (p. 83). Weitzman comments that 'successful symptomatic treatment may be taken as evidence for this second alternative, which might be extended and elaborated in ways entirely compatible with analytic theory' (p. 307). If we adopt this point of view, we rescue Freudian theory from disproof, but only at the risk of making it untestable. There is no doubt that until the lack of relapse and symptom substitution after behaviour therapy was firmly established, Freudian theorists predicted with great confidence that these consequences would follow upon symptom treatment; in fact, they based their firm refusal to even consider these new methods on these hypothetical 'facts'. If it should now turn out that after all there is nothing in the theory to justify one in making such predictions, then clearly the theory is not saying anything at all, certainly nothing which is experimentally testable.

This latter view is not only taken by philosophers like Popper and Kuhn, but also by some psychoanalysts themselves. Rapaport (1959), in his lengthy work on the structure of psychoanalytic theory, makes the point that psychoanalysis is essentially a *postdictive* system. It can rationalize events after their occurrence, but cannot predict these events. But clearly, if a system cannot predict, then it cannot be falsified, and hence loses all claim to scientific status; if all possible consequences are compatible with a given theory, that theory can 'explain' everything and predict nothing. It follows that such a theory is completely useless. We feel that this is too strong a condemnation of Freudian theory, even though pronounced by one of his best-known followers; we believe that the almost unanimous deduction from his writings that relapse and symptom substitution should follow symptomatic types of treatment is in line with the spirit and the (great majority of) words of Freud's writings. However, clearly the ultimate choice must be left to the reader; he must decide on the basis of his own understanding of Freud's writings whether the facts outlined in the paper here reprinted lead us to say that Freud's theory of the neuroses has been disproved, or rather that it is meaningless.

REFERENCES

ALEXANDER, F. (1937) *Five Year Report of the Chicago Institute for Psychoanalysis.* 1932-7.

BENNETT, A. E. & SEMRAD, E. V. (1936) Common errors in diagnosis and treatment of the psychoneurotic patient – a study of 100 case histories. *Nebr. Med. J.*, **21**, 90-2.

BOND, E. D. & BRACELAND, F. J. (1937) Prognosis in mental disease. *Amer. J. Psychiat.*, **94**, 263-74.

CARMICHAEL, H. T. & MASSERMAN, T. H. (1939) Results of treatment in a psychiatric outpatients' department. *J. Amer. Med. Ass.*, **113**, 2292-8.

COMROE, B. I. (1936) Follow-up study of 100 patients diagnosed as 'neurosis'. *J. Nerv. Ment. Dis.*, **83**, 679-84.

COON, G. P. & RAYMOND, A. (1940) *A Review of the Psychoneuroses at Stockbridge.* Stockbridge, Mass.: Austen Riggs Foundation, Inc.

CURRAN, D. (1937) The problem of assessing psychiatric treatment. *Lancet*, II, 1005-9.

De CHARMS, R., LEVY, J. & WERTHEIMER, M. (1954) A note on attempted evaluation of psychotherapy. *J. Clin. Psychol.*, **10**, 233-5.

DENKER, P. G. (1937) Prognosis and life expectancy in the psychoneuroses. *Proc. Ass. Life Insur. Med. Dir. Amer.*, **24**, 179.

DENKER, R. (1946) Results of treatment of psychoneuroses by the general practitioner. A follow-up study of 500 cases. *N.Y. State J. Med.*, **46**, 2164-6.

DUHRSSEN, S. & JORSWIECK, E. (1962) Zur Korrektur von Eysenck's Berichterstattung uber psychoanalytische Behandlungs erg ebnisse. *Acta Psychother.*, **10**, 329-42.

EYSENCK, H. J. (1949) Training in clinical psychology: an English point of view. *Amer. Psychologist*, **4**, 173-6.

—— (1950a) The relation between medicine and psychology in England. In W. DENNIS (ed.), *Current Trends in the Relation of Psychology and Medicine.* Pittsburgh, Pa.: University of Pittsburgh Press.

—— (1950b) Function and training of the clinical psychologist. *J. Ment. Sci.*, **96**, 1-16.

—— (1954) A reply to Luborsky's note. *Brit. J. Psychol.*, **45**, 132-3.

—— (1955) The effects of psychotherapy: a reply. *J. Abnorm. Soc. Psychol.*, **50**, 147-8.

—— (1963a) Behaviour therapy, spontaneous remission and transference in neurotics. *Amer. J. Psychol.*, **119**, 867-71.

—— (1963b) Behaviour therapy, extinction and relapse in neurosis. *Brit. J. Psychiat.*, **109**, 12-18.

—— (1964a) The effects of psychotherapy reconsidered. *Acta Psychother.*, **12**, 38-44.

—— (1964b) The outcome problem in psychotherapy: a reply. *Psychotherapy: Theory, Research and Practice*, **1**, 97-100.

—— (1966) *The Effects of Psychotherapy*. New York: International Science Press.

EYSENCK, H. J. & BEECH, H. R. (1971) Counter conditioning and related methods. In A. E. BERGIN & S. L. GARFIELD (eds.), *Handbook of Psychotherapy and Behavior Change*, pp. 543-611. New York: Wiley.

EYSENCK, H. J. & RACHMAN, S. (1965) *The Causes and Cures of Neurosis*. London: Routledge & Kegan Paul.

FENICHEL, O. (1930) *Ten Years of the Berlin Psychoanalysis Institute*. 1920-30.

—— (1945) *The Psychoanalytic Theory of Neurosis*. New York: Norton.

FREUD, S. (1936) *The Problem of Anxiety*. New York: Norton.

—— (1962) *Two Short Accounts of Psychoanalysis*. Transl. J. STRACHEY. London: Hogarth Press.

FRIESS, C. & NELSON, M. J. (1942) Psychoneurotics five years later. *Amer. J. Ment. Sci.*, **203**, 539-58.

GLOVER, E. (1952) Research methods in psychoanalysis. *Int. J. Psychoanal.*, **33**, 403-9.

HAMILTON, D. M., VANNEY, I. H. & WALL, T. H. (1942) Hospital treatment of patients with psychoneurotic disorder. *Amer. J. Psychiat.*, **99**, 243-7.

HAMILTON, D. M. & WALL, T. H. (1941) Hospital treatment of patients with psychoneurotic disorder. *Amer. J. Psychiat.*, **98**, 551-7.

HARDCASTLE, D. H. (1934) A follow-up study of one hundred cases made for the Department of Psychological Medicine, Guy's Hospital. *J. Ment. Sci.*, **90**, 536-49.

HARRIS, A. (1938) The prognosis of anxiety states. *Brit. Med. J.*, **2**, 649-54.

HARRIS, H. I. (1939) Efficient psychotherapy for the large out-patient clinic. *New England J. Med.*, **221**, 1-5.

HODGSON, R., RACHMAN, S. & MARKS, I. M. (1972) The treatment of chronic obsessive-compulsive neurotics: follow-up and further findings. *Behav. Res. and Therapy*, **10**, 181-90.

HUDDLESON, J. H. (1927) Psychotherapy in 200 cases of psychoneurosis. *Mil. Surgeon*, **60**, 161-70.

JACOBSON, J. R. & WRIGHT, K. W. (1942) Review of a year of group psychotherapy. *Psychiat. Quart.*, **16**, 744-64.

JONES, E. (1936) *Decennial Report of the London Clinic of Psychoanalysis*. 1926-36.

KELLY, E. L. & FISKE, D. W. (1950) The prediction of success in the VA training program in clinical psychology. *Amer. Psychologist*, **5**, 395-406.

KESSEL, L. & HYMAN, H. T. (1933) The value of psychoanalysis as a therapeutic procedure. *J. Amer. Med. Ass.*, **101**, 1612-15.

KNIGHT, R. O. (1941) Evaluation of the results of psychoanalytic therapy. *Amer. J. Psychiat.*, **98**, 434-46.

LANDIS, C. (1938) Statistical evaluation of psychotherapeutic methods. In S. E. HINSIE (ed.), *Concepts and Problems of Psychotherapy*, pp. 155-65. London: Heinemann.

LUBORSKY, L. (1954) A note on Eysenck's article 'The effects of psychotherapy: an evaluation'. *Brit. J. Psychol.*, **45**, 129-31.

LUFF, M. C. & GARROD, M. (1935) Diagnosis and prognosis in psychiatry. *J. Ment. Sci.*, **84**, 893-946.

MATZ, P. B. (1929) Outcome of hospital treatment of ex-service patients with nervous and mental disease in the U.S. Veteran's Bureau. *U.S. Vet. Bureau Med. Bull.*, **5**, 829-42.

MILES, H. H. W., BARRABEE, E. L. & FINESINGER, J. E. (1951) Evaluation of psychotherapy. *Psychosom. Med.*, **13**, 83-105.

NEUSTATTER, W. L. (1935) The results of fifty cases treated by psychotherapy. *Lancet*, I, 796-9.

ORBISON, T. J. (1925) The psychoneuroses: psychasthenia, neurasthenia and hysteria, with special reference to a certain method of treatment. *Calif. West. Med.*, **23**, 1132-6.

RACHMAN, S. (1971) *The Effects of Psychotherapy*. Oxford: Pergamon.

RAPAPORT, D. (1959) The structure of psychoanalytic theory: a systemizing attempt. In S. KOCH (ed.), *Psychology: A Study of a Science*, Vol. I, pp. 55-183. New York: McGraw-Hill.

ROSENZWEIG, S. (1954) A transvaluation of psychotherapy: a reply to Hans Eysenck. *J. Abnorm. Soc. Psychol.*, **49**, 298-304.

ROSS, T. A. (1936) *An Enquiry into Prognosis in the Neuroses*. London: Cambridge University Press.

SCHILDER, P. (1939) Results and problems of group psychotherapy in severe neuroses. *Ment. Hyg. N.Y.*, **23**, 87-98.

SKOTTOWE, I. & LOCKWOOD, M. R. (1935) The fate of 150 psychiatric outpatients. *J. Ment. Sci.*, **81**, 502-8.

STRUPP, H. N. (1963) The outcome problem in psychotherapy revisited. *Psychotherapy*, **1**, 1-13.

THORLEY, A. S. & CRASKE, N. (1950) Comparison and estimate of group and individual methods of treatment. *Brit. Med. J.*, **1**, 97-100.

WEITZMAN, B. (1967) Behaviour therapy and psychotherapy. *Psychol. Rev.*, **74**, 300-12.

WENGER, P. (1934) Uber weitere Ergebnisse der Psychotherapie in Rahmen einer Medizinischen Poliklinik. *Wien. med. Wschr.*, **84**, 320-5.

WILDER, J. (1945) Facts and figures on psychotherapy. *J. Clin. Psychopath.*, **7**, 311-47.

YASKIN, J. C. (1936) The psychoneuroses and neuroses. A review of 100 cases with special reference to treatment and results. *Amer. J. Psychiat.*, **93**, 107-25.

Epilogue

Having examined a fair number of the most highly regarded empirical studies of Freudian concepts, most of them selected because they were considered by experts to reflect favourably on psychoanalytic hypotheses and theories, what is our verdict? Can we agree with Kline (1972) that 'far too much that is distinctively Freudian has been verified for the rejection of the whole psychoanalytic theory to be possible'? Or should we agree rather with Sears (1947) that 'other social and psychological sciences must gain as many hypotheses and intuitions as possible from psychoanalysis but that the further analysis of psychoanalytic concepts by non-psychoanalytic techniques may be relatively fruitless so long as those concepts rest in the theoretical framework of psychoanalysis'? Or should we accept the even more far-reaching conclusion voiced by Eysenck (1972a) after a searching examination of the evidence presented in Kline's book, namely 'that this conscientious, scholarly and well-documented summary of the most convincing evidence for Freudian theories leaves the reader little option but to conclude that if this is the best that can be offered by way of support, then the only conclusion can be that there is no evidence at all for psychoanalytic theory'. Obviously the reader is free to come to his own conclusion on the basis of the evidence here presented, but we may perhaps be allowed to put forward a number of points which may be helpful in coming to a decision.

Note that all good judges are agreed that psychoanalytic theory, as Farrell (1961) points out, 'is not a unified theory – it does not contain certain fundamental, or primitive concepts which appear in certain basic postulates, and from which the rest of the theory is developed. Hence it is not possible to refute "the theory" by testing directly any of its lowest level generalizations; nor is it possible to refute it by deducing an empirical consequence from any generalization, and indirectly testing it by directly testing the deduced consequence.' Farrell concludes that 'it is misleading to frame the challenge in the one big question: can psychoanalytic theory be refuted? We must reformulate it and ask: can each of the different parts of psychoanalytic theory be refuted?'

There are six main divisions of the theory:

1. The theory of instincts, or dynamics.
2. The theory of development.
3. The theory of psychic structure.
4. The theory of mental economics, or defence.
5. The theory of symptom formation.
6. The theory of treatment.

Some of these part-theories have been examined in more detail than others, and of course the division itself is in part arbitrary; however, it does cover most of the ground. We have looked at the studies reported in support of the various theories very much from the technical point of view, i.e. by using the same criteria that Kline (1972) has advocated: 1. Stringency of sampling procedures and use of adequate control groups. 2. Validity of tests used. 3. Quality of the statistical analysis of results. 4. Relevance of the conclusions to psychoanalytic theory and possible alternative hypotheses. We have differed from Kline in applying these criteria a little more stringently than he; it did not seem to us that he was entirely impartial in looking at the studies he surveyed, but tended to overlook reasonable alternative hypotheses, accepted tests of poor reliability and no proven validity, paid little attention to problems of sampling, and was rather naive in considering the adequacy of the statistical treatment given to the results. In doing this we have not exceeded the stringency of criteria adopted by experimental psychologists in other fields; if anything, we have been inclined to bend over backwards to temper the wind to the shorn lamb. If in spite of this leniency our main conclusions must be rather negative, this is the fault of the data rather than an overly critical attitude on our part.

What are the main faults we have found? They are precisely those pointed out by Eysenck (1972a) in his discussion of the Kline (1972) book.

(1) *Failure to discuss alternative hypotheses.* This is perhaps the most pervasive fault in all these writings. Most workers in the field seem to believe that having made a deduction from Freudian theory, and carried out a study which more or less gives results in partial agreement with prediction, this is the end of the story. They fail to consider the duty incumbent upon any scientist to consider alternative

hypotheses which might equally well, or even better, explain the results found. Nor do they consider it their bounden duty to try to anticipate such alternative hypotheses, and incorporate proper controls into their experimental design which would make it possible to discriminate between Freudian and alternative hypotheses. This is an elementary point in experimental design and evaluation; it is curious that it has been practically universally disregarded in the writings of psychoanalytic psychologists, and that even somewhat critical writers like Kline (1972) fail utterly to take it into account. We have been able to suggest many alternative hypotheses for almost every discovery made by the authors of the papers here reprinted, and to us at least, many of these alternative hypotheses seem much more straightforward and reasonable than those accepted without question by the writers themselves. Future work will have to concern itself with this problem more seriously than has been done in the past; concern with alternative hypotheses is almost the hallmark of a scientific contribution.

(2) *Indefinite nature of the theory.* We have argued that those philosophers who deny that Freudian hypotheses can be falsified experimentally are mistaken, but the behaviour of many experimenters in this field would seem to justify the comments made by such men as Popper and Kuhn in this context. Even Kline (1972), who has many cogent criticisms to make of the notorious habit of psychoanalysts to fall back on 'reaction-formation' whenever their predictions are stood on their heads, falls into the same trap, as for instance in discussing the finding that men who gave more dependent answers on the TAT preferred women with small breasts, rather than the predicted size of mammary gland. He admits that 'dependency, of course, is a trait claimed to be part of the oral character, who, according to psychoanalytic theory, should be concerned with breasts. The fact that small rather than large breasts were preferred would have to be attributed to reaction-formation . . . This then, could be regarded as support for the Freudian aetiology of the oral character' (pp. 91-2). It is this easy recourse to concepts like reaction-formation, turning black into white at a moment's notice, which has given psychoanalytic theorizing a bad name; we would have to predict under what circumstances reaction-formation can be invoked before taking such arguments seriously. As it stands, the findings go straight counter to the theory they were believed to test; to claim that they actually support the theory is hard to swallow. Unless psychoanalytic theoreticians and experimenters clear up this particu-

lar Augean stable the suspicion will remain that Freudian theory is too indefinite to allow proper testing.

(3) *Lack of statistical sophistication.* The statistical treatment used in the studies here reprinted, and in those summarized by Kline (1972) and others, is at best rudimentary, and at worst poor. This statement has been exemplified several times in our detailed discussion of experimental studies, and there seems little point in adding to the evidence. We feel that a much more sophisticated approach, using modern methods of multivariate analysis, would be more likely to throw up useful results than does the simple-minded use of straightforward correlations and *t*-tests. When such simple tests are used, it is mandatory to judge the significance of each not by itself, but against the total number of tests carried out or implied in the design of the study. Thus when a study generates several hundred correlations or comparisons (which is not unusual when such tests as the Rorschach, the TAT, or the Blacky pictures are used), it is clear that several of these would assume statistical significance at the 5 per cent or 1 per cent level by accident; to single these accidental values out and ascribe statistical significance to them runs counter to the logic of scientific inference and statistical treatment. Future work will have to adopt more rigorous methods of analysis if it is to be taken seriously.

(4) *Failure to review the evidence.* Writers often come to conclusions which are important for psychoanalytic apologetics, but which are not based on a proper review of the evidence. Thus, for instance, Kline (1972) agrees with Kiesler (1966) 'that spontaneous remission is a myth propagated mainly by Eysenck'. Now as we have seen in our discussion of Eysenck's (1952) paper, the existence of spontaneous remission is a very powerful argument against some of the main foundations of Freudian theory; one would have expected both Kiesler and Kline to have surveyed the evidence in depth. Yet neither author has made any attempt to look at more than a few isolated studies; when a thorough review was undertaken by Rachman (1971) he came to the conclusion that 'the available evidence does not permit a revision of Eysenck's (1952) estimate of a gross spontaneous remission rate of approximately 65 per cent of neurotic disorders over a two-year period'. Greater scholarly attention is clearly called for in evaluating discrepant and disconfirmatory evidence. Kiesler and Kline may of course be right in their submission, and Rachman wrong; nevertheless, failure to survey the literature properly does not

inspire the reader with confidence that the author has in fact done his best to come to an unbiased and balanced conclusion.

(5) *Embracing contradictory positions.* Kline (1972) and others often adduce as evidence in favour of Freud's theories findings which can only be so interpreted by a complete change of that theory into its opposite. Speaking of Cattell's (1957) factor of motivation, Kline says: 'Although the factor alpha, with its emphasis on desire and lack of reality, is not unconscious, it yet appears to be not unlike the *id* component as defined by Freud.' Now the most important aspect of this *id* component was precisely that it was unconscious; how can a conscious factor, derived from questionnaire responses, be equated with a factor supposedly entirely unconscious? Such an identification (which is also made by Cattell, who sometimes indulges in this sort of verbal game), would necessitate a complete reversal of Freudian theory, making the *id* conscious; we doubt if Freud would have regarded this as support of his position! Other examples come readily to mind, e.g. the equally serious mixing up of the hypothesized repressed homosexuality which is supposed to cause paranoid delusions, and the observed greater homosexual activity of paranoid patients. We can only accept the latter finding (if it is replicable!) as evidence of conscious, not of repressed, homosexuality; consequently this alleged support of Freudian theorizing in fact disproves the main point of Freud's theory. Writers in this field will have to be much more precise in their predictions and their evaluations if they are not to be accused of bias and failure to recognize the contradictory nature of the evidence.

(6) *Non-replication of experiments.* It is a curious feature of the literature which we consulted in our efforts to find the most persuasive and positive studies that there is hardly any attempt to replicate findings. This failure to attempt replication studies does of course run through psychology as a whole, but in no field that we have come across has it reached quite the same proportions. We have quoted one study (aesthetic preferences as evidence of sexual symbolism) to show how easily apparently positive findings can on replication be reversed; we suspect that many of the studies here reprinted would on replication turn out to have insignificant results, or results diametrically opposed to those originally reported. There is an urgent need for more replication of studies in this field, made even more urgent by the habit of journal editors to reject studies with negative outcomes. This affects all statistical calculations in a very important manner, making the achievement of 'significance' difficult if not

impossible to evaluate. If of five similar studies four give insignificant results, while the fifth, which (by chance) gives results apparently significant, and if only the fifth study is published, while the others are rejected, then the reader cannot tell, from the information available to him, whether the alleged 'statistical significance' of the printed study is indeed what it is claimed to be, or not. We feel strongly on this point because we have come across several studies using e.g. the Blacky pictures, which replicated published work, but where the outcome was quite insignificant; none of these were published, either because the writer did not feel it worth while to write them up for publication, or because the editor rejected them. Here is another area where improvement of the present position is urgently required if the published work is to be taken seriously.

(7) *The non-Freudian nature of Freudian theories.* It is interesting to ask why so many authors choose to speak of the 'Freudian theory of symbolism' in connection with the notion that rounded shapes denote females and pointed ones males. This symbolism has been known for many centuries, and is well-nigh universal; Eysenck (1972b) has quoted examples of its explicit use in mediaeval times.[1] As in so many contexts, Freud simply took over existing knowledge without acknowledgement; Ellenberger (1970) has given many other examples. Whyte (1960) has similarly discussed the hundreds of writers who posited an 'unconscious' long before Freud was born;

[1]Even among the ancient Greeks and Romans sexual symbolism of this type was very well known; the Golden Ass and other writings bear ample witness to this. Oddly enough, the Greeks seem to have held a theory of dreams not unlike Freud's; thus Plato (whose views on this were of course not shared by many people in his time) taught that dreams could be the product of the 'appetitive part of the soul', when the control of the rational part was relaxed in sleep. In their interpretation of dream symbolism, the Greeks seem to have inverted Freud (or perhaps we should rather say that Freud seems to have inverted the Greek view!); to judge from the few stories about famous dreams that we find in authors such as Herodotus, or in the records of miraculous cures at Epidaurus, they seem to have had overtly sexual dreams which were interpreted as having non-sexual significance. If a Greek dreamed that his mother enticed him into her bed, he would probably conclude that his motherland, i.e. his city-state, was going to bestow some exceptional honour upon him. It is curious that no one seems to have interpreted the Oedipus legend along these lines! It is an interesting *jeu d'esprit* to consider how one would test experimentally which (if either) of the two theories of dream symbolism was correct, and to what extent the use of dream symbolism of one kind or another depended on the cultural habits and mores of a particular age. Freud's theory may to some extent be a self-fulfilling prophecy; people are told how to symbolize certain feelings, and dream accordingly. This would explain the frequent observation that patients of Freudian analysts dream Freudian dreams, patients of Jungian analysts Jungian dreams.

the notion that he discovered symbolism and the unconscious simply will not bear examination. In any consideration of Freudian contributions, and their experimental testing, it is important to be clear as to just what in a given theory of Freud's is due to other writers preceding him by years or even centuries. It is sad that so many modern authors lack the historical knowledge to make such judgments, and simply follow Freud's claim to originality when these are patently false. Freud's theory of why symbolism is used in dreams is original (and probably wrong); the notion of symbolism as such is not Freudian (and probably right). It is this mixture of originality and established knowledge which caused Ebbinghaus to say (in his Ph.D. thesis), in a similar context, that 'what is new in these theories is not true, and what is true is not new'. This is a serious matter, because what attracts many people to Freudian theory is precisely those aspects which are 'true but not new'; they are then willing to swallow also those bits which are 'new but not true'. Historical sophistication is needed by anyone writing about Freudian theories, or assessing research allegedly testing Freudian concepts (Andersson, 1962).

Even such celebrated experimental methods as word association, usually credited to psychoanalysis and making up its most important tool, were well known long before Freud; indeed, people like Galton (1881), who may be said to have used the method for the first time in a proper clinical and experimental fashion, came to conclusions which sound thoroughly Freudian – even to the precise hydraulogical imagery later used by Freud. The results, Galton says, 'gave me an interesting and unexpected view of the number of the operations of the mind and of the obscure depths in which they took place, of which I had been little conscious before. The general impression they have left upon me is that which many of us have experienced when the basement of our house happens to be under thorough sanitary repair, and we realize for the first time the complex system of drains and gas and water pipes, flues, bell-wires and so forth, upon which our comfort depends, but which are usually hidden out of sight, and with whose existence, as long as they acted well, we had never troubled ourselves.' (Galton also describes the resistances which he had to overcome in obtaining insight along these lines.)

Another anticipation of Freudian theories, perhaps the most famous of all, is Plato's image of the tripartite division of the mind into the rider controlling an obedient and socialized horse and another, undisciplined and vicious one (*Republic, Phaedrus*). The similarity to

Freud's notion of ego, super-ego and id has of course been noted by many writers; what interests us here is that in evaluating the Freudian notions few authors take the trouble to dissect out that portion which is 'true but not new', i.e. the contribution of Plato, and that portion which is 'new but not true', i.e. the contribution of Freud. Obviously a proper evaluation of Freudian theory in this field must be of his, and only of his contribution; if the attractiveness of the whole idea is due to content borrowed from Plato, then the idea should be credited to its true author.

What, then, is our main conclusion? We would say that the studies looked at in this volume give little if any support to Freudian concepts and theories, for reasons already discussed in detail; that several of the studies dealing in particular with treatment and with 'single case' investigations give results powerfully challenging Freudian hypotheses; and that the quality of the studies allegedly supporting psychoanalytic views is so poor that very little of interest can in fact be gathered from the results reported. Can we say that the results disprove Freudian theory – or rather, that they disprove the various parts of Freudian theory which they were designed to test? In some cases we think that such a claim could be made, particularly in the important area of treatment, spontaneous remission and effectiveness of 'symptomatic therapy'; we believe that it is very difficult for orthodox psychoanalysis to accommodate the findings reported on previous pages, and that in so far as this failure is concerned the results do disprove in a very real fashion quite fundamental tenets of Freudian theory. But for the most part 'disproof' is too strong a term; all that can be said is that studies which were widely believed to support and prove Freudian theories fail, on examination, to provide any such proof. There is not one study which one could point to with confidence and say: 'Here is definitive support of this or that Freudian notion; a support which is not susceptible of alternative interpretation, which has been replicated, which is based on a proper experimental design, which has been submitted to proper statistical treatment, and which can be confidently generalized, being based on an appropriate sample of the population.' After three-quarters of a century this is a serious indictment of psychoanalysis; whether it can be interpreted as an overall disproof is of course another matter.

We believe that this question can best be approached in the following manner. Scientific theories are never disproved; like old soldiers, they simply fade away. Anomalies exist at all times which could be taken to constitute disproof, yet until these anomalies reach sufficient proportion to give rise to a wholly novel conception (in Kuhn's terms, a new paradigm) there is confidence that the anomalies will be reconciled with the theory in some way or another. Simple falsifiability is therefore a useful attribute of a scientific theory, but falsification does not usually mean abandonment of the theory; anomalies are tolerated until a new and better theory is available. What seems to matter is really a sort of balance between positive and negative instances; a theory which has predicted many successful experimental outcomes can tolerate quite a number of anomalies before it gives rise to a search for a new paradigm. A theory which fails consistently to predict successful experimental outcomes can ill afford many anomalies or disproofs, but it may nevertheless survive, due to the vagaries of the *Zeitgeist,* far beyond its proper period.

We feel that psychoanalysis is in the latter position. It has consistently failed over the years to produce positive evidence of its predictive powers; thus it is in a highly vulnerable position. In recent years the evidence against certain vital tenets of psychoanalysis has become too strong to be brushed under the carpet; the lack of therapeutic effectiveness is one example, the existence of spontaneous remission another. We have here a situation which, according to Kuhn, is ripe for a new paradigm to arise, and such a paradigm is indeed in the process of completion in the form of behaviour therapy and the theories associated with it (Eysenck and Rachman, 1965). The adequacy of this new paradigm cannot here be assessed; it would require another volume the size of this to do that adequately. But it is fair to say that this new paradigm is much more closely associated with academic theory and laboratory research than is psychoanalysis, and that in the clinical field it has given rise to several techniques which have been demonstrably efficacious in removing symptoms and restoring patients to mental health, without relapse or symptom substitution (Eysenck and Beech, 1971). New paradigms seldom succeed in *disproving* their predecessors; what usually happens is that the problems and alleged solutions characteristic of the old paradigm do not appear relevant, interesting and important any longer, and younger scientists start to think and work along the lines of the new paradigm. This is what is happening in the field that was once occupied by psychoanalysis, and unless more cogent research than that reviewed here is produced soon to redress the balance we would predict that interest in psychoanalysis, which is already flagging, will slowly die. Certainly the experiments here discussed would not persuade its critics that psychoanalysis is worth preserving.

This dismal conclusion is sometimes disputed by analysts and philosophers friendly to their cause who feel that psychoanalysis tends to be considered in the wrong frame of reference. A good example of such advocacy is given in a book by Ricoeur (1970), a well-known French philosopher; he states:

> I do not dispute the legitimacy of reformulating psychoanalysis in operational terms; it is inevitable and desirable that psychoanalysis be confronted with psychology and other sciences of man, and that the attempt be made to validate or invalidate its results by those of other sciences. However, it must be realized that this reformulation is only a reformulation, that is, a second operation with respect to the experience on the basis of which the Freudian concepts have arisen. Reformulation can only deal with results that are dead, detached from the analytic experience, with definitions isolated from one another, cut off from their origin in interpretation, and extracted from academic presentations where they had already fallen to the rank of mere magical phrases.

Ricoeur adopts an extreme subjectivism.

> The psychologist speaks of environmental variables. How are they operative within analytic theory? For the analyst, these are not the facts as known by an outside observer. What is important to the analyst are the dimensions of the environment as 'believed' by the subject; what is pertinent to him is not the fact, but the meaning the fact has assumed in the subject's history. Hence it should not be said that 'early punishment of sexual behaviour is an observable fact that undoubtedly leaves behind a changed organism'. The subject of the analyst's study is the meaning for the subject of the same events the psychologist regards as an observer and sets up as environmental variables.

For the analysts, therefore, 'behaviour is a segment of meaning'; the real history is merely a clue to the figurative history through which the patient arrives at self-understanding. This means, of course, that (as Ricoeur recognizes) the whole matter of psychoanalysis is *endopsychic*; it fails to touch the external world at any point at all. There is no possible check on the theory on which the psychoanalyst operates, and equally there is no check on the extent to which he communicates with his patient (other, perhaps, than the outcome of the therapy?).

This sort of experimental, or even existentialist, understanding of psychoanalysis is favoured by many analysts who would willingly forego recognition in terms of orthodox science. To those who prefer this view, we have nothing to say; we are entirely concerned with the scientific meaning of psychoanalytic theories, and the possibilities of testing them empirically. We believe that in this attitude Freud himself would have sided with us; he would certainly not have favoured the consequences which follow from Ricoeur's point of view. As Slater (1972) has pointed out,

> if the events, the phenomena with their meanings are enclosed in an inner world that makes contact with the external world at no point whatever, then these events and the phenomena and their meanings are irrelevant to any events in the external world. Those who are concerned with the patient's external world, his family, his doctor, his employer, his judge and his jailer, will be properly advised not to pay the slightest attention to what the patient's analyst may have to say. Is this the conviction which Ricoeur wished to bring home to us? If so, is it one we can accept?

Slater points out here very neatly the dilemma which besets psychoanalysts – if they choose the scientific definition of their discipline, then they are exposed to scientific test and possible disconfirmation, while if they choose the existentialist definition of their discipline, it dissolves into utter and complete irrelevance to life and society. It is important to follow through both courses to their ultimate conclusion; when confronted with apparent scientific disproof, it is certainly appealing to analysts to try to silence the critic by appeal to such arguments as those deployed by Ricoeur. But the relief is only apparent; they would be jumping from the frying pan into the fire. Solipsism is no escape from proof, and those who embrace it will by definition have no fellow-travellers to join them. For this reason we do not believe that many analysts or psychologists will choose to follow Ricoeur; however dangerous life among critical and empirically-minded psychologists may prove to be, at least it carries within itself the seeds of renewal and improvement, of the eradication of error and the possibility of ultimate success. It has been said of psychoanalysis that it constitutes the premature crystallization of spurious orthodoxy; it is only by submitting to the critical process of experimental verification, and by accepting the results without hiding behind non-scientific attitudes, that psychoanalysis can give the lie to this judgment.

REFERENCES

ANDERSSON, O. (1962) *Studies in the Prehistory of Psychoanalysis*. Nostedts: Svenka Bokforlaget.

CATTELL, R. B. (1957) *Personality and Motivation, Structure and Measurement*. Yonkers: New World Book Co.

ELLENBERGER, H. F. (1970) *The Discovery of the Unconscious*. London: Allen Lane, The Penguin Press.

EYSENCK, H. J. (1952) The effects of psychotherapy: an evaluation. *J. Consult. Psychol.*, **16**, 319-24.

—— (1972a) The experimental study of Freudian concepts. *Bull. Brit. Psychol. Soc.*, **25**, 261-8.

—— (1972b) *Psychology is About People*. London: Allen Lane, The Penguin Press.

EYSENCK, H. J. & BEECH, H. R. (1971) Counter conditioning and related methods. In A. E. BERGIN & S. L. GARFIELD (eds.), *Handbook of Psychotherapy and Behavior Change*, pp. 573-611. New York: Wiley.

EYSENCK, H. J. & RACHMAN, S. (1965) *The Causes and Cures of Neurosis*. London: Routledge & Kegan Paul.

FARRELL, B. A. (1961) Can psychoanalysis be refuted? *Inquiry*, **4**, 16-36.

GALTON, F. (1881) The visions of sane persons. *Royal Inst. Proc.*, **9**, 644-55.

KIESLER, D. J. (1966) Some myths of psychotherapy research and the search for a paradigm. *Psychol. Bull.*, **65**, 110-36.

KLINE, P. (1972) *Fact and Fantasy in Freudian Theory*. London: Methuen.

RACHMAN, S. (1971) *The Effects of Psychotherapy*. Oxford: Pergamon Press.

RICOEUR, P. (1970) *Freudian Philosophy: An Essay in Interpretation*. New Haven: Yale Univ. Press.

SEARS, R. R. (1947) *Survey of Objective Studies of Psychoanalytic Concepts*. New York: Soc. Sci. Res. Council.

SLATER, E. (1972) Freud: a philosophical assessment. *Brit. J. Psychiat.*, **120**, 455-7.

WHYTE, L. L. (1960) *The Unconscious Before Freud*. London: Tavistock.

Author Index

General Index